Dhuuluu-Yala
To Talk Straight

Dhuuluu-Yala
To Talk Straight

Publishing Indigenous literature

Anita M Heiss

Canberra 2003

First published in 2003 by Aboriginal Studies Press for the Australian Institute of Aboriginal and Torres Strait Islander Studies

GPO Box 553, Canberra ACT 2601

Reprinted 2011

The views expressed in this publication are those of the author and not necessarily those of the Australian Institute of Aboriginal and Torres Strait Islander Studies

© Anita Heiss 2003

Apart from any fair dealing for the purpose of private study, research, criticism or review as permitted under the Copyright Act 1968, no part of this publication may be reproduced by any process whatsoever withou the written permission of the publisher.

National Library of Australia cataloguing-in-publication data:

Dhuuluu-Yala (to talk straight): Publishing Indigenous literature.

Bibliography.

ISBN 0 85575 444 3.

1. Aboriginal Australian literature - Publishing.
2. Publishers and publishing - Australia.
3. Australian literature - Aboriginal authors

070.50899915

Produced by Aboriginal Studies Press

April 2003

Foreword
By Kim Scott

Publishing Indigenous Literature

There are certain concepts any discussion of publishing Indigenous literature must address. Concepts like Indigenous identity, like culture, colonisation, and readership. There are issues of fraud, hoax and appropriation to consider. The long neglect—the silencing—of Australia's Indigenous voices must be noted. And then, this relatively recent blossoming of…is it a genre? A marketing niche?

Anita Heiss invites us to contemplate the 'publishing of Indigenous literature'. I'm glad she's put this book together. Reading it gave me an overview I didn't previously have, and an historical perspective I lacked. I was also ignorant of what a comparison with Indigenous writing in other countries would reveal. All of which, for me at least, makes *Dhuuluu-Yala*—To Talk Straight a valuable and necessary work.

Beyond that, however, it provokes me to consider issues surrounding Indigenous writing. It made me think, and that's what I like books to do.

Some might place Australian Indigenous writing within the realm of Australian Literature, but there is a wider context; that of the emergence of Australia, as a nation, at the same time as some of the stories which have grown from our land continued or were adapted, or died forever. Australian literature, in such a context is a sickly stream.

That historical perspective can't be over-emphasised. Land was stolen, a particular power relationship has been imposed and maintained between Indigenous and non-Indigenous people, and serious effort has gone into disconnecting Indigenous people from land, from language, from culture, and from one another. Reading the representations of Aboriginality in many non-Indigenous stories, one could also add that serious effort has gone into filling Indigenous people with shame. And then, more recently, there are examples of appropriation of different sorts.

I don't believe it's propaganda, or cliché to say such things. I think it's only when such truths can be accepted that we can move on to more sophisticated discussion and sharing of stories which belong here, and which empower us all.

Increasingly, enlightened Australians recognise how important Indigenous culture is to the connection of Australia (as a nation) to its land. Indigenous writing is an important, although undervalued, part of making that connection. Yes, it is a by-product of colonisation, but it can also be part of the continuation and regeneration of a prior Indigenous culture.

Unfortunately, since we live in times arguably characterised by fraud, hoax, and appropriation of Indigenous cultural material and identity, it would seem there is in some quarters a desire to exclude Indigenous people from being a necessary part of this connection of land to nation state.

Anita quotes the Aboriginal and Torres Strait Islander Arts Board Director, Cathie Craigie, as saying the 'great Australian Novel' must include 'Aboriginal undercurrents, acknowledgements or whatever. If you want to show the psyche of Australia you've got to do that. For me I think that all Australian writers have to be able to put that stuff in, but there are certain things they can't talk about.'

Is Cathie suggesting that the 'Great Australian Novel' is most likely to be written by an Indigenous author? Given that Indigenous writing is often filed under 'Australiana' in the bookshops, would such a piece of literature be an authentic product, having transgressed the niche of Indigenous writing?

What is it that non-Indigenous authors can't talk about anyway? Sacred stories, perhaps. But surely it's inappropriate for even an Indigenous writer to publish such things. Personally, I'd argue that most Indigenous material, and especially efforts to articulate Indigenous identity are also best left to Indigenous authors, and I think Anita would agree with me, but otherwise… Well, the point is that her book provokes us to consider, and have our say on such issues.

Some non-Indigenous writers complain that they are 'not allowed' to write about Indigenous characters and material, but let's not forget that there are constraints upon Indigenous writers, too. The historical context of cultural disconnection, and the low levels of literacy which is the legacy of oppression means that indiscriminate publication—even by an Indigenous author—is often not the best way to return and consolidate language and stories in communities. And how to write for an audience of whom only a minority are those with whom one most identifies, yet serve to empower that minority, and facilitate cultural consolidation and regeneration, is a serious challenge for any writer.

The 'straight-talking' in this work, developed from Anita's PhD thesis forced me to consider the complexity of much of what is discussed. Even the tittle, *Dhuuluu-Yala*, heightened my awareness of the compromise between a regional Indigenous focus, and the demands of a wider audience, whether Indigenous or not. I don't know how to pronounce this title. It is not my Indigenous language. So what is the role, and function, of Indigenous languages in national publishing?

Anita points our that one of the recommendations following the First National Aboriginal Writers' Conference was that local, community owned publishing houses be established. This would help meet the needs of local communities over and above that of national, and particularly mainstream, audiences.

A number of Indigenous publishing houses are discussed in this book, although these are not local in their focus.

Anita says that research for this book clarified that, 'there is yet to be fostered a general Aboriginal reading audience, although many writers are writing with the aim of providing something for their Aboriginal communities and families.'

Do Indigenous writers need to take responsibility for cultivating an Indigenous readership? Or is that the role of educationalists? Is this the task of Indigenous publishing houses? And how important is the printing of spoken Aboriginal English in developing a wider reading audience?

Many Indigenous writers use a variant of 'Aboriginal English'. Does that necessarily make it good Indigenous writing? Anita quotes Rachel Bin Salleh: 'Sometimes an author simply might not write well…writing in Aboriginal English does not necessarily constitute an Aboriginal or Torres Strait Islander book, and there are many factors that make up Aboriginal writing.'

It's probably similarly varying factors; of audience, of language and dialect, of diverse Indigenous histories and cultures of origin which, when coupled with the relatively recent demand for, and proliferation of, Indigenous writing make it all the more difficulty to define the stylistic characteristics of Indigenous writing. Personally, I hope it remains difficult to do so, and that the diversity and energy of Indigenous Australia resists easy categorisation.

One of the frustrations putting together a book like this must be the difficulty of keeping up with recent achievements and new writers, so I regretted the absence of names like Ambrose Mungala Chalarimere, and Boori Pryor. Of course, given the pace of change and the delays involved in publication, there will be readers who will want to add names of their own, and so I too am guilty of omission.

I want to say that I was thrilled to see reference to a small West Australian Publication, *From Our Hearts*, an anthology compiled by participants in a series of writing workshops.

Anita provides a very comprehensive discussion of what Indigenous writing has been. Of course, we don't yet know what it might become, and I'm glad she has resisted saying what it should be. I would hate Indigenous writing to shy away from being 'literary' writing, in the sense of that writing which puts words to what has previously been non-verbal, and allows us to share our experiences, to communicate and refine our sensibilities, and to celebrate Indigenous cultural continuity and inclusiveness.

Anita's discussion of Indigenous writing and publishing in other countries reveals a range of opinions as to the role of the writer, and how writing might best be published and supported.

She also helps remind us of the dangers of a prescriptive or intentionally political approach. There's two particularly wise voices which appear here.

Firstly, Sandra Phillips: 'The more that Aboriginal writers and Aboriginal editors talk about what makes good writing good, the more we can get people away from the concerns about technicalities and more concerned about how many characters you've got, what your characters do, can you evoke emotion…'

Secondly, Emma LaRocque, who says that Indigenous writers, 'like all writers everywhere, must have access to and must avail themselves of good conscientious editing and editors,' and there needs to be a, 'distinction between editing as a craft and editing as ideology.'

Publishing Indigenous Literature. Those three words of this book's title imply a tension and delicate balance between commercial interest, 'literature' and the imperatives of Indigenous concerns. This book holds much. Open and unpack it for yourself.

Contents

Preface		vi
Acknowledgements		ix
Part 1	**Authorship**	1
Chapter 1	Indigenous Writing and Identity	2
Chapter 2	The Effects of Identity on Writing	17
Chapter 3	Indigenous Discourse	25
Part 2	**Editing and Publishing**	47
Chapter 4	Publishing the Indigenous Word	48
Chapter 5	Editing Indigenous Literature	66
Chapter 6	Indigenous Cultural and Intellectual Property Rights	83
Part 3	**Readership**	89
Chapter 7	Selling Indigenous Literature to the Reader	90
Chapter 8	Recognition of Authors	106
Chapter 9	Festivals, Conferences and Awards	126
Part 4	**Canadian First Nations' Literature**	153
Part 5	**Maori Literature**	189
Appendix A	Catalogue of Indigenous Literature	220
Appendix B	Select Bibliography of Canadian First Nations' literature	235
Appendix C	Select Bibliography of Maori literature	245
End Notes		250
Bibliography		272
Index		283

Preface

Dhuuluu-Yala is a Wiradjuri phrase meaning 'to talk straight' and this book is straight talk about publishing Indigenous literature in Australia. The book also includes broader issues for writers, such as engaging with readers and reviewers.

Dhuuluu-Yala was originally written as a thesis focusing on the production of Indigenous writing. Both the thesis and this book have been inspired by my own experiences as an Indigenous author and the experiences I gained from working with Aboriginal publishers and participating in writing workshops with Indigenous people.

The research contained in the book is current up to the mid-1990s although some references to developments in the late 1990s/2000 have been included. Since this time there has been some significant change in the institutions that support the production and publication of Indigenous literature, for example, staffing structures have changed within Indigenous publishing houses. While this change in particular is significant, and may well influence the content and quality of books by or about Indigenous people, the issues identified at the time of writing the book remain current and to a large extent unresolved.

Writing for entertainment and education has increasingly become an important aspect of reviving and maintaining Indigenous history and culture, and a logical and necessary move in the development of Indigenous expression. In *Dhuuluu-Yala* I acknowledge that ongoing journey and take a close look at the journey a writer's work takes—from inception to [hopefully] broad readership.

The history of defining Aboriginality in Australia and the experience of "being Aboriginal" have both impacted on the production of Aboriginal writing today. These twin themes are the major focus of the work.

The growth of the Indigenous publishing industry and an Indigenous literary and publishing culture have arisen as a result of the pioneering roles of Aboriginal writers gone by who paved the way for the growing pool of emerging Indigenous writers. The development of this new Indigenous arts practice has also been fuelled by the increasing desire and need for an authentic Indigenous voice in Australian literature. Although support mechanisms for Indigenous writers have improved and the scope of opportunities has broadened because more publishers are seeking Indigenous authors, opportunities are still to a large extent, limited by existing publishing practices. As a result, authors are continuing to choose self-publishing paths.

Part 1 of the book focuses on authorship and includes a brief history of the publishing of works by Indigenous authors in Australia (including the first Indigenous newspapers). This Part has two themes: what makes and forms the identity of the Indigenous author; and, what the focus of Indigenous authorship is. There is significant discussion around the authors Colin Johnson (Mudrooroo) and Roberta Sykes in light of the roles they have played in the history of Indigenous writing in Australia and their profiles as Aboriginal writers. There has been widespread discussions in their respective communities. This community discourse is an essential feature of authorship and authority.

In Part 2, publishing and editing issues are discussed in the context of the process of bringing writing into the public domain. Aboriginal and Torres Strait Islander cultural and intellectual property rights are also briefly discussed. Of interest in this part are the reflections of Aboriginal authors across literary genres. It would appear that there is a consistent experience particular to Indigenous authors that reflects the fact of their being Indigenous regardless of the literary genre they are working in. In many respects this phenomena has been a product of the fact that there are so few Indigenous editors employed in the publishing industry. In other respects, it is reflective of the qualities a work will have as a result of the identity of its author. The research outcomes in Parts 1 and 2 of the book indicate that within the publishing industry a line can be drawn that divides, *relevancy to the public*, from, *relevancy to Indigenous people and communities*. This theme is developed and leads into a discussion of 'readership' in Part 3.

In Part 3 the essential appeal and importance of Indigenous literature is covered as are problems, such as marketing Indigenous literature to a largely disinterested public or indeed, to alienated Aboriginal communities. The discussion here includes some analysis of the extraordinary success of Sally Morgan's *My Place*. Information of interest to emerging or established authors, for example, support mechanisms, writers' associations, awards, festivals and conferences is also included to show how and why a good knowledge of the machinations and infrastructure of the publishing industry is indispensable to the emerging or established author.

Part 4 and Part 5 trace respectively the publishing experiences of Canadian First Nations' and Aotearoa peoples. In these Parts, the history of writing and publishing Indigenous literature in Australia is compared with the experiences of First Nations' Canadian writers and Aotearoa writers. The comparison shows that there are some essential differences, such as the fact that Canada and Aotearoa have a national culture of revering their writers, that directly impact upon the status of 'the aboriginal author' and/or their publisher in Australian, Canadian and Aotearoa jurisdictions.

A catalogue of Indigenous literature is included at Appendix A, a select bibliography of Canadian First Nations' literature is at Appendix B, and a select bibliography of Maori literature is at Appendix C.

Dhuuluu-Yala, while considering the history of Indigenous publishing and literature, also canvasses contemporary thought on the role of the Indigenous author and related literary production. These thoughts and opinions are as ever-changing and evolving as the cultures of Indigenous Australia itself, but once stated, whether in 1990 or 2002, remain a record of the way in which Indigenous literature has, and continues to impact on national and international audiences.

The issues covered in the book highlight the challenges faced by authors, editors and publishers of Indigenous manuscripts and show what is at stake for authors and publishers of Indigenous literature. The book is intended to be as accessible as possible to authors, publishers, readers and critics, and to engage relevant parties in discussions that will impact on, and assist the development of Aboriginal writing and publishing in the future.

Anita M Heiss
Sydney 2003

Acknowledgements

Dhuuluu Yala had its real birth on the Mohawk reservation of Kahnawake, Canada in 1995, when I first set foot in the office of the *Eastern Door* newspaper. I'd like to take this opportunity to thank the staff and all the members of the community of Kahnawake who have remained friends.

To Peter Kirkpatrick whose supervision during my PhD ensured I completed, passed, and remained almost sane—thank you.

To all my friends who read and proofed drafts of my thesis and provided immeasurable support and somehow still remain friends, I hope you think it was worth it!

To the staff and Boards of the Australian Society of Authors, and the Aboriginal and Torres Strait Islander Arts Unit of the Australia Council, who have inspired, supported and done so many things-in-kind for me that I will always be indebted, thank you.

To my deadly tidda Sandra Phillips and her team from Aboriginal Studies Press thanks-a-million! Thanks Sandra for your guidance and calming presence along the way.

And finally, heartfelt thanks to my very-supportive family who continue to be my life's foundation and rock of security, maintaining my belief in what is possible with hard work, determination and encouragement from those who share a common vision.

Part One

Authorship

Chapter 1
Indigenous Writing and Identity

Much has been written about the pioneers of Indigenous writing and publishing in Australia. The most noted and acknowledged Aboriginal writers include David Unaipon, poet, playwright and social commentator Kevin Gilbert, poet and activist Oodgeroo Noonuccal, novelist Monica Clare, and playwright Jack Davis. These writers pioneered Aboriginal Australian writing, paving the way and opening the doors to publishers, and alerting the wider community as to the strength and value of Aboriginal literature.

Although all the writers mentioned above have now passed on, the influence of their written works and politics is still evident in the works of today's new writers. Present day writers will be the focus of this book. Among others, the basis for the research and discussion in the book are the novelists Melissa Lucashenko, Alexis Wright, Bruce Pascoe and Kenny Laughton; the poets Kerry Reed-Gilbert and Lisa Bellear; playwright, Cathy Craigie; and biographers/auto-biographers Ruby Langford Ginibi, Herb Wharton, Jackie Huggins and Jeannie Bell.

The 1990s saw increased discussion on the issue of non-Aboriginal writers writing about Aboriginal society and culture and highlighted the need to define authenticity in Aboriginal writing. As a result, part of the discussion in this book centers on the issue of authenticity in Aboriginal writing and the role the individual Aboriginal author plays in maintaining his or her credibility.

The debate around authenticity and voice reached a peak in 1997 when white male taxi-driver Leon Carmen outed himself as Wanda Koolmatrie, descendant of the Pitjantjatara people in South Australia and author of the 'assumed Aboriginal autobiography', *My Own Sweet Time* (Magabala Books, 1994). It was a particularly shocking incident in the long history of appropriation and exploitation of Aboriginal culture and identity in Australia and raised issues and problems for Aboriginal authors including increased surveillance of Aboriginality in the publishing industry, in particular, the introduction of the Proof of Aboriginality form in Publishing Agreements.

This fraud also highlighted the lack of understanding in the broader community of the need for and role of Indigenous publishing houses, and indeed, who is employed in these publishing houses. (In fact it is widely accepted that the absence of Indigenous people in publishing houses generally is the fundamental reason why Leon Carmen's fraud went undetected for so long). Bigger issues include Carmen's claims that it is easier to get published in Australia if you are a 'black' woman than a 'white' man, and that there is no difference between 'black' and 'white' writing, or men's or women's writing. These are some of the issues that caused me to write this book and that are commented on by some of Australia's most recognised Indigenous writers.

The works of Colin Johnson and Roberta Sykes, and to a much lesser extent Sally Morgan, have been well received, arguably on the basis of their Aboriginal content and authorial identities. Irrespective of the literary quality of the works, their notoriety was to a very large extent generated by the fact that it was unusual for an Aboriginal person to have written and have had published a book. The community discourse around the identities of Colin Johnson and Roberta Sykes has therefore been very troubling for the mainstream publishing establishment and no doubt for the authors themselves. The success of Sally Morgan's work is discussed in Part 3, Readership. I now turn to discussing the controversy surrounding the identities of Colin Johnson and Roberta Sykes.

Colin Johnson

Colin Johnson was recognised as the first Aboriginal novelist to have written and published across a range of genres, including fiction, poetry, plays and academic writing. He is also recognised as an authority on Aboriginal writing in Australia.

Since publishing his first novel in 1965, Johnson, like Sykes, arguably can be regarded as someone who has made a successful career partly built on perceptions of his identity and his role in the Aboriginal literary arena. He has worked as a teacher of Aboriginal studies and in some circles remains a well-respected and highly profiled authority on Aboriginal writing. His critical texts are still set on courses here and in Aotearoa.

His authority though has now been questioned along with his identity, since his sisters have stated that he is not of Aboriginal descent, but that his father was of Creole descent,[1] and that his Black background may well be Afro-American.

Colin Johnsons's decision in the Bicentennial year to change his name to Mudrooroo followed in the steps of Kath Walker who, at the same time became Oodgeroo Noonuccal. He says of the name change,

> We were having all the protests, and I was talking to Oodgeroo, Kath Walker, and she was saying that Aboriginal writers should Aboriginalise their names. Oodgeroo means 'paperbark', and 'Mudrooroo' in my dialect means 'paperbark', too, and she was saying that the paperbark tree should be our working totem, because we are engaged with putting words on the paper. So it was very appropriate.[2]

I choose to refer to the writer here as Colin Johnson as I believe that despite the relatively widespread usage of pseudonyms throughout Australian literary history, the assumption of an Aboriginal name is an act that requires community validation. It has been asked whether Johnson may have believed by Aboriginalising his name that somehow his Aboriginal identity would be consolidated.

Johnson's first novel *Wildcat Falling* was published in 1965 and still sells today as the first novel by an Aboriginal author. With the theme of 'outsiderness', *Wildcat Falling* remains a popular novel, but it must be asked: would it have done so well if Johnson was not thought to be Aboriginal?

By contemporary standards Mary Durack's Foreword to *Wildcat Falling* could be called essentially racist. In her first line, she promotes Johnson's identity, but goes on to suggest that he was anything but her stereotype of an Aboriginal:

> He was nineteen years old and part-Aboriginal…he showed little obvious trace of native blood, but had what most darker people have lost, the proud stance and sinuous carriage of the tall, tribal Aboriginal…An above average IQ could, however have been more burden than advantage had he inherited the typical instability of the out-camp people. We observed that Colin was not apparently lazy. He found jobs for himself about the place and did them well. He also had a sense of time and he began to seem—was it possible? —even dependable.[3]

There we have it: Johnson's introduction to the literary world as a noble savage.

In 1990 Johnson published *Writing From the Fringe: A Study of Modern Aboriginal Literature*. At the time, he was regarded as the authority on Aboriginal writing, and anything associated with it. He was an 'acclaimed Aboriginal writer', with several collections of poetry and novels under his belt, with a profile on both the national and international levels. He established the Aboriginal Writers, Oral Literature and Dramatists' Association with Jack Davis in Western Australia (currently defunct), served on the Aboriginal Arts Unit Committee of the Australia Council, and has been a judge of the David Unaipon Award for new Aboriginal writers.

In 1994 he published *Aboriginal Mythology: An A-Z Spanning the History of Aboriginal Mythology from the Earliest Legends to the Present Day*. This book was thought to be the first by an Aborigine to collate and explain the many elements of Aboriginal culture: song cycles and stories, artifacts, landmarks, characters and customs. He provided information and insights about topics ranging from dolphins and medicine men, to Yothu Yindi.

In his book *Aboriginal Mythology* he also writes about matters widely understood as existing within the restricted context of 'women's business'; providing detail in his alphabeticised entry 'M' for 'Menstrual blood'. This foray into this subject matter was not taken lightly by some of the elder women at the 1996 Aboriginal and Torres Strait Islander Writers' and Playwrights' Conference in Brisbane. In response to *Aboriginal Mythology*, and to comments he made previously on an ABC-TV program in relation to the literary success of Sally Morgan, Colin Johnson roused anger and a reaction from many Conference delegates, particularly the female delegates. A statement was prepared but never distributed through the media that strenuously disowned Colin Johnson.[4]

In the same year, 1996, Johnson went on to win the $10,000 Ruth Adeney Koori Award (RAKA) for *Us Mob* (a series of lectures which looks at issues around Aboriginality in Australia in the 1990s). Questions that could be asked include: should Johnson retain the Ruth Adeney Koori Award (RAKA), and should he have been nominated again in 2000? Should he repay the senior writing fellowship from the Australia Council he received? Should his titles be retained in the Black Australian Writers Series (BAWS) through University of Queensland Press (UQP)?

Following discussion at the community level for some years, in 1997 Johnson's identity came under public scrutiny. Andrew Wilkins, a director of Hyland House which has published six of Johnson's works said, (following the Leon Carmen outing in 1997), that Johnson had assured the publishing house he was Aboriginal and until there was 'conclusive evidence' to the contrary, its support was 'incontrovertible'.[5] Hyland House also said that Johnson feels that, 'his life qualifies him as an Indigenous writer, and that it's up to anyone who believes differently to prove it.[6]

UQP are also defensive of Johnson's (and Sykes') position in BAWS saying,

> Historically, Mudrooroo's Aboriginal heritage was not in question in the public arena until well after his UQP publication of his poetry. Sykes has not been promoted as an Aboriginal person by UQP, and there continues to be support from members of the wider Aboriginal community particularly for recognition of her work in higher education for Indigenous Australians.[7]

But it is the views of members of the Nyoongar community that Johnson says he is from, that should also be acknowledged and respected in this debate. Community members Tom Little, Lorna Little and Graeme Dixon in their joint essay, 'The Mudrooroo Dilemma', believe, that it is Johnson himself who has fuelled the fires by his 'Que sera sera' attitude. They further believe that by not taking the opportunity, (and he has been given several), to defend himself against allegations that he is not Aboriginal, he has done a further disservice to himself.[8]

Graeme Dixon, winner of the David Unaipon Award for his volume of poetry *Holocaust Island* (1990), thinks that it is ironic that over the years Johnson has become the arbitrator of what is and what is not an authentic style for Aboriginal writer. Dixon believes that Aboriginality has a great influence on the theme and style of a book.[9] He also points out now, that if Johnson is not Aboriginal, then questions related to the worth of his writings come to the fore. These are questions that non-Aboriginal academics and literary people, the very ones who helped put Johnson on the Aboriginal author's platform, should also ask themselves. Is Aboriginality an important or relevant criterion in writing? If Mudrooroo is not Aboriginal does his writing lose any of its value or worth?

Dixon's view is that, "It may be true that Mudrooroo's institutionalised childhood caused him to relate to Aboriginal people, but [even] so, for the good of all, he should come clean and tell the true story of Colin Johnson."[10] Little and Little add,

> It has been said by some Aboriginal academics that Mudrooroo's writing, while of a high academic standard, lacks the empirical and experiential detail that seems to be common to most Aboriginal writing so that it reads like the writings of the 'armchair anthropologists' of the nineteenth century.[11]

Little and Little also point out that the dilemma faced by the members of the academic and literary community is just as bewildering. By lionising Mudrooroo as the 'one true voice' of Aboriginal literature, some non-Aboriginal academics have allowed the works of other Aboriginal writers to be ignored or demeaned. The profiling of Colin Johnson as *the* Aboriginal writer also fails to recognise the true diversity within Aboriginal and cultures that other Aboriginal writers are likely to portray. On a practical level, Little and Little realise that, "There is also a great risk of so far alienating Aboriginal writers that they refuse to be part of a system which has so badly treated them, or even worse, begin to write what they think non-Aboriginal academics and readers want to hear."[12]

Johnson does himself no favours and gains no integrity (or identity) by responding to the backlash in the Afterword to *Race Matters: Indigenous Australians and "Our" Society* (1997). In his essay titled, *Tell Them You're Indian*, he sidesteps the issue of his Aboriginality by claiming that blood and genetics have nothing to do with it, saying, "The question of blood is what else but a clinging onto Victorian classifications of race, classifications which reached their fulfilment in the Nuremberg race laws (1935)."[13] Contradicting this point further on, however, Johnson says that genetics (bloodlines) is the key to Aboriginal identity, saying,

> Any basic Aboriginal identity, owing to the many contradictions combining in such an identity, can only rest on a genetic connection to those who have come before us. This is because so much of traditional Aboriginal culture has been destroyed and, with it, any passing on of traditions.[14]

Aside from this sweeping generalisation, and aside from what Johnson himself thinks about Aboriginal identity, Robert Eggington of the Dumbartung Aboriginal Corporation in Perth is adamant that the determination of Aboriginality must include the determination of bloodlines as well as an acceptance of the person by the elders. He says, "Unless you've got Aboriginal blood, you can't claim to be Aboriginal. I, as an Aboriginal person, with English blood as well, can't declare myself to be Japanese. Spiritually it's offensive. It generates a form of commercialism."[15] Eggington describes Johnson's position as deceptive and, "an example of the on-going and continued spiritual colonisation of our people…a continuation of genocide."[16] As a spokesperson for the Aboriginal community in Perth, Eggington says that until such time as Johnson goes back and talks to the elders of the area he will be regarded as, "a renegade spiritual thief on the run."[17]

Nyoongar writer Dr Rosemary van den Berg blames the literati, academia, publishers and 'ignorant Aborigines' who uphold Mudrooroo's right to maintain his false identity. She asks,

> Where does that leave Indigenous people, the Nyoongar people, whose cultural identity he has stolen and made use of for his own ends? Are we to accept this state of affairs? What can we, as Nyoongars and as Aborigines do, especially when this man's white wife is legitimately called Mrs Nyoongar. It is a farce and an insult to my people, the Nyoongars of the south-west of Western Australia.[18]

Responses from the white intellectual community to Johnson's outing have been relatively few. Thomas Shapcott said in his review of Johnson's Pacific Highway Boo Blooz in 1996 that, "The volume can now only be read in the light of recent disclosures about the author's 'background,'"[19] meaning it can be read as yet another book about Aboriginality by a non-Aboriginal person. In a newspaper article Beatrice Faust pointed out that if the Aboriginal community rejects Johnson then we lose the kudos of his vigorous output, but if we defend the value of the work, then we undermine the unifying basis of Aboriginality in shared blood.[20]

It is sad but true that after 30 years as 'the Aboriginal author' Johnson must now reassess everything he has thought about himself and his writing. But it is perhaps more important that he find out who he is rather than continue to write as an Aborigine. One can't help but feel sorry for someone if they honestly believe their identity was something that it is not. But Johnson must learn to live the life of who he really is: genetically (non-Aboriginal), spiritually (a Buddhist) and practically (an academic in a white education system).

Johnson spent many years as a monk, and the rest of his life as a writer and academic who has rarely attended any Aboriginal Australian writers' workshops or conferences since the 1980s.

However, a few Indigenous people supported Johnson through his 'outing' and continue to support the literary works he continues to produce. Ruby Langford Ginibi has said, "He has not got to prove himself to anyone, let alone his own family."[21] Editor Rachel Bin Salleh has also remarked that irrespective of Colin Johnson's identity, his texts will always have a place in the 'history' of Indigenous Australian literary production,

> Over the years he has made some relevant points and has impacted quite heavily on Aboriginal literature as we know it. Whether he is Aboriginal or not, his experiences are relevant. His work should be deconstructed in their correct context—whether he is or not—and studied with these issues in mind.[22]

Bin Salleh believes Johnson has made a phenomenal impact on the Indigenous literary canon and that his intelligent writing and thinking are a bonus for Aboriginal Australia in that they have opened doors for many Aboriginal people and contributed to making publishing houses take notice of what Indigenous Australians are saying. She also believes that Johnson has a story to tell, and that his voice does not need to be silenced, but put into context. She says, "It is a more constructive path to take if we debate and educate rather than shoot down. At least then as Indigenous peoples we have a benchmark for what we may want to see, expect, discuss and conceptualise."

With Bin Salleh's comments in mind, Johnson's comments on Aboriginal literature and publishing in Australia have been included within this book as an acknowledgement of his role, such as it has been, in literary and academic debate in Australia.

Some mention must also be made here of Western Australian writer Archie Weller whose own identity as an Aboriginal writer also came into question in 1997. Weller is not discussed within this book as he has not been given the same profile as Johnson, nor has he set himself up as an authority on Indigenous writing or been written about near as much as Johnson by members of the Western Australian Aboriginal community. Further, Weller's work has also been largely fictional whereas Johnson's has included cultural and theoretical criticism.

Roberta Sykes

It is interesting that 'outings' like those of Leon Carmen and Colin Johnson in 1996-97 attracted so much publicity and, more importantly, condemnation. By comparison it would appear that being Aboriginal was far more important in the 1990s, and some would say impressive or 'useful', than it was in the 1960s and 1970s when Roberta Sykes began her career in the Aboriginal movement (or what she generally terms the 'Black Movement'). Beatrice Faust recalls that when Julia Freebury, the then doyen of the reform movement in NSW, challenged Roberta Sykes during the Whitlam era, asking that she prove that she was genuinely Aboriginal and 'not the R-and-R offspring of a Black American serviceman,'[23] that the challenge didn't cause much of a stir, (compared to the storm that questions about Johnson's identity have). Faust puts this down to the fact that challenges like those from the Dumbartung Aboriginal Corporation and the Nyoongar community to Mudrooroo, "[show] that Black pride has become more than a slogan…Indigenous people are now more militant about exploitation of their culture."[24] But even with Leon Carmen's outing and the national sense of outrage and debate over his actions, no questions were raised of Sykes. The woman who launched one of Johnsons's books, and who has for decades been defined in the press as an 'Aboriginal writer and activist'[25], even though Birri Gubba discourse has attempted to unsettle these perceptions.

However, it was as early as 1972 that John A. Newfong outed Sykes as not being Aboriginal in *Identity*, then the only national Aboriginal publication in Australia. Then editor of the publication, Newfong, the first Aborigine to become a professional journalist said of Sykes,

> Originally from Townsville, she is of White Australian and Black American descent and has moved around the more radical section of the Aboriginal Advancement Movement in the last six months....[26]

And in Brisbane's *Sunday Sun* in 1973, Sykes' own mother Rachel Paterson, was quoted as saying that, "her father was a Negro soldier. His name was Master Sergeant Robert Barkely of the US Army."[27] Not long after that statement though Sykes was being defined in the press as "one of two Aboriginal women from Sydney who have surveyed country Aborigines' views", and praised at the conferring of her doctorate in education from Harvard as 'the first Aboriginal to be awarded a doctorate from Harvard University'.[28]

Like the Nyoongars who commented on Colin Johnson, respect must also be paid and a voice given to the Birri-Gubba people of Townsville where Sykes is from. Birri-Gubba elder Doris Prior said in relation to the Sykes controversy: "I'm sick of people jumping on the bandwagon...There are people who take our art without permission, sell it overseas and make millions out of it. I think Bobbi's trying to do the same thing with her book."[29] Clan elders challenged Sykes to appear before a Clan meeting in Townsville to explain her actions they believe insult their Birri-Gubba culture by claiming the Clan's snake totem as her own. The elders also say that contrary to Sykes' story that says she was raised poor, she had a relatively comfortable childhood with little or no contact with the Aboriginal community when she was growing up.[30] Another member of the Birri-Gubba nation and Director of Aboriginal Studies at the University of Southern Queensland, Associate Professor Gracelyn Smallwood, alleges that Sykes '...has constructed an identity closely aligned to the snake totem in a desperate search of Aboriginality. There is no evidence to show she understands the seriousness of such an action.'[31]

Reviews of Sykes' autobiographies[32] even suggest her books are more of a 'whodunit' mystery about her paternity, and to white followers of her work it might be interesting, but for Aboriginal writers and community members generally hearing the stories of someone who has made a literary and academic career out of being a victim—a victim of racism based on her skin colour rather than her Indigeneity, has become too much to bear.

In 1997 Sykes won the $20,000 Kibble Literary Award for women writers for *Snake Cradle*, on literary merit not recognisant of Birri-Gubba perspective.

Whites Writing on Blacks

Another contentious area is that of non-Aboriginal writers writing in the area of Aboriginal studies. For some white writers, credibility arises from the view that they are providing a voice (however indirectly), to Aboriginal Australia. Nevertheless, this attitude is unacceptable to many Aboriginal writers who are tired of competing with white writers for the opportunity to write and be published in the areas directly related to their lives or life opportunities.

In discussing the role of non-Indigenous writers it is important to distinguish between the fictional and non-fictional and the historical and literary areas of writing. There are fiction writers like Thomas Keneally, Xavier Herbert, Peter Bulkeley and Phillip Gwynne, who have obviously seized upon the Aboriginal character and at times lifestyle, and written about them in their works of fiction. While academics and historians like Catherine and Ronald Berndt, C.D. Rowley, Henry Reynolds, Peter Read and Heather Goodall, have exposed the atrocities of the white man against the Black man since invasion, they have also, regardless of their altruistic reasons, managed to create successful academic and literary careers for themselves in the area of Aboriginal studies and history. Other white writers like Adam Shoemaker, Stephen Muecke and Bain Attwood have also made careers out of teaching what they have learnt about Aboriginal society and culture. The number of articles published by individual writers of this ilk proliferate.

There are strong and original arguments coming from people who believe that white writers should not write about Aboriginal issues, especially sacred matters. Sandra Phillips, who as in-house editor at both Magabala and UQP, was committed to working with Aboriginal authors, believes there are definite criteria determining whether a non-Indigenous author can adequately represent Indigenous societies and cultures through their writing:

> For a non-Indigenous author to achieve a true feel to their representation on Indigenous subject matter and character they would need to be very enculturated within Indigenous culture. And if they are not, they are writing as outsiders to that culture and their representation would be vastly different to the representation defined, developed and refined by an Indigenous writer.[33]

Co-author of *Auntie Rita*, Jackie Huggins also feels strongly that writing children's literature (Dreamtime/creation stories) should be exclusively done by Aboriginal people because, she says,

> Much of what has been written about Aboriginals by non-Aboriginals has been patronising, misconstrued, preconceived and abused. We've had so much destructive material written about us that we must hold together the very fabric of the stories that created us. Out of all the material written about, for and by Aboriginal people, this is perhaps the most sensitive genre. We never refer to these stories as 'myths', how can the bible be a myth?[34]

Huggins also asks that white writers not write about Aboriginal spiritual characters, because too often they are used tokenistically or for creative effect, rather than in ways that reflect understanding of the protocols and responsibilities that come with the telling of such stories. She comments, "The problem with some writers is that they have 'made up' what they don't know. This dangerous methodology only serves to alienate socially aware readers and those people whom it is meant to benefit."[35]

Although Huggins is adamant that non-Aboriginal writers should not be writing Dreamtime/creation stories, she does believe that white writers can, in some instances, write on Aboriginal themes, such as on historical evidence and colonial literature. She cites an historian at the University of Queensland, Ray Evans, who writes in a way that Huggins finds very acceptable and hard-hitting. She also makes the distinction between works of fiction and history:

> I think in order for us to educate other people, particularly students especially at universities like this [University of Queensland], we need those qualities. But I don't think the same degree should be given with writing fiction and stuff. I don't like it, never have liked whitefellas writing about Black stuff. It seems like they all feel that, "If they didn't nobody else would," and I find that very patronising as well. And that they're doing us a favour.[36]

Eastern Arrente author of the novel *Not Quite Men No Longer Boys* (1999), Kenny Laughton admits that there is no one area where he would be totally comfortable with non-Aboriginal people writing on Aboriginal Australia, especially in relation to language, culture and history. He says, "I reckon that is our business and we should be the ones writing it; and receiving the appropriate recognition and status as the custodians and experts on that history."[37]

Author of the ground-breaking autobiography *Fringedweller* (1980), activist Robert Bropho adds to the discussion of the problem of white people writing about Aboriginal society, culture and issues,

> When a white author decides to write a book he hears direct from the Aboriginal person broken words which the white man calls 'broken English', he hears it and then he twists it around and his mind is taking up the sounds of that and he's putting the flavour of the white mind into those words that go into the lines and become chapters in that book.[38]

A Waanyi woman from the Gulf of Carpentaria, novelist, anthologist and editor Alexis Wright in a paper presented at the Tasmanian Readers' and Writers' Festival in 1998, said she writes so that her people have their own books, in their own communities, written by their own people, countering the damage done by whites writing in the area. She adds,

> I do not like the way we are being treated by successive governments, or the way our histories have been smudged, distorted and hidden, or written for us. I want the truth to be told, our truths, so first and foremost, I hold my pen for the suffering in our communities. Let it not be mistaken: suffering is widespread in our communities. I do not write stories of 'getting on and getting by'. 'Getting on and getting by'—these words were used to describe the subject matter and mood of an anthology of Aboriginal stories published recently, which contained two of my short stories. But neither of my stories was about, as described in the preface, 'celebrating and expressing a hearty optimism'. What I know of our struggle gives me no cause for celebration or hearty optimism.[39]

(The anthology that Wright refers to is *Across Country* [ABC Books, 1998] compiled by white editor Kerry Davis, author of the preface.)

While most authors are definite either way on the issue, Cathy Craigie says the issue is debatable more along the lines of content and style rather than politics. Craigie's problem with whites writing in the area is that she doesn't feel they capture the whole essence of the experience, rather that they are writing it from their own perspective. She adds, though, that the mythical great Australian novel must have some Aboriginal content and recognition,

> I believe that any writing that's done on any theme that comes out of Australia, must or should have Aboriginal undercurrents, acknowledgement or whatever. There is no such thing as the great Australian novel unless it has included that side. If you want to show the psyche of Australia you've got to do that. For me I think that all Australian writers have to be able to put that stuff in, but there are certain things that they can't talk about.[40]

Like Craigie, van den Berg says that while non-Aboriginal writers can write about Aboriginal issues they cannot live the Aboriginal experience or write about it, and that, "It does not matter how many of the 'experts' on Aboriginal issues write about the Indigenous people, they are still outsiders looking in."[41] The concern here is the factor of how the identity of an author will influence their *perception* or 'take' on 'history' and or experiences.

Aboriginal Research Fellow, Christine Morris, at the Australian Key Centre for Cultural and Media Policy at Griffith University in Brisbane said in 1996, that she believed the issue of non-Indigenous people writing in the Aboriginal area came down to subject matter and context.[42] Morris, in line with Huggins, believes that non-Indigenous writers should stay away from, "…anything that comes under customary law or depicts our basic world view and values," including Dreaming stories, traditional political systems, trading systems, intermarriage systems and child rearing.[43] On the other hand, Morris doesn't have a problem with non-Indigenous writers writing about issues that cover Black/white relations, for example, issues around first contact and invasion, political relations between Blacks and whites, recording oral histories and the stories of children taken away from their families, (which would cover the works by people like Henry Reynolds and Carmel Bird). These works of course cover the roles whites play in the oppression of Blacks, something Morris says has not been covered strongly in Australian history books, and should be.

The strongest arguments against non-Aboriginal people writing in the area have been responses to the negative representation of Aboriginal people in books written by white people. These negative portrayals have led to greater support for the creation and development of Aboriginal literature in Australia today, but as far back as 1957 Frederick Macartney in *Australian Literary Essays* had observed how,

> Most of the authors of these writings have little if any first-hand knowledge, and they seem seldom to go to reliable authorities for information, or not very thoroughly, content instead, apparently, with accounts by 'our special reporter' or others who travel among the remnant tribes over well-defined motor-tracks where the foot of white man has never trod.[44]

Bundjalung author of *Don't Take Your Love to Town* (1988), Ruby Langford Ginibi, admits that she has written much of her work to redress the negative portrayal of Aboriginal people in print saying, "For many years we have been misrepresented by misinformed people and have never had a voice!"[45]

Alexis Wright is also strident in her critique of the ways Aboriginal people have been portrayed in print in Australia, saying,

> In Australian literature we have remained almost invisible or often at the mercy of being misrepresented by others. And I include in this the bulk of academic writings and books about Aboriginal people where most of our people would not have a clue about what was written about them.[46]

A few white authors have discussed their own roles as 'outsiders', at times justifying their place. In a letter to the editor of *Australian Author* responding to Marlo Morgan's fictitious work *Mutant Message Down Under*, author Di Morrissey from Byron Bay wrote,

> As a novelist who tries to be faithful and sensitive when writing about Aboriginals by having my work checked by Aboriginal friends, I think it painful that here is yet another example of abuse of Aboriginal culture. I know legally one can argue that anyone can write about anything, Greek mythology or Aboriginal myths, but I do think as Australian writers we have a moral responsibility to do the right thing by our native culture. There are resource centres where one can find accurate and helpful information when writing anything in connection with Aborigines.[47]

Children's writer and one-time Board Member of the Australian Society of Authors, Nadia Wheatley points out the no-win situation for white writers. She suggests that writers who don't include Aboriginal characters and themes in their work run the risk of painting a white Australian monoculture and inadvertently foster racism. On the other hand, those who do include Aboriginal characters and themes may depict Aboriginal people tokenistically, including them to make white writers and readers feel better. At worst, and however unintentionally, they create a new form of exploitation and appropriation.[48] Wheatley talks about the appropriate methodologies for research that will produce good writing as well as engender mutual respect and politeness,

> After all, if I wish to write a story about executives, I make sure I go and meet some, and I try to understand how they think and feel and talk; once the story is written, I go back and check it with them, to make sure I haven't made any stupid blunders. Or if I wish to write a story featuring gay characters, I am very careful to try not to use words or stereotypes that might hurt real gay people.[49]

The practical experiences of some white writers follow on from the concerns identified by Wheatley. During a study of the effects of newly developing literacy on a predominantly oral society, Mari Rhydwen, author of *Writing on the Backs of Blacks: Voice, Literacy and Community in Kriol Fieldwork*, says that the most frequent challenge to her from communities was, "What gives you the right to write about us?" This question had the effect of turning the focus of her project to the legitimacy of the very processes of linguistic research. She says in the introduction to her book,

> My confidence in answering that question dwindled increasingly over the years to the point where I felt I had no right whatsoever and fieldwork often became an exercise in evasion, doubt, embarrassment and shame. Rather than abandon my work, I decided to include writing about the experience of being a non-Aboriginal academic doing linguistic work on Aboriginal languages in Australia in the 1990s.
>
> Ethnographic writing is rightly under scrutiny and those of us who write about 'other' people must be prepared to be questioned by these people whom we research. They will often tell us that our perceptions are influenced by the specific cultural basis of our analysis.[50]

To give these white writers some idea of what is 'right' Jackie Huggins observes in an article, *Respect V Political Correctness*, that,

> The best books written about Aboriginals by non-Aboriginals are by those who have some relationship and friendships with Aboriginal people. Having a respect and knowledge of Aboriginal culture, history, social issues and what was happening to Aboriginal people in the era in which they are being written about is imperative to how one writes the Aboriginal characters and situations.[51]

Managing director of Fremantle Arts Centre Press (FACP) in Western Australia, Ray Coffey sees the issues for non-Aboriginal writers who dominate the field of books published on Aboriginal topics this way:

> It has been our great concern as a non-Indigenous publisher to be aware of the problems, and the possible problems, to always be vigilant and ever-concerned that as far as possible proper protocols operate. [We] endeavour to address and minimise…problems. Only when all proper care is given and sensitivity is taken, and the correct authorities are adhered to, [can]…a space for discussion, debate and understanding be opened up by non-Indigenous writers and publishers within the broader Australian community…[52]

Coffey comments that from the point of view of the publisher there is no essential difficulty posed by the non-Aboriginal person writing about Aboriginal characters and experiences, "…as long as they are up front about their own identity as non-Aboriginal." This comments suggests that readers can make their own judgment about the value and accuracy of the work. Unfortunately, because books are to some extent written to inform, it is crucial that the information contained in the book is *authentic* and *credible* and accurately reflects and presents, for example, Aboriginal phenomenology. Marlo Morgan's *Mutant Message Down Under* is a classic example of the capacity of a non-Aboriginal writer to lead readers astray. Because Morgan is not an Aboriginal woman she obviously could or would not be privy to sacred men's business. In her book she suggests that she is, and unfortunately her work has been read by many Americans in and outside the academic system, and become a best-seller in the United States.

Reviewers of Aboriginal theatre also flag the issue of authenticity in writing. Geoffrey Milne comments that while some reviewers on the ground may feel that plays by and about marginalised groups are worth reviewing, they often find it hard to convince their editors of the importance of such reviews.[53] Milne acknowledges the people who, "understandably argue against the right of non-Aborigines or non-Greeks (for example) to write about Aborigines or Greeks (for example)."[54] He cites an example of the problems that exist in the area in relation to writing about Aboriginal people and issues, noting Gordon Francis' play, *God's Best Country* about a Northern Territory cattle station's buy-back by a Land Council.[55] The play was generally favourably reviewed by non-Aboriginal reviewers in Perth (and later in a different production in Melbourne), but it was vigorously attacked by Galarrwuy Yunupingu in the *Sunday Territorian* in April 1987 on the grounds of its inherent prejudice and racism.[56] Milne states that Yunupingu's comments were repeated on Territory radio, prompting a public debate in Australian theatre criticism: how often has the opportunity arisen for a Black voice to be heard among the predominantly white voices in the regular arts media?[57]

Aboriginal writers competing with non-Aboriginal writers in attracting contracts with mainstream publishers, coupled with the lack of resources within Indigenous publishing houses, has led to self-publishing becoming a real option in Australia. It has been taken up some of the country's well-known writers, like Lionel Fogarty, Romaine Moreton, Norm Newlin, Kerry Reed-Gilbert, Jennifer Martiniello and myself.

One of the things that has become clear as a result of researching this book, is that whatever is being written, either by emerging or established writers, a general Aboriginal reading audience is yet to be fostered. Many writers are writing with the aim of providing meaningful records for their Aboriginal communities and families. The fact that many writers write in the oral tradition of story-telling and make use of what is commonly referred to as 'Aboriginal English' should ensure that such an audience will develop over time because the works being published are of increasing relevance to Aboriginal people and communities.

This book now goes on to consider other issues such as editorial practices within Aboriginal and mainstream publishing houses, intellectual property and copyrights for Indigenous writers, support mechanisms for Aboriginal writers and how the Aboriginal publishing industry compares with those in Canada and Aotearoa. The analyses in the book will however continue to be focussed on the impact that Aboriginality has on writing produced by Aboriginal people.

Chapter Two
The Effects of Identity on Writing

This chapter considers the definition of Aboriginality in the context of literary works and the further question of definitions of the 'Aboriginal writer'. Some preliminary remarks and discussion from established Australian Aboriginal writers and the publishers of Aboriginal works are introduced. The question of the effect of Aboriginality on writing is raised in order to demonstrate how Aboriginality forms Aboriginal literature stylistically, and further, how as a result of Aboriginality, a distinct Aboriginal literary discourse can be identified within the Australian literary canon. The important question of Aboriginality, although not defined in the introductory chapter, is a continuing theme throughout the whole of this book.

Defining Aboriginality

Historically, governmental definitions of Aboriginality did not emanate from Aboriginal communities. In general, Aboriginal people or communities have not perpetuated or accepted governmental labels such as, half-caste, quarter-caste, quadroon and so on. This phenomena is not mirrored by, for example, Native American sistas and brothers who have been categorised historically by governments by blood quantum. First Nations' North Americans have accepted these definitions/labels.[58]

In Australia definitions of Aboriginality based on blood underpinned the racist notion that Aborigines fathered by white men were more intelligent and indeed more tractable than their 'full-blood' counterparts. Blood-based definitions of Aboriginality were used to justify 'integration' into European society and also underpinned the later and official policy of assimilation. Being defined as 'half-caste' or 'part-Aboriginal' not only detracted from someone's Aboriginality, forcing even Aboriginal people to question their identity, but also supported the policy of assimilation designed in 1951 and amended in 1965 at the Native Welfare Conference, which stated in part:

> The policy of assimilation seeks that all persons of Aboriginal descent will choose to attain a similar manner of living to that of other Australians and live as members of a single community—enjoying the same rights and privileges, accepting the same responsibilities and influenced by the same hopes and loyalties as other Australians.[59]

The assimilation policy was developed from the racist notion that European society is superior/more highly valued socially than Indigenous cultures. Arguably, everyone in Australia is racially mixed, so why were/are Aboriginal people singled out to be divided into part, quarter, half-caste or full-blood? Eve Fesl points out that these terms were used, and are still used, to divide and rule Aboriginal people through such processes of assimilation.[60] The issue of how much Aboriginal blood someone has is directly linked to the assimilation process, as the less blood you have the easier, in the eyes of the government, it will be for you to assimilate, and 'be white'.

Tony Birch believes that the intervention of the government in the lives of Aboriginal people has both erased and reconstructed categories of 'Aborigines' to suit the governmental policy in vogue. He says,

> Attempts to gain full understanding of the identities of Aboriginal people are not possible, as our communities, which frame our identities, are multi-layered and diverse. Aboriginal people realise this in a positive way. Non-Aboriginal representations of our cultures have failed to recognise this, often deliberately so. This has resulted from attempts to re-imagine us, and re-present us as objects suitable for, and benefiting non-Aboriginal society. These negative categories and imagery serve one end; to deny self-identity and therefore self-determination by capturing and controlling definitions of 'the other' in the colonial imagination.[61]

Birch adds that the categories of 'caste' imposed on Aboriginal people, were established not only to break up Aboriginal communities, but to enable legislation to be enacted that would legitimise the practice of utilising Aboriginal labour at a minimal cost.[62]

Today though, defining Aboriginality has become part-and-parcel of being Aboriginal. Defining and declaring Aboriginality is inextricably linked with access, and on the odd occasion, equity. For the purposes of access, federal and state governments require a 'certificate of Aboriginality' signed and sealed by an incorporated Aboriginal organisation. Similarly, applications for the recently released 'Aboriginal Label of Authenticity' require an artist to supply two letters / certificates that confirm the Aboriginality of the artist.

And so it has become necessary for Aboriginal people to define ourselves: for the purpose of broader community acceptance; for the purpose of census counts; for access to employment/education opportunities; and, to satisfy the pluralistic underpinnings of the complex of Australian society, a complex that continues to struggle to assert a 'national' identity—an identity, it seems, that will never be split from its migrant beginnings and that requires the acceptance of Aboriginality.

The problem and practice of classifying Aboriginality has been something 'given' to and 'expected of' Aboriginal people. It is something we seem to have accepted and run with and our own organisations have accepted the requirement of a 'certificate' or 'confirmation' of Aboriginality. There are many good reasons for this though. In the case of publishing for example, a Proof of Aboriginality form was introduced as a guard against exploitation in light of the 1997 outing of Leon Carmen as 'Wanda Koolmatrie'.

Marcia Langton comments that even with the imposed need to categorise, the difficulty Aboriginal people face when trying to define Aboriginality themselves is compounded by past government policies:

> The label 'Aboriginal' has become one of the most disputed terms in the Australian language. There are High Court decisions and opinions on the term and its meaning. Legal scholar, John McCorquordale, has noted sixty-seven definitions of Aboriginal people, mostly relating to their status as wards of the State and to criteria for incarceration in institutional reserves…In one legal case, whether or not an Aboriginal person lived in a 'native's camp' even became an important issue of definition".[63]

Although much of Langton's discussion is in relation to Aboriginality and representations, (or misrepresentations), of Aboriginal people and issues in film and media, her comments on Aboriginality as a 'field of intersubjectivity'[64] are very relevant to literary production. The three categories of cultural and textual construction of Aboriginality that Langton discusses are ubiquitous in, for example, definitions or creations of Aboriginal characters in books.

The categories discussed by Langton are:
- the social interaction of Aboriginal people with other Aboriginal people;
- the cultural and textual construction of Aboriginal ideals/icons/stereotypes by non-Aboriginal people; and
- the constructions created when Aboriginal and non-Aboriginal people interact socially[65]

In contrast to these definitions of Aboriginality, artist and writer Nellie Green from the Badimia people of Western Australia believes that for Aboriginal people,

> The notion of Aboriginality is inseparable from that of identity and identifying with the land we come from. This concept is intrinsically linked to the sense of belonging or the homelands of Indigenous people. The manner in which someone might feel 'Aboriginal' can be determined by how immersed in Aboriginal culture and lifestyle that individual is and how they identify within their community.[66]

She adds,

> Aboriginality is not something that can be or should be classified or measured. Rather, it is an inherent identifying quality that cannot be dismissed or denied. The Aboriginality of a person is not determined by how much Aboriginal blood that person may have. Nor is the Aboriginality of that person lessened because they might have 'mixed blood'.[67]

Ruby Langford Ginibi recognises the influence the general Australian image has over Aboriginal identity, suggesting that the only 'real Aborigines' in the eyes of many whites are the ones sitting on a desert rock with a spear. She says,

But we urban Kooris define ourselves as traditional people too, because we at sometime in our lives come from some tribe, or tribal area. We never asked for the degree of caste that white people have endowed us with, and are always being stereotyped and blamed because of it![68]

Sonja Kurtzer reinforces the point that 'Aboriginality' is something that has been introduced to Aboriginal people from 'white society'. While she admits that the actual concept of Aboriginality didn't exist before colonisation, she sees the impact of this in the way the Indigenous community restrains the Indigenous author by expecting to have Aboriginality 'authentically' represented to the hegemonic culture.[69] Kurtzer points out that historically, Aboriginal Australians referred to themselves and each other according to kinship groups, skin groups, or on the basis of their relationship to totems, the Dreaming or particular areas of land.[70]

For the purposes of the administration of federal government programs and policies, a 'working definition' of Aboriginality was accepted in 1978. This definition was, "An Aboriginal or Torres Strait Islander is a person of Aboriginal or Torres Strait Islander descent who identifies as an Aboriginal or Torres Strait Islander and is accepted as such by the community in which s/he is associated".[71]

This definition is supported and endorsed by public institutions such as the Australia Council for the Arts—the major sponsor of Aboriginal arts in Australia. The Council establishes Aboriginality through three social elements: descent, identification and acceptance.[72]

Since 1977 when Kath Walker was in the literary limelight, Aboriginal writers have been defending and defining their identity. The following excerpt of an interview in *Meanjin* [73] shows the frustrations of Walker with the questions of an ill-informed interviewer:

Interviewer
What proportion of the people generally thought of as Aboriginal are in fact mixed-blood, and do you think –

Walker
Look, you're mixed blood yourself, so why pull this into the scene? You know, when people say to me, Are you a full-blood? I say, No, are you? Now find me a full-blood in the white field. Now what's that got to do with it?

Interviewer
Only in so far as whether there'd be some people who have lived in cities for a couple of generations, and who mightn't want to move, that's all...

Walker
But for God's sake! No-one recognised my white blood in me all these years— why the hell should I have to declare it now? I don't want to declare it. To hell with the white blood in me! I'm Black.

2. The Effects of Identity on Writing

As Australia establishes itself in the 21st century with a growing interest in Reconciliation and Aboriginal affairs generally, it is apparent that the debate and discussion around who is and who isn't Aboriginal is a reaction, in part, to white Australia trying to understand the concept of Aboriginality on its own terms, and always in terms of how it compares with the dominant, (white-mainstream), culture. In this way, for those who don't fit the media portrayal of what it means to be Aboriginal, it can be a difficult task to convince others of your own identity. Aboriginality like sexuality is a personal issue, a personal issue that is now public for public identification.

Robyn McCarron, a Noongar,[74] also notes that the strategies associated with pan-Aboriginality or the ideology of 'Aboriginality' did alter somewhat in the 1990s, with writers asserting their identification with a region—defined by geography, language, cultural practices and kinship ties.[75] Authors in the 1998 anthology, *Across Country* (ABC Books) were also distinguished geographically and by nation to show the diversity existing in Aboriginal identification. In this way, there is a strong shift away from pan-Aboriginality, to recognition and greater understanding of the diversity of culture within Aboriginal Australia. This includes Aboriginal experiences. In terms of Aboriginal literature and those who create it, it is important to see how Aboriginal writers define themselves and their peers.

Jackie Huggins pointed out at the Brisbane Writers' Festival in 1997 that Aboriginality is largely based on the experience of community life. Huggins argues that it is simply not sufficient to have Aboriginal bloodlines without living the Aboriginal experience.

Yet even with the diversity of Aboriginal cultures, and without resorting to pan-Aboriginality, it must be recognised that there is a shared sense of Aboriginality nationally, (and internationally with other Indigenous peoples), regardless of the geographical location or socioeconomic experience of the individual. And so while writers may write of their own individual experience as an Aboriginal person living in a remote, rural or urban setting, they can also express through their writing a unified sense of belonging to a larger Aboriginal community.

To close this preliminary discussion of Aboriginality I cite the then Aboriginal and Torres Strait Islander Social Justice Commissioner, Mick Dodson to sum up what I feel about the categorisation of us as a people:

> Since their first intrusive gaze, colonising cultures have had a preoccupation with observing, analysing, studying, classifying and labelling Aborigines and Aboriginality. Under that gaze, Aboriginality changed from being a daily practice to being a 'problem' to be solved.[76]

So what makes an Aboriginal writer?

Attendant to the question of Aboriginality is the question, What makes an Aboriginal writer? Is an Aboriginal writer someone who is genetically Aboriginal and who writes, or can an Aboriginal writer also be someone who is not genetically Aboriginal, but who writes on Aboriginal issues?

Although this book does not attempt to give a final definition of Aboriginality, it does discuss how Aboriginal writers define themselves and their peers. Numerous interviews with Aboriginal writers suggest a variety of views, all of which relate to the notion of one community, many experiences.

In line with Huggins' views, Jeanie Bell, Murri author of *Talking About Celia* (UQP, 1997), says that to be an Aboriginal author it is important for people to have lived the experience,

> I find it a bit hard to imagine that anyone can really tell a story of an Aboriginal or Islander without having actually lived as one themselves. How can they talk about Aboriginal people and culture if they haven't actually done it? How can you possibly know what people feel and how they cope?[77]

Bruce Pascoe, novelist and publisher from Victoria and Wiradjuri poet, Kerry Reed-Gilbert, are clear about what defines an Aborigine: identity, descent and acceptance. These views are in keeping with public policy about Aboriginal identity. Pascoe comments that Aboriginality entails having, "an Aboriginal heritage, provable family links and acceptance by the Koori community."[78] Reed-Gilbert comments that Aboriginal people have Aboriginal families, Aboriginal blood, and belong to their Aboriginal communities,

> Nobody can just pretend to be an Aboriginal author. Again we also have people whose skin is Black and portray themselves as a Black person giving the wider community and the Black community the impression that they are an Aboriginal person when they're not.[79]

Cathy Craigie believes that an Aboriginal author's identity comes through in the writing, showing that the author has a grasp of the culture and society which they belong to / come from, and that the text will 'reach' an Aboriginal reader by, for example, addressing Aboriginal dilemmas, situations and aspirations. Craigie comments,

> You have to be Aboriginal to do it, if the content is to be factual. I think that more importantly it's the way that you write it and it's the words that you use. It's gotta be something where you capture the essence of what being Aboriginal is about. The sense of humour, language patterns move in and out. It's showing that you are aware of your own culture. When you read some of the Native American writers you can see very strongly that they have a hold of their culture, they understand it. That's where I think a few [Aboriginal] novels have come out and you can see that people don't have a grasp of that.[80]

In Kenny Laughton's view, being born Black in this country gives you an identity and a mantle that you carry wherever you go. He says,

> Aboriginal footballer, Aboriginal lawyer, Aboriginal doctor, Aboriginal author. This is not dissimilar to the categorising of Aboriginal literature. There is that neat little category that western publishers/marketers slot us into under the Aboriginal author niche and then there is the recognition we give each other. That's what we acknowledge. Our Aboriginality gives us our identity as an Aboriginal author.[81]

Agreeing with comments from the authors cited above, Rosemary van den Berg says that an Aboriginal author is one who belongs to the Indigenous / Aboriginal race of people and identifies as such.[82]

In contrast to these views, Melissa Lucashenko comments that Aboriginality is a hard thing to define, something of a continuum rather than, 'you are or you aren't'. She believes that the 'acceptance' side of any definition of Aboriginality can cause problems,

> I think it's something that you grow into, but at the same time as soon as you say that, all those people in the desert can point to us and say you're not Aboriginal because you haven't been through the lore, you haven't grown into it yet.
>
> It's like that bloke in the desert [Ray Beamish] that did the paintings with his wife, is that fraud, is that collaboration? I'm sure he speaks at least one language, and he knows the social norms of that group, so is he white or is he Black? It's complex. Genetically he's white, but in every other aspect of his life he's Black.
>
> So as an Aboriginal writer, I think you do have to write from the experience, but that experience is going to be widely different.[83]

Because Aboriginality is something that is constantly scrutinised by people *outside* the Aboriginal community, it is not surprising to find that there is little difference in the way that Aboriginal writers think about the factors that make for an Aboriginal author. When looking at how Aboriginal writers and other Black Australian writers define themselves however, there are obvious differences. Consider the way that Roberta Sykes never defines, introduces or describes herself or the community she talks about as Aboriginal but 'Black'.[84] Few Aborigines call themselves 'Black Australian' as consistently as Sykes does: we generally define ourselves proudly as Aboriginal, Koori, Wiradjuri or whatever other term makes us distinct from other groups, and certainly other groups internationally, (eg Black Americans).

The fact of this anomaly is also supported by Robyn McCarron who notes that the number of writers who have come from the Noongar community of south west Western Australia is significant, and that increasingly, "the writers have identified themselves as Noongar rather than as Aboriginal or 'Black'".[85]

Although we may share common histories and experiences in terms of colonisation, oppression and racism we are all unique in our cultures and social structures. This is something few white reviewers, impostors and journalists have yet grasped. Prominent Australian citizens who are physically 'Black' but not Indigenous to Australia, are often lumped together by publishers, readers, academics and booksellers, mistakenly or otherwise, with us, Indigenous Australian writers. This practice could suggest a lack of responsivity to community discourse on issues of identity.

The lack of Aboriginal people staffing publishing houses makes it highly likely that publishers will make many mistakes in developing, marketing and distributing books by 'Black Australians'. Therefore, while the look of 'Blackness' overrides the other elements of public policy accepted by Aboriginal Australians as being reasonable criterion for establishing a person's Aboriginality, it would seem that the racism of the Black/white dichotomy is able to be martialled at any point in the writing or publishing process to deceive and entrench the mind-set of the 'average' Australian.

Chapter 3
Indigenous Discourse

> *Current writings by Aboriginal and Torres Strait Islander people belong within a cultural and historical continuity that predates the invasion whilst utilising, adapting and challenging the written genres and forms of the colonising culture.*[86]

David Unaipon is regarded as the earliest pioneer of Aboriginal writing and publishing and is commonly thought to be the first Aboriginal writer in Australia. Unaipon published *Native Legends* in 1929 and wrote articles for the *Daily Telegraph* during 1924. Apart from Unaipon's work it is also generally accepted that written Aboriginal written literature did not fully develop into a distinct genre until the 1970s, 80s and 90s. Penny van Toorn qualifies this generally accepted view commenting that, "Aboriginal people began using the technologies of alphabetic writing and print far earlier than the dominant literary historical narrative would suggest."[87] She points out that this writing and printing was in fact used as early as 1796 when Bennelong dictated a letter to Lord Sydney's steward. Van Toorn notes that letters, poems, essays, pamphlets, newsletters, newspaper articles, petitions, speeches and traditional stories written and printed by Aboriginal people have been overlooked as legitimate forms of literature and publishing.[88]

Non-Indigenous academic, Stephen Muecke, also argues that Aboriginal people considered to be 'illiterate' have always read or written in the broad sense, but that these forms of writing have simply been valued differently by other, (mostly colonising) peoples.[89] Muecke draws on Paddy Roe, (from whom he recorded *Gularabulu: Stories from the West Kimberley* [1983]) as an example of an author who uses an "abstract signifying system of lines, dots, circles and so on," as a form of writing[90], and asks, "do we fail to call it writing because it is kept from white people?"[91] Van Toorn and Muecke show that literature and publishing do not simply include printed works in book form, but can range from dots and circles in the sand to letters, essays, articles, pamphlets and so on.

Jennifer Biddle also discusses the use of Aboriginal artwork as story-telling, particularly in the form of the art book, *Kuruwarri: Yuendumu Doors* (1987). This work highlights the historical literary creativity of Aboriginal people who combine art and language to communicate stories to the broadest possible audience.[92] For example, many Warlpiri people cannot read Warlpiri when it is written in the 'English style' but they can *read* the painted stories. By way of comparison, many Europeans could not *read* these paintings. The skill of portraying a story and comprehending it, adds, I think, another dimension to the concept of 'literacy'.

The late Judith Wright, as early as 1988, described 'Black writing' as, "a literature in its own right".[93] With the dawning of this new understanding, came the rise of a new set of literary questions and issues. By whose standards would *this* writing be judged? Who would be most likely to review and assess such work? Wright posed these questions:

> Do we go on talking from our critical heights, as though our standards are necessarily to be accepted even by those who have no cause to thank us for them? And do we continue to dismiss Black writers unless they somehow contrive to keep a lowly and conventional stand?[94]

Furthermore, by whom and how would this new literature be defined? At the outset it could be argued that any definition of Aboriginal writing should be coming from Aboriginal writers themselves. While the diversity within Aboriginal Australia might make Aboriginal literacy difficult to define, there is consensus among writers that a work must at least be written or co-authored by an Indigenous person for it to be an Aboriginal work. Direct input to the work by an Aboriginal person will result in the work being able to be construed stylistically as, Aboriginal.

Huggins and Bell find it relatively easy to define Aboriginal literature. Huggins sees it as something, "holistic, all-embracing, and written by an Indigenous person."[95] Bell defines it as a way of telling our side of the story in our characteristic style: "we were oral people, so literature wasn't something to worry about sixty years ago, but we've come a long way."[96] In this way, Aboriginal literature can be defined and judged by *writers* in terms of what has driven the production of a work and the way a work reflects the real life experiences of Indigenous people.

Alexis Wright comments that the experience of the Aboriginal writer will influence the writing of a work and that as a result, a distinct Aboriginal literature can be identified because,

> We see the world differently, our experience of the world differs from the rest of the population, and our linguistic expression will differ from what is accepted as Standard English. If Aboriginal writing causes unease it is because it challenges non-Aboriginal perceptions of standard English, or white concepts, values and ways of describing events, places, people etc.
>
> What we do as Aboriginal writers is try to second guess the world of literature, we don't enter into the discourse because our experience does not allow it. There are many people who will not share their knowledge through writing because historically, literature was used against us. They say, why bother trying to explain to them, because they would not understand so our knowledge is wasted on them.[97]

However, poet Lisa Bellear questions whether or not there is actually something that can be defined as Aboriginal literature. She says that if it does exist it is being primarily judged by non-Aboriginal people, the very people Judith Wright suggested should not be judging it. Bellear raises these contemporary questions:

> Is it Aboriginal literature because it's written about an Aboriginal person? Or is it Aboriginal because it's written by an Indigenous person about Aboriginal characters? Or is it Aboriginal just because it's written by an Aboriginal person, even if it's about someone surfing down Byron Bay.[98]

Bellear is, however, adamant that she would not describe anything written by a non-Aboriginal person writing about Aboriginal culture as 'Aboriginal literature'.

Cathy Craigie also feels that it is hard to define Aboriginal writing, but says at the very least works should be by Aboriginal writers and reflect Aboriginal culture, (which relates, in turn, to how one defines 'Aboriginality'). Craigie comments,

> The thing that binds us as Aboriginal people—[though] we have different languages and cultures, there's a general essence of what Aboriginal is and it's the way that you set things up. It's your thinking. I would expect Aboriginal people to understand land issues a lot easier [than whites]. It's the content really, the way you handle the content.[99]

Agreeing with Craigie, Melissa Lucashenko doesn't see Aboriginal writing as a separate genre, but more an issue of content, and that in order for her to define Aboriginal literature she needs to consider the definition of Aboriginality. As she points out,

> To me there are people who are biologically white, but culturally Black and people who have lived in the communities for donkey's years and basically see the world through Black eyes. But they're not the people who are likely to write books, so that complicates it a bit. Aboriginal writing to me at the moment is a protest literature I suppose and it's centered around land and social justice and legal stuff.[100]

Non-Aboriginal academic, Kateryna Olijnyk Longley, admits that it is hard to sum up the body of Aboriginal writing specifically arising from Western Australia. Referring to the work of the writers Glenyse Ward, Jack Davis, Jimmy Chi and Sally Morgan, she says the writing, "accommodates many distinct cultural groups and literary (or anti-literary) approaches," and that, "Aboriginal literature has done more than any other writing to change the direction of literary history in Western Australia over the last few years."[101]

While Aboriginal writers have not generally complained about being boxed into exclusively Aboriginal categories, most *are* writing on Aboriginal issues and experiences. Sandra Phillips points out, though, that we sometimes want it both ways commenting,

> We, as Aboriginal people involved in writing and publishing, want people to recognise the connections between our work and the common basis of

Aboriginal writing or writing by Indigenous people. We want that recognition. At the same time we want recognition of our difference; so we want it both ways and we need to be able to articulate why we can be believed in both ways. The UQP Black Australian Writers Series is chock-a-block with diversity. There would be few titles that I can think of that are the exact same style as others.

The similarities though to my mind as an editor having worked on titles in the last two years is the complete rootedness in this country—Australian characters, mannerisms, landscape depictions, it's from here, and you don't get enough of that sort of sense from many Australian writers. So it's Aboriginal from here but it's also in terms of its non-Indigenous characters from here.[102]

Opposing the previous definitions of Aboriginal literature, Herb Wharton answers the question, "What is Aboriginal literature?" with another question: "What is Aboriginal literature? It's a bit like defining Evonne Goolagong-Cawley, she's an Aboriginal tennis player. Does she play Aboriginal tennis? She's a great tennis player, full-stop."[103]

Is there an Aboriginal style?

At the time of his outing as Wanda Koolmatrie, Leon Carmen claimed that he perpetrated the fraud to show that there were no differences between Black and white writing, or men's and women's writing.[104] After speaking with a number of Aboriginal writers, editors and readers, however, it is clear that Carmen's claim is unfounded.

Throughout the history of Aboriginal Australia, most aspects of Aboriginal society, culture, religion and history were passed on to family and community via an oral tradition that included approximately 200 distinct Aboriginal languages spoken by 600 Aboriginal nations. This involved storytelling to pass on information over generations and this practice endures today. Storytelling was the oral literature, the artform likened to dance, performance and visual arts (which also pass on information). It is this storytelling, or 'oral' technique, that contributes to a distinct Aboriginal style of writing.

The oral tradition is still very evident in Aboriginal writing today. Many authors use 'Aboriginal English' out of respect for its speakers and so as to reach Aboriginal readers. Rather than using Standard English (which they may not be trained in) or an Aboriginal language (which they may not be able to speak or want to write down), many Aboriginal writers choose Aboriginal English. Aboriginal English is an Aboriginalisation of the English language and often needs to be translated to aid understanding by non-Aboriginal audiences. The use of Kriol in Aboriginal writing, (for example, Lionel Fogarty's works), is also common. Kriol is believed to have developed as a common language during the period of first contact as a result of the need for communication between

Aboriginal and non-Aboriginal people.[105] There is a great difference between what is spoken and what is written in the Anglo world, but in Aboriginal society, spoken and written traditions are more closely aligned. Many writers do not want their manuscripts Anglicised (or 'gubbarised'[106]) by editors, who often seem fixated with 'correcting' Aboriginal expressions of English.

Kenny Laughton acknowledges what many writers also affirm, that Aboriginal people tend to write how we speak: "so it's not the Queen's English or remotely Edwardian or Shakespearean, it's Blackfella lingo."[107] But Laughton also acknowledges that Aboriginal writers can 'play the game' when required, being articulate in a variety of styles and able to write what audiences want. He adds,

> We have also developed our own literary language in a sense, our slang some white linguists call, 'Aboriginal English'. I don't necessarily agree with this label as it only makes the white interpreters (who wrote on Aboriginal English) as the experts, once again. But I admit that we do use our own slang, and even though our language and tribal groups (whether you be bush or urban) are diversely different, we still link up through some of this common (equally recognisable) slang (i.e. Koorie, bunji, gammon, etc).

Alexis Wright also comments on the significant linguistic differences between Aboriginal languages and English,

> Early colonial observers chose to denigrate Aboriginal languages as being like gibberish. In fact, Aboriginal languages have a great complexity, which derives from the genius of our people to describe their complex relationships with each other and within their world. Each language contained about 10,000 words which is about the same as any average citizen in any country of the world.[108]

Wright gives an example of her own recording of oral literature for an anthology of land rights stories and essays for the Central Land Council published by IAD Press:

> One exceptional memory man from the Tanami Desert region, wanted to do two tape recordings of the exact same story, one for himself for his particular local audience, and another one for me. There was no saying, "I will send you a copy." He wanted the two recordings there and then.
>
> So we sat down in the spinifex one windy night and he went through his story in Warlpiri. It was about 40 minutes long. Then he went through it again as soon as the first tape was finished and told the exact same story, 40 minutes, and that was for me. He said he did not call himself boss, that is, the senior traditional owner, yet I believed he knew everything about his country. These are our great orators who can recall thousands of site names in their head, each with a sacred song, a Dreaming, and an inter-connected sacred history over vast areas of land. And they might say to you, I cannot read or write, but I got it all along in my brains and I have to say it straight and the right way.[109]

Another example of the recording of oral literature (done well) is contained in the highly regarded, *Gularabulu: Stories of the Kimberley* by Paddy Roe and Stephen Muecke, first released in 1983. Muecke, as scribe, discusses the differences between the people who analyse material and the storytellers: the first set consider material that needs to be studied in an academic sense, and the second tells a story in a traditional sense. Understanding the significance of the storyteller, and he himself as the listener, Muecke says that to represent Roe's works honestly, the stories were presented in the text word for word, from taped recordings. Muecke also included Roe's hesitations as well as his own interventions to show that there could be no doubt as to the authenticity of Roe's stories. He also explains to the reader how he transcribed the storytelling and Roe's use of Aboriginal English. Muecke believes this was the first time that an Aboriginal narrative had been presented in its true form, explaining the common effects of editorial changes that had impacted on works in the past. He says,

> Presenting the stories as narrative art is a way of justifying a writing that tries to imitate the spoken word. When language is read as poetic, it is the form of the language itself, as well as its underlying content, which is important. Just as it would be unjustifiable to rewrite a poet's work into 'correct' English (in other words to take away the poet's 'license'), so it would be unjustifiable to rewrite the words of Paddy Roe's stories.[110]

Muecke also explains that, while some parts of the text might be difficult to understand, it is important to not only listen to the language but the content of Roe's story. When Aboriginal people express themselves without intervention and speak out clearly like Roe does, then the culture will live on, even as times and people change. The integrity of Meucke's work is also found in the fact that Muecke acknowledges the importance of 'Aboriginal English'. Meucke comments that,

> Aboriginal English is a vital communicative link between Aboriginal speakers of different language backgrounds. It also links Blacks and whites in Australia, so, as it is used in these stories, it could be said to represent the language of bridging between the vastly different European and Aboriginal cultures.[111]

The reader can open any page of *Gularabulu* and see an example of Roe's story-telling technique and use of Aboriginal English. Here's just a sample from the story 'Living Ghost',:[112]

Well this fella used to look after that trough he had —
oh he had childrens too —
he had childrens —
he had about five or six children —
and an old lady —
mother for the children —
old man —

> *so this old man had a bicycle* —
> *you know he gotta go back to station to get his tucker*
> *every Friday* —
> *he must go and get his tucker* —
> *he carried, ration in the bicycle (laugh)* —
> *hard work* —

Aboriginal speech patterns put into the written form provide Aboriginal writing with character, passion, authenticity and humour. An example of the great effect of Aboriginal English is Alf Taylor's characterisation of Barney in his story *The Wool Pickers*:

> Um gunna take Auntie Florrie to dat French River Place, somewhere. And next we be goin' to see that Nyoongah bloke. You know, he was locked up in jail for twenty years an' come out to run his own country. Wass his name?[113]

Another great storyteller and an author whose writing is largely based on the oral form, Ruby Langford Ginibi says Aboriginal writers choose Aboriginal English as a way of writing because,

> We, Aboriginal people, come from an oral tradition, where our legends, and laws, were handed down by word of mouth, from generation to generation, it is we, who have always had to conform to the standards of those invaded, learn the Queen's English, so us Mob can write our stories so you Mob can comprehend what we are on about.[114]

Colin Johnson believes that oral literature is often relegated to the status of children's stories and hacked to pieces by editors who do not pause to think why oral stories, (commonly referred to as 'Dreamtime stories'), even existed and what they signified.[115] He points out that oral literature is important, though, as it "describes Aboriginal life in Australia before invasion."[116] He also notes that generally when Aboriginal oral literature has been collected and published,

> Little or no regard has been paid to how it was told, that is to the discourse of the story. Content was considered more important. Sometimes the very ones at fault have been academics, linguists who should have known better. Other whites were exploiters after a quick quid. They obtained a version of a story, then rewrote it for publication as a children's story.[117]

In his first book on Aboriginal writing, *Writing from the Fringe*, Colin Johnson warns Aboriginal writers that if they write according to white styles, in white genres and with white theories, then they run the risk of being judged by white standards. However, as Perth based poet and journalist Rod Moran points out,

> At the heart of this book there is a paradox. While issuing this warning Mudrooroo himself is employing some of the most ratified 'white', indeed colonial, literary theory. It includes French phenomenology, deconstructionism and semiotics. He nowhere reflects on this paradox and what it might mean for his aesthetic overall.[118]

A number of Aboriginal writers suggest it is the language and the use of it that gives their writing an Aboriginal style. Sandra Phillips, editor of books by Lisa Bellear, Jeanie Bell, Alexis Wright and Melissa Lucashenko, notes that there are obvious differences in language between Black and white writers. She comments, for example, "Jeanie Bell's sentences weave and flow rather than being manipulated to suit conventional sentence structure. They match the language to suit the style of communication."

A wide reader, Melissa Lucashenko, also notes the familiarity Aboriginal works have for her, compared to non-Aboriginal works. She says, "It strikes a chord. Language, and the way people are socially, would tell me if an author is Aboriginal or not. The details could give it away." But she also adds that when you have whitefellas who have lived a Black life then they could write a book that was, to her, for all intents and purposes, Aboriginal-sounding. Lucashenko comments,

> A lot of older white writing is about landscapes and it feels dry and false to me. More modern [Aboriginal] writing is more oral and is closer to what I call an Indigenous style. It's about standing back and noticing what people are doing and slotting it into an Indigenous context. The little details.

In terms of her own personal style Lucashenko says she can write in different styles including academic and 'street-style'. She adds, "I think the style that's closest to my real style is short words, short sentences, very clear, very direct and fairly confronting but again, acknowledging that it's a complex work."

Jackie Huggins who can and does write in many styles, (for example academic, biographical and autobiographical), admits there is a definite style inherent in Aboriginal work compared to non-Aboriginal work, "it's grammatical too, syntax, how we write. It can be the slickest writing, but you can still tell that it's Indigenous."

Known for her hard-hitting political poetry, Kerry Reed-Gilbert says that it is the use of colloquial language that sets Aboriginal writers apart from non-Indigenous writers who more often employ a 'high' literary language, especially in their poetry,

> I think in relation to poetry itself that a majority of non-Aboriginal people write in a way that people can't understand what they are talking about. When there is a language barrier anyway amongst people it is a lot harder to understand what a person is trying to say when you can't understand the words they are saying. I find they use words that are jargon or so big and they end up losing their audience. Now me, I lose them cause they don't like what I'm saying, that's different to not being able to understand me.[119]

Gilbert's views are supported by van den Berg, who says Aboriginal writers often have a more straightforward style of writing, "that denotes a people who are not really into the 'posh' English of white writers. Much like my own style of writing. I don't like using big words to describe things or to tell a story when simple words are just as clear and easier to read".[120]

Supporting both van den Berg and Gilbert, John Muk Muk Burke believes that Aboriginal writers are very rarely academic in their writing but often very deep saying, "most of us don't use big words in our writing. Some of us write what looks like very simple stuff but it is in fact very serious and very deep and layered and layered."[121]

Laughton uses the contrast between white and Black writing to define an Aboriginal style saying that non-Aboriginal authors also have a distinct cultural advantage, having used the written form of recording language for hundreds of years longer than our writers,

> Our stories were an unwritten form. Translated and passed down through many generations by story telling and the corroborree. So in a sense, the art of writing as a means of saving or at least recording our language, culture, history, in comparison to say the European or Asian cultures, is a relatively new medium for Aboriginal people.

Kombumerri writer, lecturer and consultant in Aboriginal matters, Mary Graham offered the Australian Publishers' Association Residential Editorial Program in 1999 some basic differences between writing based on oral story-telling and European writing. These differences include:

1) A different logic between Aboriginal and non-Aboriginal thinking. All perspectives are valid and reasonable in Aboriginal society with no absolutes, where even contradictory things are negotiable.
2) There is a different sense of time for Aboriginal people, with the idea of beginning/middle/end being a foreign concept, meaning the Aboriginal view is not linear.
3) An individual is a member of a group, and while Europeans would say this leads to 'conformity', Aboriginal people see this as not being isolated from their community.
4) Stories don't 'belong' to an individual in Aboriginal society as they do in non-Aboriginal societies and it is against lore to tell someone else's story. And regardless of geography, all stories are traditional.
5) The place for authority is well defined in Aboriginal society and the older people in communities work out of a distinction between power and authority. Grey hair is a good thing, denoting authority, and it is a good thing to have children and grand children.
6) Land is the basis of all life for Aboriginal people and the relationship between land and people sets the tone for the relationship between people, and for this display of manners. All the creative process, culture, comes out of land itself.

7) Decolonisation is demystifying and defining Aboriginality is a new concept. There is a notion of universal 'assumed knowledge' in our culture, which means there is no necessity to describe.

8) Contradiction is an issue for the writer, that is, the editor should emphasise craft in editorial comments rather than the 'utopian' idea of perfection. There is not utopia in Aboriginal culture. The pure/spontaneous thing is natural to an Aboriginal writer.[122]

The differences described by Graham contribute to defining an Aboriginal style of writing.

Another example of an Aboriginal style of writing is given by Sandra Phillips who cites a manuscript she read as part of the David Unaipon Award,

> I read it and said I think this is a non-Aboriginal woman. It can be quite easy to read something and figure it out. I have no doubt that it's not an Aboriginal person. It comes through in the language of the cover letter. And when people are Aboriginal they say I'm from here or there, this is who I am. That's the identifier. But you can't base statements like that on total credibility either, but that's part of the picture of the presentation. These are the sorts of things that a non-Indigenous editor mightn't pick up.

Cathy Craigie, who mixes different styles in her writing, says she prefers using Aboriginal English. So too does Alexis Wright. In an interview with Alison Ravenscroft Wright comments that she writes the way she speaks, and that this comes from her attachment to traditional land in the Gulf of Carpentaria. She adds that Aboriginal people generally need to be able to write their own work their own way saying, "we need to choose our own voices."[123]

Along with all the arguments which say that Aboriginal voices are distinctly different to white styles of writing—partly due to the use of Aboriginal English, and partly due to the content of the writing—it must also be recognised that within the editorial processes of Aboriginal publishing houses, new styles are actually being created. Two books released by Magabala Books in 1999 used the form of storytelling for the purposes of autobiography. The books were *Jinangga* by Monty Walgar (as told to Cloud Shabalah) and *Holding up the Sky: Aboriginal Women Speak*, an anthology of nine women from around Australia. Both books, even though telling the stories of ten different people, are written in the same style—short, simple sentences, occasional Aboriginal English, and little dialogue —with content based on experiences of Aboriginal people living in a variety of situations and locations. More noteworthy in this context is the anthology of women's writing whose nine stories are by women from such different locations as Broome, Beagle Bay, Perth, Yarrabah and northern New South Wales.

The voice in each of these stories is so similar to the next and it is, at times, difficult to tell the authors apart. Having followed closely on the release of

Walgar's life story, one must ask if these works are really in a 'Magabala House Style' as opposed to an Aboriginal style.

In what genres do we excel?

Considering the number of published poets and autobiographers we have, it would be hard to ignore these as our main genres for writing, but as we move more into fiction, and even erotica, this is changing. Aboriginal writers are telling their stories through the printed word in poetry, fiction, autobiography and biography, essays, histories, short stories, plays and film scripts. But we are still categorised and known largely for life-writing. (See Appendix A for a Catalogue of Aboriginal Literature.)

Editors, Josie Douglas and Marg Bowman, from the Institute of Aboriginal Development Press in Alice Springs, believe that when Aboriginal writing first began to emerge during the 1960s, poetry was the most popular genre,

> Aboriginal people were writing in a time of great political change and activism, land rights and the right to vote were all part of this era. Poetry at this time carried the voice of protest and was used as a political tool. Aboriginal poetry today still carries a political message. Even those themes that might normally be considered apolitical can't escape the political nature of Aboriginal people's experiences. Black poetry is a commentary on Black lives, showing the diversity and range of the Aboriginal experience.[124]

Regardless of why the poetry is being produced, non-Aboriginal, Werner Arens says there is no way that you can by-pass the contribution that Aboriginal poets make to a, "new consciousness in the white and Black community with regard to Australian self-image."[125]. He cites the poetry written over two decades by Kath Walker, Jack Davis and Kevin Gilbert as the force behind bringing to public attention the existence of, "a second cultural tradition in Australia."[126] *In Writing from the Fringe*, Johnson sees the practicality of writing and publishing affecting the genres in which Aboriginal people appear, noting the costs of publishing a novel are far higher than running off short photocopied manuscripts of poetry through a community organisation.[127]

Although Jackie Huggins acknowledges that poetry is a popular genre with Indigenous writers, she points out that, "the life-story, biography and autobiography will always be around because for most writers, that's the first book that they write." Autobiography is a genre in which Aboriginal people throughout Australia are choosing to write, documenting their life experiences and expressing both their own anguish and the anguish of their fellows. Autobiographies are the history and text books of Aboriginal Australia. Writing autobiography is a way of retrieving and reclaiming a past that in many parts has not been either written down or recorded accurately. Autobiography is a key place for Aboriginal people to start writing, empowering us to use (and at times change) the English language, a language that was once used against us, describing us as 'barbaric' and 'savage'.

This type of writing plays a number of roles, not only because it provides a vehicle for the author to learn to write about their own history, but also because it educates and often entertains a wider audience who may have a narrow perspective on Aboriginal Australia. Perhaps most importantly, it also makes available first hand accounts of sometimes disturbing and hitherto hidden aspects of Australian history. Lisa Bellear bases much of her poetry on first hand experiences and comments that the genre of autobiography is also a very important component of our culture, "given that for 208 years we've been silenced and told that our stories aren't of worth."[128]

One of the most widely read autobiographies in Australia is Ruby Langford Ginibi's *Don't Take Your Love to Town* which has appeared on the NSW Higher School Certificate Curriculum for many years. Ginibi says that she decided to pick up a pen in 1984 to write her autobiography because she realised there was nothing taught in the school curriculum about Kooris:

> I thought if I wrote about my experiences as an Aboriginal person, it might give the other side, the 'white side', some idea of how hard it is to survive between the Black and white culture of Australia, and they might become less racist and paternalistic towards our people.[129]

Some autobiographies cross into biographies as life-stories are retold to family members or trusted writers. Biographies are also a vehicle for writing about history and recording facts about significant Aboriginal people, communities and moments in time. Authors published in the genre of biography include Jeanie Bell, (*Talking About Celia*), Mary Coe, (*Windradyne—A Wiradjuri Warrior*), Eric Wilmot, (*Pemulwuy: The Rainbow Warrior*) and Rosemary van den Berg (*No Options, No Choice- the Moore River Experience*).

Due to the profile of co-author Jackie Huggins, one of the more well-known biographies is *Auntie Rita*, a book of dialogue between mother and daughter and the first of its kind. The story tells of Rita Huggins' forced removal from her traditional lands as a child, her resettled life on Cherbourg Aboriginal reserve under the Aborigines Protection Act, right through to the rise of Aboriginal political activism in the 1960s and her life in Brisbane.

Regardless of genre, 'rewriting history' can be an appropriate phrase for much of the work currently being penned by Aboriginal writers in recent years. Aboriginal authors are rewriting the history books that have conveniently left out the facts around invasion, colonisation and attempted genocide. Aboriginal people today are documenting the history of a people misrepresented, or not represented at all in history books of the past. As Langford Ginibi comments,

We are writing our histories too. We are telling our stories, and saying the same things about our dispossession in the hope that people will understand us better. And the writing of our stories, our biographies, and autobiographies are our documentation of our histories and stories. From our Aboriginal perspectives, and they need to be read, and heard all over this great land, because for too long, we have had other people defining, and telling us who we are.[130]

In *Us Mob* Johnson agrees that so many Indigenous historical narratives are being written because he believes that while Indigenous people have no 'true' past, they can have no 'self'.[131] He adds, "It is our [sic] past and only we can write it, for in a sense we need history and it is not 'ours' until we do the writing ourselves, giving importance to those stories which now matter to us."[132]

Another cultural and historical work published as part of UQP's Black Australian Writers Series is Jackie Huggins' *Sister Girl*, a long-awaited collection of the author's writings over ten years. In this, her first book to follow *Auntie Rita*, Huggins gives 'an Aboriginal view', (as opposed to 'the' Aboriginal view which is a much misused phrase) on a wide range of political and personal topics that have directed her in her life's work. The first line of the first chapter opens discussion on a very important topic: "is it possible for white Australians to write 'Aboriginal history'? Obviously not when you consider, as Huggins points out, that there still exists the missing written history of Aboriginal women and their role as pioneers in Australian colonial society—a role defined and substantiated by testimonies of six Aboriginal women interviewed by Huggins who proved that they, and their 'sister girls' lived through times where, "the Black woman's entire day seemingly revolved around catering for the white family's needs."[133]

Sister Girl is classified in the genre of history and essays, but because of Huggins' real life experiences, roles and responsibilities as an Indigenous woman with a profile and power in Australia, it is also an autobiographical work giving a very real insight into the psyche of a contemporary Murri woman and the society from which she comes. In *Sister Girl* Huggins points out what most of us as Blackfellas often say, that when you are born Aboriginal, you are born political, and her writings in *Sister Girl* are testament to that belief. As Huggins says, "political awareness and action is a way of life."[134]

Within the non-fiction genre there are also Aboriginal writers who are publishing academic books. Authors like Aileen Moreton-Robinson have published writings in the area of native title, whiteness, race, and feminism in anthologies and journals, nationally and internationally. Her book *Talkin' Up to the White Woman*, is a thesis which interrogates feminism and its practices in relation to Indigenous women of Australia and provides a new standard in Indigenous non-fiction writing in Australia (UQP 2000).

While these kinds of works are written, styled, structured, directed at, and reviewed largely by white-mainstream academic institutions and individuals, they are indeed defined as Aboriginal literature. While the 'style' and 'language' may be regarded as colonised, it is the message of the work, and the delivery of that message on issues such as whiteness or race, that provides the obvious 'identifier' or clue as to whether the book has been written by an Aboriginal person or whether the book has entailed consultation with Aboriginal people as to the content and 'tone' of the message presented. It can perhaps be claimed that to some degree there is an overarching 'Aboriginal ideology' that can be identified in Aboriginal writing, in particular in the policy orientated statements that generally emanate from public institutions. For example, compare, "Aboriginal people should assume responsibility of their health care", with, "The Aboriginal community should retain the control of their health care". Obviously the latter phrase is more likely to have resulted from consultation with Aboriginal people because it avoids the paternalism inherent in the first phrase. However, it is also the case that the rhetorical perspectives of either phrase position 'the Aboriginal' in ways that majority interests in Australia could never be positioned. However, without our own voices in and out of literary genres, our influence on the public policies of the State are diminished.

Although much Aboriginal history and real life experience is written in the non-fiction genres, there is a growing pool of fiction writers that touch on the politics of being Aboriginal and the realities of Aboriginal experiences in their novels. While we have a smaller, yet growing pool of writers in the area of fiction than other genres, there is a strong core of published authors making names for themselves and their works can be found on university reading lists and course guides around the country.

Alexis Wright says that what she is doing in the novel as an Aboriginal writer is trying to make sense of her own world: "I care and I don't care about genres, discourse, standard English, expectations or assumptions, reality or chronology. If I challenge the lot it does not really matter because I have nothing to lose."[135] Unless she is asked to write otherwise, she says she chooses to write fiction because she feels she would fail if she tried to write factual history.[136] In writing *Plains of Promise*, for example, Wright says she tried to create a set of characters that are very real to her, and although a lot of the story comes from her own experience, the characters are not from her real life. Wright says fiction is the one way of saying all the things that need to be said to the reader, without exposing people from her traditional area to the kind of scrutiny that a conventional history book would have risked.[137]

Other fiction writers that include personal experience in their work include Doris Pilkington, John Muk Muk Burke, Melissa Lucashenko and Steven McCarthy.

As the pool of fiction writers grows, so does the pool of Aboriginal playwrights, who also include Aboriginal politics and experiences in their genre. And while it is true to say that few Australian plays appear in print, it is also true that even fewer Aboriginal plays are published. That does not mean they are not being performed and work-shopped however. The published works include those of Roger Bennett, (*Funerals and Circuses*), Jack Davis, (*Kullark, The Dreamers, No Sugar, In Our Town, Honeyspot, Barungin, Moorli and the Leprechaun*), Kevin Gilbert, (*The Cherry Pickers*) and Robert Merritt (*The Cake Man*). Other plays like Craigie's, *Murri Time* and *Koori Love* are not published but have been work-shopped and toured throughout New South Wales and Queensland, while Owen Love's, *No Shame* has toured Queensland and was performed at the 7th Festival of Pacific Arts in Samoa in 1996.

Jack Davis believed that theatre offers an opportunity to use all the talents of speech and body movement present in Aboriginal oral literature and dance since time began. He was not surprised that his Aboriginal background was a great asset in theatre, saying,

> The Nyoongah language was always full of humour and music. Theatre in a bush arena, is the very essence of an Aboriginal corroborree and performances there are often full of brilliant dance and mime. There was and is great opportunity for theatre to draw upon the rich Aboriginal oral literature.[138]

Eva Johnson is another playwright who has made a huge contribution to the representation of Aboriginal women, and was the writer/director of the First National Black Playwrights Conference in Canberra in 1987. She is the author and co-director of the play, *Tjindarella* which debuted at the First Aboriginal Women's' Arts Festival in Adelaide in 1984. The play examines Aboriginal oppression and highlights the effects of government policy on the forced removal of children from their parents and culture.

Kooemba Jdarra Indigenous Performing Arts in Queensland has also been very successful with its production of *The 7 Stages of Grieving* performed by AFI Award winner Deborah Mailman. The story of an "Aboriginal Everywoman", the play has been staged in Sydney, Melbourne, Tasmania, Canberra, Western Australia and Brisbane. *The 7 Stages of Grieving* was also published by Playlab Press and the publication includes the script, reference material, support articles and the national tour program.

Bran Nue Dae, a piece of musical theatre also showed the success of Aboriginal writing for performance as did Wesley Enoch's, *Sunshine Club* musical that graced the stage at the Sydney Opera House in 2000. Katherine Brisbane, co-founder and publisher of Currency Press, the main publisher of Australian plays, commented in her paper to the IDEA'95—2nd World Conference of Drama/Theatre and Education that,

> *Bran Nue Dae* in 1989 was a turning point in the short history of Aboriginal writing for theatre. Twenty years of evolution: in writers, political activists, actors, dancers, singers and song-writers, preceded it... Encouraged by the public statements [of the 60s], individual voices began to be heard. Poetry and song came first; drama followed.[139]

Brisbane now feels that the most important new Australian voice in drama, and one that will in due course be widely heard in other countries, is the Aboriginal one.[140]

Just as the theatre provides a mechanism for appealing to large audiences because of its entertainment value, so too do children's books by Aboriginal authors and illustrators. These books are increasingly being used in education, to teach young people, (and indeed older people with literacy problems), about Aboriginal society and culture and in particular about Aboriginal creation stories. Perhaps the more marketable Aboriginal works, are in fact, those in the area of children and juvenile literature because of the large educational market. Well known names from various states and territories and Aboriginal nations grace the covers of many award-winning children's books.

Although better-known for his political poetry, Lionel Fogarty also writes children's stories and published *Booyooburra: A Story of the Wakka Murri* in 1993. Fogarty says,

> My own initiative to write this story was to bring truth to the children's eyes and truth to the children's minds. With a little bit of information or a little tiny bit of a story from back then, you can bring it into the reality of today, because those stories are thousands and thousands of years old, and are still the essence of knowledge today.[141]

Authors like Narelle McRobbie, (*Who's That Jumbun in the Log*), use Aboriginal words and illustrations to get messages across to children. She says her love of writing short stories for children has been furthered by her commitment to keeping languages alive. McRobbie says it was her mother, (to whom the book is dedicated), who instilled traditional language into her thoughts.[142]

Other writers whose family background and fluency in language affected their work include the late Daisy Utemorrah whose first collection of stories, *Do Not Go Around the Edges*, won the Australian Multicultural Children's Book Award in 1992 and was also short-listed for the Children's Book of the Year in the same year.

Margaret Dunkle published, *Black in Focus: A Guide to Aboriginality in Literature For Young People* in 1994, which focuses on books for young people on Aboriginal themes from 1960 onwards. Nearly 1000 titles by Aboriginal and non-Aboriginal authors were culled to 300 books with Aboriginal themes that were appropriate for young people. The books were reviewed with the assistance of Pat Torres, Jackie Huggins and May O'Brien, all with young Aboriginal people in mind as readers. The reviews highlight the large number of inappropriately written books in one genre alone.

With the exception of Melissa Lucashenko's novels for young adults and my book, *The Diary of Mary Talence*, we are lacking in books in the young adult range, as our major focus has been children's books and adult fiction.

The short story form, though, continues to be popular with Aboriginal writers. In the anthology, *Across Country* (ABC Books, 1998), names such as Herb Wharton, Alf Taylor and Alexis Wright give strength and credibility to this collection compiled by non-Indigenous editor Kerry Davis whose 'specialties' include 'Indigenous literature.'[143] What you'll find in *Across Australia* is 30 short stories by 18 Indigenous writers from across Australia except Tasmania, which is a noticeable gap: a few yarns from story-teller and author Ida West or Jimmy Everett would have added flavour to the collection. *Across Country*, unlike glossy *Indigenous Australian Voices*,[144] not only showcases established writers such as Bruce Pascoe, Herb Wharton and Alexis Wright, but also provides a forum for many new and emerging writers to showcase their work in a collection that will gain wide coverage. New writers like Fabienne Bayet, Harold Hunt and Janice Slater mix their blend of writing with those that have been published for years.

Although Aboriginal writers are clearly writing across all genres, the question of whether or not there is an 'Aboriginal genre' or 'Aboriginal discourse' as such is not as clear. Sam Cook (ex-Magabala staff member) says she finds it difficult to categorise Aboriginal writing as she does not agree with pigeon-holing Indigenous publications into western genres. She says this is because,

> Our works are so much more. For example most of the titles considered children's books should also be considered art books and even cultural literacy resources. I see no reason why we cannot extend the definition of the genres to accommodate our differences.[145]

Aboriginality and writing

Kerry Reed-Gilbert whose poetry in, *Black Woman, Black Life* is heavily influenced by her identity, is clear about the role of Aboriginality in writing, saying, "Aboriginal identity is who we are as writers, as people. We live our lives as the Indigenous people of this land, we write as Indigenous people of this land."

Jeanie Bell agrees that Aboriginal identity plays a definite role in the way she writes and in the reasons for Aboriginal authors writing,

> It [identity] gives you an opportunity to write, to look at your own position and how you feel about yourself and where you see yourself in relation to history, and your community in terms of the bigger picture. But it also reaffirms who you are, and it's a statement to the world of, "This is who I am and I'm proud of who I am."

Kenny Laughton says it is important to retain our Aboriginality in our writing, believing that we have a moral obligation to be role models, proving that, "we as Aboriginal people can not only achieve but mix it with the best of them, in any field, be it sport, work or writing." Finally Alexis Wright is adamant that she doesn't want her Aboriginality separated from her writing as it is, she says, "what's producing the writing. Without it I wouldn't be able to write the way I do."[146]

As publisher at FACP, Ray Coffey says the number of autobiographical works, family and community histories by Aboriginal writers is evidence that through personal testimony, there is an obvious attempt to establish and project a sense of Aboriginal identity.[147]

The concept of Aboriginality is certainly a difficult thing to grasp for contemporary Australians; indeed, sometimes even for Aboriginal people themselves, especially those who have been denied access to family, culture and community due to government policies of the past. The effects of the differing experiences of Aboriginality, though, are nevertheless evident in writings by Aboriginal people, regardless of genre. The act of writing often becomes more than something creative for some Aboriginal people who seek to use the process as a vehicle for analysing, processing, determining, understanding and asserting their identity. The process of writing also allows individuals, like Sally Morgan for example, to follow their journey of discovering their Aboriginality and document it for their own and other's benefit.

The way in which Aboriginal people have been categorised by race in terms of where they fit into literature is no different to the way in which they have been defined in sports, history, the arts and politics. Although many would like to be regarded and critiqued for their writing, rather than their race, 'Aboriginal author' is also a cementing of identity for the writer, and a categorisation that doesn't offend most Aboriginal writers. Most writers are proud of their identity as well as their ability to write in a profoundly white world, because, in the words of Ruby Langford Ginibi, "we are reclaiming our history, our heritage, and our identity, and that's very important to our cause."[148]

As to whether or not publishers are more wary since the Johnson/Sykes controversies, Ray Coffey, speaking for FACP, says they probably aren't, "because we have always been fairly careful." As a publisher of only Western Australian writers Coffey says it is perhaps easier for them to check on the credentials of writers who present as Aborigines, "we are perhaps more easily able to determine whether an individual is known and recognised by the local Aboriginal community as being Aboriginal".

In response to the never-ending questions around whether or not a particular writer is or isn't 'Aboriginal', Bruce Pascoe raised some interesting points at the 1998 Spring Writing Festival, when in the "Land, Life and Literature" session he asked if Bryce Courtney was really South African, or 'just jumping on the bandwagon' and whether or not David Malouf was really Lebanese or 'just trying to sell books.'[149] He taunted the audience with, "I'm surprised you haven't put that question to him because it's a crucial literary concern".[150]

Post-Colonial—NOT!

In terms of the academic world, the literature of African countries, Australia, Bangladesh, Canada, Caribbean countries, India, Malaysia, Malta, New Zealand, Pakistan, Singapore, South Pacific Island Countries and Sri Lanka, are often defined as 'post-colonial literatures'. Ashcroft, Griffiths and Tiffin suggest,

> The term 'post-colonial' is used generally to describe all cultures affected by the imperial process from the moment of colonisation to the present day. It is also considered as the most appropriate term for the new cross-cultural criticism which has emerged in recent years and for the discourse through which it is constituted.[151]

They go on to say that the idea of 'post-colonial theory' is a reaction to equate European theory with what they term as post-colonial writing.[152] But it might also be suggested that the term 'post-colonial' is simply a term used to describe much contemporary writing.

In terms of defining Aboriginal writing as post-colonial literature, it appears that there are two distinct views. Firstly, that of the literary establishment who use the term as a way of describing a genre in which Aboriginal people write; and secondly, that of most Aboriginal writers who see the term implying that colonialism is a matter of the past and that decolonisation has taken place, which of course is not the case. In this way, most writers do not even consider the term in relation to their writing at all, which makes this discussion difficult.

As comments by writers below show, the term 'post-colonialism' is largely meaningless to Aboriginal people, bearing in mind the political, social and economic status we currently occupy. Kathryn Trees, in a joint paper with Colin Johnson, asks the questions,

> Does post-colonial suggest colonialism has passed? For whom is it 'post'? Surely not for Australian Aboriginal people at least, when land rights, social justice, respect and equal opportunity for most does not exist because of the internalised racism of many Australians.
>
> In countries such as Australia where Aboriginal sovereignty, in forms appropriate to Aboriginal people, is not legally recognised, post- colonialism is not merely a fiction, but a linguistic manoeuvre on the part of some 'white' theorists who find this a comfortable zone that precludes the necessity for political action.

> Post-colonialism is a 'white' concept that has come to the fore in literary theory in the last five years as Western nations attempt to define and represent themselves in non-imperialist terms.[153]

Unlike some other Pacific Nation writers who accept the term 'post-colonial,'[154] claiming to write from a post-colonial experience, there are few, if any Aboriginal Australian writers who agree with or use the term at all, least of all in relation to their writing. Its relevance to Aboriginal people appears to be non-existent. As high numbers of Aboriginal people continue to be incarcerated and die in prison, and the community still experiences infant mortality rates the same as Third World nations, and we continue to need government assistance in attaining housing, education and basic health care, it is apparent that colonisation, as Aboriginal people interpret it, is alive, even before considering the current Liberal Government's approach to Native Title, and its failure to acknowledge the damaging effects of government policies that led to the Stolen Generations.

Sandra Phillips quite strongly believes that we are still colonised and that it makes those in the literary and publishing community feel better to think we're post-colonial. She adds,

> But if only they'd realise the way in which they carry themselves in society today still is colonial. They take an ownership stand, saying if we didn't colonise these people they wouldn't be able to create this stuff.

Jackie Huggins is offended by the term post-colonial, preferring the term 'neo-colonial' but feels that, along with the term 'post-modernism', they are all just yuppie buzz words which,

> Convolute the whole process of writing that says there isn't a colonial mentality still in existence. In Queensland for sure you can see it. I think because we live so close to a certain member of Parliament here it's exacerbated unusually.[155]

Lisa Bellear is straightforward in her reaction to the term, saying,

> I know that if you are widely read and well-travelled then you would see the total inappropriateness of using that word [post-colonial] and the more that you try to justify using that word in a sense that you offer the definitions and framework, theoretical constructs, the more full-of-shit you are… . How can people use it when you know what's going on in this country.

Herb Wharton acknowledges the term but says he doesn't worry too much about or agree with a lot of the things academics say because,

> When they're describing Australian literature, there's no cut-off date for the history of Australia. The literary history or the recorded history. 1788 is when Europeans came. But Australian history and its literature and stories were there all the time.

Cathy Craigie like myself, thinks it's hard to believe there is any such thing as post-colonial when you are the people who've been colonised:

We're still in Aboriginal time, Murri time, we're still in there doing the same things. For me it's a continuation of a culture that's thousands and thousands of years old. It's not something that you cut off because white man has come in.

For Craigie the term post-colonial only fits the white system, rather than acknowledging our own time-frame. She explains, "my definition of time is endless, it's past, present and future."

In contrast, both Lucashenko and Laughton agree that their writing reflects the effects of being colonised. Lucashenko, who was born in 1967, says that everything in her life, including her writing, is touched by or has risen out of colonialism, not being able to grow out of anything traditional. She dissects the issue of post-colonialism, saying,

> What's post-colonialism? Then you have to ask what's colonialism?, which is the process of coming in and taking people's land and sovereignty away from them. The process of actually taking that has almost ended, but it hasn't quite ended because of Mabo and Wik where it's politically still going on, and psychologically, because people in the bush are much closer to that stuff I think, than people in the city, so to them they are far more in the colonial period than we are. In some senses, people have discovered how to be Black living in Redfern, living the urban lifestyle, and that's sort of edging towards post-colonialism to me. I'm not saying that we're not oppressed, I'm saying that what I define as a colonial era is ending and now the oppression is still there, but the circumstances of our oppression are changing.

Although not accepting the use of the term, Kenny Laughton can see why Aboriginal writing has to be called post-colonial. He says,

> Let's face it, prior to the arrival of white man, our history, everything about us was recorded by mediums other than the written word. But our ancestors were prolific storytellers, they must have been; for these stories to be passed on from generation to generation, for hundreds of thousands of years. So the 'post-colonial' label is one that would sit comfortably with the anthropologists and the linguists and the historians, maybe even with some of our Aboriginal 'academics' as they would have been the first to use pen and paper to form their opinions on Aboriginal Australia.

> But I don't necessarily accept it. Not as an Aboriginal author, especially knowing the depth, the intricate knowledge, and the elaborate ceremonies that were the blue prints for the Dreamtime generation stories. Our first form of written history may be classed as 'post-colonial' but our stories could almost be described as 'post-history'.

In her book *Literary Formations: Post colonialism, Nationalism and Globalism* (1995), Anne Brewster says post-colonialism may be,

> Useful when describing certain aspects of post-invasion culture in Australia, (such as the relationship between Australia and the United Kingdom or the West), as a discourse it has not been scrupulous in distinguishing between the

very different formations of colonisation and the decolonisation in 'settler' and Indigenous cultures.[156]

Brewster understands fully the irrelevancy of the term post-colonialism to Aboriginal people generally, and writers specifically, and says that through her own studies she realised that, "the discourses of post-colonialism and feminism diverged from that of Aboriginality."[157]

Muecke agrees saying, "Australia seems to be caught in a post-colonial syndrome, because, unlike America, independence has not been fully achieved either historically, through war for instance, or symbolically: the Fourth of July."[158] And while some advocates of the definition, like Samoan writer Albert Wendt,[159] write out of what they say is the experience of being colonised, it is hard not to agree with Bruce Pascoe who says that, "All our writing is influenced by the stories and culture which have developed for 200,000 years. Colonial we aren't. Colonised we are."

Part Two

Editing and Publishing

Chapter Four
Publishing the Indigenous Word

The whole thing about publishing is to do with the Indigenous people controlling the public perception of who we are—of providing an authentic representation of Aboriginal culture, rather than a version that has been filtered through non-Aboriginal interpretation.[160]

Sam Cook,
Indigenous Graphic Designer

The chapters in Part 2 will focus on the publishing of Aboriginal written work in Australia including a brief history of Aboriginal print journalism, profiles of the three Indigenous publishing houses and consideration of the mainstream houses currently catering for the increasing level of Aboriginal writers producing books for publication.

Aboriginal participation in print journalism

In his anthology, *For the Record: 160 Years of Aboriginal Print Journalism*, Michael Rose documents the extent to which printed journalism has contributed to the pool of published materials by Aboriginal writers in the media.

The Aboriginal or Flinders Island Chronicle, (September 1836 – December 1837), is considered to be the first Aboriginal newspaper in Australia. It was handwritten and sold for two pence, and was believed to be the work of three Aboriginal clerks employed by G.A. Robinson, Commandant of the Aboriginal Settlement on Flinders Island.[161] There is no evidence of the level of influence Robinson had over the reports published in the paper, or even how many Aboriginal people could actually read it, but many of the articles were written in the first person, in the style of a journal, and signed by Thomas Brune, 'Aboriginal Youth' of Flinders Island.[162]

It was over a century before the next Aboriginal paper appeared. This paper was published through the Aborigines Progressive Association (APA) in Sydney. The Association, lead by William Ferguson and John Patten, also instigated the 1938 'Day of Mourning' Protest and Conference in Sydney and was foremost in the campaign for full citizenship rights for Aborigines, Aboriginal representation in parliament and the abolition of the NSW Aborigines Protection Board. Between April and September 1938 APA also produced six editions of *The Australian Abo Call: The Voice of the Aborigines*, a tabloid newspaper. It is said that the title of the tabloid caused a split between Patten (President) and Ferguson (Secretary), "who objected to the title and to the fact that the paper was financially supported, at least for a time, by the radical, right-wing Australia First Movement".[163] Rose says of *Abo Call*,

> *Abo Call* is a fascinating journalistic record of the era. Much of the reportage concerned the campaigns being waged by the APA, and the affairs of the Association itself, but there were also articles about conditions on Aboriginal reserves as well as some attempts to document past injustices suffered by Aboriginal people.
>
> The various editions also included letters to the editor, some of which contained valuable elements of reportage about living conditions for Aboriginals. The letters also indicate the enthusiasm among Aboriginal people for a newspaper which reported on their concerns.[164]

The publication of the *Westralian Aborigine*, a tabloid paper published by the Coolbaroo League in Perth, followed in the 1950s. This paper covered local issues and events and was popular with its readers.[165]

Between 1965 and 1970 the New South Wales APA published *Churinga*, the style of which was replicated by the Aboriginal Advancement League in Perth in 1976 when they published *Harmony*. Both papers took a conciliatory approach to race relations.

A more militant voice was found in *Alchuringa* which was reinvented between 1971 and 1972 and published by the National Aboriginal Theatre Foundation and the Aboriginal Tourist and Economic Development Association. Kevin Gilbert's influence was evident in the contentious and assertive editorial approach taken by the paper.[166]

The 1960s and 1970s saw an increase in the number of newsletters and newspapers published by Aboriginal communities as methods of communicating and disseminating information to their members, particularly in relation to the political movements of the time. In what Rose describes as a 'Black Power' tone",[167] the newspapers *Koorier, Koorier 2* and *Koorier 3*, appeared in the late 1960s and were followed by *Black Action* in Tasmania and Black Liberation and *Black News Service* in Brisbane, while Palm Island's *Smoke Signal*, (later *Black Knight*), was also published during this period with the help of author Bill Rosser.

Sydney, a focal point of much political activity as a result of the continuation of the 'Day of Mourning' Protest begun in 1938, and the 1965 Freedom Rides, continued the political tradition with *Koori-Bina*, published between 1976 and 1978. This paper was produced by the Black Women's Action Committee in Redfern. *Koori-Bina* reported on political events, race relations and issues of importance to Aboriginal people, often from a women's point of view. The paper was incorporated into A.I.M. (Aboriginal and Islander Message) in 1979 and was published until 1983.[168]

As a result of appalling race relations in Queensland, it is no surprise that *N.Q. Messagestick* was one of the longest running and much needed Aboriginal publications emanating from Queensland. It began as a typed 'rag' in 1975 but by 1984 was being professionally printed. The paper was, "committed to putting on the public record the perspective of the Aboriginal communities affected by such matters [as tourism, mining and inappropriate development of land]."[169]

Perhaps the most highly profiled and memorable of all Aboriginal publications was the magazine *Identity*, which was established as a quarterly in 1971 (and folded in 1982). *Identity's* literary focus was something new in Aboriginal publications and the magazine profiled the works of many well-known writers, such as Kevin Gilbert, Jack Davis and John A. Newfong. *Identity* was published by the Aboriginal Publications Foundation in Perth and became a forum for Aboriginal people to write, debate and discuss issues relevant to them, as well as to record history and publish artwork, poetry, reviews and photos. *Identity* moved to Canberra in 1979 and was then only published occasionally with artwork and political articles given a greater focus than journalism and literature.[170]

The *Koori Mail* and the recently established *Aboriginal Independent Newspaper*, are the only national Aboriginal and Torres Strait Islander newspapers currently in operation. The *Koori Mail* was established in early 1991 by Owen and Sue Carriage from the South Coast of NSW. The fortnightly paper was taken over by Budsoar Ltd in 1992, and is jointly owned by five Aboriginal organisations on the North Coast of NSW.[171] The paper is currently self-funded and Aboriginal owned, with a board of directors comprising one member from each of the five Aboriginal organisations who own it (Bundjalung Tribal Society, Bunjum Aboriginal Co-operative, Kurrachee Co-operative Society, Nungera Co-operative and Buyinbin).[172] The *Koori Mail's* readership, both Black and white is estimated at 80,000 including Australian, European and American readers. The paper includes contemporary news and information, community and personal profiles, arts, education, a cartoon feature, health features and poetry.

In 1997, the *Koori Mail* was joined by the *Aboriginal Independent Newspaper*, the only privately owned Aboriginal media in Australia, in that it was independent of all government funding. Begun by a group of Nyoongar Aboriginal people in Western Australia, the paper was a subscription-based paper distributed throughout Western Australia, the Northern Territory and South Australia. Disbanded in 2001, it was soon followed by the launch of the *National Indigenous Times* in April 2002. The *National Indigenous Times* is a newspaper for the Indigenous and non-Indigenous people of Australia and the Torres Strait and aims to promote the achievements and ambitions, hopes and aspirations of individuals and communities.

Aside from the journalistic endeavours listed above, it is the books published by Aboriginal authors that have really stolen the show in terms of measurements of Aboriginal literary and publishing standards. The works of Unaipon, Walker

(Oodgeroo Noonuccal), Davis, Gilbert and so on are the achievements in publishing that are often cited as 'Aboriginal publishing.' Interestingly, these pioneers and their published works didn't come from Aboriginal publishing houses, but no doubt inspired the development of such houses and new writers.

Indigenous publishing houses

Having considered briefly the history of Indigenous publishing in terms of print journalism and magazines, I now turn to discussing the important role of Indigenous publishing houses in Australia including the Institute of Aboriginal Development Press (IAD Press) in Alice Springs, Magabala Books in Broome, and Aboriginal Studies Press in Canberra. Brief mention will be made of Pascoe Publishing owned by Aboriginal writer and editor Bruce Pascoe. I then go on to discuss the roles mainstream publishers like UQP, FACP, University of Western Australia Press (UWA Press), Hyland House and Currency Press have played in developing and promoting Aboriginal writing in Australia.

In 1997 there were no all-Black publishing houses in Australia. Sandra Phillips, who has worked at both Magabala Books and as an editor at UQP, believed that publishing houses that identified as Indigenous entities still tended to have disproportionate non-Indigenous inhouse influence. Although there was usually Indigenous representation on the board and among the staff. And while all published works must go under the editorial knife there remained too few Aboriginal editors.[173] More recently, though, Philllips has been appointed Managing Editor of Aboriginal Studies Press, and Josie Douglas has been appointed Publisher of IAD Press.

At the time of interview, Lisa Bellear did not think that it could be said that there was an Aboriginal publishing house in Australia:

> If an Aboriginal publishing house has a white manager, publisher and editor, does it make it an Aboriginal publishing house? I would say it doesn't make it an Aboriginal publishing house, nor if you have an Aboriginal committee in this Aboriginal publishing house that leaves the decisions up to the white man or the white woman.[174]

Institute of Aboriginal Development Press, Alice Springs

Established in 1972 and based in Alice Springs, the Institute of Aboriginal Development Press is the publishing arm of the educational college, the Institute of Aboriginal Development. The Press specialises in language dictionaries, teachers' guides, Aboriginal art and children's books. Their list includes oral histories, poetry, children's books, reference titles, (bush food, natural history etc), Indigenous history, (land rights, Stolen Generations etc), and cross-cultural information. This Press is different to other publishers because of their role in publishing language dictionaries. No other publishing house in Australia is directly involved with cultural maintenance or revival. IAD's aim is to, "reach out to all corners of Australia, providing a voice for Aboriginal people that recognises the diversity of our cultures."[175]

Like Magabala Books and Aboriginal Studies Press, IAD Press is governed by a Board of Management made up of Aboriginal people and comprising all senior office bearers from other Aboriginal organisations in Central Australia. For instance, in 1999 the Chairperson of IAD Press was the General Manager of the Central Australian Aboriginal Music Association (CAAMA).

In 2000 IAD Press had a staff of seven with three of those staff Aboriginal: Josie Douglas (then Assistant Editor), Louise Wellington (Book Designer) and Denella Hampton (Reception/Sales Person). Manager Simon MacDonald says of the number of non-Aboriginal people working at IAD Press,

> We actually have a higher proportion of hours spent by Aboriginal people than non-Aboriginal people (because some of our non-Aboriginal staff are not full-time while Josie and Louise and Denella are full-time). Each person is almost a department in their own right. There's no real hierarchy, more lateral.[176]

All books that are published through IAD are written, edited, illustrated, researched or contributed to by Aboriginal people. MacDonald claims that only Aboriginal authors are published or else there is at least a 50% collaboration between Aboriginal and non-Aboriginal writers. IAD Press's list of published writers includes poet Marjorie Bil Bil, autobiographer Yami Lester and historian and novelist Kenny Laughton.

In terms of funding, MacDonald says that half IAD's income is derived through book sales, and this money is what pays the wages. Production money is sought from ATSIC and the Australia Council for the Arts, while the Institute of Aboriginal Development supports the Press in kind to the value of $60,000 per year.

While celebrating their 25th anniversary of publishing in 1997, IAD Press launched their new imprint Jukurrpa Books, aimed at giving the work of Aboriginal story-tellers greater public prominence. The new imprint focuses on children's stories and novels by Indigenous authors.

IAD Press, alongside Jukurrpa Books, accepts unsolicited manuscripts from Aboriginal and Torres Strait Islander authors on a regional and national basis. The Press receives between 20 and 30 manuscripts a year and publishes between 10 and 12 of these. In 1999 the Jukurrpa diary sold 5,000 copies. MacDonald describes the process of finding manuscripts,

> Over a year we don't necessarily receive manuscripts. We find out about a project that isn't even in written form yet. Someone wants to tell a story or a group want to say something or they've got an idea. *Going for Kalta* came to us [IAD Press] as an idea, and it was worked up in the press for 15 months before

it actually got to the printers, and it had been working up with them [the authors] for 12 months before it got to us. Good books take a long time.

In terms of IAD Press's distribution, MacDonald says that the people who want to study, learn, read about, or familiarise themselves either with their own language or learn an Aboriginal language, will read language learning dictionaries and word lists bought largely from IAD directly or from specialist book shops. Alternatively, IAD has an Australia-wide distribution, so the general book buyer also gets to see IAD books. MacDonald says IAD's distributor also gets books into stores that aren't specifically book-selling outlets, for example, tourist centres.

Magabala Books, Broome

Magabala was established in 1987 with a grant from the Australian Bicentennial Authority's National Aboriginal and Torres Strait Islander Program, (a somewhat controversial program because of its link to the Bi-centenary and boycotts of such funding programs by other Indigenous groups). The Kimberley Aboriginal Law and Cultural Centre (KALACC) also provided an establishment grant of $287,000.[177] Glenyse Ward's, *Wandering Girl*, published in 1988, established Magabala in the scene. Ward's book was launched by the then Prime Minister Bob Hawke, and the initial print run of 5,000 sold out in two months, putting it on Sydney's best-seller list while the rights to publishing in the United Kingdom were taking up by Virago.[178]

Magabala Books Aboriginal Corporation is based in Broome, and takes its name from the Yawuru word for the bush banana, which disperses its seeds over the landscape. In this way Magabala Books, "spreads the seeds of Aboriginal culture far and wide, by providing Aboriginal and Torres Strait Islander people with a contemporary medium to express the richness and diversity of their cultures."[179] Magabala publishes children's books, autobiographical and historical works, as well as fiction and poetry. There is a Management Committee at Magabala made up of local Aboriginal people and some Aboriginal people in the publishing industry.

Magabala Books became an independent Aboriginal corporation in March 1990, with the objective of restoring, preserving and maintaining Aboriginal and Torres Strait Islander cultures by,

- assisting and encouraging Aboriginal and Torres Strait Islander people to pass on their history;
- making the wider community aware of the wealth of Aboriginal and Torres Strait Islander tradition and culture;
- protecting and educating Aboriginal and Torres Strait Islander groups and individuals on matters pertaining to copyright;

- recording, promoting and publishing a body of Aboriginal and Torres Strait Islander cultures;
- promoting acknowledgment of and respect for Aboriginal and Torres Strait Islander cultures through the use of various printed and electronic media and through published works;
- providing employment and training for Aboriginal and Torres Strait Islander people.[180]

In 1989 Merrilee Lands, Magabala's publicity and information officer discussed the unique environment of the Magabala office saying, "anyone can just walk into our office-you don't need to make an appointment. And because we virtually do everything here up to pre-print stage, our authors can come in any time and watch their book being produced."[181] However, Magabala Books is disadvantaged by its remoteness, not only from major cities, but also from its authors, so Lands' comments should be taken with a grain of salt. The Australian Publishers Association Residential Editorial Program (which will be discussed later) highlights the problems that arise for Magabala as a result of its establishment in such a remote location:

> Editors need to be given the opportunity to *meet with authors* more frequently. Several editors admitted that they had not met authors whose work they had edited and that they perceived this as a major problem in developing their manuscripts.[182]

As at October 1996, Magabala's policy was to publish works that Aboriginal or Torres Strait Islander authors have had major input to. A policy with integrity would also entail employing an Aboriginal or Torres Strait Islander editor. Although publishing priorities are in the Kimberley region of Western Australia, Magabala increasingly provides advice and publishing services to Aboriginal and Torres Strait Islander people elsewhere and publish manuscripts received from authors across Australia. The works published are those that have been assessed by the publishing house's Aboriginal Management Committee, taking into account,

- the fulfilment of Magabala's objectives as Aboriginal and Torres Strait Islander Publishers;
- the intended readership and sales potential;
- quality and/or importance of the manuscript.[183]

Magabala's titles have won a number of prestigious literary awards and commendations and in 1992 the house was awarded the inaugural Black Books award for initiative and achievement in the publication of works by Aboriginal and Torres Strait Islander people.[184]

One-time editor at Magabala Books, Rachel Bin Salleh, says she does not underestimate the complexities involved in the balancing act that Magabala

Books performs, explaining that, "social responsibility must combine with professional expertise and marketing savvy."[185]

Magabala is far ahead of Aboriginal Studies Press in the numbers of works by Aboriginal writers that have been published. In an article in *Publishing Studies* in 1997, then publisher at Magabala Books, Bruce Sims, said that authors varied little at Magabala, in that most of them were first time and often one-time authors, which also meant, "a heavier load of explanation and consultation".[186] Comparing Magabala to his prior experience with Penguin, Sims said he required a mental turnaround when negotiating contracts with authors, as one of Magabala's stated aims was to provide maximum income to Indigenous authors.[187] However, authors such as myself still only received the standard 10% royalty return as per a standard author contract. Because Magabala is one of the largest publishers of children's books by and for Indigenous people, it is obvious that their illustrators are as important as their authors. Bin Salleh says,

> A large proportion of our books contain a visual element, and it is through this visual element that many of the books have very firm sales. We try to retain having an input of a majority of 51% by an Indigenous author or editor. Where possible we utilise Indigenous illustrators, rather than non-Indigenous ones.[188]

Before Sam Cook worked with Magabala Books for five-and-a-half years, she had no previous publishing experience, but had a background in the area of design and the arts. Cook started with Magabala as a trainee designer. Cook says of being thrown in the deep end, that,

> I basically had to rely on my own initiative to shape and mould the responsibility and position of Indigenous Designer in Aboriginal Publishing. Upon reflection, I am amazed we got to what I feel is a confident position as we were behind the eight ball in all respects, from limited knowledge of the industry to poor quality technology, to constantly being considered niche and not quite taken seriously by the mainstream publishers.[189]

More importantly she notes the importance of design in producing Indigenous titles and says the integrity of utilising designs, colours, symbols and language in a culturally appropriate manner is paramount.[190]

Cook also notes the difference being Aboriginal makes in working in an Indigenous publishing house, saying she has certain insights about the Indigenous community in general, including a healthy respect for the cultural diversity that exists among the Aboriginal population. She says she has a strong regard for Aboriginal consultative and decision-making processes.[191] In her time with Magabala Books, Cook produced 37 titles.

Aboriginalisation of the Indigenous publishing industry is something that is seen as vital to the development of Aboriginal writing and publishing, and Magabala's failure to pursue this policy is the reason Cook left in 2000. The trainee manager of Magabala Books in 1994, Blanche Bowles, stated in an interview for the *Report on Strategies for the Further Development of the National Aboriginal and Torres Strait Islander Arts and Cultural Industry* (1994) that:

> Magabala has an Aboriginalisation policy to fulfil all roles and positions within Magabala with all Aboriginal people or Torres Strait Islanders. That was one of the specific requirements of the objectives of the constitution that was put in place by the people that initially set up. It was to provide economic independence and culturally appropriate nests of materials being submitted…
>
> I do not know if you know, but if you are an Aboriginal person and you go into the communities you are going to be more spoken to by the community members than if you are a non-Aboriginal person—especially if they do not know you and they do not know your family background…You might go out there with the best intentions of obtaining materials…and you might be out there for three months and not get anything. So you know that is probably one of the reasons why it is essential that Magabala does come out Aboriginalised, to be able to keep getting that information.
>
> If you are recruiting and having the staff members on board that come from various areas, various backgrounds from Queensland or from South Australia or from the Northern Territory, then that makes your market bigger because they all have family members who will be far more readily wanting to submit information or art work or everything else, and still maintaining cultural control.[192]

Aboriginal Studies Press, Canberra

Established in 1964 Aboriginal Studies Press was originally established for whites to publish on Aborigines. It could be said that it was a press for anthropologists, historians and academics, as Oodgeroo Noonuccal was the only Aboriginal person publishing at the time, and her work was poetry.

Housed within the Australian Institute of Aboriginal and Torres Strait Islander Studies (AIATSIS) in Canberra, Aboriginal Studies Press is the publishing arm of the Institute, and publishes works by authors in all fields of Aboriginal studies including art, biography, contemporary studies, education, history, health, housing, land rights, language, physical anthropology, prehistory, psychology, social anthropology and women's studies. It has recently begun to publish fiction, poetry, plays and children's literature.

Aboriginal Studies Press has a set of Corporate Objectives[193] which are,

- to inform and educate the general public, and Aboriginal and Torres Strait Islander people in particular, about past and present Aboriginal and Torres Strait Islander histories and cultures;
- to publish works of the highest quality which provide accurate information and conform to the highest ethical standards;
- to produce a wide range of publications;

- to promote both the Press and the Institute through publications and related materials and activities.

In 1999–2000 there were over 100 titles in print and approximately six new titles being published each year.[194] Aboriginal Studies Press sees the increase in manuscripts submitted by Aboriginal authors in recent years as, "a welcome trend."[195]

Aboriginal Studies Press accepts unsolicited manuscripts that are refereed and considered for publication by the Publications and Products Advisory Committee. In 1999 the Committee comprised Marcia Langton (Deputy Chair of Council), Jackie Huggins (Council), Russ Taylor (Principal), Kingsley Palmer (Deputy Principal), Stephen Wild (Director of Research), Nick Thompson, Frank Thompson, Lindsay Mackerras, Dianne Hosking (Director of Archives and Production) and Penelope Lee (Manager Publications).[196]

As the Press moves into the area of poetry and plays it still only publishes those by non-Aboriginal people. The 1998 release of *The Great Forgetting* written by Geoff Page, perhaps got the go ahead for publication by this Indigenous press because of the illustrations by Aboriginal artist Bevan Hayward (Pooaraar). The plays *Black Mary and Gunjies* by white writer Julie Janson show yet again the failure of the press to introduce Aboriginal writers into their list of new works and genres. Although Director of Publishing David Horton said, "the new books represent a change in direction,"[197] it was a pity that he referred to the move away from academic writing, instead of a move towards supporting more Aboriginal writers.

Aboriginal Studies Press's best known titles are probably the two-volume *Encyclopaedia of Aboriginal Australia* and *The Two Worlds of Jimmy Barker* (which was the first book by an Aboriginal author published by the Press in 1977, 13 years after its establishment).

Mainstream Publishing Houses

Rachel Bin Salleh believes the general issues faced by Aboriginal authors wishing to be published are that many authors do not understand publishing processes, how to develop their work, or understand how royalties work.

Aboriginal authors have varying degrees of understanding of the publishing industry. Kenny Laughton believes that the publishing process is an industry in itself, "remote from the author and also from the readers," which is what Laughton thinks makes it so hard for new writers to get their material even looked at by the large mainstream publishing houses.[198]

At the First National Aboriginal Writers' Conference, held at Murdoch University in February 1983, authors questioned how they could ensure the continued growth of Aboriginal literature without continually bowing to pressure from publishers for commercially viable manuscripts.[199] Among the solutions were, local community controlled publishing houses, the establishment of a guild of Black Writers, and the creation of a national Aboriginal publishing house.[200]

The now defunct Aboriginal Writers, Oral Literature and Dramatists Association (AWOLDA), situated in Perth, managed to organise three conferences (1983, 1984, 1987), where discussion revolved around editing issues: for so long as the products of Aboriginal creative endeavour must go through mainstream publishing houses, there will always be changes to the style,

> There will be a denial of such things as the Aboriginality of language and the text will be edited towards what is considered a saleable product in a market place where the majority of consumers are white.[201]

Findings from the 1999 Australian Publishers Association (APA) Residential Editorial Program suggested that a program might be initiated which develops a wider understanding of the cultural issues being addressed by Indigenous publishing projects. Proposals included a series of industry seminars on Indigenous publishing issues.[202] It was also suggested that the APA along with publishing houses be encouraged to develop a list of consultants appropriate to the needs of their Indigenous publishing lists.[203]

While many Aboriginal writers have come through our own publishing houses, few have come through the mainstream. The reasons for this can be found in the responses of authors below.

Kerry Reed-Gilbert, who published her work *Black Woman Black Life* with Wakefield Press, says the reason that Aboriginal authors aren't picked up so much by the mainstream presses is because, "we are not a dollar industry…and I think too because the majority of our work is controversial or confronting to the wider target group".[204]

Kenny Laughton believes that the reason Aboriginal authors are left off mainstream houses lists is simply because of the stereotype that Aboriginal authors only write about Aboriginal issues. He adds to Gilbert's comment about profit and the publishing industry, saying,

> The big companies are no longer risking their money on new authors. They are sticking with the proven, well known authors, to bring home the bacon. Not enough of our works have been recognised by the literary world; and it will take this for Aboriginal authors to become attractive to the big companies.

Laughton acknowledges that it can also be the content of Aboriginal works that will affect the decision of publishers, especially when it is,

> Aboriginal history pricking white Australia's conscience i.e. the massacres or the stolen generation…this is far too controversial for mainstream Australia so the big companies won't take the risk of a community backlash on their product. So it's safer not to go with Aboriginal authors, especially if they have an opinion that doesn't reflect the sometimes rose-coloured glasses conceptions

some white Australians have of controversial topics, such as racism and Asian immigration.

Laughton suggests that "true-blue Aussie icons like Alan Jones and John Laws" would have no problem attracting mainstream publishing contracts, even though they mightn't be able to write 'jack shit'. Because they are icons, "people are going to buy their product anyway."

Sam Cook echoes this comment, believing that few Aboriginal authors are picked up by mainstream publishing houses because these houses are profit-driven and will only go with what she calls 'a safe bet'. This means that the author in question would already have had to prove themselves to be 'mainstream friendly'. She adds, "the mainstream would rather read books about Indigenous people not by Indigenous people…They need that filtration because without it, the Indigenous experience may be too confronting."

Cross-cultural studies lecturer at the University of Western Australia, Tom Little, comments that several local Nyoongar writers were looking at the feasibility of setting up a Nyoongar publishing house because mainstream publishers were unwilling to recognise the writers and their importance. Little comments, "the greatest strength of contemporary Aboriginal writing is its truth, and it is not being heard by the mainstream."[205]

In response, though, Ray Coffey from FACP says few people, whether Aboriginal or non-Aboriginal, are picked up by mainstream publishing. Citing his own press as an example, he says they receive approximately 500 manuscripts from writers per year but publish only 30 books—that's 6% of what they receive. He says the percentage is probably lower for larger publishers.[206] Out of that pool of writers, Coffey says they receive one manuscript per year from Aboriginal writers and would publish one book by an Aboriginal writer every three years. Bin Salleh is also practical in her analysis of the situation, considering the reality that publishers today do not accept unsolicited manuscripts, many now only taking them from agents.

Muecke argues that the appearance of Aboriginal literature over the past two decades is not just in response to conditions of repression and struggle but is also a consequence of the publishing industry being in a state of readiness, even eagerness, to publish work by Aboriginal writers.[207] He argues that the relationship of Aboriginal writers to the publishing industry is one of 'positive effects'.[208] In contrast to what the Aboriginal authors have said above, Muecke says,

> The story of Aboriginal relations to the publishing industry is not one of persecution and struggle as the repressive hypothesis might lead us to believe. Oodgeroo Noonuccal (Kath Walker) did not have to fight to get published back in 1964, Jim Devaney had to talk her into it. Mudrooroo Narogin (Colin Johnson) had no trouble getting *Wild Cat Falling* published under the patronage

of Mary Durack. With Jack Davis as editor of the journal *Identity* writers such as Archie Weller got a start.[209]

On behalf of IAD Press MacDonald says it is the whole process of working with Indigenous people that has turned mainstream publishers off. They won't devote the time and money to such a long process without pre-determined outcomes,

> Historically it's been too difficult. The process that's in-house involves often an Aboriginal person whose first language isn't English, or who has never been taught English properly or used it, who's still writing to the best of their capacity. It's a too hard basket topic for commercial mainstream publishers. IAD Press invests in their authors. We spend 25% of our editorial energies on working with authors. It's that very difficult path that editors tread. That non-invasive role that has to be invisible afterwards, but has to be present during the process.

Pascoe Publishing, Apollo Bay

Established by husband and wife team Bruce Pascoe and Lyn Harwood, Pascoe Publishing produced the quarterly journal *Australian Short Stories* (ASS) for 16 years out of Apollo Bay in Victoria. In that 16 years, *Australian Short Stories* published some of the biggest names in Australian literature including Helen Garner, Elizabeth Jolley and Matt Condon, and in the 1990s began to give space to some emerging Aboriginal writers.

While Pascoe is "a proud member of the Wathaurong Aboriginal Co-operative"[210] and identifies as Aboriginal, Pascoe Publishing has never been promoted as an Aboriginal publishing house, or functioned on behalf of, or for Aboriginal writers and communities, and therefore be recognised as an Aboriginal publishing house. Having said that, Aboriginal writers did feature sporadically in Australian Short Stories and a special edition of the journal was produced in 1990 as a result of a trip Pascoe had undertaken with story-teller Maureen Watson to Aboriginal communities from Melville Island to Burrunga that year.[211] In later years, Pascoe often made references in his editorials to Aboriginal history and issues and dedications of editions were made to people like Noel Pearson (ASS, no. 46, 1994) and Mick Dodson (ASS, no. 57, 1997).

In 1994 though, Harwood and Pascoe claimed they were getting more writing from Aboriginal people because they had been working with Aboriginal communities. Pascoe stated:

> Aboriginal people have had their stories hacked around by white editors, who think that the uneducated writers need more grammar or better spelling, when in fact a lot of editors have been stuffing up rhythm. So you have to be careful, and we always guarantee that if they don't want it changed, it won't be changed. It's a matter of process too, in a way, that we actively encourage Koori

writers. I suppose there's a bias there, but I'm prepared to argue that with anyone. In the first place we want to get those people in the magazine and we want their second story to be better than their first, so it's the same process.[212]

The fact that *Australian Short Stories* was essentially a general literary journal, that it was not promoted to Indigenous writers specifically as a place welcoming manuscripts, and that Pascoe himself did not identify strongly with his Aboriginal identity until the 1990s[213], could well explain why Pascoe Publishing was not seen as an Indigenous publishing house by Indigenous writers, and that a missed opportunity has resulted now the journal has been sold.[214]

University of Queensland Press, Brisbane

In 1997, UQP was the only mainstream publishing house in Australia with an Aboriginal editor, Sandra Phillips, and over the years it has demonstrated a true commitment to Indigenous publishing through the Black Australian Writers Series (BAWS). In fact, UQP could be seen to be the only mainstream press ever to have displayed such a commitment to Aboriginal literature and its authors.

The BAWS testifies to the diversity of Indigenous writing in Australia. Launched in 1990, it evolved out of the annual David Unaipon Award (which attracts texts by unpublished Indigenous authors from across the nation). This award has been judged by well-known writers such as Jack Davis and Jackie Huggins. The late Oodgeroo Noonuccal was a founding judge and series consultant, and the Series is made up of the Award winners and other Aboriginal and Torres Strait Islander authors such as Melissa Lucashenko, Alexis Wright, John Muk Muk Burke, Jeanie Bell and Herb Wharton.

Current senior editor, Sue Abbey says UQP was publishing books by Aboriginal people before the Unaipon Award was established, and now the Press and the Unaipon judges, "understand and practice the importance of fostering a writing career for winners."[215]

Sandra Phillips who was (and remains) the only Aboriginal editor employed in a mainstream publishing house, made these comments on the commitment of UQP to Aboriginal writing:

> It is an Australian owned independent publisher with a very strong history of publishing Aboriginal and Torres Strait Islander writers which you will not see reflected in any other mainstream press in the country, with the exception of Fremantle Arts Centre Press.[216]

The audience of the BAWS is determined, Phillips says, by the author, citing Jeanie Bell who was concerned with the Murri community nationally and particularly in south-east Queensland. She adds, though, that the prime motivation for Aboriginal writers has been to write for the non-Aboriginal audience, to educate and inform through an entertaining medium.

Fremantle Arts Centre Press, Western Australia

FACP are carefully building their list of Aboriginal writers, which already includes Paddy Roe, Butcher Joe Nangun, Sally Morgan, May O'Brien, Kim Scott, Alice Nannup and Stephen Kinnane—all of whose works have generally sold well and been well received critically. FACP produced its first book by an Aboriginal writer in 1983, (*Gularabulu: Stories from the West Kimberley* by Paddy Roe), and has continued to do so. FACP is an incorporated association and has a Board of Management of ten. Two members are from the Press staff, including the General Manager and Ray Coffey, (Publisher and Managing Director of FACP, having been in that position since 1989 and with the Press since 1978 when he started as Managing Editor). The rest of the membership is made up of people with backgrounds in writing, the arts, libraries, business, academia and publishing. There are no Aboriginal people on the Board or on staff.

The Press seeks to publish for a general readership, with some books produced and/or promoted as crossovers into specialist markets such as schools and tertiary. Coffey says that FACP has a strong commitment to supporting Aboriginal authorship and publishing Aboriginal works:

> It is part of our commitment since inception to encourage, support and publish work by people who have had limited access to publication. Historically this has included women, and, for example, it continues to varying degrees to include people from a non-English speaking background, and working class backgrounds.

Coffey says that FACP has always had a developmental role with respect to writers and writing, and to fulfil this role they receive a small grant from the Western Australian Department for the Arts. He adds, "certainly in this area we do consider Aboriginality as a criteria, as one of our particular concerns is to identify gaps in the record and disadvantage with respect to the artform...and [we] seek to help redress this".

University of Western Australia Press

In conjunction with the Centre for Indigenous History and the Arts Aboriginal Programmes at the University of Western Australia, UWA Press intends to publish a series of books by Indigenous writers, to be fuelled by an Indigenous Writers' Prize, the Marrwarnging Award, established in 1999. Recognising they had only published one book by an Indigenous author, *Bulmurn* by Richard Wilkes, and contemplating the further publication of works by Indigenous authors, UWA Press identified the need for greater knowledge of Indigenous cultural issues and Indigenous publishing to enhance and facilitate the development of the series.[217] With financial assistance from the Literature Fund of the Australia Council, Anthea Wu, Editorial and Production Manager of UWA Press, was provided with training in three key areas, including an Aboriginal Cross Cultural Awareness

Workshop at the Centre for Staff Development at UWA, Kimberley Cross Cultural Training with Olive Knight of the Kimberly Land Council, (this training took place in Broome, Derby and Fitzroy Crossing), and work experience at Magabala Books in Broome. Wu says that the cross cultural training received at the Centre for Staff Development, (facilitated by Tom Little), and with the Kimberley Land Council provided her with, "a basic foundation in the key elements of the history and culture of the Indigenous peoples of Western Australia," greatly enhancing her ability to communicate with Indigenous writers.[218] Wu's time with Magabala Books (August 1998) increased her understanding of the challenges and opportunities faced by staff there, both Indigenous and non-Indigenous.

As a result of her training in Perth and the Kimberley region, together with discussions with staff at the Centre for Indigenous History and the Arts at UWA, Wu began to build a network among Indigenous people associated with publishing: Sam Cook, (formerly of Magabala Books), Rachel Bin Salleh and Tazuko Kaino, (Magabala Books), Sally Morgan, (Centre for Indigenous History and the Arts, UWA), Mary Ann Jebb, (Noongar Land Council), and Irene Jimbidie, Karrayilli, Fitzroy Crossing.

UWA Press currently engages the services of professional freelance editors who give each manuscript a structural edit and copy edit. The idea of training Wu in structural editing was to increase UWA Press's in-house knowledge base in structural editing, which would enable them to work more effectively on the development of manuscripts. The decision to take this direction was directly related to observations of how long manuscripts are in development at Magabala Books, and how deeply Magabala is involved in the development of the manuscript before it goes into production.

On the future of Indigenous writing, Wu says that, "there has been a lot of personal history and oral interviews in Indigenous literature to date, and I think it is now beginning to broaden into other genres of literature. For us, the direction of our Indigenous list depends very much on the winners of the Marrwarnging Award.[219]

Aside from the efforts made by UWA Press, there are no other examples of mainstream publishers attempting to understand the cultural differences affecting Aboriginal writing production or publishing. There is a clear need for cross-cultural training for non-Indigenous people working in the publishing industry because, as IAD Press have pointed out, "too many people within publishing are treating secret/sacred material as a marketable product."[220]

Magabala also supported the notion of cross-cultural training so that workers had an understanding of the variations in cultural processes and languages within Aboriginal and Torres Strait Islander cultures, and between Aboriginal and Torres Strait Islander and 'mainstream' cultures.[221]

Hyland House, South Melbourne

Hyland House has two of Australia's most celebrated writers, Lionel Fogarty and Kevin Gilbert as well as a number of books by Colin Johnson on their list. Michael Schoo from Hyland says that at the time of printing Fogarty, Gilbert and Johnson, Hyland had a broad publishing policy, and those working at the house had a genuine interest in the issues being discussed by Aboriginal writers.[222] More recently though, the house has had less expertise in the areas of poetry and adult fiction and is moving more into young adult fiction. Schoo says Hyland would love to receive manuscripts from Aboriginal writers in this genre.

Hyland do not have a specific policy on publishing Aboriginal writers and Schoo says that when Johnson was published the house would have relied on his, 'own cultural identification', and his history of writing as an Aboriginal person. Schoo adds it might be different today though, and any books published by Johnson from now on would have an explanatory note on the back of the book about the public debate that occurred regarding his identity.

Currency Press, Sydney

Currency Press have published a selection of plays by both Black and white writers that offer a rare insight into the pain and the humour of Aboriginal life in Australia. As a form of social commentary they document the diversity of the Aboriginal experience and as "dramatic texts they offer an opportunity to enter into the life of our Indigenous people through the imagination of the writers".[223] Publisher, Katherine Brisbane, says Currency's criteria for publishing Indigenous writers is the same for any writer: "we look for writers who have something to say of significance to Australians and the skill…to say it. And we publish if we think we can find sufficient market for the work and make it worth our while."[224]

Currency publish between 30 and 35 books a year but receive many more submissions, and in terms of Aboriginal works Brisbane says, "there is rising public interest in Aboriginal writers and issues generally at the moment and courses in Aboriginal literature and art, which is encouraging."[225]

Currency Press have published the work of Jack Davis, Roger Bennett, John Harding, Robert J. Merritt, as well as Jane Harrison's first play *Stolen* (1998) which looks at the complex and controversial issues surrounding the Stolen Generations. The four television dramas that made up *Women Of The Sun*, winner of the 1982 United Nations Association Australia Media Peace Prize, were also published by Currency in 1983. The popular musical *Bran Nue Dae* by Jimmy Chi and Kuckles was jointly published by Currency Press (and Magabala) in 1991.

Having considered the role of Indigenous publishing houses in Australia, their philosophies and their objectives, the next chapter will discuss the role of the Aboriginal editor in such houses and the way in which editorial practice is impacting on the creation and publication of Aboriginal works.

Chapter Five
Editing Indigenous Literature

When considering the impact of editorial practices on Aboriginal writers in Australia, a number of issues are of obvious importance in terms of their influence on the specific style of Aboriginal writing. For example: non-Aboriginal editors altering or 'gubbarising' Aboriginal text; non-Aboriginal editors not understanding the context of some Aboriginal writing; and the lack of Aboriginal editors trained and employed in Australia. Quite often a further issue is simply the fundamental difference in the perception of the white editor and the Aboriginal author as to perfunctory editorial processes: the editor may see editing processes within the context of negotiation whereas for the Aboriginal author, the context is, compromise.

As an Aboriginal editor, Sandra Phillips questions the ability of non-Aboriginal editors to effectively edit Aboriginal works while at the same time maintaining the integrity of the work. Several authors praise the editing skill of Phillips and have commented on how 'fortunate' they were to work with a Murri editor.[226]

The issues covered in this chapter have been discussed by Aboriginal people in the industry for years. It was not until the release of a report sponsored by the Australia Council for the Arts on a scheme for the training of Indigenous editors in 1997, that there was broader industry acknowledgment of the problems editing processes pose for Aboriginal authorship. The report found, although those participating in the 'inquiry' didn't believe that Indigenous books could only be edited by Indigenous editors, there was a growing sense that a body of trained Indigenous editors was an industry priority.[227]

Before considering the existence and place of the non-Indigenous editor in the development of Aboriginal writing, it is firstly important to consider the role of Indigenous editors in Australia.

There are currently four 'industry trained' Aboriginal editors in Australia, Sandra Phillips (Aboriginal Studies Press), Josie Douglas (IAD Press), Ruth Gilbert (Magabala Books) and Rachel Bin Salleh (ex-Magabala Books). As the most well established and recognised Aboriginal editor in the country, Sandra Phillips is popular with Aboriginal authors, particularly those who have published through UQP. Phillips has a long history in the publishing industry. Her interest in editing began at high school where she edited the school magazine. From there she went on to co-edit the *Aboriginal and Islander Student Handbook*, produced by the Aboriginal and Torres Strait Islander Studies Unit at the University of Queensland between 1985 and 1988. In 1994 she edited the book, *Racism, Representation and Photography* for the Inner-City Education Centre in Sydney.

Following this work Phillips applied for the position of trainee editor at Magabala Books, a job which took her to Broome for eight months, where she worked editing and publishing. Undertaking the traineeship was, she says, "a reflection of my commitment to the decision to work inside of publishing where I thought you really should start from the bottom and work your way up."[228]

From Magabala, Phillips moved to UQP becoming editor for the Black Australian Writers Series. She was specifically employed to work on the series and also to make recommendations on any other manuscripts written by non-Aboriginal people. Phillips points out how her role as 'Aboriginal editor' was different to those of editors in other houses because most other editors dealt with specific genres, (for example fiction or non-fiction). Phillips was required to work across several genres—poetry, fiction, non-fiction, short story and novel. Phillips is now the Managing Editor at Aboriginal Studies Press in Canberra.

From her experience in both an Indigenous (Magabala) and mainstream publishing house (UQP), Phillips came to see a number of issues around non-Aboriginal people editing Aboriginal writers' works. UQP though was a little different, she believes, because the original editor [Sue Abbey] of the Black Australian Writers Series was also the editor of poetry, somebody Phillips thought, "understands experimentalism in language and who is much more open to new ways."

Having said that, Phillips believes that, regardless of genre, the relationship between the editor and author has to be very strong. She believes relationships can be forged across culture and race and religion, adding, "unfortunately they don't get much testing in Australian publishing because most publishing professionals are from Anglo backgrounds, so you can't forge relationships across those barriers." Phillips says that she is able to edit effectively and in a culturally sensitive way because she is able to understand the politics behind what writers are saying. She cites one example,

> One author asked me how I felt about the portrayal of an Aboriginal man [in relation to domestic violence] and I said that they weren't being over the top, they are being balanced. We knew that a lot of Aboriginal men haven't been able to cope with colonisation and how that then gets carried out in their lives and particularly within Aboriginal communities and against Aboriginal women, so we can talk about that stuff.

Phillips appears frustrated at times with the editorial process because she feels many Aboriginal people are too concerned with the grammatical and technical side of writing, rather than concentrating on what Phillips says determines good writing: characterisation, timing, tension, reader fulfilment. She says,

> The more that Aboriginal writers and Aboriginal editors talk about what makes good writing good, the more we can get people away from the concerns

around technicalities and more concerned about how many characters you've got, what your characters do, can you evoke emotion.

In this way Phillips hopes writers will understand that the issue is not the grammatical side—the use of Aboriginal English or the unintended lapses in standard grammar—but the heart of the work which is the key to its success as good writing.

A Wardaman woman from the Top End, Josie Douglas, was Assistant Editor at IAD Press at the time of interview and had worked there for six years. Douglas started at the Press selling and packing books but had a personal interest in promotional activities and soon took on a promotional role, working in sales and promotions consecutively. During her early years at the Press, Douglas would go to book fairs to learn more about the industry. She knew she wanted to stay in publishing but didn't know what area she wanted to work in until she began editing and realised, "yeah, this is what I want to do."[229] Douglas is now the publisher of IAD Press.

Douglas says she's happy with her role and staying in Alice Springs, and would, "just like to be a very good editor. One that is industry standard but also working at the Press." She has also considered doing some freelance work at a later stage, but says, "I don't think you become a good editor in a year or two. To become a good editor you're learning all the time. Even experienced editors 10-15 years down the track, every book you approach you learn from."

For Douglas one issue in terms of editing is that the dictates of publishing say that the bottom line is there is only so much money to spend on the production of each book. For example, if you've got a manuscript with 208 pages and you can only produce a 98 page book then you have to edit. She says,

> You're going to get a manuscript and you have to say, "We can't publish it in its entirety, something has to go." You give it back to the author or authors and say, "What do you think can go? What do you want to be taken out? It's up to you. You tell me what's really important and what you want to stay. You advise me on what you think can go, but we're going to have to cut, because this book is only x amount of pages." As an Aboriginal person, sometimes I can see how important those stories are, but we haven't got room for all of them.

Douglas admits that authors generally react pretty well to editorial advice, but says the process is still one of compromise so far as the author is concerned: "If you talk to the old ladies I worked with on my last book they'll say, 'no they're all important'. And of course they are, but what ones really need to go in and what ones do you think can be left out."

Like Phillips, Douglas says that as an Aboriginal person she relates better to another Aboriginal person. Understanding Aboriginal people, through the use of language, and as a result of understanding kinship/community links, she is able to communicate with Aboriginal people in ways that white editors might not be able to:

> You may have contacts, they may be related to me or to my partner, or I know them through community connections, so there's that personal relationship that comes into it as well, or they know who I am. They can place me within my family, within my community. And negotiation then is a lot easier.

She gives an example of when the dynamics of a situation are dictated by the cultural differences in a meeting with authors,

> We've sat around a table with Aboriginal authors and gudyia [white people] mob sitting there, and the authors don't say anything. These are traditional people, they just don't say anything. Away from the table, outside having a cup of tea or cigarette, or you might bump into them shopping down the street, and they'll say, "Hey, I want to tell you this." It's just about you as a person being able to communicate. There's no shame job talking with me, not like talking with somebody you don't know from a bar of soap. It's about connection and not being shame job, which is still part of our culture.

Rachel Bin Salleh is the third editor and was once employed at Magabala Books 3.5 days per week. She first began her job there as a project officer, employed to finish two oral history projects: one was an interview with a woman that is now in the anthology, *Holding Up the Sky*, the other project has not yet been completed. Bin Salleh switched from project work to editorial work and has been editing Aboriginal and Torres Strait Islander works for approximately eight years. Rachel was recently replaced at Magabala Books by Ruth Gilbert.

The first thing Bin Salleh says she sees hindering Aboriginal people's ability to write is mainly the fact that, "many feel that their stories are simply not just good enough. I say 'stories', as there are many authors that are illiterate, and so there is a need for a second party to help them."[230]

In terms of issues that editors face when working with Aboriginal authors, Bin Salleh points out that sometimes an author simply might not write well. She says that Aboriginal and Torres Strait Islander people have to be aware that writing in Aboriginal English does not necessarily constitute an Aboriginal or Torres Strait Islander book, and that there are many factors that make up Aboriginal writing,

> There are examples of not too good writing that may have a wonderful yarn through it; it is these yarns that are full of life, rich in substance and fulfil the reader immensely with the experience that the author has had. It is possible to capture the narrative of the author and fine tune, without treading on too many toes and insulting the authorship of the author. It is possible to take a manuscript like this and develop it, if the author is willing to do some work and maybe tidy up areas that can cause ambiguity. This is the main area, ambiguity.

Bin Salleh says that Indigenous authors that she has worked with, (many first time authors and traditional people), speak/narrate/talk/discuss their lives with a complex beat of time, (as defined by Western society)—and they usually refer to everyone as 'he', or jump from person to person without making that distinction.

This is a trait of Aboriginal English, and as an editor Bin Salleh then has to be aware of where the author is coming from. And while she says authors are quite willing to help out in terms of these areas, the process does take some time. She explains:

> I have helped out authors, by suggesting changes and have changed mainly tenses, (simply to give the reader a better understanding of what the author is saying), in areas of high ambiguity. It is hard to explain to authors that really want to do it right, (in their sense of right—they think that high English is the only way to go). I explain to authors that there of course will be some changes, but it is their voice that needs to be heard, their story that needs to be told and a good story/yarn/narrator can carry a book long and far.

Bin Salleh comments that authors often feel that they are 'right' and this again supports the view that the editorial process is, for authors, a process of compromise.

Aboriginal designer, Sam Cook, comments that the editorial process used at Magabala is different from the processes used in mainstream houses and this is essentially because Magabala has staff at all levels working closely together. In an interview with Maria Mann, Cook commented that she did not feel like an 'editor's tool' churning out whatever was decided by someone else. She was involved from the start of the process in deciding whether or not to accept a manuscript for publication, whether there might be cultural impediments to publication and what formats are most appropriate for the work in question.[231] She adds that it is extremely important that the Indigenous identity of material is not lost in the editorial process. She cites an example, "if a person is talking Kriol, I think it is offensive to clean that up to high English because of some non-Indigenous convention."[232]

Indigenous editors Vs non-Indigenous editors

The issue of working with non-Indigenous editors as opposed to Indigenous editors has been discussed by Aboriginal writers who have gone through the process themselves. Kenny Laughton sums up the issue: "I have many reservations about non-Indigenous editors interpreting our works, using their style which undoubtedly is influenced by western ideas and concepts, taught at mainstream institutions."[233]

From his experience at FACP Ray Coffey says that for a large number of Aboriginal writers and would-be-writers, if being edited by a non-Aboriginal is an issue, then it is an issue.[234] The primary question for Coffey as a publisher is whether or not a writer is comfortable working with his or her editor. In principle however, Coffey says whether an editor is Aboriginal or non-Aboriginal, there shouldn't necessarily be a problem,

> The skill of editing, when done well, is about being sensitive, sensitive to the needs and intentions of the text and sensitive to concerns of the writer. This

sensitivity is of equal importance to the other editorial skills of being able to conceptualise the whole shape of the work, identify unclear or overstated passages in a text, knowing grammar and how to spell, etc. Sensitivity to the text and the author are very specialised abilities. Part of it can be taught certainly, but a big part comes down to natural attributes, of disposition and personality.

Bin Salleh agrees that it is not just the technical skills and abilities that make a good editor, especially in terms of Aboriginal writing. She comments that you can't say an editor just edits because,

> The process of editing an Aboriginal/Torres Strait Islander author requires the editor to disseminate all aspects of Indigenous life. It is not just the text you are editing, it is all the issues that are a part of being Aboriginal/Torres Strait Islander that you edit. I don't just edit—I liaise with communities, am a gate keeper (sort of) for knowledge, do contracts, copyright issues, license issues, deal with the author/community, deal with ownership/law. There is no fine line as to what is editing in an Aboriginal publishing house.

Coffey's and Bin Salleh's comments lead to the conclusion that a more holistic approach to editing is needed. Bin Salleh adds that many non-Indigenous editors are not fully aware of the issues that surround an Indigenous person, and this fact can hinder the ability of Aboriginal people being published:

> They [non-Aboriginal editors] are not aware of issues such as 'country', ownership, Aboriginal society [whether that is an urban or non-urban setting]. Many do not understand that there are protocols that are a part of Aboriginal / Torres Strait Islander society and so are ignorant of the way they may go about things. Also the 'time' factor is slightly different for Aboriginal people. It is through this, that many editors would hinder the process of mainly developmental work with an author. Not necessarily impacting on the Aboriginal/Torres Strait Islander person's ability to write, rather a major slowing down of the publishing process.

Considering Bin Salleh's point, it can easily be seen where the non-Aboriginal editor may fail in the holistic approach to editing Aboriginal writing.

The benefits of having Aboriginal editors editing Aboriginal works are also pointed out by Colin Johnson who notes that the meanings of standard and Aboriginal English words and constructions can be lost on an inexperienced editor, who may not know the oral and cultural traditions upon which a work rests.[235] Although some publishing companies may be sensitive to Aboriginal manuscripts, there is still an inclination to edit works so that they fit into particular genres aimed at mainstream audiences.

In terms of non-Aboriginal editors, Douglas says it's really up to the author, and even with mainstream houses authors can specifically request that the manuscript be freelanced out to Aboriginal editors. She says authors might well find a non-Aboriginal editor they are happy to work with but, "it's up to them also to be 'political' and say, 'I want an Aboriginal editor on this. Just freelance it out, I'll suggest somebody'." Douglas says that IAD have never been asked to freelance out to Aboriginal editors interstate or at other publishing houses, probably due to the fact that she is the in-house editor at the Press.[236] Douglas has been asked to do some freelance editing for *Lonely Planet*, but due to other work and family commitments turned these down.[237] Sue Abbey from UQP says that UQP have freelanced editorial work to Aboriginal editors.[238]

Josie Douglas says that while there appears to be a continuous process of both negotiation and compromise between Aboriginal authors and white editors, these are still two essentially different things. 'Compromise' is agreeing to drop something in order to keep something else, and 'negotiation' is generally related to the technical aspects of the book's production.

At least one non-Aboriginal editor, Peter Bibby, says he had little need to edit the manuscripts he received at Magabala, because many of them were based on a spoken tradition, and Magabala tries to let the author's voices speak freely. He commented that this is important for several reasons but primarily because the Kimberley is made up of different tribal groups, ranging from those who live on the coast to those who may live 300 miles away. He added, "You need someone who knows the area and the different groups to understand why the stories are important. It is no good having an editor or translator up from Sydney."[239] (Interestingly Bibby was the editor of Carmen's fraudulent work, *My Own Sweet Time*).

Finally, Katherine Brisbane from Currency Press, retells a story about the effect of editing on two authors (one Indigenous, one non-Indigenous):

> The poet Robert Adamson described an incident in his experience. He had been sitting on a jetty with Kevin Gilbert, each with a copy of their first published books of poetry. Adamson was excited and proud at having his work in print. Gilbert was angry and threw his book into the harbour. The quality of his poems had been destroyed, he said, by the addition of punctuation. The profound feelings he expressed had, in his views, been 'civilised'.[240]

Editorial Experiences of Aboriginal writers

The personal experiences of individual authors within the editorial process range from the easy approach Kerry Reed-Gilbert found with Wakefield Press to the nightmare Jackie Huggins experienced with Aboriginal Studies Press. Bruce Pascoe, Jeanie Bell, Melissa Lucashenko and Lisa Bellear all cite positive experiences with working with Sandra Phillips, either while she was at Magabala or UQP.

The most positive experiences of Aboriginal writers going through the editorial process appear to be those with Aboriginal editors, and in particular, experiences working with Phillips. Bruce Pascoe, who was in the publishing industry for over a decade working on *Australian Short Stories*, says Phillips is the best editor he has met and that, "Working with a Murri helps."[241]

Jeanie Bell, who started working with Phillips on the biography, *Talking About Celia*, says she was fortunate to have Phillips go through her manuscript, and to meet with her to discuss the changes. Bell says she was offered a Sydney-based non-Indigenous reader for the manuscript, (before Phillips was given the task), who listed for Bell what she thought would improve the text. Bell says,

> There were things that I was prepared to change, things that I wasn't. There were things she said that I could give more information about. She was talking about writing for a student audience. She was saying that I needed to explain more about what the Federal Council for the Advancement of Aboriginal and Torres Strait Islanders was. And I thought there's been so many books written about that stuff and this is not what this is about. This is one woman's story.[242]

Lisa Billear, who received an offer from UQP to publish Dreaming in Urban Areas (as it was highly commended in the David Unaipon Award) first worked with white editor Sue Abbey on the manuscript and recalls thinking to herself at the time that it would be good to have an Indigenous person in the publishing world.[243] Eventually Sandra Phillips began at UQP and started working with Bellear, who noted one difference between working with an Aboriginal editor and a non-Aboriginal editor: "The poems that got selected were different to those in the original collection."

Bellear says that although strictly speaking it is not the role of the editor to talk to the writer about cover designs and layout, Phillips did include her in those decisions. Considering the final product Bellear says, "It was great that the words are by a Murri woman and the editing is by a Murri woman. I was just fortunate."

Another Phillips fan is Melissa Lucashenko whose work with Phillips on *Steam Pigs* included some minor revisions (cutting back some of the length). Lucashenko says the editorial experience was "pretty good" and of Phillips she says,

> It was really good that she was a Murri woman my age, so you really couldn't ask for a better relationship. There were things that she suggested that I didn't totally agree with at the time but I went with because they weren't important to me and now I can see that she was right.[244]

Jackie Huggins also worked with Sandra Phillips on her collection of essays *Sister Girl* and says, "There were things I didn't have to say to Sandra. We just knew intuitive, camaraderie."[245]

On working on *Black Woman, Black Life* with Wakefield Press, Kerry Reed-Gilbert said of the white editor: "I had no hassles and they made no changes to my words and were willing to listen to suggestions in relation to the prints in the book, that is, which print went with which poem."[246]

When asked about his experience with the editorial process, Herb Wharton talked about the actual changes and proofing that needed to be done. He said that when he sent UQP 200 pages of *Unbranded* he knew he hadn't done the best he could, and after a week called them and asked for it back. Wharton got the manuscript back with comments on it, and realised then that he had been repeating himself a lot, but at other times he had to ask why they wanted something removed.[247]

Although having worked very little with editors, Kenny Laughton says that when he did, he found the experience interesting and stimulating. Marg Bowman, (non-Indigenous editor at IAD Press), was Laughton's second editor on his novel *Not Quite Men, No Longer Boys* and he says that the few times he did manage to sit down with her and go through the work, he really enjoyed it. Laughton enjoyed the experience because he finds writing is often isolating, so having the opportunity to bounce ideas or thoughts off anyone else made a pleasant change.

In contrast to these positive experiences, John Muk Muk Burke, author of *Bridge of Triangles*, had a bad editorial experience with a young, non-Aboriginal woman in Sydney, who he says wanted to change a lot of things. Burke admits that as a writer he may have been a bit precious about his work, but there were a number of clashes between the two in relation to issues and content central to his work. Burke offers one example:

> All that book is based on my life, I didn't write it as autobiography. It's all fictionalised. But every incident is based on real things and my mum's sister was actually murdered, and those were the things that I had to write about. She [the Editor] said, "You're just harping on about that murder too much." And I didn't want to tell her that it was all true and so I was really pissed off. I won out in the end. I said it's my work and I want it like that.
>
> She didn't know where I was coming from and she never once asked, "Is this really personal to you?" I got the impression that she thought that it was truly a work of fiction and that it wouldn't make much difference if you changed a few things to make it a more interesting story.[248]

Ruby Langford Ginibi has published four books with four different publishers: *Don't Take Your Love To Town* (Penguin, 1988), *Real Deadly* (Angus and Robertson, 1992), *My Bundjalung People* (UQP, 1994), and *Haunted By The Past* (Allen and Unwin, 1999). While many of the issues related to the publishing process were not necessarily related to 'editing' as such, but rather to copyright, misrepresentation of Ginibi's work and promotion issues, Ginibi also experienced four different editors, culminating in a positive experience for her most recent work, *Haunted By The Past*.

Ginibi worked with white editor Susan[249] on *Don't Take Your Love To Town*. Susan had been recommended to Ginibi by Billy Marshall-Stoneking, one of the ABC crew that took her up to Alice Springs in 1985. Ginibi's mother had told him that she was writing her life story and he read it, recommending that because there was a lot of women's business in it and that he was an American male, that Susan, a friend of his wife's and a writing teacher, should edit it.[250]

In terms of the editorial process, Ginibi says she was happy. Susan wrote out the basics of editing for Ginibi who studied what she was being told but said to Susan, "Don't gubbarise my text. Don't edit out my voice." Ginibi admits that the editor's input made the story better, and her natural voice comes through strongly in the book.

Ginibi's next book, *Real Deadly* (1992) was published by Collins Imprint (Angus & Robertson) with the key person working with Ginibi, senior editor Tom Tompson. In terms of the editorial process, Ginibi says that there was not much editing of *Real Deadly* because, "It's written orally, like we talk," and that it was Tompson who came up with the title, *Real Deadly* during one of his visits with Ginibi at Alawah Hostel to discuss the manuscript.

On leaving Angus and Robertson, Ginibi says that Tompson bought up all the back copies of Australian authors to form his own publishing house. "He took my book. He bought the rights from Collins Imprint, not only me, but some of the biggest Australian writers. 70 nearly 80 well-known authors that he took.".. Ginibi says,

> He presented the book to the Blind Institute to make an audio book. He organised for a Greek…to read the text…
>
> I rang him up and got him on the phone and called him everything I could lay my tongue to. They turned around after me complaining so much and got a Koori one from Melbourne.

Ginibi says that after she complained so much Tompson gave the copyright back, but there are no books left in print and she is looking for another publisher to reprint.

In 1991 Ginibi won the inaugural History Fellowship from the NSW Ministry for the Arts to research her book *My Bundjalung People*. It took her four years to get all the information together to write the book and, to the author's dismay, the publisher employed a white editor. Ginibi says,

> All the historical content that I did so much painstaking research on was edited out of the text. I never realised this had been done until after it was finished. So you see, some publishers only dress up our Koori manuscripts, making 'pretty stories' so they are easily saleable.[251]

Ginibi says, "The manuscript kept coming back edited. And it had to be sent back to me all the time to check it. It got that way in the end that I got sick of 'cut this' and 'cut that.'" When asked why she thought the publisher wanted to cut things out, Ginibi said that UQP couldn't see the relevance of some things to the story,

But this is a journey that I took to connect up with my people after 48 years absence. So everything in the damn thing was relevant. I can't remember specifically what they wanted to remove, but there was stuff that I jacked up on and said "You're cutting too much. Don't go cutting too much of my story."

Penny van Toorn was the final editor Ruby Langford Ginibi worked with, this time on *Haunted By The Past*. Ginibi says that van Toorn, a Research Fellow in the English Department at Sydney University, went through all the drafts of *My Bundjalung People* at the State Library of NSW, and saw how much had been cut from the original manuscript. Ginibi says she received a phone call from van Toorn requesting a meeting, and so began a two year process of working on her son Nobby's story.

Ginibi recalls that van Toorn would arrive at her place about 11am on Friday and stay until 3pm. Ginibi says of van Toorn's commitment to the book,

> This woman is a deadly woman. And what I like about her was that when I offered to pay her for it she wouldn't take a damned thing. She even paid for something for the computer. She was one trying to make up for the rip-offs. A caring person. One minute we'd be laughing with the stuff and the next minute we'd both be crying.

In terms of the process with van Toorn, Ginibi says her advice was, "Hey look, this is his life story. You've got to go back and start from the beginning, and to what led him to here. While I was hand writing she was on the computer, and it worked."

Haunted by the Past was published by Allen and Unwin and the experience for Ginibi was 'excellent', working with senior editor Sophie Cunningham and then Annette Barlow. The difference between a good publisher and other publishers, says Ginibi, is, "They [Allen and Unwin] consult, and they come and talk to you. The editors even come to your place and sit down and talk, asking 'What do you reckon about this?'". Ginibi also thinks she was lucky that in-house editor Annette Barlow didn't want to change anything in the text, she said,

> They'd consult with me, and I said "What about the cover?" They paid Nobby for the cover because he did the artwork. I always say to anyone who's working with me, "Don't gubbarise my text. Don't Anglicise my text, because that's how we speak, how we talk. We say 'comin' and 'goin' and 'tidda' or 'brud' or whatever". This is how we talk, this is our voice.

She adds,

> We have always been disadvantaged because we have to rely on white editors, who tend to Anglicise our text too much always, correcting the way we talk and using the proper English, though now they are bringing into the schools our Koori English. It's the way we talk, it's our voice, and I might add, it's as relevant as any other spoken English.[252]

Perhaps the worst editorial experience of all Aboriginal writers that I spoke to involved that of Jackie Huggins, but also included her mother Rita, the subject of the book *Auntie Rita*. The problems within the process were heightened because the book was being published through an Indigenous publishing house, Aboriginal Studies Press in Canberra.

Huggins admits that like so many authors she had completed her manuscript, submitted it, and expected to get it back in book form. Of course, she realises now, that doesn't happen. In terms of editing and reworking *Auntie Rita* Huggins put her life on hold, was receiving no income, and raising her son alone while living with her brother and mother to save paying rent. Huggins chose to do this with a sense of urgency because she wanted to complete the book before her mother died. She describes the process as difficult, beginning with an editor who she believes demonstrated little "knowledge of Indigenous peoples culture or literature" to working with another editor, Alison Ravenscroft, who embraced Aboriginal family and community politics. For Huggins, Ravenscroft 'saved the day!'

Like many authors, and previous to working with Ravenscroft, Huggins worked on the editorial changes asked for by the publisher as soon as they arrived and returned the work only to wait for months on end without a response. The first period Huggins waited was for three months, and then she finally rang the editor in Canberra saying,

> "What's happening with my mother's book?" And the editor said, "Well you know we've got the *Aboriginal Encyclopaedia* that we're trying to get out, and it's made it very difficult." So my mother and I marched down to Canberra and mum was really upset by this stage, and we walked into the room and I said, "Look, you've gotta give us some feedback, we've given you all these changes." The editor said, "We're so busy," and I assumed their priority was the *Encyclopaedia*. The editor took my mother off in a corner somewhere and was trying to talk to her. I said, "What are you telling her about?" My mother said to the editor, "Well…I'm gonna sit out here with my blanket and pillow until you help us with our book." The next day things started to happen in terms of the feedback.

These were fairly extreme lengths for any author to go to, to say nothing of it happening in an Aboriginal publishing house. Huggins says that everyone in the Press at the time was white, right down to the copy girl. For Huggins, things had got so bad she felt she had no support and no one to ask for help.

Huggins worked further on the book for the next three months and then got a call from the editor who had contracted a freelance editor to work on *Auntie Rita* because the Press was so busy. Huggins couldn't understand why the Press hadn't done it six months before. Huggins was living in Brisbane though, and the new editor lived in Melbourne: the Press said they didn't have any Brisbane-based editors on file (a file Huggins later found out didn't even exist).

Alison Ravenscroft had limited contact with Aboriginal people before, and Huggins told the Press the job needed to be done by someone, "who knows the scene, you don't want to go through all that educating and explaining and so on." But Ravenscroft was the editor and she wanted to meet the two Huggins women and so went to stay with them for two weeks. In that time she did what the women did normally, including going to a funeral at Cherbourg. Huggins explains how well the process worked commenting,

> She sat down and started to edit and talk to Mum and got her stuff on tape and filled it out which was great because there were things that Mum told Alison that she never told me for the book. Mum built up an immediate rapport and trust with her and Alison started to relax and was immersed in our home life. We had to go to a funeral in Cherbourg and she experienced that too. A young relative had been bashed to death by her boyfriend at the age of 23, and on the way up there I told her the background of the family. I could tell it really affected her and on the journey home Alison said, "Jackie, let's you and Auntie Rita and I pull in here for a counter-lunch." I said, "Are you kidding, this is a red-neck country town, they don't serve Blacks here." She apologised but these are the kinds of examples that she experienced, and it touched her deeply, it changed her, it transformed her.

Huggins says that Ravenscroft then became an advocate for her and a 'buffer-zone', so she got what she wanted without having to speak to other people at the Press, especially in the final production stages. Huggins says things worked out with Ravenscroft because, "We immersed her in our culture."

Huggins also credits the original editor who gave editorial advice on character development and the need to fill in gaps in Auntie Rita's life, however, she also gives a good example of cultural insensitivity:

> When one of the corrections went down I said my mother had received her exemption from the mission when she was 23 years old. In the margin the editor wrote, "An exemption? What do you mean, a tax exemption?" I was furious. I saw the editor the next day and said, "Listen, my mother was earning two bob a week for her domestic service work, and 15 pence of that went to the Department of Native Affairs. So she was obviously not earning enough money to even pay tax."

Training for Indigenous Editors

It is clear there is a need for cultural awareness training for non-Aboriginal editors, to assist them in a holistic understanding of Aboriginal writing. Bin Salleh says editors need to be educated and made aware of what the issues are and what process to use when editing a book by an Indigenous author. She suggests setting up a publishing education program for editors that is taken to publishing houses.

The idea of training is supported by Arts Training Northern Territory who in their report to ATSIC note that where non-Indigenous people are involved in the publishing process because of their industry expertise, the involvement needs to be based on training and education which ensures that their skills are used in a context which places Aboriginal and Torres Strait Islander people in control. By doing this, an important issue of Aboriginal management in selecting non-Aboriginal staff would ensure that non-Aboriginal expertise is utilised in ways that enhance Aboriginal control.[253]

Jane Arms' report on a proposed scheme for the training of Indigenous editors in Australia in 1997 stated that, "in a country with an increasing number of emerging Black writers there are only two trained Indigenous editors".[254] Considering the growing number of published fictional and autobiographical works, then, it was understandable that the report found,

> The clear need in Indigenous publishing is for a group of well-trained Indigenous editors, especially now that Magabala, Fremantle Arts Centre Press, and the Aboriginal Studies Press all have substantial Indigenous lists. Wakefield Press, and the University of Western Australia Press are also both looking at establishing Indigenous publishing imprints. There is a growing sense that a body of trained Indigenous editors is the first priority, that a single mentor program would not begin to address the immediate needs of Indigenous publishing. A more structured approach to training is needed.[255]

Arms' report goes on to say that in many houses (eg Magabala, UQP, Random House, IAD Press, Penguin Books and others), those who are qualified to train Indigenous editors do not have the time to set up a formal training program, let alone put it into practice. Such a training package being successful would require support in the way of funds from bodies such as the Australia Council.

This report also came up with a series of recommendations related to proposed training for Indigenous editors. In summary they are,

- that all trainee Indigenous editors be automatically offered places in the proposed residential course for senior editors (their places to be paid for from the Aboriginal and Torres Strait Islander Arts Board [ATSIAB] special initiative fund);
- that trainee Indigenous editors undertake supplementary training—a basic skills course in copy editing, a structured industry placement, computer skills training, and two weekend residential courses in editing—before being able to enter the proposed industry residential course;
- that costs to send basic trainees to basic skills course be funded by ATSIAB or appropriate state bodies;

- that the Literature Fund convene two weekend residential courses for Indigenous editors;
- that the costs of the residential weekends be carried by ATSIAB;
- that the cost of airfares and accommodation for the industry placement be made from ATSIAB funds and the rest of the costs be borne by the host publishing house.[256]

With a special funding allocation in 1998 from the ATSIAB to implement its national Indigenous arts policy, the Literature Fund developed a strategic initiative aimed at individual training programs for Indigenous and non-Indigenous editors. The purpose of the programs was to provide training opportunities for Indigenous editors, and for non-Indigenous editors to work with Indigenous writers to enhance their editing skills.

Following the recommendations of Arms' report, the Australia Council established a grant to provide training for Indigenous editors. Approximately 120 Australian publishers were contacted in early 1998 and were invited to submit proposals for individual training programs for editor(s). Five proposals were received, and the four publishers received a part of the total budget of almost $46,000.

IAD Press also received funds from the Literature Fund to enable its senior editor Marg Bowman to train Indigenous editor Josie Douglas on a one-to-one, in-house basis. This allowed Douglas to take part in industry placements and seminars, including a seven day editorial workshops in Alice Springs in May 1999 which was also attended by Rachel Bin Salleh and 11 other participants. Douglas says she was quite surprised by the number of other editors there that were working with and editing Aboriginal authors.

> They were asking questions to Rachel and I about different issues: protocols, cultural issues, cultural sensitivity issues that they've come across in their manuscripts, and dealing with white authors who are writing about Aboriginal issues. So the editors I spoke to are working on Aboriginal authors and then white authors writing about Aboriginal issues. I was really amazed, although I shouldn't be amazed, but I thought this day and age people would know about us. I was amazed at the ignorance they had.

The Australian Publishers Association Residential (APA) Editorial Program, was also established as a result of the recommendations of Arms' report. This program was an Australian first and was held over 6 days in 1999 in the Blue Mountains of New South Wales. Participants included Melissa Lucashenko, Mary Graham and Josie Douglas. Aside from intensive editing workshops with mentors, there were sessions and discussions devoted to "Listening to the Voice of the Author", "Conceptual Editing", "Commission Fiction and Non-Fiction" and "Indigenous Writing and Editing".

The "Indigenous Writing and Editing" session addressed issues relating to the editing of Indigenous materials and the cultural issues which are important for the future of Indigenous publishing, for example, What is it to be Indigenous? and, What is the motivation behind Indigenous writing?[257] Bruce Sims discussed the contractual issues involved in Indigenous publishing in this session.

Along with the Indigenous-specific session, there was continued input from participating Indigenous writers and editors, helping to raise consciousness amongst editors as to their role in facilitating adequate Indigenous assessment of manuscripts prior to publication, and sensitivity to Indigenous authors' issues.[258]

Findings of the Program included[259]:

a) the smallest presses are those committed to training Indigenous editors;
b) many publishing projects do not receive the benefit of expert Indigenous assessment and consultation before being accepted;
c) participants generally benefited from Indigenous input in the course and felt that more Indigenous consultants needed to be engaged when publishing projects were being assessed.

Melissa Lucashenko discussed how dealing with an Aboriginal manuscript is vastly different from dealing with other manuscripts. She suggested that editors could either insulate themselves from that fact, or they could try to understand/ accept/engage with it.[260] She noted the dangers that awaited editors who think they may have consulted adequately but still manage to step on people, stressing the importance of consultation, and that the process involves talking to more than one person. She commented that if you approach an author with good intentions, you will be respected, but that if you come in ignorance you can do damage.[261]

The APA Residential Program also found that:

> It is the editor's role as gatekeeper to ensure that they have full knowledge of what they are publishing, and whose right it is to tell particular stories; and towards whose interests the publishing project is directed. The white writer and editor has particular issues to address in clarifying the ownership of Indigenous content.[262]

In terms of training Aboriginal editors through mainstream publishing houses, Colin Johnson says that the problems may lie in the training itself. He argues that training implies that one will become literate in white genres and thus become part of the European culture actively colonising any work outside the mainstream.[263] Surely that does not have to be the case, though, if we have Aboriginal people in mainstream publishing houses who are already culturally sensitive to the issues relevant to Aboriginal society and have a working knowledge of Aboriginal literature. Surely we are capable of maintaining that sensitivity while learning the skills commonly used to develop good writing?

Surely as professional Aboriginal people we can combine the techniques of good writing with the storytelling that is being done to produce a work that is appropriately written and edited and available to a wide audience.

As flagged in this chapter, the editor of Aboriginal writing has a larger role to play in the production of Aboriginal writing than simply editing text. That role includes being aware of cultural and intellectual property rights and issues and these will be explored in the next chapter.

Chapter Six
Indigenous Cultural and Intellectual Property Rights

The need to secure protection by law of Indigenous Cultural and Intellectual Property rights was again brought to public attention in 1999 with the launch of the National Indigenous Arts Advocacy Association's (NIAAA) Label of Authenticity. In the same year, Our Culture: *Our Future—The Report on Australian Indigenous Cultural and Intellectual Property Rights* was published. The work of NIAAA and the Report written by Terri Janke were responses to the increasing level of appropriation of Aboriginal culture and voice, highlighted by the recent spate of artistic frauds (Elizabeth Durack/Eddie Burrup and Leon Carmen/Wanda Koolmatrie) in the 1990s.

The issue of protecting intellectual and cultural property rights is so important, Janke's initial report has generated much discussion and debate. Discussion has also touched on issues relevant to the creation of written literature, an issue that has been considered by both Indigenous and non-Indigenous authors and Indigenous communities in recent years.

Copyright and intellectual property laws are becoming increasingly relevant to Indigenous people. When research projects become published manuscripts and include traditional stories, copyright usually ends up with the non-Indigenous author because of the requirements of the *Copyright Act 1968* wherein a work must be original, have been reduced to material form and have an identifiable author.

The *Copyright Act* as it stands is unsuited to protecting Indigenous culture, because it is, "focused legally on individualistic commercial concepts, rather than notions of communal ownership or the cultural integrity of a work".[264] The Act also fails to accommodate the fact that Indigenous cultures, stories, information and knowledge are passed from generation to generation by oral means. In fact, reducing them to material form is, tantamount to the destruction of them.

Generally, under the *Copyright Act*, once stories are published in books and other documents, the person responsible for translating the oral story into written form is recognised as the owner of the copyright for the text.[265] Similarly, when a performance of a previously unpublished story or dance is recorded on film or audiotape, the maker of the recording is acknowledged legally as owning the film or tape.[266] In this way, copyright only protects the material medium rather than the idea or concept.

It is also the case that the person who first reduces an oral literature to material form is recognised as the author of the ensuing work,[267] and can exercise the exclusive rights granted to authors under the *Copyright Act* to reproduce the work in material form or to broadcast the work.[268]

It is no secret that over the last two hundred years Indigenous Australians have provided copious amounts of information for PhDs, research theses, governmental reviews etc, but few have ever benefited personally in terms of financial or academic gain. Pat Torres comments,

> This situation is in part due to the fact that many people who have provided specialised information to academics and others have not been seen as co-authors, writers or owners of the information or the copyright holders.[269]

In terms of recognising joint copyright and providing shared royalties to communities, Torres points out that,

> The payment of consultancy fees and royalties to key people within Aboriginal communities for their specialised and culturally unique knowledge is paramount towards the legitimisation of the worth and integrity of the information being provided...That payment not only legitimises the worth of the information from a mainstream Australian viewpoint, but it honours the concept of fees for service that is provided to other people with specialised knowledge and which is accepted as a given fact within business and academic circles.[270]

Janke also asks, "Whilst there is a strong argument for interviewees and contributors to be joint owners of copyright of resulting work, what about the communal interests of the group who are the 'Indigenous owners' of a story?"[271]

One example of a successful joint copyright /royalties arrangement however is *Jandamarra and the Bunuba Resistance* (Magabala). Howard Pederson, whose 15 year relationship with Banjo Woorunumurra led to the creation of the book, holds joint copyright with the Bunuba people, and all royalties are going back to the traditional owners. Another example of joint copyright is witnessed in *Love Against the Law: The Autobiographies of Tex and Nelly Camfoo* (Aboriginal Studies Press, 2000), recorded and edited by anthropologist Gillian Cowlishaw with copyright held by the three. But what happens when the non-Indigenous author is less sensitive to Aboriginal culture than Pederson and Cowlishaw? Interestingly, both these books came out of Indigenous publishing houses, who, by definition and by their own philosophies, *should* be protecting the rights of the communities they have been set up to represent.

In line with this concept Bruce Sims, one-time publisher of Magabala Books, acknowledges there are some areas of concern when working on Indigenous books, considering in the first instance the recording of the material. At the APA Residential Editorial Program in 1999, Sims acknowledged that copyright at present is held by the person who takes the tape or photo and that the person recorded or photographed has no further rights. However Sims believes that copyright must be assigned back to the person telling the story from the person doing the recording.[272] He notes that in terms of collaborative works, where the author is often white, that there are a range of options for dealing with the situation in contractual terms. Firstly, all copyright may be assigned to the Indigenous writers or an escape clause might allow joint copyright until an established cut-off time, with ownership then reverting to an Indigenous writer. Or the third option may be to have an 'heir letter' attached to the contract that assigns royalties to someone else.[273] The final issue for the publisher concerned is permissions. Sims says the publisher must educate the author about what a permission is, and what permissions might be sought for a property.[274]

Nadia Wheatley looks at the questions of copyright faced by non-Indigenous authors who may, for example, want to write a Dreaming story. She asks,

> Do we need to get permission from the community whose story it is, in order to re-tell it and make money out of it? Or can we just claim full copyright and full royalties? If we don't have to get permission, why do people like Lionel Fogarty and Pat Torres have to? And if we don't want all the hassle, why can't we just make up a Dreaming?[275]

Wheatley is aware of the protocols facing authors regardless of race, when it comes to reproducing a Dreaming story from someone else's area. Her question of what to do if an author can not access the necessary permission, or simply can't be bothered, and what next to do, is a relevant one. And if the protocol is not followed, is there any mechanism for retribution? At this stage it appears not.

Currently the Copyright Agency Limited collects royalties for the copyright of literary works but Janke and others maintain that this is not appropriate for Indigenous cultural works, and that any Indigenous collecting society or societies would be voluntary or set up under *sui generis* (stand alone) legislation.[276] The authorisation of use of cultural materials then would be based on the premise of prior informed consent of rights given to the society under license rather than as an assignment of rights.[277]

Janke advocates for further investigation of Indigenous collecting models able to distribute monies to communities (setting up trust arrangements, and the like) and an agency that can address specific Indigenous issues like communal ownership, and assisting Indigenous writers and publishers in developing models of practice and protocols. Informants would also then be empowered about income streams so that they can strike deals at the time of speaking with authors.[278]

IAD Press also express their concerns with copyright as a publisher saying that the greatest problem area in the field of copyright for them to date is that of oral history, as it is riddled with unresolved difficulties. Related to this is the contentious area of copyright itself: whether ownership of a story is vested in an individual, family or kinship group(s), community/ies, language group(s). This issue is particularly difficult when it comes to royalty payments time,[279] especially when you consider the average 10% payment due to the owner of the copyright of the text then being divided between perhaps multiple owners. It could lead to the question of whether such copyright terms are worth the financial outcome and administrative process that new laws would create.

Due to all the copyright issues facing publishers and authors, IAD Press believes a specific strategy is needed to address the problems. They believe ATSIC needs to provide assistance for Copyright Council regional workshops focussed specifically for Aboriginal people with the aim of increasing their knowledge and understanding of their rights and entitlements.[280]

An added problem for traditional artforms is that copyright lasts for the author's life plus 50 years; therefore, because Indigenous stories are passed on through generations, they do not qualify for copyright protection. As Janke comments, "Many works of Indigenous arts and cultural expressions have been in existence since time immemorial and those that are newly created today will remain significant beyond this period."[281] In addition, Pat Torres had the following concerns about the 50 year cut-off date,

> Copyright exists in Australian law, material that is put into books, is only copyrighted for 50 years after you are dead. So your children and your grandchildren will not own the copyright of your work.
>
> So it does not take in the life, cultural and traditional realities of Aboriginal people. It is okay if you are making a book that is made up about any kind of story, but if it is a Dreaming story and it is your tradition and your culture, having a 50 year life on your works is really acting against us.[282]

Intellectual Property

In Janke's view, 'Indigenous Cultural and Intellectual Property Rights' refers to Indigenous Australians' rights to their heritage, and that heritage consists of,

> The intangible and tangible aspects of the whole body of cultural practices, resources and knowledge systems developed, nurtured and refined by Indigenous people and passed on by them as part of expressing their cultural identity.[283]

The term 'heritage' also includes literary, performing and artistic works (including music, dance, song, ceremonies, symbols and designs, narratives and poetry) as well as languages, spiritual knowledge, Indigenous ancestral remains and other aspects of Aboriginal society and culture.[284]

In discussing the need to develop strategies for the protection of Indigenous Intellectual and Cultural Property rights, Janke advocates for the *Copyright Act* accommodating:

> Moral rights for Indigenous custodians which provide the Indigenous cultural group whose traditions is drawn upon to create a copyright work with rights of attribution, false attribution and cultural integrity:

However, this might only cover Indigenous cultural works within the copyright period and will not refer to Indigenous material currently considered in the public domain.[285]

Janke also advocates for the protections of Indigenous languages within literary and performance work—including books, songs, plays, poetry and other works, as well as translations into Indigenous languages.[286]

The appropriation of Indigenous spirituality is another concern of Indigenous peoples. Janke's report compares this appropriation to the commercialisation and derogation of rituals, including medicine wheel ceremonies and sweat lodges, belonging to North American First Nations' peoples by non-Indigenous people. Janke cites Marlo Morgan, author of *Mutant Message Down Under* as an example of such appropriation as the book had been marketed as a true account of the author's "real spiritual experience among a group of Aboriginal Australians known as 'Real People'."[287]

In terms of those adopting Indigenous persona like Leon Carmen /Wanda Koolmatrie and Elizabeth Durack/Eddie Burrup, Janke says that laws relating to fraud and misrepresentation may offer assistance where false documents are used or when contracts and agreements are signed. She also suggests that laws relating to misleading and deceptive conduct under the *Trade Practices Act 1974 (Commonwealth)* may also be useful.[288] Janke also points out that there is no protection against culturally inappropriate treatment of Aboriginal works,

> For Indigenous people, cultural integrity in reproductions of Indigenous cultural material is important. Under customary law, Indigenous custodians are collectively responsible for ensuring that important cultural images and themes are not reproduced inappropriately. The Indigenous creator must be careful not to destroy or misuse the cultural knowledge embodied in a work. Although an author is the creator of the artwork, song, or story, he or she cannot authorise reproduction of it without ensuring the reproduction complies with Indigenous customary law. Such rights are not recognised under current copyright laws.[289]

Sam Cook believes that Aboriginal intellectual property rights—all of the knowledge that has been accumulated over tens of thousands of years by Aboriginal people—must be protected. She says that with the movement of Aboriginal people away from their traditional lands, usually forcibly, ownership of information is not as clear-cut as it used to be, adding,

> We must guard against utilising a design in the wrong context. Traditional designs invariably belong to certain community groups, and the relevant elders and/or traditional owners must give permission before they can be reproduced. It would be wrong, for example, for an image from one region to be placed alongside a story from another region of Australia, unless permission has been obtained.[290]

Contracts

To an extent, Aboriginal writers face the same professional industrial problems as all authors. Thus they need to know how to protect their rights in a contract. They need to know: how to apply for Public Lending Rights and how to access the Copyright Agency Limited; what rights (electronic, digital, moral) they should retain and what the publisher is entitled to; and what they should be paid for a piece of work or a public appearance. At the same time, some Aboriginal writers face additional contractual and copyright issues, because there are sometimes matters of community ownership and collaboration that may need to be considered.

In her "Report on Preparation for Indigenous Writers' Series", Anthea Wu recommended that UWA Press contracts, "be modified in accordance with…suggestions from Bruce Sims," (described above) given at the Residential Editors Program.[291] However, in October 1999, Wu says that the Press had not yet incorporated these changes into their contracts as they had not yet created their first contract for their Indigenous list.[292]

As few mainstream publishers have extensive Indigenous lists, the issues discussed in this chapter have yet to be taken on board by most, aside from the efforts of UWA Press and perhaps Fremantle Arts Centre Press who have published a number of successful works by Aboriginal authors. Because of this, only authors with contract advice from legal representatives who are 'up-to-speed' with intellectual property rights for Indigenous people would, at this stage it appears, be benefiting from the new discussions on such protection issues.

As an editor, Rachel Bin Salleh says she can't even start editing until issues of ownership, authorship and copyright have been sorted out. She says it is these areas that cause the most headaches because people are generally not aware of the issues, but they can halt the book process for good. She adds,

> In a sense getting correct ownership of a story is more important than the process of editing or publishing. Also, if a section in the book is appropriate. Maybe there are sections interwoven into a book about men's law or women's business. Is it appropriate to be there? I mightn't think so, but maybe the women/men do. Maybe they are unaware that it has been included? If so then negotiations must start as to what should be there. How it should be portrayed. Who is the custodian for the story, is it appropriate for that person to be telling that story. There has to be some amount of tact—as these questions can be quite offensive to a lot of people.[293]

Issues around protecting the intellectual property and copyrights of Indigenous authors are key to developing an authentic voice in the literary field in Australia. These issues are not the only ones concerning writers though, as the need to improve the marketing and distribution of Aboriginal created works has also become a high priority. A look at the current strategies employed by publishing houses and suggestions for further improvement will be examined in the next chapter on selling Black writing to the white reader.

Part Three

Readership

Chapter 7
Selling Indigenous Literature to the Reader

Issues around access to publishing, the influence of the non-Indigenous editor and the need for protection and acknowledgement of intellectual property and copyrights are of utmost importance to Aboriginal writers. The marketing and distribution of Aboriginal works, the appropriate reviewing of Aboriginal books and the need to foster audiences interested in reading and hearing works by Aboriginal authors are equally important factors in growing Aboriginal authorship and readership. This part focuses on the latter issues.

Marketing and distribution

Writers generally complain about lack of marketing in relation to their books, so complaints from Aboriginal authors are not surprising. However, some of the reasons why the marketing of works by Aboriginal authors are unsuccessful are particular to Aboriginal authors. While the authors interviewed for this book had a cursory interest in publishing and marketing processes, they were very interested in having their books reviewed or profiled and available for purchase at literary festivals and bookstores.

The attitude of publishing houses to Aboriginal works fundamentally influences the marketing of Aboriginal writers and their works, therefore the marketing and promotion of Aboriginal writing is an area of much importance. There is a great divide between publishing a book and having the book published read. It appears that publishers do little to help the promotion and eventual distribution of titles published by Aboriginal authors.

It is generally accepted that the superficial interest in marketing Aboriginal works is a product of assumptions made by publishing houses as to the tastes of the 'reading public'. As a result of the assumption that the 'reading public' is not interested in works by Aboriginal authors, the lack of profile given to Aboriginal works contributes to a general lack of recognition and appreciation of Aboriginal writers. Further, publishers often mistakenly assume that Aboriginal works are of interest to a select [read Aboriginal] audience. Some publishers claim to have good marketing and distribution strategies, but admit there are areas that need developing so that the promotion of Aboriginal authors and their works is more rigorous and far-reaching.

Even though libraries are the most frequented cultural institutions in Australia,[294] the need to promote the books that make up library shelves does not seem necessary to booksellers or publishers. Aboriginal books are rarely seen in book shop catalogues, and only in recent years have they started to be reviewed by mainstream papers. This is no doubt due to increased publication of Aboriginal books.

7. Selling Indigenous Literature to the Reader

Sandra Phillips in an interview with Lisa Bellear on community radio in Melbourne, suggested that the lack of promotion of Aboriginal writing stemmed from an ignorance of the Aboriginal and Torres Strait Islander community generally, regardless of how powerful Aboriginal and Torres Strait Islander literature might be. Phillips is also quick to point out that the low profile of Aboriginal writers within the wider literary world is a direct result of the low profile we have within our own communities. Comparing Aboriginal writers to First Nations' writers, she comments,

> In terms of the profile of Indigenous artists in this country, there is absolutely no comparison to the way that Native Canada treats its writers. They are seen as very important carriers of messages and the fact that there were no writers on the arts workshop panel at the Reconciliation Convention (1997) is a slap in the face for the writing community. How did all that get through without anybody saying "excuse me how about these people."[295]

There are a number of Aboriginal writers who are concerned about the negative experiences that have stemmed from trying to have their books marketed and distributed. It is not unreasonable for any author to expect that their book, at the very least, is available for purchase. Lisa Bellear is clearly not happy with the marketing and distribution of *Dreaming in Urban Areas*. Although UQP's distribution is done by Penguin, Bellear notes that on occasion in the past she would turn up to festivals and her book wouldn't be there even though she was on the program. Bellear commented,

> I get treated very well here but in terms of the marketing, they don't know how to promote Indigenous writers and they only promote certain Indigenous writers. I get support from a number of women at UQP and I'm thankful for that, but it's like let's get specific and talk marketing because they haven't got it right.[296]

Sandra Phillips, who was the Indigenous worker Bellear referred to, says the book's jacket is the selling point. Because of this she says it should have Aboriginal art on it; it needs to be inviting and affirming of Aboriginal culture and society as opposed to what publishers or corporations go for.[297] Phillips adds that the marketing issue is a more fundamental issue of how confident the house is in an author, and where they will place that confidence, for example, through the size of the print run and the resources in people and dollars put into marketing. From Phillips' comments it seems clearly necessary that publishers need to do larger print runs when supporting the release of new books with promotions and marketing strategies.

Among other UQP authors, Jeanie Bell says that aside from a launch in Musgrave Park and another at the Woodford/Malaney Festival, from her author perspective it appeared that the marketing of *Talking About Celia* never happened, so she was surprised to hear that a lot of people around the country said they'd seen it in book shops. One woman even told Bell she saw the book in a second hand book shop not long after its release.[298] Melissa Lucashenko admits she knows little about marketing and promotion, saying, "I sort of left it in their hands because my main aim was to get it published."[299] These authorial perspectives of UQP's marketing could be seen as much as a comment on the lack of inclusion of Indigenous authors in the marketing process, or even the authors lack of understanding of this process, rather than sole comment on the publisher's marketing capacities.

One of the reasons offered by Cathy Craigie for the lack of promotion and marketing of Aboriginal writers by their publishers is that there are what Craigie calls 'racist factors' in Australia, a sort of 'cultural cringe' or unofficial discrimination policy because there hasn't been a reconciliation between Black and white Australians.[300] She says when that reconciliation happens, Aboriginal people in Australia will have the same respect and acknowledgment as the Maori in Aotearoa. She also adds that marketing and distribution of books is about economics and, in terms of Aboriginal theatre, 'bums on seats'. She believes that publishers and publicists don't think anyone out there is interested in Aboriginal works that do not dilute what really happened, which is another example of the 'racist factor', something that Aboriginal writers who want and deserve attention have to challenge all the time.

While there are many complaints by writers generally in relation to the lack of promotion for Aboriginal works, there are also suggestions as to how to improve the situation. Phillips says marketing can be improved by quantifying the interest shown in Aboriginal writing and books and maximising that interest. She says there is not enough confidence in book selling. That lack of confidence, she says, is demonstrated in small print runs and little or no marketing,

> These are big issues and I think any Aboriginal person working in publishing fights those battles and they are really tough battles because they are about money, and that's what we need to recognise: that publishing is a cultural endeavour but also publishing houses are a business.

While many authors complain that their books are not valued or supported by large print runs, Ray Coffey from FACP says that most publishers are cautious with print run sizes these days because of the high costs of production, printing and warehouse storage. FACP would see a 500 print run for poetry as small and 1000 as large, with general non-fiction and adolescent fiction small at 3,000 and large at 5,000 copies. Children's picture books however would be small at 5,000 and large at 10,000 copies.[301]

Simon MacDonald from IAD Press says the print runs reflect community interest: a print run of 500 copies is usually sufficient to have kept the cost of producing the book down while also providing sufficient copies for resale or trade. MacDonald also comments that it is more usual to see print runs of 3-3,500 copies for childrens' or art/cross cultural titles and 4-5,000 copies for fiction.[302]

Both Coffey and MacDonald explain that the point of the print run is to recover costs (editorial, design, marketing, printing) and that often the publisher is likely to come out no better than the author.

Kenny Laughton believes that technology is one facility that Aboriginal authors now have at their disposal to promote and market themselves. Despite the potential of the internet however, in reality he narrows the issue down to financial security, via private funding or community arts funding. He says marketing and promotion of is the author's hardest task, but vitally important: "It's what makes or breaks you."[303]

Considering the success of Marlo Morgan's fictitious tale *Mutant Message Down Under*, one might question: what made her work so marketable? Lynne Spender, then Executive Director of the Australian Society of Authors, questioned the marketing campaign of Morgan's work which allegedly cost HarperCollins (US) approximately $250,000 with a first print run of 250,000; prompting Spender to ask,

> Did the possibility of selling half a million books lead HarperCollins to conveniently ignore the genuine objections to the book and the allegations that the good doctor is a phoney? And if the book sells, do its credentials matter?[304]

Jackie Huggins, while acknowledging that bigger publishers are better at marketing and distribution, comments that it is often the author who does all the work of marketing and selling. In the case of *Auntie Rita*,

> We flogged our books off everywhere. The Institute did nothing for us and I keep reminding them and telling them about that. You're your own marketing machine. We sold about 2,000 ourselves. I used to carry a box of books around in the car. People keep asking me for copies wherever I go. I just went to a breakfast this morning and these two women from the Health Department said, "I read Auntie Rita and did you bring any books today." They wanted to know where they could get it from and there's only one place you can get it from in Brisbane, the book store at the University of Queensland because they have it on English, Anthropology, Sociology and Politics courses.305

Recognising the problems associated with distribution for small publishers, Huggins says a stronger strategic marketing plan is needed if more books are to sell. She cites another example from her own experience:

> I rang up to get a box of books for a talk that I was doing for women in Queensland in the public service and they wanted copies of my book, and when I rang up they [Aboriginal Studies Press] said that those women would have to pay for the postage there. I said, "Hang on here, I am doing you a favour in terms of doing your job for you, in terms of selling these books which you could never do, you'd still have them sitting in the warehouse down there.

In defence of publishers, there are obvious efforts by some to improve the sales and status of Aboriginal writers. Ray Coffey says FACP's approach to marketing is the same irrespective of the writer's background, and is always individually tailored to the content and the perceived market for each book. He comments,

> Aboriginal writing, like any writing, is certainly marketable if it is readable and accessible to a readership. Clearly the great majority of potential readers for any book is non-Aboriginal. The size of the potential Aboriginal reading population is generally too small to make publishing largely to that market viable.

While Sam Cook admits that there is a long way to go to improve the level of marketing and distribution of Indigenous books, she is also quick to point out that human resources and financial budgets present the major restraints. She comments,

> There are many possibilities and exciting options we have in front of us and it is a matter of finding the time in the publishing schedule to really workshop ideas and put things in place. I think Magabala's choice of Australian Book Group was a step in the right direction because I feel they are the best distributor to promote our titles and we have sales to reflect this but we really have a long way to go in this area.[306]

Cook says that while she would like to say that Magabala's books are aimed at an Indigenous audience, the reality is that, "Until the publishing house is 100% Indigenous there will be a strong focus on non-Indigenous markets. I believe that in the future of Indigenous publishing there has to be a balance struck between both Indigenous and non-Indigenous markets."

Rachel Bin Salleh says that many of Magabala's books are marketed towards all social and reading classes of Australia, and that educational and specialist bookshops are major retail outlets. She says Magabala's mission is to produce books for Aboriginal people by Aboriginal people, and so they focus on making books accessible to Indigenous communities who are more likely to particularly seek out Aboriginal works. When she edits a book, though, Bin Salleh says it is always with the readership within Indigenous communities, as well as the wider Australian and international readership, that are foremost in her mind.[307]

Clearly, book publishing needs to take into consideration commercial marketability. Even so, the Arts Training Northern Territory Report of 1994 said that publishers did not see all writing, or all of Aboriginal and Torres Strait Islander writing, in commercial market terms. In their report they quoted UQP as saying,

> University of Queensland Press has a commitment to the publication and development of Aboriginal and Torres Strait Islander writing as an affirming and valuable discourse in world literature.
>
> The Press does not operate on a market-based rationale in determining which Black writing manuscripts to publish. As with emerging ground breaking

literature, readership is largely unidentified, particularly in areas of political and combined genre writing (eg autobiographical fiction) and market demand can be difficult to predict.[308]

In relation to the domestic market, IAD Press added to the same report,

> The market in Australia is small and unsophisticated in its expectations of Aboriginal-authored works. It is mainly limited to children's/Dreamtime stories, auto/biographies, art books and academic works (the latter generally about, rather than by, Aboriginal people).[309]

In contrast to IAD's comments though is the view from FACP:

> There is, as commercial publishers have shown in recent years, an increasing demand for books which deal with aspects of Aboriginal culture and history. Both for Aboriginal and non-Aboriginal readers. This demand, and therefore the potential market for publication, exists at local, regional, national and international levels.
>
> If publications are produced with a clear and accurate idea of the particular market for each production, then reasonable returns can be made for those with a large market, and costs can be minimalised for those that do not.[310]

Promotional strategies for maximising potential within export markets and with links to tourism have yet to be developed in a coordinated way but would appear to offer promise. As Magabala Books noted in the 1994 report,

> Cultural tourism is a developing market which it is imagined would not be difficult to break into. However, there are still airport gift shops, Aboriginal run galleries and art centres which are not aware of the books available.
>
> It is apparent that insufficient funds are being made available. It also needs to be stressed that this is not a peripheral requirement but a core operation. The mainstream market is huge and extremely competitive.[311]

Rachel Bin Salleh comments that Aboriginal literature is generally marketable to all walks of life: "Even though we talk about the Aboriginal or Indigenous experience, all the experiences are human, and suffering is universal. So, the Aboriginal experience is relevant to Australians today as it is a part of the overall history of Australia." She further comments that the book publishing industry should be telling ignorant booksellers,

> Just because it's Aboriginal doesn't mean that it goes into the Australiana section for mild mannered tourists. I find that no matter what you do, how you market a book, it goes into the Australiana section. Death by association. If we have a biography, autobiography and the person happens to be Aboriginal then it goes into this section. Any other coloured writer of this genre would go in the right section—bestsellers, biography, autobiography etc.

Bin Salleh cites an example of going to a bookshop in Melbourne and finding in the Australian section Archie Weller's science fiction/fantasy book *Land of the Golden Clouds*. Bin Salleh says she sees this all the time and it disadvantages the author because their books do not really get the maximum exposure that they should.

In a positive light, Simon MacDonald from IAD Press is confident that Aboriginal literature is generally marketable, because IAD's books are being sold to non-Aboriginal Australia and non-Australian readers. He comments,

> There's an international hunger and interest and it's probably not being serviced very well unless you come to Australia which is why it's good that Herb Wharton will pack up his bags and go to Paris tomorrow. More of that activity needs to be supported so that Aboriginal authors can travel.[312]

MacDonald goes on to say that the education market is targeted title by title and that *Take Power*—an anthology celebrating 20 years of land rights in Central Australia and edited by Alexis Wright for the Central Land Council—is a good example of a secondary school text covering Aboriginal studies, cross cultural studies and history. This is the kind of book that MacDonald believes could be put on many curricula.

Kenny Laughton was the first of IAD Press's authors to be sent on tour, with assistance from the Australia Council. MacDonald says there's no doubt that the tour assisted sales of his book, but that he would be struggling to say that without the tour the book wouldn't have gone so well, because that outcome can't be measured:

> We had a brilliant author who would speak to anyone, and when people did speak to him they recognised him for his qualities alone, intrinsic qualities. Nearly all the people in the media in Sydney said, "Hey you're a pleasure to talk to." So we had a gem to work with to begin with. Kenny has the press and IAD firmly in the centre of his priorities as well.

In terms of my own experiences with marketing and distributing my satirical commentary *Sacred Cows*, it became obvious shortly after its release that I was doing a disproportionate amount of work given my royalty-based return. I estimate I have conducted 95% of the marketing and 90% of the distribution for 7.5% of the recommended retail price. The publisher-chosen illustrator received 2.5% royalty return. So, following *Sacred Cows*, I self-published *Token Koori* in 1998. While the response to *Token Koori* has been generally good with almost 700 copies sold in the first 11 months, and publicity both locally and nationally, with invitations to readings arriving regularly, the marketing and distribution of this book has not been easy. Self-promotion and distribution does have its downfalls, the most obvious having to carry a box of books with you everywhere you go. But as Jackie Huggins commented above, authors published by mainstream publishers also have to do this. If you want your book to be out there, to be read, reviewed and appreciated, and hopefully bring in some of the estimated $3000 income that the average Australian author is supposed to get annually,[313] then you have to do a lot more than just write it.

7. Selling Indigenous Literature to the Reader

As part of my grant application to the Australia Council for funds associated with printing costs for *Token Koori* I was required to develop a distribution and marketing strategy for the book. Even without the grant (that I was fortunate enough to receive), this strategy was an invaluable tool to ensure maximum publicity and distribution. I was offered a contract for publication from Aboriginal Studies Press who wanted to use *Token Koori* as the first in a series of creative works by young Indigenous authors, however the Press couldn't match my strategy and/or give me more than the usual 10% royalty, so I declined their offer.

Once the books were printed I had to market them. I had a niche market and so targeted Indigenous media associations nationally, placed an advertisement with order form in the *Koori Mail*, and did interviews on radio stations with Aboriginal issues or arts programs. My marketing plan included three key strategies.

Firstly, *Token Koori* was launched at the 1998 Sydney Writers' Festival. This was a major coup as it gave recognition to a self-published work. This is quite uncommon in the mainstream literary world. Being on the Sydney Writers' Festival program also brought with it a large amount of publicity, something an individual author would probably rarely be able to afford to buy.

Secondly, a press release was sent via email, fax and hard copy to media outlets relevant to my audience. These included, *Arts Yarn Up, Deadly Vibe, Koori Mail*, AWAYE (Radio National), SBS (Radio) Indigenous Program, Arts Yarn Up (Koori Radio), ICAM (SBS TV), and the National Indigenous Media Association of Australia, responsible for sending press releases out to its membership (which includes the Broadcasting to Remote Aboriginal Communities Service).

Thirdly, review copies were sent to literary journals including the *Australian Multicultural Book Review, Australian Women's Book Review, Heat, Meanjin, Scarp, Ulitarra* and *Five Bells*.

Aside from the marketing of books for sale, there is also the marketing of works for public performance and invitations for Aboriginal writers to attend literary events. The belief that people won't pay to see Aboriginal writers perform their work was implied by Lydia Miller, Project Coordinator of the Festival of the Dreaming, who wrote in 1997: "The State Library of NSW forums are free. There is no entry fee as we wish to encourage people to access as many events as possible with the Paperbark Literature program and the Festival generally."[314] This statement seems to assume that people won't pay to attend Aboriginal literary events, as opposed to other Indigenous arts events. This is simply not true. At the NSW Writers' Centre's Spring Writing Festival Indigenous sessions in 1996 (Tiddas' Business: New Aboriginal Women's Writing), 1997 (Literary Fraud or Artistic License?, Young Black and Talented, and Native Tongues) and 1998 (Land, Life, Literature, and Yarnin' Up), there were almost full-houses and participants paid a $5 entrance fee. $5 is not a large fee, but the fact that people interested in literature will pay a small fee is proved by the attendance levels at this event.

There have been varying degrees of promotion of Aboriginal writers at other literary events, and oddly enough it is the mainstream events that provide more support and coverage than Aboriginal-organised ones. Publicity for Spring Writing in 1997, for example, ensured good attendance at the Aboriginal sessions. Executive Director of the NSW Writers' Centre, Irina Dunn, puts the success of the these sessions down to some positive publicity provided the day before the session by the *Sydney Morning Herald*. Dunn believes the article, "Helped to focus on the festival, but generally the resurgence of Aboriginal culture over the last few years has made people a lot more interested in an Aboriginal perspective."[315]

In contrast, promotion of the Paperbark program of the Festival of the Dreaming was not as effective as it could or should have been. A colour flier was scheduled to be available in all venues on 1 September 1997, with a mail-out due the first week of September. However, Dunn stated that she didn't even receive a program or invitation to attend Paperbark at all, which leaves one wondering if a peak literary organisation in the host city didn't see a program who else didn't—or, more to the point, who did?

Blackbooks is presently the only specialist distribution service for Indigenous books and resources. They have a comprehensive catalogue and shop that claims to be Australia's leading specialist distributor of books and resources by, for and about Aboriginal and Torres Strait Islander people and issues. The aim of Blackbooks is to maintain a quality service that provides culturally appropriate information. They also have a policy of 'checking out' new stock before including it in material offered to their customers.[316]

At the Festival of the Dreaming in September 1997, the three Indigenous publishing houses launched the *ABC Of Indigenous Publishing* celebrating 65 years of combined Indigenous Australian publishing (Aboriginal Studies Press 30 years, IAD Press 25 years, and Magabala Books 10 years). This catalogue of publications by and about Aboriginal society and culture, also includes works published by mainstream presses like UNSW Press, FACP, UQP, Hyland House, Spinifex Press, Allen & Unwin Australia, Hale & Iremonger, Wakefield Press, UWA Press and Prospect Media.

While this catalogue is useful in listing publications currently in print, it fails yet again to list books specifically written by Aboriginal authors. Julie Janson (*Black Mary*) appearing next to Jimmy Chi and Kuckles (*Bran Nue Dae*), and Herb Wharton (*Cattle Camp: Murrie Drovers and their stories*) listed alongside Henry Reynolds (*Dispossession: Black Australians and White Invaders*) can confuse or mislead those not familiar with Aboriginal literature. Members of the general community often comment to me that they want to read books by Aboriginal authors, but that they don't know who these authors are. The problem with the catalogue therefore is that it doesn't point readers wanting to read works by Aboriginal authors to Aboriginal works. By contrast, the Blackbooks catalogue lists works by genre and author.

Reviewing

Another way to sell books is through positive reviews. While the saying goes that, any publicity is good publicity, it is certainly the case that a good review in a widely-read and reputable paper or journal will also contribute to an increase in sales. Review copies are counted by publishers as part of their marketing strategies, but the reviewer and criteria for reviewing Aboriginal writing, are other aspects of the process that can affect how well a book is marketed to the reading audience and, in turn, how many books sell.

In *Born of the Conquerors* Judith Wright asks some very relevant questions about the role of critics and reviewers in relation to Aboriginal literature. She asks,

> Can we apply the critical standards we use in evaluating new contributions to our own literature by those who inherit and live within the dominant culture and language, to those who have had no such education, training and background—and who moreover, may bitterly and thoroughly reject all the bland assumptions of that culture and feel that language an alien imposition?[317]

Alexis Wright also comments,

> We have not had the opportunity to receive an appropriate education to even get close to the standards set by the gatekeepers of the English language to get heard or published, or reviewed, or at times when we do publish and are reviewed we are unfairly ridiculed by the cross-culturally inept.[318]

Emmanuel S. Nelson is also aware that ethnocentrism and paternalism exist even within reviewers sympathetic to the Aboriginal cause.[319] He points to an article by John Beston in 1977 which asserts that Oodgeroo Noonuccal and Jack Davis are ineffective when they attempt poetic forms other than short lyrics, prescribing his own cure for their alleged literary ailment, "They need the discipline of traditional [European] verse form."[320] Nelson adds that while critics are commending or condemning Aboriginal writing from a range of perspectives, few seem to be taking notice of what it is that Aboriginal writers are saying. He says that it is to the artists themselves we should turn, "If we are seeking an appropriate critical approach to Aboriginal writing."[321]

Colin Johnson believes that a writer should write for their own people secure in the knowledge that the work is accepted on Aboriginal merits, rather than the notoriety a book will generate because it is a best-seller.[322] In terms of reviews of the content of Aboriginal work, Jackie Huggins, comments, "The only ones who know our stuff, the only ones who can review our stuff are our own mob. Others just don't understand the argument." But Judith Wright makes a valid point when she says, "This critical dilemma can result in a refusal to try to criticise the work at all. So the Aboriginal voice, with all it has to say to us, may be silenced by critical consent."[323]

In reaction to the small numbers of Aboriginal reviews of Aboriginal writing, Ian Anderson, in a letter to *Australian Book Review* in 1993 commented that,

> In 1992 there were 24 books reviewed which contained significant amounts of Aboriginal and Torres Strait Islander subject matter…What is disturbing…is that the majority of this reviewed writing is written by non-Aboriginal people (approximately 19 works) and all were reviewed by non-Aboriginal people. Even given errors in my allocation of writers this is hardly an impressive record.[324]

The fact that there are few Aboriginal reviewers has been somewhat redressed in recent years with the increased pool of Aboriginal writers reviewing books by and about Aboriginal people, including John Muk Muk Burke (*The Australian's Review of Books, Ulitarra*), Melissa Lucashenko (*The Australian's Review of Books*), Bruce Pascoe (*Going Down Swinging, Ulitarra*), Alexis Wright (*Australian Book Review*), and myself (*Meanjin, Southerly, Ulitarra, Australian Book Review, Courier Mail, Sydney Morning Herald*).

In practical terms, many writers comment that white reviewers don't understand the essence of their Black writing and the message they wish to get across. John Muk Muk Burke who received many reviews for *Bridge of Triangles* was happy with most of them but believes Adam Shoemaker hated his book and that the review lacked humility. Shoemaker's review titled, "A Bridge Too Far" described Burke's work as, "…a disquieting piece of work," but also said Burke was a writer with "obvious talent".[325] Shoemaker also asks, to Burke's disappointment no doubt,

> So what do we do with this? Is *Bridge of Triangles* an existential story of the human condition or is it an overwhelmingly pessimistic literary gestalt? Even more: where and how does Burke place Aboriginality in all of this maelstrom? The answer seems to be that the author has gone for a flicker of Black Australian optimism, but little else.[326]

In response, Burke commented,

> Why couldn't he just say, "Look I'm not Aboriginal and this book can't really speak to me—et's be honest." Shoemaker said, "The author doesn't know what he's saying," and it wasn't that at all, *he* didn't know what I was saying. And he didn't have the humility, he didn't have the wherewithal to say, here is something that is really challenging.[327]

In contrast to Shoemaker, who commented on there being too much death in the book, P.A. Danaher's review focussed more on the positive saying, "despite this catalogue of depressing, even tragic, events, Chris's story is by no means uniformly bleak. There are moments of quiet humour."[328] Danaher suggests that the book should be set for study by senior students and adds that the book's, "prose style is appealing, describing poverty and racism with a curious mixture of innocence and compassion."[329]

Ruby Langford Ginibi gives an example of a review from non-Aboriginal reviewer Mary Rose Liverani, who wrote of Ginibi's *Real Deadly*:

> If a white had written this manuscript it would have gone straight on to the publisher's reject pile. In publishing *Real Deadly*, Angus and Robertson may have opened up a Pandora's Box. What if those armies of unpublished writers clamouring to be heard start claiming Aboriginal ancestry?[330]

In her published response to Liverani, Ginibi wrote,

> The alienation and dispossession forced me outside the social mainstream; it's not a question of rejecting social norms. We Kooris were not allowed into your social enclaves. Liverani talks about us Kooris as though we had a choice, which shows how little she knows of the Aboriginal experience of Australia.[331]

A comment on this type of reviewing is made by student of Aboriginal literature, Cliff Watego, who analyses the role critics and reviewers play in influencing audiences, and even more so, the publishing industry:

> [White] critics make the frequent mistake of making evaluations (from within their Eurocentric world view) of literature from the Black view point. Because publishers and editors rely heavily upon critics they also fall into the trap of not recognising the essential character or fibre of Black literature.[332]

A final example of how Euro-centric thought can affect commentary on Aboriginal works can be seen in a review of Kenny Laughton's *Not Quite Men, No Longer Boys*, where Theresa Kuilboer wrote: "I've got to be honest, I prepared myself for the inevitable cliches of how tough it was to be an Aborigine, but to my surprise, Laughton simply continues his tale with self-effacing humour and a keen insight into human nature."[333] It is clear Kuilboer had preconceived ideas about what the content of Aboriginal writing would be, and the tone in which the story would be told, which led to surprise when her expectations weren't met.

What made Sally Morgan so marketable?

In 1987 Sally Morgan from Western Australia became a national identity because of her family history *My Place*, which tells the story of Morgan's family and the suppression of its Aboriginal heritage. It is also an autobiographical book following Morgan's own search for her identity once she realised she wasn't part-Indian as she had been led to believe.

The work became and remains the most popular book ever published by an Aboriginal author. And the question why? remains.

Although applauded by the white academic world, and far from a fraud, Sally Morgan came under attack with the success of *My Place*. One of the reasons Morgan's Aboriginal identity was questioned was because she did not regard herself as Aboriginal until she traced her family. She made little reference to her 'being Aboriginal' in *My Place*, except for saying, "I was excited by my new heritage."

My Place's success arguably lay in the fact that it was not confrontational to the white-mainstream way of perceiving Aboriginal Australia, providing instead a somewhat gentler view of one woman's experience growing up in Western Australia and later in life searching for her Aboriginal identity and heritage. The fact that the work has sold over 400,000 copies and is listed on university and school reading lists across Australia is proof of that claim. However, the issue still stands that Morgan's work interprets only one Aboriginal experience—an experience that highlights one family's denial of their Aboriginal heritage and identity and the experience of Sally Morgan not knowing who she really was. *My Place* does not give the story of someone living as an Aboriginal person, knowingly and acceptingly.

Marcia Langton notes that Morgan's story is about finding her Aboriginality in adulthood, and that it has an appeal to a large audience because,

> Morgan assuages the guilt of the whites, especially white women, who were complicit in the assimilation program and the deception into which families like Morgan's felt they were forced.[334]

Aboriginal student of literature, Sonja Kurtzer agrees that the success of Morgan's *My Place* proved that white audiences would welcome and accept only certain kinds of Indigenous stories. She believes that while there was a growing desire to hear stories by Indigenous people, "There was a limit to just what kinds of stories 'white' Australia would accept as 'authentic'".[335] Kurtzer cites Glenyse Ward's *Wandering Girl* as one of those authentic voices not so well embraced by white audiences. Although also written as autobiography, and fulfiling the desire of white audiences to hear directly from Indigenous writers, Ward's story through the eyes of a 16 year old girl who survived a disturbing past as a domestic servant for a white family in south-west Western Australia, was a story that did not sit comfortably with the reader, as it described blatant acts of racism and discrimination. Ward's work was therefore not going to be anywhere near as marketable as Morgan's to a non-Indigenous readership.

Kurtzer comments that discussions on life writing at the 1996 Aboriginal and Torres Strait Islander Writers' and Playwrights' Conference in Brisbane saw many delegates concerned that Morgan's work had been so well embraced by 'white' audiences while other stories of despair, devastation, Black deaths in custody, poverty and loss, weren't.[336] Kurtzer also points out the predicament that

Indigenous writers are in when writing for white audiences who desire the truth and authenticity of the story, but aren't ready for what the story actually says.

Works like Connie McDonald's *When You Grow Up*, Glenyse Ward's *Wandering Girl*, and Jackie and Rita Huggins' work *Auntie Rita*, to name a few, cite far harsher life experiences, discrimination and the impact of racist government policy. However, these works have not had near the same success as Morgan's work, arguably because their content and strong Aboriginal identification were more challenging to potential readers. But it must be remembered that most of the reading and reviewing public is not Aboriginal Australia, so it is not Aboriginal people who are judging what is and isn't 'acceptable' Aboriginal literature, and what is or isn't an 'acceptable' Aboriginal history, lifestyle and identity.

This is supported by author and historian Jackie Huggins of the Bidjara and Birri Gubba Juru people who notes that Morgan's,

> Accolades and confirmation have come from whites due to the minuscule Aboriginal reading audience…It cannot be denied that among those who have read *My Place* are (usually patronising) whites who believe that they are no longer racist because they have read it. It makes Aboriginality intelligible to non-Aboriginals, although there are different forms of Aboriginality which need to be considered also; otherwise those remain exclusionary and the danger is that only one 'world view' is espoused.[337]

Although by descent Morgan is an Aboriginal woman, and her book was in fact an autobiography, the issue of her Aboriginal identity is what raised discussion in both literary circles and Aboriginal communities. Huggins comments in relation to Morgan:

> I read the first three chapters and thought I was reading the life of a middle-class Anglo woman. I could not identify anything which told me Morgan was an Aboriginal person except the part about our common Aboriginal Study Grant…Overall there is little which indicates the writing and story of an Aboriginal.[338]

Huggins is explaining that as well as Aboriginal content, there is also an Aboriginal style of writing missing from Morgan's work. Huggins goes on to explain the dangers (and perhaps the motives) behind academics highlighting only one work like *My Place*, suggesting that those who persist in placing *My Place* as the only Black text on the reading list inevitably create twentieth-century welfare dependency of a different kind. She asks,

> Why is there an inherent expectation that we all read in a hegemonic, shared, unquestioned, glamorous, applauding way? Why is *My Place* the only experience told of Aboriginal life? Has Aboriginality now been understood by those who read it because it appeases white consciousness and perhaps it might even have been the poor old Abo's fault, not theirs? Or a bit of both?[339]

Gamilaroi playwright Cathy Craigie is also sceptical about the reasons behind Morgan's success in the white community:

> Like Alan Duff's book [*Once Were Warriors*], Sally Morgan's work didn't show why things happened and that's why white people liked it, felt great about it. What she should have showed is, "This is a fact of life, that Black velvet was a fact of life for all those white pastoralists, that all this sort of stuff happened." But I think that you've got to balance it up and you shouldn't just take one side or the other and we have a responsibility as writers to do that.[340]

Following Sally Morgan's success, perhaps the greatest of Sally Morgan's attackers was, ironically, Colin Johnson, whose own identity came under attack in 1997. He dismissed *My Place* for being within the 'battler genre', individualistic rather than community based, stating that the book was a milepost in that it marked a stage where it was considered, "OK to be Aboriginal as long as you are young, gifted and not very Black."[341] Since becoming published both Johnson and Morgan have been profiled and praised as Aboriginal writers, 'the big names' in Aboriginal literature, and one can't help but think that Johnson felt somewhat threatened by Morgan.

How do we sell Black writing then?

The marketing and distribution of our products is one of the biggest issues facing Aboriginal writers. While Laughton simply asks publishing houses for, "a crack at it with the same opportunities and commitment towards our aspirations as they afford our non-Aboriginal counterparts," Herb Wharton claims that good Aboriginal writers, "have got more chance of having a bigger market overseas in Europe or Asia than say America."[342] He goes on to explain that,

> The trouble with publishing houses like UQP is that they don't have international distribution. If you're published by one of the big ones like Penguin, they're multi-nationals and overseas owned and if you're published by one of them, chances are you will get marketed over there, but most Australian publishers don't have that clout and so you really have to chase up your own contacts.

Bellear also believes that there needs to be more Indigenous people working in the industry, occupying roles in legal matters, business issues and every facet of the industry, particularly in the key decision-making areas. She adds,

> People in the publishing industry have to do more, not only in employment but how they promote writers. A practical example is the brochure for UQP Black Writers Series doesn't have Graeme Dixon on it who did *Holocaust Island* and the significance of that is that Graeme was the inaugural David Unaipon Award winner. But they have three books by Herb Wharton and there's no disrespect to Uncle Herb but, three books by one person and you don't even have the inaugural David Unaipon Award winner. Marketing did that.

Rosemary van den Berg offers a number of suggestions to make the publishing process more accessible to Aboriginal writers starting with changing the minds of mainstream publishers about the 'Aboriginal image', and letting them know that they can publish many Aboriginal writers if they choose.[343] She also suggests that more Aboriginal publishing houses need to be set up to deal with the demands of Aboriginal writers, commenting that, "Aboriginal people have found their voice through writing and their books should not be rationed out, as everything else is rationed out to Aboriginal people."

There are some real practical issues facing Aboriginal authors and their publishing houses in trying to provide efficient and effective marketing and distribution of books by Aboriginal authors. These issues also need to be dealt with and supplemented by other mechanisms that will further support the development and promotion of Aboriginal writing. These support mechanisms will be considered in the following two chapters.

Chapter Eight
Recognition of Authors

Like the artform itself, the support of Aboriginal writers and writing is something of a new phenomenon in Australia. Unlike the situation for Aboriginal visual and performing arts, (theatre and music), new structures are still being devised to support Aboriginal people contributing to the literary world. The structures that can also (and in some cases already do), support Aboriginal authors are many and will be discussed in this chapter. Discussion includes funding opportunities for Aboriginal writers; policy development within State and Territory Arts Ministries; practical support from Indigenous and mainstream literary organisations; and industry training opportunities.

Funding

Financial support to authors via writers' grants, publishing and promotional grants, fellowships, scholarships, and funds to participate in conferences, workshops and festivals are keys to supporting creative expression. They are also crucial to supporting both the development and continuity of Aboriginal literature. The Australia Council for the Arts is undoubtedly the largest administrator of funds for established or emerging authors. Regional organisations, such as State and Territory Arts Ministries are also important institutions for authors.

The *Report on Strategies for the Further Development of the National Aboriginal and Torres Strait Islander Arts and Cultural Industry* found that publishers support investment in writing through fellowships. An IAD Press representative commented that, "More fellowships and ongoing funding arrangements should be created to avoid project-oriented funding which perpetuates writing as an activity carried out outside the author's 'real job'."[344]

Australia Council for the Arts

The Australia Council is a service organisation and a Commonwealth Statutory Authority created under the *Australia Council Act 1975*. One of its roles is to provide advice on cultural matters to the Commonwealth Government through the Minister for the Arts. The 1996–1999 Corporate Plan of the Australia Council presents the Council's role and aims for the period and, within its set goals, the Council aims to promote the unique Aboriginal and Torres Strait Islander cultures as integral to Australia's national identity.[345] Within its policy the Australia Council has specific provisions for Aboriginal and Torres Strait Islander Arts, and endorses the National Aboriginal and Torres Strait Islander Arts Policy which includes respect, authority, rights, responsibilities and diversity. The Australia Council also has a specific Aboriginal and Torres Strait Islander Arts

Board (ATSIAB) staffed largely by Indigenous people involved with administering grants to Aboriginal or Torres Strait Islander people. In recognition of the diversity of the Indigenous community, and in a desire to make the *Australia Council Grants Handbook* as accessible as possible, consumer information is written in Torres Strait Broken/Creole, Pitjantjatjara and Warumungu languages from the Northern Territory, where English is often a second, third or fourth language. No other Aboriginal languages are translated in the handbook.

I have been fortunate enough to receive two writers' grants and one publishing grant through ATSIAB. On two occasions the funding was essentially to subsidise wages while I completed manuscripts. Personally though, being offered a writers' grant was more a sign of faith in my ability to complete a manuscript, something important to me.

In 1997 the Australia Council for the Arts initiated a review into Indigenous writing with the aim of improving ATSIAB's Grants Program to Indigenous writers. MC Media & Associates conducted a national survey and the preliminary findings were that more than half of Australia's Indigenous writers are writing poetry and a quarter write for children. Other significant categories of writing, involving less than 20% of the respondents, included storytelling on radio and TV, print feature writing and speeches. At least 12% of the respondents were involved in multimedia, this usually entailing writing pages for web sites.[346]

Apart from writers working as professional journalists or academics, most writers earn very little income from their writing with most earning less than the standard $3000 per year estimated by the Australian Society of Authors as the average for an Australian author.

State Policies and Funding

In March 2000, the NSW Ministry for the Arts launched its *Policy for the Promotion and Support of Indigenous Arts and Cultural Activity in New South Wales*, which followed the Government's *Cultural Development Policy* in March 1995 and the *Statement and Commitment to Aboriginal People* in 1997.

Premier Bob Carr, in 1996 Minister for the Arts in NSW, was also the first head of an Australian State to offer a formal apology to Aboriginal people in relation to the Stolen Generations, an apology endorsed by the Parliament, alongside a resolution affirming a commitment to reconciliation.

The Carr Government's commitment to supporting Indigenous arts has been shown through the establishment of an Indigenous Arts Fund within the Ministry for the Arts, the appointment of Indigenous people to the NSW Arts Advisory Council and its committees (these members also form the Indigenous Arts Reference Group), the creation of a regional Indigenous Cultural Officer's position based at Regional Arts NSW, and the release of a paper entitled

Indigenous Arts Protocol: A Guide (1998). This guide was developed to promote Indigenous arts in Indigenous and non-Indigenous communities.[347]

The NSW Policy is based on seven principles that begin with acknowledging the significance of Aboriginal Australia as the oldest living culture it the world, the history of colonisation and its impact on Aboriginal communities, the need for self-determination, and recognition of intellectual and moral rights of Indigenous peoples.[348]

Hopefully this new policy will be implemented in a way that supports Indigenous writers more financially. The Ministry's *1998–99 Annual Report* reveals how insignificant funds are to literature. Sadly, in 1998-1999 no money at all was allocated specifically to Aboriginal literary projects.

It appears that the NSW Ministry for the Arts may be leading the way in its attempts to nurture, promote and protect Indigenous arts and cultural activity. Other State and Territory bodies have been slower to develop policies and strategies.

Arts Queensland is the State government's major funding, advisory and advocacy body for arts and cultural development. The Queensland rhetoric is, building partnerships with the arts and cultural industry, local, state and federal governments, and the business community in areas such as, "enhancing our Indigenous cultural industry."[349] The Department is currently implementing some of the recommendations of a report they commissioned from Sharenne Bell, *Arts, Business, Culture: A Report on an Indigenous Cultural Industry in Queensland* (1998). In 2000 Colleen Wall was the Principal Consultant for Aboriginal and Torres Strait Islander Arts for Arts Queensland, with responsibility for managing the implementation of the recommendations from the report.

Arts Tasmania also has a number of policies relevant to supporting Indigenous arts and culture, which are published in its *Arts Grants and Loans*, and implemented through the appointment of an Aboriginal member to the Tasmanian Arts Advisory Board and its Panels. This panel is responsible for funding decisions.[350] The policy requires that applications contain Aboriginal and Torres Strait Islander references to ensure relevant consultation has occurred within the community, and an endorsement from the community must be received prior to the application being lodged. Due to the historical and social issues involved in identifying as Aboriginal in Tasmania, Arts Tasmania says that applicants may, "elect to express their Aboriginality," and that the Board, "cannot support applications which infringe on other artists' and communities' ownership," the focus here being on copyright ownership.[351]

As the Aboriginal Arts Project Officer (a position established in the mid-1980s) Sam Cook commented that the Arts WA's policy on Indigenous art is loosely based on the Australia Council's, and there has been extensive consultation with the Aboriginal community to make certain, "it is as relevant and current as it can be."[352] The draft policy states the principles that guide the assessment panel process and identifies key areas for work until 2003:

> With a firm commitment to Aboriginal arts ArtsWA will facilitate and actively promote programs that encourage participation in arts and cultural activities by Aboriginal people and Torres Strait Islanders.[353]

The policy respects and acknowledges the Aboriginal peoples of Australia as traditional owners and also acknowledges that Aboriginal and Torres Strait Islander authority and self-determination are essential to the arts. While acknowledging diversity, it also endorses the rights and aspirations of Aboriginal and Torres Strait Islander people.[354]

ArtsWA also provides practical and financial support to organisations to ensure the employment and development of Aboriginal people and Torres Strait Islanders in all aspects of the arts industry, including support to Magabala Books to encourage the training and development of Aboriginal and Torres Strait Islander artists, writers and arts administrators.[355]

In 2000, ArtsACT did not have an Indigenous policy but did have an Indigenous Arts Officer. Arts South Australia also has an Indigenous Arts officer and is in the process of developing a policy.

Aside from relevant policies, funding allocations from arts organisations need to reflect the importance of literature as an entertaining or educational experience in Australian society. In 1995, the Cultural Industries Statistics Working Group of the Cultural Ministers' Council released its findings on Attendance at Selected Cultural Venues. The proportion of population attending venues and activities shows that local, state and national libraries were visited more than any other arts related venue. Administrators also take into account the amount of revenue generated by the industry and the amount of money spent nationally on books compared to the amount of funding allocated to the development of the artform.

Indigenous organisations

National Indigenous Arts Advocacy Association (NIAAA)

NIAAA is the national Indigenous arts and cultural service and advocacy association which supports the continued and increased recognition and protection of the rights of Indigenous artists. NIAAA also provides culturally appropriate advice, information, referrals and support services to Indigenous artists and organisations. It is government funded through agencies such as the Australia Council and the Aboriginal and Torres Strait Islander Commission, and is a not-for-profit organisation.

The organisation supports initiatives that recognise and protect all forms of Indigenous artistic and cultural expression, and through greater awareness, education and protection of the rights of Indigenous artists, NIAAA envisages that professional opportunities to Indigenous artists in all artforms will be encouraged and increased.[356]

NIAAA's promotional material cites the above as their platform and reason for existence, and although they claim to work for the benefit of artists 'across all artforms', the organisation does not at present provide any services (advice or referral) to writers. NIAAA produces resources advising on computer generated artwork and copyright, reproduction of artwork, Indigenous dance, and issues of cultural and intellectual property in dance. However, when information was requested from NIAAA relevant to Aboriginal writers, I was referred to the Australian Copyright Council and VISCOPY, which again deals with visual artists.

That literature lacks priority, or indeed a role within this national organisation can be put down to a number of factors:

a) literature is a new artform for Aboriginal people and the issues and structures around more traditional artforms like visual arts and dance have been talked about and worked on for much longer than we have been writing and publishing;

b) visual arts far outweigh any other artform in the level of revenue generated each year. It is estimated that Aboriginal visual artists generate over 50% of the $100 million visual arts revenue per annum in Australia;[357]

c) NIAAA has for many years had a board made up heavily of visual artists and curators.

As part of the Indigenous portfolio at the Australian Society of Authors, myself and Executive Director, Jose Borghino held discussions in 1999 with Chris Bonney from NIAAA with the aim of developing a working relationship between the two organisations. The purpose was to develop processes that would support and nurture Aboriginal and Torres Strait Islanders practicing the artform of writing. NIAAA are yet to respond to the suggestions made. The establishment and growth of a relationship between the two organisations, it was hoped would support the development of policy to protect the rights of Indigenous authors, while coordinating some practical projects such as a mentoring program between established and emerging writers.

Gadigal Information Services

Gadigal Information Services (GIS) is a community based media/arts and information service for the 36,000 strong Indigenous community in Sydney. It began in 1994 as a reaction to years of the mainstream media portraying Indigenous Australia in negative stereotypes and only ever telling one side of the story. GIS is the home of Koori Radio, which grew out of Radio Skid Row and has diverse programming which takes in other marginalised Indigenous groups such as Torres Strait Islanders, East Timorese, Burmese and Palestinians.

The organisation supports all artforms including visual arts, theatre and literature. It supports writing via the Gadigal Writers' Group, established in Sydney following the 1996 Aboriginal Writers and Playwrights Conference held in Brisbane. Although the initial meeting was well attended, subsequent meetings were not so well attended. There is currently a core of three or four members.

The Group, essentially Cathy Craigie, Kerry Reed-Gilbert and myself, were successful in organising writers events in 1996. In 1997, Gadigal hosted, "Singing and Talking Up Loud", featuring poets and writers in public venues. One event held during the Festival of the Dreaming featured Melissa Lucashenko, Kerry Reed-Gilbert and Kapu, a spoken word artist from Aotearoa.

GIS also ran a series of workshops for writers interested in writing for radio. Supported by the NSW Writers' Centre and the Australia Council, three participants from the workshop, Fiona Smith, Helen Anu and Goie Wymarra were successful in selling their radio-plays to the ABC radio drama unit, and presented their works as part of a panel discussion at the 1997 Spring Writing Festival.

GIS coordinated the Indigenous component of the 1997 Spring Writing Festival and sponsored two of the panels, Young Gifted and Black, and Native Tongues, which profiled Briar Grace-Smith of Aotearoa and Kateri Akiwenzie-Damm from the First Nation of Objibwe in Canada.

Literature is one of the major artforms constantly profiled by GIS after music, and the organisation is one of the few that gives it such attention and recognition. In 1998 it was the administering body for a series of Master Classes for established writers.

Aboriginal Publications Foundation (APF)

With Jack Davis as Managing Editor between 1972 and 1979, the primary function of the APF in Perth was the production of the magazine *Identity*. The role of the APF, as stated in the magazine, was as a referral body to the Aboriginal Arts Board (now ATSIAB). The organisation had broader aims:

- to publish books, pamphlets and other publications by and for Aboriginal Australians;
- to commission such works for publication;
- to organise training for Aboriginal Australians in literature, visual and other relevant arts and crafts;
- to provide scholarships, fellowships, advances and other assistance for Aboriginal creative artists of promise;

- to conduct competitions, arrange exhibitions and in other ways recognise and reward distinguished performance by Aboriginal Australians and the literary, visual and related arts and crafts.[358]

Aboriginal Writers, Oral Literature and Dramatists Association (AWOLDA)

After the demise of the AFP, Jack Davis was concerned that there was nowhere for Aboriginal writers to send manuscripts for assessment, so he began toying with the idea of an Aboriginal writers' association. Including oral literature in the concept he drew up some objectives and memoranda for AWOLDA. Murdoch University assisted Davis and Marlene Chesson in setting up an AWOLDA Conference, and a committee was established including Davis, Marlene Chesson, Keith Chesson, Eddie Bennell and Alma Toomath, who intended to raise funds to establish a centre where resources and reference material to promote Aboriginal writers and house their written works.[359]

Because writers were busy writing and AWOLDA needed a full-time organiser, the organisation didn't go much past the First National Conference of Aboriginal Writers, held at Murdoch University in 1983, organised jointly between AWOLDA and the university's School of Human Communication. A successful outcome of the Conference was to produce a volume of writing edited by Davis and Bob Hodge, *Aboriginal Writing Today: Papers From the First National Conference of Aboriginal Writers Held in Perth, WA in 1983* (1985).

Comparisons with other Aboriginal organisations

When you consider that other artforms have substantial government and community support to encourage participation, development and profitability, it is frustrating to see that literature does not receive or enjoy the same support. Visual arts has organisations like NIAAA, Aboriginal artists cooperatives like Boomalli in Sydney (which are duplicated in many cities and regional areas around Australia), Aboriginal galleries like Yirribana who display work, and university degrees in fine arts which introduce new people to the artform while providing employment for practicing artists. There are dance schools like the National Aboriginal and Islander Skills Development Association (in Sydney), Aboriginal Dance Theatre Redfern, and the national touring company Bangarra, which all provide places of learning and support for aspiring and established Aboriginal dancers.

Aboriginal writers, or aspiring Aboriginal writers however don't have access to these kinds of Indigenous-specific support mechanisms that can provide structures for the development of their artform.

Mainstream Organisations

Writers in Sydney have organisations like the NSW Writers' Centre and the Australian Society of Authors, the Copyright Council and the Australia Council for the Arts located nearby, should they choose to access them. These organisations exist to assist writers in every aspect of their artform, from providing workshops on how to write, to funding assistance and information on rights.

The following cases will show that Indigenous membership of some key organisations is low, but not necessarily because the organisations are not providing specific assistance to Aboriginal authors.

NSW Writers' Centre (NSWWC)

The NSWWC has been instrumental in increasing the profile of Aboriginal writers while providing the reading community with access to some of the newest voices in Aboriginal literary circles.

Established in 1992 as a resource and information centre for writers, it aims to encourage people in the activity of writing, and provides people who are interested in writing with advice and assistance on how to get their writing published, whether in book form or on the internet. Executive Director Irina Dunn sees the broader picture and the role of literature in Australian society. She comments,

> Believing in a writing and literary culture we are trying to foster readers with a focus on Australian writing, because we are interested in developing the literary aspect of Australian culture, which is important to a national identity, and the way it reflects our values and also creates and establishes them.[360]

Dunn explains that the Writers' Centre was formed because many people felt, as other artforms had a base, writers also needed their own building too. The Centre now houses a library for writers, a writers' studio, a venue for book launches and offices for a number of other arts organisations, and is also the home of the annual Spring Writing Festival.

The significance of the NSWWC in relation to the growth and nurturing of Aboriginal literature is that it has previously supported Aboriginal writing from the grassroots, with representation on the Centre's Management Committee in 1997, 1998 and 1999. Dunn comments on the importance of Indigenous board members:

> I was interested in having someone on the Board who was plugged into Aboriginal literary culture to bring writers to the centre. So Cathy Craigie was elected to the Board. Cathy was important in getting young writers for the Spring Writing program, which is a very major and practical role for her. Cathy

is proficient in the area of Aboriginal literature and had proven results from her tutoring, so she was able to bring a lot to the Centre, through her teaching and her links in the Aboriginal community which you really need, and I don't think a white person can do that.

Although the Writers' Centre doesn't have specific a policy in relation to Aboriginal literature, it does have a philosophy that is inclusive of new forms of writing, which includes Aboriginal writers and writers from non-English speaking backgrounds.

In practical terms the Writers' Centre has also coordinated and administered projects for and by Aboriginal writers. In 1996 the Australia Council gave the Writers Centre $25,000 for Community Writing Projects and Dunn made her first focus Aboriginal and NESB projects, commenting:

> That's the place that is most under-funded, and it's those developmental programs that really give people confidence with writing, especially when being tutored by an Aboriginal or NESB tutor because they understand the difficulties of moving from one education system to another, or one language to another.

Other work with Aboriginal writers includes the coordination NSWWC did for the Australia Council in 1996, organising travel for the Aboriginal Writers and Playwrights Conference in Brisbane. The NSWWC sends free newsletters to a number of Aboriginal arts workers / writers, and in 1993 held the Blackbooks catalogue launch.

The Victorian Writers' Centre (VWC)

The VWC does not have any formal policy about Indigenous writers, although Director Christine McKenzie says she is keen to develop more support networks for Indigenous writers in Victoria.[361] And while not as active as the NSWWC, the VWC has had some Koori participation in their functions. Boori Pryor read at La Mama Theatre at a VWC function in 1998 and Lisa Bellear has also read at the Centre's poetry readings and discussed her work on a number of occasions. In 1999 Pryor attended the Castlemaine Festival to discuss his work, an event organised by the VWC.

Tasmanian Writers' Centre (TWC)

In early 1999 the TWC hadn't actually initiated any projects supporting or nurturing Aboriginal writers during the two years they had been operating, and their database is not set up to distinguish Indigenous writers.

Although the TWC hadn't coordinated any projects themselves, they were aware of other organisations that had been working in the area of Palawa writing, such as the Tasmanian Department of Education and Community Development, which put together an anthology of young Aboriginal people's writing in 1998 entitled *Two Rivers* with images by Barbie Kjar. The project was initiated by the Aboriginal Education Unit of the Department and its key players Phillip Kelly and Tony Woodward. *Two Rivers* was launched by Tasmanian author Aunty Ida West in late 1998.

Northern Territory Writers' Centre (NTWC)

In early 1999, the NTWC had 62 Aboriginal and Torres Strait Islander writers on their database, but only a handful (perhaps four or five) were members. "This makes it difficult to get information to them. The limited budget of the NT Writers' Centre does not allow us as to send newsletters to non-members,"[362] said Executive Director, Marian Devitt.

In 1997 the NTWC organised for Dino Hodge (a Darwin writer/historian) and Francis Good (Senior Archivist Oral Records from NT Archives) to travel to Nhulunbuy and Yirrkala to deliver two seminars on writing oral histories. Good also provided practical training on collecting oral histories. Good subsequently collaborated with the NT Writers' Centre by facilitating transcription services for a collection of oral histories undertaken by Peg Havnen. This resulted in the publication in 2000 of *Under The Mango Tree: Oral Histories with Indigenous People from the Top End*.

In 1998 the NTWC made an unsuccessful application for funding from the Australia Council. Part of that application was to fund a specifically Indigenous newsletter which Devitt thinks would be more appropriate than the general one she produces for her members. Devitt realises that Aboriginal people tend to have different networks from the mainstream and that information travels differently. She admits though that many of her 140 strong membership would have associations with Aboriginal people through their work, marriage or residence in remote or regional communities, so the newsletter could well be read by a number of Aboriginal people already.

In 1997 the NTWC produced the *Handbook for Central Australian Indigenous Writers* to redress the disadvantage suffered by Indigenous writers in the Territory. The 70 page handbook includes information on: professional training opportunities; the NTWC; books by Indigenous writers (although the list also includes works by non-Indigenous people); competitions and awards; history and oral history resources; publishing opportunities; Indigenous media; funding and sponsorship; arts organisations; and library and electronic resources. The *Handbook* project, coordinated by then Project Officer at the NTWC Terry Whitebeach, was the result of a Community Cultural Development Grant funded project in previous years, but an application to follow up the project with some, "practical workshops and seminars for Aboriginal writers" was unsuccessful.

In November 1998, the NTWC funded Whitebeach to deliver a workshop in Tennant Creek for Aboriginal writers and she also supported Aboriginal author John Muk Muk Burke in delivering a workshop on his novel *Bridge of Triangles* in Alice Springs. The Centre offered the workshop to the Institute of Aboriginal Development in Alice Springs which declined the offer.

In 1999 however the first Indigenous Writers Creative Writing Course started at Batchelor College for Indigenous Tertiary Education in Alice Springs, jointly administered by the Institute of Aboriginal Development in Alice Springs and the college.

In spite of Devitt's efforts, Whitebeach, who has been heavily involved with writing in the Northern Territory, says she finds very little support for Indigenous writers in the NTWC program, citing one workshop she ran in Barkly in 1998 which largely targeted Aboriginal writers. To be jointly funded by Barkly Arts (the community arts centre for the Barkly region around Tennant Creek) and the NTWC, Whitebeach says the NTWC reneged on their part of the financial deal and she ended up footing the bill for accommodation and travel allowance herself. She comments,

> There has never been a follow-up to the NT Aboriginal Writers' Conference, and generally I find there is very little commitment, or thought about what would be appropriate or desirable for Aboriginal writers. There is nothing in the 1999 program for Central Australia that targets Indigenous writers. In contrast, Peter Callinan, Barkly Arts officer…has a real commitment to Indigenous artists, and is always on the lookout for opportunities for them. A writing tour he organised for two Barkly writers, increased the literacy levels of school students faster in a weekend than had happened in a year of ESL programs, was the conclusion one ESL teacher had at the community school they were working in.[363]

In 2002 this circumstance has changed considerably.

Queensland Writers' Centre (QWC)

In 1999 the QWC had 10 Aboriginal and Torres Strait Islander members that they knew of, but considerations for diversity are implemented in all planning, which is witnessed in their newsletter with regular feature articles on Indigenous writing both about and by Indigenous writers.

In 1996 the QWC ran a Writer-in-Community Project with widely acclaimed writer and story-teller Herb Wharton. During this project Wharton visited 38 state and private schools and spoke with up to four classes per day, a total of approximately 3,000 students and their teachers. Taking in both south-western and far-northern Queensland, Wharton visited Murgon/Cherbourg, Dajarra, Doomadgee, Burketown and Mornington Island as part of his tour. In their Final Acquittal of funds in 1997, QWC stated,

Response to his sessions was always warm and receptive, and there were many questions from students concerning both the writing process and Herb's life experiences as first an Aboriginal drover, and then as a writer…Many of the schools were unused to writing activity and obviously relished the experience. Many had prepared by either reading Herb's books or by buying them and other Aboriginal texts for their libraries.[364]

"Wordpool", QWC's literary cabaret for local Queensland writers, offers fast-paced and funny nights of readings, discussions and improvisations by some of Australia's best language innovators. In 1997 "Wordpool" featured me in "Acid Tongue(y)" and in 1998, Lisa Bellear and Melissa Lucashenko in "Brace Yourself Gladys". In 1999 playwright Wesley Enoch was part of the event.

QWC received funding in 1999 to undertake an Indigenous mentorship scheme—the first of its kind in Queensland, if not Australia. In its strategy, QWC claimed,

> A project of this nature is consistent with QWC's mission and commitment and, in particular addresses its goal to facilitate specialised development opportunities for specific sectors of the community, including young and emerging writers, rural and remote writers, and writers from diverse backgrounds.[365]

In October 1999 Wesley Enoch worked alongside Hilary Beaton (Executive Director of QWC) to present "Words at Play" as part of the QWC calendar of workshops and seminars. The workshop took participants through the elements of play writing, focussing on characterisation, setting, movement and dramatic effect.

WA State Literature Office Inc (WASLOI)

Western Australia has the State Literature Office, and aside from the name being different, it functions exactly the same as other state writers' centres, with regular newsletters and services for members. While the WASLOI does not run anything aimed specifically at Indigenous writers, they toured Indigenous writer Margaret Brusnahan around schools in the Pilbara in 1999. As the then State Literature Officer Susan Hayes commented that as an organisation, "we are aware that we probably don't do enough in the area of Indigenous writing and to this end we are trying to recruit an appropriate member to our Board."[366]

Hayes highlights an issue that arose in 1998 in a grant application to the Community Cultural Development Fund of the Australia Council for a project called "Write Off Centre". The project involved a series of workshops with young writers who lived outside the metropolitan area and who, for whatever reasons, did not have easy access to writers' centres, colleges etc. In all the three locations targeted, the youth groups and drop-in centres which agreed enthusiastically to host the workshops (with support letters provided), indicated that some of the young people at the classes would be Indigenous people. The application was turned down by the Community Cultural Development Fund because WASLOI, "had not observed the correct protocols as far as Indigenous participants were concerned." Hayes was informed that she would need letters of agreement from communities whose members might attend the workshops (particularly in the Pilbara location). In response to this experience Hayes wrote,

> The prospect of seeking permissions from all the communities who might (or indeed might not) have people wanting to attend workshops was extremely daunting, particularly in a vast state like WA, and we universally shrugged our shoulders and decided not to bother any further. This is one reason why we tend to steer clear of projects involving Indigenous pupils. Adhering to the procedures and protocols demanded by the funding organisations are far beyond the resources of overworked understaffed arts organisations and it seems that each year it gets harder.

ACT Writers' Centre

The ACT Writers' Centre does not specifically refer to Indigenous writers within its policies, but does have an unwritten policy to support the multicultural and Indigenous groups who received seed-funding through the Centre in 1996-97 to run workshops. The Centre also provides practical support in the form of a free venue space, despite half of the writers being non-members.[367] The Centre also held workshops for Indigenous people interested in writing in March 1998. Author Kerry Reed-Gilbert was one of the tutors and Canberra poet and project coordinator Steve Kelen was the other. The Centre said that an important part of the workshops was the 'writing for publication' component, as well as exploring other strategies to have work published.

Australian Society of Authors (ASA, National)

The ASA is located in Sydney and aims to promote and protect the professional interests of Australian literary creators. The agency provides practical advice on copyright, contracts, rates of pay and negotiates with publishers and multimedia producers (among others).

Since the organisation was first formed in 1963 the ASA has become a national organisation, with varying levels of membership covering writers from every genre.

In 1997, then Executive Director Lynne Spender said there were few Aboriginal writers on their membership database, one reason being [that] when the organisation was first set up it was not considered politically correct to ask people about their ethnicity, as it arguably had nothing to do with their professional writing.[368] Over time however, it became very clear that racial identity did indeed have something to do with professional writing, particularly in relation to Aboriginal identity. Although only 10-20 out of the 3000 ASA members identify as Aboriginal or Torres Strait Islander there could be more, said Spender, as membership forms do request information about ethnicity but few answer the question. Spender also recognised that there's still a sensitivity about putting something in the newsletter asking, "Will all Indigenous writers please let us know that you are Indigenous."

The ASA receives project funding from the Australia Council who are interested in whether or not organisations are accommodating Indigenous authors, whether they are aware of them, and whether or not they have special programs set up for them. Spender admitted that, "While it is an economic thing on one level, there is not one person on the Management Committee who would object to special efforts being made for Indigenous writing."

In 1993 the ASA made resources available for their Deputy Chairperson to attend the Black Women's Writers' Conference in Brisbane, and in 1994 held a seminar at the Sydney Writers' Festival where Magabala's Chair Robyn Hannigan spoke about the different issues faced by publishers of Indigenous material. The ASA in the same year invited representatives from Blackbooks to speak at their Management Committee meeting.[369]

There is nothing specific to Indigenous writers in the ASA's Memorandum of Articles set up in 1963, but like the NSWWC, the organisation does have a corporate plan and an annual achievements list for the coming year. In 1996 they listed the promotion and protection of Indigenous writers. Spender observed,

> It's becoming something that we're very conscious of. For example before each of the State writers' festivals happen we send out a letter asking that they not only have panels, but that Indigenous people are there as part of the host arrangement because we know that that's important.

These efforts and the fact that the Management Committee made a decision in 1997 to support Australians for Native Title (the Committee unanimously agreed that the issue was part of their charter to support Indigenous writers—although the decision caused some unrest and the resignations of some members), is further reason for Indigenous writers to be part of the ASA.

The ASA has also had Indigenous-specific issues of *Australian Author*, the ASA's professional journal. "We try to get Indigenous writers to do them rather than us pontificating," Spender remarked. Examples of this can be seen in the spring 1994 edition which featured the Aboriginal flag on the cover and included articles by Jackie Huggins and Pat Mamajun Torres about material written by white writers on Aboriginal issues. The 1997 autumn edition of the *Australian Author* had as its feature article, "Tricky Business: Whites on Black Territory" by non-Aboriginal Willa McDonald, who included comments by Aboriginal writers Kerry Reed-Gilbert, Connie Nungulla McDonald, Sandra Phillips and myself.

Spender says that nurturing Indigenous writers and their interests is,

> Becoming not only more of an issue but more acceptable as an issue that we should be addressing. I'm sure that as more Indigenous writers get published there is more awareness generally in the community and certainly more awareness amongst the Committee of Management who are probably the best read people in terms of what's happening in publishing, changes in trends and so on.

As a referral service, the ASA receives a lot of calls from people who want to include some Aboriginal work in their own writing, and who are increasingly concerned about cultural appropriation. The ASA refers people to GIS, Blackbooks and other organisations that offer appropriate resources or starting points. The week of Spender's interview she had already received two calls in relation to Aboriginal literature and writers.

In a move to introduce more Aboriginal members to the organisation and promote the services of the ASA to the Aboriginal literary community in 1998, I was elected to the Management Committee. The Committee, which runs the organisation, is made up of 14 members who are all writers, and who are elected by the full-membership. The Chairperson and office bearers give power to the Executive Director to run the office.

With my appointment to the ASA in March 1998 I established the Indigenous Portfolio to acknowledge and recognise the contribution that Aboriginal writers and writing are making to the growth and development of Australian literature generally. The portfolio aims to support and nurture Aboriginal writers around Australia and encourage as many as possible to become members and utilise the services and skills available through the organisation. The aims of the Indigenous Portfolio as endorsed by participants of the 1998 Master Classes for Aboriginal writers are:

- to raise the profile of Indigenous Australian literature;
- to develop support mechanisms for Indigenous authors in the mainstream industry;
- to lobby for the employment of Indigenous people in every aspect of the writing/publishing industry;
- to formulate policy to protect the cultural rights of Indigenous authors and their material;
- to encourage literary/publishing organisations to adhere to cultural protocols relating to Indigenous Australia.[370]

Areas of concern to Aboriginal authors that can be supported by the ASA include: the lack of Indigenous editors currently trained and/or employed in Australia in both Indigenous and non-Indigenous publishing houses; the lack of marketing of Indigenous works to the education sector; and the lack of knowledge Indigenous authors have concerning their rights as authors, or in relation to contractual agreements and copyright issues.

So far the Indigenous Portfolio has already been active in contacting organisers of literary festivals, encouraging them to follow protocol and have traditional welcomes by local Aboriginal spokespeople. The ASA hopes that festivals will embrace such protocol.

In 2000, the ASA released Discussion Papers on Aboriginal and Torres Strait Islander Intellectual and Copyright Issues and on a code of ethics for non-Indigenous writers writing in the area of Aboriginal studies.

Training Opportunities

Culturally Appropriate Professional Training Opportunities for Central Australia Indigenous Writers

This project was initiated by Terri Anne Whitebeach who was Literature Officer at the NTWC at the time, and was funded by the Community Cultural Development Fund and the Literature Fund of the Australia Council with the Northern Territory Department of the Arts and Museums. It was designed as a research project to look at the needs of Aboriginal writers in the Northern Territory, and the project was taken over by Alexis Wright in June 1997.

The success of this project obviously lay in the opportunity the Project Officer had to disseminate a great deal of information to Indigenous writers on publishing opportunities, while assisting writers in preparing manuscripts for submission to publishers and generally acting in a liaison capacity.

After meeting with service providers in Central Australia, Whitebeach's interim report[371] on the project made the following observations:

- Literacy is a major focus;
- Mentorship is seen to be the most appropriate model in many instances for assisting Aboriginal writing to develop;
- Community Development Employment Programs (CDEPs) may provide a useful focus for training;
- There is a need for oral history recording training;
- Individual projects and writers need to be identified.

Whitebeach's report also highlighted the issue of diversity in Aboriginal writing and writers, listing elders, youth, song writers, poets, oral historians, biographers, autobiographers, community historians, fiction and faction (creative non-fiction) writers.

In her second report in September 1997,[372] Whitebeach discussed the individual writers and projects she was assisting as part of this project. They included:
- Mentoring and editing the work of Warumungu writer Rosemary Plummer to a point where the writer could send work to *Overland*, the NT Literary Awards and to Magabala Books;
- Assistance offered to Eileen Mosely with oral histories and documents she has collected about the St Mary's residential facility for Aboriginal children near Alice Springs;
- Assisting mentee Yaaltje Ninu to approach funding bodies, and decide on issues of relevance in developing cultural practice in creating a children's picture book from the elder's stories and descriptions of extinct or endangered species of animals that were once prolific in the area.

In her third report Whitebeach notes that there is no uniform group of 'Aboriginal writers' in Central Australia, rather a plethora of needs, abilities, skills and interests. In working on the project Whitebeach established a number of links with key Aboriginal organisations in the NT to assist her in providing the necessary support for writers. Her network included:
- Tangentyere Council (Alice Springs Arrernte organisation responsible for town camps)—Whitebeach found that the training officer at this organisation was most anxious to be involved in the development of writing programs for town campers (urban Aboriginal people) with the women's story telling project and other literacy-linked activities being high priorities;
- IAD Press—discussions between Whitebeach and the Press's Manager Simon MacDonald focussing on training of an Aboriginal editor so that writers' work "is treated sympathetically and within an appropriate cultural context";
- Batchelor College[373]—discussions with the interim Coordinator highlighted areas such as training in computer skills, grammar, punctuation and creative writing development.[374]

In her final project report in 1998, Whitebeach stated that,

> Aboriginal literature in the Northern Territory flows from a rich storytelling tradition derived from an ancient culture. Despite over two hundred years of alien cultural imposition, in the Northern Territory Aboriginal story telling still maintains its traditional continuity while incorporating and adapting the strength of European literature. With increasing literacy, both in the vernacular and in English, there is currently a resurgence of self-expression by Aboriginal writers which promises to develop into a fresh and culturally unique contribution to Australian literature. This parallels in many ways the cultural contribution made by Aboriginal art to the Australian and indeed to the international art world.

> For Aboriginal writing to reach its full potential as a cultural industry, an investment in training and resources is necessary.[375]

Recommendations were also included in Whitebeach's report, and they include,
- that a creative writing course be developed in consultation with the major Aboriginal educational providers. The course must be culturally appropriate and structured for modular delivery on remote communities;
- that Aboriginal Literature offices be established in Darwin and Alice Springs with staff and resources to service each region.

The creative writing course recommended in Whitebeach's Report came to fruition in July 1999 when ten students enrolled in the inaugural two-semester long Creative Writing course at the Alice Springs campus of Batchelor College.

The *Report on Strategies for the Further Development of the National Aboriginal and Torres Strait Islander Arts and Cultural Industry* commissioned by ATSIC in 1994, also highlighted the need for training in remote areas, with a submission from IAD Press stating,

> Training at professional level happens on the east coast, with the odd writer-in-residence making a bush trip for a few weeks a year to conduct workshops with a limited number of people. Enthusiasm is raised, only to die again when the writer-in-residence returns east.[376]

To resolve the problem, IAD Press proposed a strategy that would provide assistance to take professional level writing and publishing workshops to bush communities on an ongoing basis to ensure effectiveness. They saw the need for this to happen in conjunction with the establishment of community based literature development officers.[377]

In terms of general in-house staff training, Simon MacDonald says IAD Press trains Aboriginal staff to industry standard but doesn't necessarily hang on to them because they can't pay industry rates sometimes, relying on personal commitment from the individual. MacDonald sees his own role at IAD Press is to make himself obsolete. There is no trainee manager at IAD Press because staff work their way up the ranks. For example, Assistant Editor Josie Douglas was in the role of front-desk person and got wide experience, not just as a receptionist and sales person, but travelled overseas and attended book fairs, mixing with other publishers, mainstream and niche. MacDonald says,

> She's moved vertically in the same press and is now in line to be the IAD Press editor. The IAD Press Manager will take a bit longer, because you don't get the experience of manager for four or five years, and you've got to be in there that long to get a sense of what the industry is about. There are about six or eight occupations in the publishing industry which one can choose as a strand as one's own to begin with.[378]

Mentorships for emerging writers

Mentorships are becoming more popular in Australia as funding bodies and literary organisations work together to develop the growing pool of emerging writers. No larger pool exists than within the Aboriginal literary community, where writers are brimming with stories, but desperately need the skills to put them on paper in a readable format.

As mentioned briefly above, the QWC was funded by ATSIAB in 1998 to present an Indigenous mentorship program, designed to assist the long-term development of Aboriginal and Torres Strait Islander emerging writers in Queensland. The program began in 2000, and over a 12 month period, mentors worked with emerging writers, and travel to regional venues to meet with them.

For the purpose of this project, 'Indigenous emerging writers' were defined as writers ranging from those with no work previously published in book form right up to and including those with no more than two books published. Applications were invited from Indigenous emerging writers working in the genres of prose fiction (including young adult and children's fiction), non-fiction (including autobiography and history) and full-length stage play.

The mentors chosen were Judith Lukin-Amundsen, Melissa Lucashenko, Getano Bann, and the emerging writers were Walter Waia, Audrey Evans and Albert Holt, with mentoring support from Sandra Phillips and Mary Graham.

Mentors worked with each emerging writer (assessing and editing their work, as well as working with them face to face or by phone/fax/email/etc) for a minimum of 60 hours each over a 12 month period. Mentors also travelled to regional venues and emerging writers travelled to meet with mentors where necessary throughout this period.

Sandra Phillips, whose role at UQP involved her acting as editor, mentor, artistic director and friend to Aboriginal writers, believes that, "mentoring is a skill that usually comes only with life experience, where one develops the necessary strength, insight and selflessness."[379] Phillips is not talking about mentoring in its conventional form, but also, "mentoring in 'disguise'. I am young, I am still learning, and I have learnt much from the relationships I have with individual writers and with the writing community at large."[380]

As someone who has been mentored herself, Douglas says mentoring is about being on an equal footing and sharing information, teaching your mentor as much as you are being taught. She comments,

> There's not that many of us within publishing and I think that if we are going to be blazing the trail, then it's really important that we are good at what we do. That we are professional high standard editors, because we can then take on that training role. I'm all for using those people out there that have skills because we have to, we have to serve our authors. No good having an

Aboriginal editor and an Aboriginal graphic designer who can't do the job and the author is being criticised more because of the bad editing, or the sloppiness of the design. We need expert people being trained well.[381]

This chapter has highlighted Government funding opportunities and the policies of inclusion and support for Aboriginal writers as well as the organisations that act on behalf of writers and Indigenous artists. These support mechanisms along with the limited training opportunities for Aboriginal people interested in building a career in the writing and publishing industry are simply not enough, and the following Chapter will consider the roles that literary festivals, conferences and awards play in nurturing Aboriginal writers.

Chapter Nine
Festivals, Conferences and Awards

Aside from grant funding, fellowships and the support available from organisations, participation in literary festivals, writers' conferences and workshops, and literary awards can also benefit emerging and established authors. These aspects of the supra-structure for literary endeavour are discussed in this chapter.

Literary Festivals

Writers' festivals provide recognition, promotion and employment for writers, and are increasingly becoming avenues for Aboriginal voices. In the late 1990s newer festivals like the Byron Bay Writers' Festival were yet to recognise the important contribution Aboriginal writers make to Australian literature, while other festivals like the Sydney Writers' Festival increased the level of participation by Aboriginal writers in the festival. This reflects the fact that more and more Aboriginal authors are establishing themselves in the field.

Writers' festivals provide authors and spoken word performers with the opportunity to showcase and sell their work, participate in debate and discussion around literary issues, and network with other writers. In this context, more experienced authors can also provide inspiration, motivation and support to those still developing skills and reputations. These are the larger, immeasurable benefits that stem from participating in writers' festivals.

Alexis Wright, who has been a regular festival goer since the release of her novel *Plains of Promise* and her non-fiction work *Grog War*. She comments that writers' festivals have generally been a very positive experience for her in terms of support, acknowledgement of hard work, and the opportunity to talk to other writers and make contact with other writers and the industry. She adds, however,

> That it is difficult to encourage Australian audiences to believe that Aboriginal writers had anything worthwhile to say so our sessions are poorly attended. In this, we are not far down the ladder to other Australian writers as it is often the overseas writers people are flocking to see and who the organisers are promoting, to the detriment of local writers. However, I have been on sessions with notable writers—Australian and overseas guests, which were well attended in Brisbane and Melbourne. How I got to be on these panels by the way, was through advocacy by others on my behalf with the festival organisers who might not have thought an Aboriginal writer was capable of delivering on the issue being discussed.[382]

Wright also questions the programming of some literary festivals, commenting,

> Sometimes, I wonder how festival organisers put together programs because they do not include Aboriginal voices on sessions re land, the meaning of the

land and others (magic realism), spirituality, but have included some white fellas who really have nothing to offer. I found this in Melbourne in 1996 when they had a session called Whites on Blacks which I found offensive.

Wright also believes the Aboriginal traditional owners who contributed to *Take Power: Like This Old Man Here* (Jukpurra, 1999), an anthology she edited celebrating 20 years of land rights in central Australia 1977–1997, are the kinds of authors who could be invited to literary festivals. Even though she advocated for their participation, no invitations were forthcoming.

In terms of Aboriginal participation in literary festivals Lisa Bellear comments,

> Unless you get a $100,000 grant to put on a festival you are not obligated to include Aboriginal people…it's just that you have to be seen to be doing the right thing. So many festivals/events will only include Aboriginal/Islander people if they get a grant. What's that got to do with inclusion?[383]

Some of the more well known festivals ensure inclusion of Aboriginal writers and discussion of Aboriginal works in their programs.

Sydney Writers' Festival

For many years the Sydney Writers' Festival was hosted by the Sydney Festival in association with the State Library of NSW and was held in the month of January. In 1998 the Writers' Festival became its own entity. Meredith Curnow, Program Manager of the Festival since 1998, commented, "We do not have specific policies on putting the program for the Festival together in terms of the program content."[384] The Festival does however have a Mission Statement which acknowledges Aboriginal and Torres Strait Islander writing:

> The Sydney Writers' Festival will reflect the diversity of the lively nature of literary culture and Sydney. It will be a professional, innovative festival that presents ideas, debate, performance and the best writers and writing from Australia and around the world. It will aim to become a festival of international stature that reflects Sydney's unique position in the Asia Pacific region and makes the most of Sydney's natural and cultural environment.
>
> It will reflect the range of writing from literary and popular fiction, poetry, screen writing, journalism to serious non-fiction in order to attract a wide audience of readers and writers. By representing the work of young writers and cutting-edge topics, it should be attractive to young audiences and create new audiences for writing as well as attracting and consolidating established literary audiences.
>
> In demonstrating an on-going commitment to Aboriginal and Torres Strait Islander writing, the Festival acknowledges both Australia's ancient origins and capacity for reconciliation.[385]

Aboriginal involvement on the Sydney Writers' Festival committee prior to 1998 included participation by Cathy Craigie (1993), Gerry Bostock (1994/95) and Philip McLaren (1996). Margaret Burke, who coordinated the Sydney Writers' Festival prior to 1998 says that Indigenous involvement was a very high priority in the years that she was involved in co-ordinating the festival.[386] She notes that the Festival in the past had many impressive guests including Glenys Ward, Archie Weller, Herb Wharton, Burraga Gutya, Archie Roach, Ruby Hunter, Ruby Langford Ginibi, Gerry Bostock, Keith Saunders, Lionel Fogarty, Pat O'Shane, Sam Watson, Jackie Huggins and others.

The 1993 Festival had sessions programmed which included 'Indigenous Women Writers' and 'The Screen Scene' which promoted Aboriginal films and scripts by Archie Weller, Bryon Syron, Lydia Miller and others. Tranby Aboriginal College also had a writing workshop as part of the Festival led by Jackie Huggins and Lionel Fogarty, and there were also book launches for *Yinto Desert Child* by Pat Lowe and Jimmy Pike and, *True Country*, by Kim Scott.

The 1994 Festival included the book launches of Rosemary van den Berg's *No Option! No Choice!* as well as the late Kevin Gilbert's *Black from the Edge*. 'Aboriginal and Torres Strait Islander Theatre: On the Edge' was a panel with Eva Johnson, Gerry Bostock and Lydia Miller which questioned mainstream definitions of literature, and the panel, "Coming Home", profiled the experiences of some of those who were victims of the government policy of stealing Aboriginal children. Tranby ran a writing workshop again in 1994 with Ruby Langford Ginibi talking about collecting, researching and writing oral histories.

At the 1995 Festival Roberta Sykes launched the mythical Wanda Koolmatrie's *My Own Sweet Time*, and in 1996, Melissa Jackson and Ronald Briggs gave an introduction to the life, times and achievements of David Unaipon in a session titled, 'Australia's Leonardo: David Unaipon'. The 1996 Festival in particular had a number of Aboriginal and Torres Strait Islander writers participating in Aboriginal-specific panels, including a tribute to three literary pioneers, Kevin Gilbert, Oodgeroo Noonuccal and David Unaipon. Held again in the Domain in 1997, the event drew large crowds to pay homage to dead writers, including eulogies from Barbara Nicholson, Cathy Craigie.

Burke recognises a strong relationship between Magabala and Blackbooks who were very supportive of the Festival, and says, "I hope that those years set down roots for continuous and serious involvement of Indigenous Australian writing on the Sydney Writers' Festival program."[387]

I have only been involved in Sydney Writers' Festivals since 1996, but have learned that when Koori writers show interest and offer assistance, the hosting bodies are generally enthusiastic about our participation. The launch of the 1996 Sydney Writers' Festival at the Atrium of the ABC Studies in Ultimo included a presentation by Magabala Books featuring Connie McDonald, author of *When You Grow Up* and myself. I was also invited to participate in two other sessions during the week. The first, "Forever Young", was a series of readings from nearly and newly published young talent which included Matt Condon (*A Night at the Pink Poodle*), Judith Fox (*Bracelet Honeymyrtle*) and Christos Tsiolkos (*Loaded*). While my work was Aboriginal and Tsiolkos' was Greek, this panel was not a set of tokens but essentially a group of young writers that happened to cross cultural boundaries. In this way it proved that Aboriginal writers can be programmed with other writers when performing to a mainstream audience interested in literature.

The second session showed how Aboriginal writers can contribute to programs highlighting cultural diversity. *The Private Lives of Photographs* was a program of readings by emerging writers of culturally diverse backgrounds, presented by the Ethnic Communities Council of NSW. The piece I chose to read at the session was a short story called *Contemporary Koori Woman*, which was considered by the organiser, Barry Gamba, the Multicultural Affairs Officer at the Ethnic Affairs Commission of NSW, to be,

> Exactly the sort of stereotype-breaking story I hoped we would have in the program. Tilly is a strong contemporary character—I think it is that contrast between her yuppie/consumer values and her Reconciliation discourse which gives the story an edge.[388]

In 1996 the Festival also recognised the importance of story-telling as a literary skill and included Herb Wharton (*Unbranded*) in a panel discussion on the importance of story-telling to cultural heritage. Philp McLaren, (*Scream Black Murder*) in, *A Night of Crime*, was also featured.

The 1997 Sydney Writers' Festival included an Aboriginal poetry session supported by The Poets' Union, Tranby Aboriginal College, UQP, Leichhardt Council, Kuri-Ngai Partners and the Dominican Sisters of Eastern Australia. "Black Lives, Black Writing" featured Lisa Bellear, Kerry Reed-Gilbert, Ken Canning (Burraga Gutya), Norm Newlin and Bruce Pascoe with myself in the Chair. Held in the courtyard of Tranby College, the venue was full to capacity and suggested that interest in Aboriginal writing was growing.

In mid-1997 I was asked by organisers to present some ideas to aid them in their desire to include relevant and entertaining Aboriginal panels at the 1998 Sydney Writers' Festival. Ideas included readings, book launches, tributes, panel discussions and a visual displays of literature. The Festival organisers themselves, particularly Meredith Curnow, seemed to be keen for Aboriginal participation.

The 1998 program gave a good cross-section of Aboriginal writing. Fiction writer Melissa Lucashenko did readings and spoke on the panel, "Gender, Genre and Geography" alongside Boori Pryor and Archie Weller. She also participated in "School Days" at the Lower Town Hall. Pryor, the top-selling author at the Festival, was involved in the Stolen Children Special Event at the Sydney Town Hall. I also launched my collection of poetry, *Token Koori*.

The 1999 Sydney Writers' Festival featured Ruby Langford Ginibi in, *School Days* and, *Writing for the City*, and Kenny Laughton speaking on "Reconciliation" before the launching of his first book, *Not Quite Men, No Longer Boys*. Philip McLaren spoke on, *The Crime of the Scene*, and Pat Torres was, "In Conversation with Anita Heiss" as well as participating in *School Days* and the panel "Reconciliation". Film Director Rachel Perkins and singer/performer Leah Purcell also featured in the Festival program in 1999 on a panel, *Black and White* chaired by Noel Tovey. Tovey's background in the theatre and his position on the Sydney Writers' Festival Committee no doubt influenced the presentation on this panel. A special performance of *Box The Pony* was also presented by Hodder Headline at the Bangarra Performance Theatre. Gordon Hookey, who is better known for his visual art than his poetry, was programmed on a panel *Dialogues Across the Islands* with Lili Tuwai from Fiji and Jean Riki from Aotearoa.

Brisbane Writers' Festival

The Brisbane Writers' Festival is one of Australia's largest, longest-running and most attended literary festivals. First held in 1967 as Warana Writers' Week, the Festival incorporated under its new name in 1996. The Festival is held on the banks of the Brisbane River at the State Library and adjoining buildings.

Although the Festival has no official policy in relation to the inclusion of any particular groups of writers, the majority of programming decisions are made by a committee with a charter to develop a program in accordance with the Association's Strategic Plan. This plan outlines the mission of the Brisbane Writers' Festival Association Inc, which is, "to bring the world of writers to the people of Brisbane."[389] And in pursuit of this mission, the Association has set goals to deliver an annual, high-quality festival with a balance of local and international writers, and present a program that reflects Australia's cultural and social diversity.

The Indigenous writers who participated in panels in 1996 program included: Lionel Fogarty, Aunty Vi McDermott and Aunty Irene Egert talked with Kerry Charlton on the panel, "Bring Your Binungs: Indigenous Writing for Young People". Award-winning filmmakers Sally Riley, Darlene Johnson and Sam Watson looked at the issues raised in recent Indigenous cinema as part of the "Black Screen: From Sand to Celluloid" session and Watson participated on the panel, "Northern Exposure: New Takes on the North". Jeanie Bell looked at the issue of being bilingual in the "Speaking the Lingo" panel, while Kev Carmody considered whether or not songwriters and prose authors compose in the same key in the session, "Songwriting: What's Love Got To Do With It"? The program also included Warrigal Anderson, Lisa Bellear, Wesley Enoch, Sandra Phillips and Colin Johnson in, "Talking It Up: Indigenous Writing, Indigenous Lives", while Lisa Bellear also read her work as part of the "Reality Bites" session.

Book launches included on the 1996 program were Mabel Edmund's, *Hello, Johnny*, launched by the Governor, HE Mrs Leneen Forde, and Lisa Bellear's poetry collection, *Dreaming in Urban Areas*, launched by Cheryl Buchanan. The 1995 David Unaipon Award winner, Warrigal Anderson, was announced and his book *Warrigal's Way* was launched by Jackie Huggins.

The 1997 Festival further promoted and showcased Indigenous writing. Uncle Herb Wharton, spoke on the "Cowboys and Drovers" panel, while the "Faking It", panel convened by Jackie Huggins considered the issue of literary fraud and the cases of 'Demidenko' and 'Koolmatrie'. Melissa Lucashenko was "All Frocked Up" as a young woman writer amongst some of Australia's best like Emma Tom and Kaz Cooke, and Kooemba Jdarra Indigenous Performing Arts presented "Urban Dreaming" an innovative and exciting dramatisation inspired by Bellear's *Dreaming in Urban Areas*.

A highly commended entry to the 1997 David Unaipon Award was announced and was Melissa Lucashenko for her first novel *Steam Pigs*. This book was launched by Jackie Huggins. The panel "Telling Stories: New Indigenous Writing" gave writers like Jackie Huggins, Alexis Wright, Melissa Lucashenko and myself an opportunity to make a contribution, even though this session was the final session on the Sunday program.

In 1998 the Brisbane Writers' festival continued to highlight the best in Indigenous writing from around Australia and included Jackie Huggins in "The Road to Reconciliation" session and Wayne Coolwell and Sam Watson discussing the editing process in the "In Black and White" panel. In "The Right to Remain Silent" session Sam Watson 'took statements' from Marele Day, Jenny Pusacker, Simon Higgins and Garrett Russell and looked at the popularity of the crime novel. The 1998 festival also saw the launch of John Graham's *Land Window*, a Highly Commended entry in the 1997 David Unaipon award.

Melbourne Writers' Festival

The Melbourne Writers' Festival was founded in 1986 and is acclaimed as Australia's premier literary event, attracting over 30,000 readers and over 150 writers each year. In 1998 the festival entered into a partnership with Melbourne's *The Age* newspaper, and the festival is now known as *The Age* Melbourne Writers' Festival.[390]

Out of the listed 157 participants in the 1998 festival only three Indigenous writers and Roberta Sykes—"one of Australia's leading Aboriginal rights activists"—were on the program.[391] Singer/ songwriter Ruby Hunter was part of the "Missing Persons" session on the Stolen Generation, but it was interesting to see that three out of the four people participating in this panel were not Aboriginal.

Melissa Lucashenko and Boori Pryor participated in *Youth Literature Days*, and Lucashenko was part of the *Reconcilable Differences?* and *The Outsider*.

Perth Writers' Festival

There has not been much written about the Perth Writers' festival, but the 1999 Festival focussed on the central theme of *Journeys*. Celebrating the Aboriginal tradition of storytelling, the Festival presented six storytellers, "…who have worked hard to preserve their heritage whilst encouraging a greater understanding of Aboriginal culture in our community."[392]

These story-tellers included Alf and Ben Taylor, Josie Boyle and Lorraine Griffiths, and Richard and Joe Walley. These sessions always attract a large audience of Aboriginal supporters and those curious about Aboriginal culture.

The Perth Festival also included writers Kim Scott, Steve Kinnane, Sam Watson, Lisa Bellear and Rosemary van den Berg, with a particular panel discussion "Through the Darkly Past" considering the emergence of powerful Indigenous writing and greater illumination of Australia's past. Aboriginal playwright and actor Richard Walley also ran a Youth Literature Workshop at the Fremantle Children's Literature Centre.

Tasmanian Poetry Festival

The Tasmanian Poetry Festival began in 1985 and within a decade grew into Australia's largest and most prestigious festival devoted solely to poetry. Between 1995 to 1997 it combined with Tasdance, Tasmania's professional contemporary dance company, to put on the Tasmanian Poetry and Dance Festival, but in 1998 it went back to poetry, with a leavening of music and sculpture as well.

Aboriginal writers that have been invited to participate include Jimmy Everett (1989) and Lisa Bellear (1999). John Harding was invited for the 1995 Festival and was publicised as taking part, but didn't attend.

Tim Thorne, Director of the Festival in 1999 commented,

> The Tasmanian Poetry Festival does not have a specific policy relating to the inclusion of Aboriginal poets, but it does have a commitment to presenting the diversity of voices that make up contemporary Australian poetry and an awareness that Aboriginal poets represent a vital component of that diversity.[393]

Adelaide Writers' Week

Adelaide Writers' Week began in 1960 but it wasn't until 1966 that the first Aboriginal writer appeared on the program when Jacaranda Press and the Festival jointly sponsored Kath Walker (Oodgeroo Noonuccal) to appear. Walker's appearance was followed sporadically by other Aboriginal writers: Kevin Gilbert (1978), Archie Weller (1987/1994), Eva Johnson (1994), Jack Davis (1992), Ruby

Langford Ginibi (1992/1994), Herb Wharton (1996), Evelyn Crawford, Kim Scott and Herb Wharton (1998) and Sam Watson, Steven Kinane and Alexis Wright (1998).

Writers' Week actually came under fire in 1972 after American beat poet Allen Ginsberg, who had been in the country only few days, took an Aboriginal performance group on stage with him at the Town Hall, and proved that it took an international artist to promote the local Indigenous culture and community.[394]

While the Festival aims to produce a program that encompasses all forms of writing and has a balance of genders and cultures, Rose Wight, Executive Officer in 1999 said, "It [Adelaide Writers' Week] is committed to the inclusion of Australian writers to adequately reflect the kinds of writing taking place in that community."[395] This commitment means the consideration of Aboriginal writers in the program, in the absence of a specific policy about inclusiveness. Wight says the numbers reflected on programs in recent years does not represent the number of invitations issued to Indigenous writers who were unable to attend.

Alexis Wright called the planning of Adelaide Writers' Week in 1998 'extraordinary' as they programmed Kim Scott's session the same time as her own:

> He was in one tent and I was in another. It seemed that the Aboriginal content ought to be dealt with with one swift blow. The people attending the festival had to then choose which session to go to and miss out on the other.

Canberra Word Festival

The Word Festival in Canberra in 1999 had a strong Aboriginal component for a three day festival with invited writers including Kim Scott (WA), Alexis Wright (NT) and myself from NSW. Unfortunately Wright was unable to attend the Festival due to unexpected family commitments at the last minute, but the opening session of the Festival, "Dreamtime: Whose time?" comprised myself, Scott and Canberra-based John Heath and followed a traditional welcome by local Ngunnawal elder Agnes Shea. Scott also participated on a panel "Who Writes the Past?" alongside Henry Reynolds and Lucy Frost and I participated in a reading as part of the session "Five Bells". Organiser of the 1999 Festival Judy Pearce said of including Aboriginal writers in Word Festivals, "We have tried to include Aboriginal writers in all our Festivals, and in our *I'd rather be reading* day in August 1999."[396]

Byron Bay Writers' Festival

The inaugural Byron Bay Writers' Festival was held in July 1997, and was organised by the Northern Rivers Writers' Centre in Lismore. As the only Aboriginal writer there I found the event an alienating and frustrating experience. While it is understood that the budget was tight for this event, it is difficult to accept that reason alone as a legitimate excuse for not having a larger representation of Aboriginal writers.

After being relocated a number of times on the program, I joked to the organisers that I was the 'displaced, token Koori' to which they became immediately defensive. I was assured that I was not the 'token Koori' because I had not been invited as an Aboriginal writer, but simply as a writer. That being the case, I said that they then had no Aboriginal voice whatsoever and that they shouldn't expect me to talk about Aboriginal issues/writing.

When I finally had the opportunity to read in the company of people like Matt Condon, I assured the audience that I was not Leon Carmen in drag, that I was Aboriginal and a woman, with the genealogy and the genitals to prove it. They laughed. I went on to say that I realised I was the only Koori on the program, in the room, and at the Festival, and it appeared that I was sitting on an absolute gold mine. I should set up an agency and call it 'Token Kooris: Blackfellas for Hire'. They laughed again. My point was meant to be funny but subtly political and I believe I got the message across.

However, it was apparent that I had pricked the conscience of the Director, Peter Barclay, who quite aggressively told me that I was not the 'token Koori' of the Festival and that they had limited funds. It appeared to me, though, that they weren't limited in having others there. My point about having Aboriginal voices at this event was not simply for the sake of tokenism. Rather, Aboriginal involvement should be based on the fact that Aboriginal writers were making big waves in the world of literature at the time. 1997 alone saw some great works in the writings of Alexis Wright and Melissa Lucashenko. The fact that Leon Carmen outed himself as 'Wanda Koolmatrie' in March 1997 also raised the whole cultural appropriation versus artistic license issue which should have been discussed at this literary gathering.

Annoyingly, when I make comments like the ones above, I am automatically invited to join committees, working groups, boards etc, to give my expert opinion. To a degree it is necessary for us as Aboriginal writers to do these things; however, I believe that if someone is paid to organise a literary festival they should at least know something about the literary scene, and that Aboriginal writing now makes up a significant part of that scene.

I sat on a panel with Mungo McCallum, Ian Cohen, and Rodney Hall, with a few interruptions from Bob Ellis in the audience. Here I was, not only the sole Aboriginal voice, but the lone female representative as well. My consolation came in the form of a dozen or so audience members approaching me as I left the stage congratulating me for my efforts and attempted restraint during a very difficult panel.

Other issues included the mis-spelling of Aboriginal with lower case 'a' on the Festival flyer, and numerous mistakes in my biographical details on the program, before being introduced by an ill-prepared MC who got the pronunciation of 'Heiss' wrong. I noted the names of Anglo writers weren't confused or disregarded as unimportant as was mine. Perhaps if I were generous I would suggest that it wasn't a race issue, but the fact that I was simply a lesser-known writer.

Since then it appears the Byron Bay Writers' Festival has changed its approach to Aboriginal inclusion, and Jill Eddington, Director / Manager of the NRWC in 2000 says, "The festival certainly has a policy of including Aboriginal writers. We have no set percentage but try to select a sound representation which is seemingly increasing each year".[397]

This increase is true. Recent years have included Melissa Lucashenko (1998/2000) Stephen Schnierer (1998), Wesley Enoch (1999), Ruby Langford Ginibi (1999), Sam Wagan Watson (1999/2000), and Boori Pryor (2000).

Spring Writing Festival, NSW Writers' Centre

Spring Writing, which began in 1992, is a very popular Sydney based literary festival held in the grounds of the NSWWC at the old Rozelle Hospital. Irina Dunn says that when they were developing the festival they,

> Very consciously decided to set up a festival that would be in tune with our grounds here, very intimate and very beautiful. We provide a showcase for well known writers and new writers. Unlike the big writers festivals where big names are kept on the stage and you don't get to meet them.[398]

She explains the emphasis that the Writers' Centre puts on Aboriginal writers participating at Spring Writing:

> As part of that interest in new writers and other aspects of Australian literary culture that don't get much attention, we really do very consciously seek out NESB and Aboriginal writers for our program because we think there are few festivals where they can showcase their work. It's very interesting to look at the way attendance at the Aboriginal and NESB sessions at Spring Writing has grown over the years.

Since 1996 the Spring Writing program has included more and more Aboriginal involvement, with the panel "Tiddas Business: New Aboriginal Women's Writing' including Romaine Moreton, Kerry Reed-Gilbert, Cathy Craigie and myself. This was followed by the launch of Gilbert's *Black Woman, Black Life* and Moreton's *The Callused Stick of Wanting*. Ruby-Langford Ginibi and Philip McLaren participated on other panels at the Festival.

The 1997 Spring Writing festival included more Indigenous voices with readings and panel discussions which included Indigenous writers from Aotearoa and North America in a session "Native Tongues", new writers with "Young, Gifted and Black" and Kerry Reed-Gilbert in the erotica session "Hot'n'Happening".

Philip McLaren, Les Murray and myself presented papers on literary fraud and the Carmen affair, which also stirred people's interest. Dunn commented,

> No doubt all the scandals have assisted too, so that now people want to hear authentic Aboriginal voices as opposed to a Wanda Koolmatrie or other literary frauds, so people are interested in what Aboriginal writers are writing about. Of course, there are other Aboriginal writers like Phillip McLaren that stand in a particular genre, and the fact that he's Aboriginal is one of his characteristics. The fact that he's also writing detective novels and has made his name in that genre is also of interest to us.

In essence, what the NSW Writers' Centre is doing via Spring Writing is fostering new talent. The reasoning, says Dunn, is, "We want to provide at least a venue, a showcase where people can see new writers and listen to what they've got to say, meet them and start to read a new strand and new thread of Australian literature."

There has been an Aboriginal component at Spring Writing for several years and for the last two years there has been an Aboriginal welcome. The average attendance at Spring Writing events that feature Indigenous writers ranges from 30-50 people.

The opening night of Spring Writing 1999 featured *In the Spirit of Reconciliation* with Burraga Gutya, Kerry Reed-Gilbert, Norm Newlin and Lorraine McGee-Sippel, alongside Debra Adelaide, Rosie Scott and Gabrielle Carey. This was possibly the most successful session at Spring Writing that year with over 70 people in the audience, a full-house.

Woodford Folk Festival

The old Malaney Folk Festival (held at Woodford since 1995) is a celebration of the best of arts and crafts Australia has to offer between Christmas and the new year. Each year the Festival has a strong program including the best in Indigenous arts and artists, including writers.

Walbira Watts has been the Coordinator of the Murri Program of the Festival for four years and has been involved for seven years (the Festival itself has been running 15 years). She says there is a designated Murri Stage because,

> Murri culture is too big, too precious to be confined to just a time slot. By having a Murri venue we can program in a culturally appropriate way to Indigenous peoples. The Queensland Folk Federation has never told us what we could and could not present there.[399]

9. Festivals, Conferences and Awards

The Murri Stage has extended over the years to three venues at the Festival: the Murri Stage, the Talking Circle (a story-telling and art space around a fire) and the Corroboree Grounds (a sand dance ground that's opened by elders).

In terms of the importance of the Aboriginal involvement in the program and other Festival programs, Watts says, "Other festivals are only catching on to it now, and some copy the Woodford style of program." Performing on the Murri Stage, and also scattered throughout the festival grounds, Indigenous musicians, dancers, storytellers and writers join together to share dance, song and culture with whoever is willing to learn. The importance of Indigenous authors being included in such a festival is highlighted by Watts:

> Indigenous authors are the scribes of the community. They record our history, our humour, our perspectives in various ways. We have always been story-tellers. This is a new medium to that storytelling is all. And I think it's important to show the diversity in Aboriginal artists, from actors to singers to authors to craftswomen etc.

Aboriginal and Torres Strait Islander writers who have been invited to perform and speak at the Festival include Cathy Craigie, Kerry Reed-Gilbert, Debbie Rose, Jackie and Auntie Rita Huggins, Ruth Hegarty, Lionel Fogarty, Maureen Watson and Uncle Herb Wharton. Book launches with performances of acclaimed works like Kevin Gilbert's *The Cherry Pickers* (1995) are also common on the Woodford program, with Watts pointing out that book sales are high and launches well attended.

A Summer Readers' Feast, Sydney 1998

As the Sydney Writers' Festival moved to May and became its own entity, the State Library still saw the need to have a literature program of some substance during the January Sydney Festival, and began it with "A Summer Readers' Feast" in 1998. I was approached by organiser Anne Doherty to assist in developing an appropriate panel and program involving both established and emerging Aboriginal writers.

We came up with Koori Readings held, by tradition, the day before Invasion Day. The panel included Kerry Reed-Gilbert, Barbara Nicholson, Lorraine McGee-Sippel, Cathy Craigie and myself. The success of the event was seen in the numbers of people in the audience in the Dixson Room, but it was obvious from the stage, though, that there were very few Kooris in the 100+ people in attendance.

This raises two issues for participants and observers. Firstly, that the Reconciliation process is working and non-Indigenous Australia is genuinely interested in what Aboriginal people have to say in the written and oral form.

Secondly, that the event was not adequately marketed (if at all) to relevant Aboriginal media and community organisations. This is a huge issue in terms of all Festivals because there are different networks in the Aboriginal community. These networks often involve contact by individual participants in order to let people know what's on and where and also includes extensive Aboriginal specific e-mail lists and arts networks.

1998 Spring Poetry Festival, ACT

The inaugural Spring Poetry Festival organised by Peter Latona was held over the long-weekend in October 1998 and left a lot to be desired in terms of organisation that included Aboriginal writers. Although I was invited as a key speaker I didn't receive a copy of the program prior to the event and my biographical details were left out of the program altogether.

Jennifer Martiniello assisted the organisers in putting together a session called *Reconciliation Readings*, which was well attended, considering it was on Sunday morning the day after the Federal election, and on the weekend of the Koori Knockout Football Carnival. The panel consisted of an equal number of Indigenous and non-Indigenous writers, reading and giving commentary on the topic of Reconciliation. However none of the Aboriginal writers' biographical details appeared on the published program, while nearly all of the non-Aboriginal writers were included.

The organisers obviously deemed it was enough to include Aboriginal people on the program, without giving them the same acknowledgement and recognition as their white counterparts. They denied that it was anything more than an administrative mistake that I didn't receive a program, and that it was an innocent omission that biographical details of Aboriginal writers were not included. What happened in 1998 was no different to what happened to Kath Walker in 1961 when she published the poem "Companionship" in the *Realist Writer*. Unlike the other poets in the magazine, her name was left out of the list of contents.[400]

With a strong broader history of exclusion Aboriginal people are sensitised to levels of inclusivity, even though some omissions may be justifiable as administrative oversight.

Shorelines—Bermagui Festival of Words

The Shorelines Bermagui Festival of Words was held for the first time in March 1999 and again in 2000, and each event had a significant Indigenous contribution considering the size of the Festival. Both the coordinators and the writers gave their services for free and the 1999 Festival included local Aboriginal writer Eileen Morgan, (*Calling the Spirits*) and myself from Sydney. In 2000 myself and poet Jennifer Martiniello spoke in forums, on panels and did sunrise readings.

There was no written policy for Aboriginal inclusion in the Festival, just a personal commitment by the Festival organisers to acknowledge the local Aboriginal community and a desire to support Aboriginal writing.

Festival of the Dreaming, Sydney 1997

The Festival of the Dreaming was the first of the four Olympic Arts Festivals to be presented in the lead up to and during the Sydney 2000 Olympic Games. It was supposed to be dedicated to the presentation and promotion of Indigenous culture, primarily Aboriginal and Torres Strait Islander, with some international input.

Held in and around Sydney from 15 September–6 October 1997, the Festival incorporated all artforms (some to a lesser degree than others). One of those components was the "Paperbark" Literature Program held between 18–23 September. The Paperbark program was poorly promoted and as a consequence, poorly attended, and to some extent, provided disproportionate voice to the invited non-Indigenous writers like Henry Reynolds, Kaz Cooke and Heather Goodall.

The distaste at the way in which the program was put together was a matter for discussion between writers for weeks leading up to and following the event. Cathy Craigie, who carried out the original consultancy for the Paperbark Program through the Gadigal Writers' Group, was concerned by many aspects of the Festival, particularly the way in which Aboriginal literature was not profiled as seriously as the other artforms. After the event she commented on the fact that *Waiting for Godot* and *Midsummer Night's Dream* were performed with Aboriginal casts:

> I think Shakespeare has enough publicity, and Beckett…Writers were quite upset. I think for writing we were just thrown out the back lane. While everyone else was up there enjoying the party we were in the back lane, and for me I find that quite sickening, that our own people are part of that.[401]

The fact that other artforms, particularly theatre, were seen as the most important aspect of Indigenous arts was obvious to most, especially Aboriginal writers. Craigie commented, "Writing wasn't seen as an integral part of anything and it really quite saddened me that something that is a new tool that we are using… and our own people [Festival organisers] didn't help put that up [support it]."

Jeanie Bell attended the Festival, and while she said her bookshop readings went well, they had small attendance figures. She commented, "I felt that the literature stuff at the Festival was kind of neglected. Like we were down there and they [the other artforms] were up there. It was a bit of a shame."[402]

Prior to the Festival, a letter sent by the then Director of the Cultural Olympiad, Jonah Jones, invited me to tender for the Literary Event Consultancy, stating that,

> The event will promote awareness and appreciation of the literary works of Indigenous writers from Australia and overseas…Works included in the event will reflect the Aboriginal and Torres Strait Islander cultural practice of storytelling and a significant component of the program will be devoted to elders. Both written and oral works across all genres will be presented. The event will promote open public discussion of the current issues affecting Indigenous writers.[403]

The Festival of the Dreaming was, "Dedicated to the presentation and promotion of *Indigenous* culture, particularly *Aboriginal and Torres Strait Islander*, with some international involvement."(My emphasis).[404]

The low profile of literature and the arguably excessive inclusion of non-Indigenous writers led to missed opportunities for Indigenous literature. Out of 38 participants listed on the program (some of whom didn't actually participate due to unforeseen circumstances, including Lionel Fogarty), seven were from Indigenous nations outside of Australia and four were non-Indigenous.

Kerry Reed-Gilbert was not invited to participate in the Festival aside from acting as MC for the tribute to her father, Kevin Gilbert, and Oodgeroo Noonuccal. This role was seen simply as a birthright to Reed-Gilbert, rather than a role as an Aboriginal writer. Reed-Gilbert was furious that she had been denied a voice while non-Indigenous participants played significant roles,

> I haven't got a problem with white writers, but don't they already get adequately promoted and their voices heard out there? Is it a question that by participating on our panels they will be comparing Black and white writing and who is the best? It makes you wonder.[405]

As an Aboriginal person, I found the fact that the scaffolding at *Black Mary* collapsed half-way through the season somewhat meaningful, considering the grumbling within the Aboriginal writing circle about yet another white writer's work being shown at the Festival. It was bad enough that Janson's work had come through Aboriginal Studies Press, the fact that it was also being produced at the Festival of the Dreaming was too much to bear. Cathy Craigie said of the work being on the program, "I found that really disgusting."

Sandra Phillips was the Editor of the BAWS at UQP when the programming was in progress for the Festival and, to the detriment of the Festival, her experience and role in the publishing industry was completely overlooked. She commented, "I'm in touch with what new authors are in publication right now and who are going to be big by the year 2000."[406]

On a positive note, the Festival did provide the opportunity for histories, cultures and contemporary literatures to be shared with Indigenous writers from Aotearoa, the United States and Canada. It was some of these writers who opened up discussion on issues faced by Indigenous writers the world over. Top Maori author Patricia Grace (Ngati Toa/Ngati Raukawa/ Ta Ati Awa) gave a memorable talk, saying, "non-Indigenous societies perceive our cultures as dead. That's why we need a great variety of story-telling, such as contemporary Indigenous writing to change those perceptions."[407]

7th Festival of Pacific Arts (FOPA)

In 1996 I attended the 7th Festival of Pacific Arts (FOPA) in Apia, Western Samoa. I was not there as a writer, but as an interviewer for the national Aboriginal Arts Program, *Arts Yarn Up*, produced by Gadigal Information Services. FOPA is held every four years and carries on the tradition of providing an international forum for Indigenous peoples from Micronesia, Melanesia, Polynesia and Australia to unite in a celebration of culture, art and traditions. A total of 24 nations and their collective 1500 delegates gathered to share histories and aspirations as dancers, visual artists, story-tellers, writers and musicians.

The Australian delegation of 60 was selected by ATSIAB after a call for applications. It included dance groups (Bapu National Dancers, Mornington Island Dancers and Torres Strait Islander Dance Group) and the band Footprince from Broome. Carnavon-based egg-carver Barry Bellotti and the Yirrkala weavers represented some important crafts, and story-tellers Aunty Maureen Watson and Pauline McLeod displayed our ongoing oral tradition in very entertaining ways. While Indigenous Australian writers were under-represented at the festival, South Australian playwright Owen Love did a few performances of "No Shame", to appreciative audiences.

The Pacific Book Exhibition held at the Nelson Memorial Library showcased the authors and publishers of the Pacific Islands including Guam, the Cook Islands, Wallis Island and Samoa. But there were was no sight of any Aboriginal Australian work.

The absence of Aboriginal writers at the Festival was a sad reflection on how little recognition is paid to Aboriginal literature in Australia as opposed to other Indigenous nations around the Pacific and the world.

Such an absence was also seen in the 5th Festival of Pacific Arts, coordinated and held in Townsville, Australia in 1988. The Festival included a visual arts exhibition, a film and video program ("Adventures in Paradise"), and a performance section which included Maureen Watson and Pat Torres only once in a week long schedule.[408]

In 2000 the Festival was held in New Caledonia and no writers at all were chosen as part of the Australian delegation.

Conferences

Like literary festivals, writers' conferences provide benefits to writers on an individual basis, but also offer an avenue for collective decision making on the artform as a whole.

The first Aboriginal Writers' Conference was held in Perth in 1983, the second in Brisbane in 1986.

In 1992 the first National Aboriginal Writers' Workshop (as distinct from conference format) was held in Gariwerd in Victoria. This was the springboard for later conferences and workshops including the 1993 Black Women's Writing Workshop in Brisbane and the 1996 Aboriginal and Torres Strait Islander Writers/Playwrights Conference, also held in Brisbane.

These conferences and workshops provide a forum for discussion and debate, a platform for artists to perform and workshop pieces, and sessions on the practical side of writing and getting published. Conferences also bring professionals together to share resources and to scrutinise the industry they work within. The following section aims to highlight the benefits of specific Indigenous writing conferences to the author as an individual and to the development of Aboriginal literature as a whole.

"Our Words—Our Ways": National Aboriginal and Torres Strait Islander Writers' Workshop

Aboriginal and Torres Strait Islander writers from across Australia gathered at the Brambuk Cultural Centre at Budja Budja, Geriwerd in Victoria in December 1992. The event was coordinated by Tony Duke and Sandra Phillips through the Centre for Blackbooks (Tranby Cooperative for Aborigines Ltd) as part of their tenth anniversary celebrations. The Workshop was sponsored by the Literature Panel of the Aboriginal Arts Committee of the Australia Council and the primary focus of the workshop was to create a forum for Aboriginal and Torres Strait Islander writers to meet and share their processes and experiences. Phillips commented, "Prior to this event there has been two very successful Aboriginal Literature Conferences in Perth in 1983 and Brisbane in 1986. With the workshop the emphasis is on sharing and participation as opposed to theory and analysis."[409]

Practical workshops led by writers like Richard Walley, Jackie Huggins and Kathy Kum Sing covered genres like fiction, play writing, women's writing and comic writing. Workshops were also held on creative writing, editing, academic writing, writing for radio/film/television and political writing, conducted by experienced writers including Eva Johnson, Eve Fesl, Bob Maza, Gerry and Lester Bostock and Lionel Fogarty.

Issues within the industry were also considered, including funding opportunities, copyright, self-publishing, ethics in writing and research, and accountability.

National Aboriginal and Torres Strait islander Women Writers' Conference, 1993

Held at the Warilda Conference Centre in Brisbane the conference included writers like Cathy Craigie, Jackie Huggins, Pat Torres, Toni Janke and Kerry Reed-Gilbert. Sessions offered included "Writing Within Bureaucracies", "Writing a Tiddas Manifesto", "Writing about Internalised Racism" and "Writing and Illustrating for Children" by Pat Torres.

Indigenous Writers' Conference, Northern Territory, 1995

This was the first ever Indigenous writers conference in the Northern Territory and immediately followed the "Word and Breath Writers Festival" in 1995. The conference was set up by Andrew McMillan who was the NT Literature Officer at the time, with the assistance of the Multicultural Arts Network. This Conference identified the training needs of Indigenous writers, and Terry Whitebeach says recommendations from the Conference were part of the impetus for the setting up of the present Creative Writing Certificate III course at Batchelor College that she now teachers and coordinates.[410]

Mogwi-Djan National Indigenous Writers and Playwrights Conference and Workshop, 1996

In April 1996, 139 writers, playwrights, editors, publishers and other industry workers descended upon the Bardon Professional Centre in Brisbane for Mogwi-Djan (a Yugarabal phrase meaning "Stories of the Land"). The conference and workshop brought together writers from each State and Territory as well as from Nauru and Switzerland. The Conference included work-shopping of plays, thanks to Kooemba Jdarra Indigenous Performing Arts Group from Brisbane. There was also an Indigenous Book Fair with a local independent bookseller displaying and selling a selection of books.

Aside from work-shopping, Mainstreet Community Theatre Company from Mt Gambier presented a performance of "No Shame", written by Owen Love and directed by Bob Maza and David Milroy. The novel, *Follow the Rabbit Proof Fence* by Doris Pilkington was launched by Carol Innes, Aboriginal Programs Officer, Western Australian Department for the Arts.

Pilkington's second book with UQP and the first book edited by Sandra Phillips at that Press, was part of an anticipated trilogy. Its launch was an occasion significant for the fact that it brought into the published world a story of immense love, courage and survival. No-one though could predict how significant that story and its place in the world were to become. Six years later the book became the film "Rabbit Proof Fence" and was released to critical acclaim and international audiences. In Australia it was met with much consternation from conservative forces who tried to politicise and deny the history it told to everyday people, though it is a story that continues to enthrall because of its powerful and simple truths.

The conference, as with most Indigenous conferences, finished up with a list of recommendations directed to the Australia Council, none of which appear to have been taken seriously to date. Several recommendations highlighted the need to separate dramatic writing from other forms of writing when programming future conferences (because of the differing practical needs of the two groups), as well as the desire for writers to move across genres. Drama has since received a focus with the 3rd National Aboriginal and Torres Strait Islander Playwrights Conference held in Adelaide in March 2000 (following others in 1987 and 1989). Other recommendations also lobby for conferences that are at least two weeks long and in format similar to the Australian National Playwrights' Conference.

In her report to the Australia Council the conference coordinator, Lesley Fogarty, commented that, "The value of conferences such as Mogwi-Djan is that they support an environment of a 'hothouse of ideas' for many people with different experiences to come together for a short, intense exchange."[411] The organisers felt the shortcomings of the conference included the fact that the program was split between talk sessions and practical workshops, and that talk sessions mainly focussed on information exchange, rather than discussions of content issues, for example, "who do you write for?" or "what is Aboriginal writing?"[412]

Sandra Phillips also commented on the Conference's shortcomings,

> Though the conference program looked, smelt and felt good, a read of it wasn't as heartening. Perhaps in trying to do a little bit of justice to everything the Mogwi-Djan agenda at times became an eclectic catch-all rather than a well-synthesised instrument designed to bring out the best and give the best.[413]

Nevertheless she also commented that, "…the Indigenous writing community has gained from the gathering, and…that our collection and individual creative energies will continue to draw inspiration from who we are and where we come from."[414]

Phillips points out that the aim of forums like Mogwi-Djan is to, "Transfer skill not in a formulaic way but almost as if by osmosis through discussion and sharing of insight."[415] She adds, "it becomes clear that a gathering of Indigenous writers needs to concern itself with not only the creative, but also the cultural and the political."[416]

Melissa Lucashenko commented that she felt a bit alienated at Mogwi-Djan:

I felt like it was full of egos. I would have liked to have gone to the playwright sessions, and then I noticed that there was one for published playwrights and one for aspiring playwrights, and to me it was off-putting to people who haven't written a play. It would have been useful to share ideas. If there's a person from Cherbourg with heaps and heaps of ideas and life experiences and enthusiasm but he's never written a play, why not put him together with someone who has and they can feed off each other. Maybe they did that for reasons of space.[417]

Mogwi-Djan was possibly the first time that Indigenous literature gained any substantial media coverage because the SBS *Bookshow* took the opportunity to attend the conference. The show also pre-taped a panel discussion with Lisa Bellear, Sandra Phillips and Lionel Fogarty prior to interviewing a number of writers at the conference centre on the role and status of Aboriginal literature at this time.

There hasn't been a major Indigenous writers' conference since Mogwi-Djan.

Indigenous Writers' Symposium

In November 1998, the University of Queensland brought together some of Australia's leading Aboriginal writers for a one-day Indigenous Writers Symposium. Organised and chaired by Jackie Huggins, Coordinator of the Aboriginal and Torres Strait Islander Unit at Queensland University, the day involved informal discussions, readings and papers on the role and importance of Indigenous writers as well as the implications of Indigenous writing in education and entertainment. The need to promote Indigenous writing and writers was also a key focus of the day.

Writers across all genres were included in the symposium: Melissa Lucashenko (fiction), Sam Watson (fiction), Jennifer Sabbioni (editor), Herb Wharton (autobiography), Pat Torres (children / faction), Michelle Buchanan (poetry), Denis Foley (poetry) and Aunty Ruth Hegarty (autobiography). The program included discussions on why Aboriginal people write, the role of poetry, fiction and life stories in Aboriginal literature, and in depth discussion between writers and their editors (Jennifer Sabbioni and Kay Schaffer, Jackie Huggins and Alison Ravens-Croft, Melissa Lucashenko and Sue Abbey, Herb Wharton and Barbara Kerr-Wilson).

The day ended with some informal readings by participants and the launch of Indigenous Australian Voices at the Wordsmiths Cafe.

Writers' workshops

Similar to the role of conferences, but structured in a more practical way, workshops provide writers with the opportunity to develop or enhance their skills in the written word. Workshops are normally conducted by more experienced and established writers, who not only provide advice and assistance, but also act as role models for aspiring writers.

Pat Torres in an interview with the consultant for the *Report on Strategies for the Further Development of the National Aboriginal and Torres Strait Islander Arts and Cultural Industry* commented that there was a need for writers to know how to present their information, and a great need for workshops to teach people the skills of how to put onto paper what, "…they might be dying to write."[418]

Aside from the workshops I conducted in regional NSW in 1996, the first ever Master Classes for Indigenous Writers were held at the NSWWC from September 6-10, 1998, with tutors Eva Toia and Janine McVeagh from Aotearoa. Indigenous writers from across Australia participated included: Lisa Bellear (VIC), Cathy Craigie (NSW), Rhonda Grosvenor (NSW), Ruby Langford Ginibi (NSW), Kenny Laughton (NT), Owen Love (SA), Bob Maza (QLD), Pauline Mitchell (NSW), Donna Morris (NSW), Bruce Pascoe (VIC), Doris Pilkington (WA), Kerry Reed-Gilbert (NSW), Rosie Smith (TAS), and Ida West (TAS).

The main aims of the master classes were to improve writing techniques and therefore the opportunities for mainstream publication. Writers learnt the skill of critiquing and how to develop fiction writing techniques. Other aims of the classes were to learn appropriate methods of facilitating writing workshops, in an environment where participants could meet and support each others writing.

The course followed a sequence that necessitated full participation for maximum benefit. Course techniques were modelled with explanation and included an opening and closing ceremony each day with tributes to the traditional owners of the land and Aboriginal writers.

Awards

As more and more Aboriginal writers move across genres and we are less categorised in bookshops under 'Austrailiana' but as writers of fiction, erotica and satire, so too the argument grows about whether or not specific awards should be made available to Aboriginal writers to better establish us in mainstream literary culture.

There have been a number of award winners within the mainstream area including Melissa Lucashenko who took out the Nita B. Kibble for *Steam Pigs* in 1998. Ruby Langford Ginibi and Kevin Gilbert both won Human Rights Awards for Literature in 1988 for *Don't Take Your Love To Town* and *Living Black* respectively. Jimmy Chi and Kuckles followed the same path in 1991 for *Bran Nue Dae*.

In 1999, *Going For Kalta: Hunting for Sleepy Lizards at Yatala* won the Children's Book of the Year-Eve Pownall Award for Information Books. It also won the 1998 Australian Excellence in Educational Publishing Award.

In 2000 Kim Scott was joint winner of the Miles Franklin Award for his historical novel *Benang: From the Heart*.

In terms of Indigenous specific awards, the success of the David Unaipon Award is a good case for maintaining old awards while establishing new ones to attract more writers to submit for eventual publication. Individual cases of writers who may not have won the Unaipon Award but received meaningful feedback in the judging process encourages the existence of such an avenue for Aboriginal writers.

It is also important to remember that while Aboriginal people can write across genres and geography and be included in mainstream festivals and programs, the perceptions of the author as a descendant of the first peoples of this land are a unique feature in the content of the work. In this way, Indigenous-specific awards recognise that distinction and acknowledge it in a way that provides the author with some financial support.

Considering the few awards with small cash prizes that are currently in place for Aboriginal writers in this country, it is obvious that the visual arts are still seen as the more important artform. The number of awards available to Aboriginal visual artists continues to grow, with cash prizes as major incentives.

Australia's most prestigious Indigenous art award, the National Aboriginal and Torres Strait Islander Art Award is administered by the Museum and Art Gallery of the Northern Territory, and was worth $18,000 in 1996. Australia's richest Indigenous art award, the National Heritage Art Award administered through the Australian Heritage Commission, is worth $40,000 in prizes. The Award focuses on the theme of heritage places and former winners include Ginger Riley Munduwalawala, the late Lin Onus and Treahna Hamm.

David Unaipon Award

While it is a giant foot-in-the-door for winning authors, Sandra Phillips says the David Unaipon Award is also of benefit to publishers, "It gives a very clear insight into the writing that's going on in Indigenous Australia." She goes on to praise the Award and the avenue it has provided to Aboriginal and Torres Strait Islander writers since 1989,

> The profile it has established over the years is enormous. May 31 each year is marked on the calendar of a lot of Indigenous writers. I think it has become part of the psyche and it does give people a deadline to aim for. It's got a continuity, a profile, an incentive. It definitely has worked to inculcate a commitment to writing.

As Craig Munro points out, when UQP established the award they wanted to do more than simply honour David Unaipon:

> UQP has published a lot of scholarly material since the 1960s, including the areas of Aboriginal studies. In virtually every case the writers were white. It was

the bi-centenary that galvanised us into feeling more political about it, and feeling that we could make a conscious change in philosophy where we published on Aboriginal topics, we would where possible seek books by Aboriginal writers, whatever the subject matter or whatever the style of book.

At the time UQP were looking at doing an anthology of writing called *Paperbark* with two Aboriginal and two non-Aboriginal editors. They discussed with us establishing an award that would provide more publishing opportunities for Aboriginal writers because we thought it wasn't just an accident that all of our books in the areas of broad Aboriginal studies had been by non-Aboriginal people.[419]

UQP set the award up with the assistance and advice of Oodgeroo Noonuccal, Jack Davis and Colin Johnson, but also sought advice from other Aboriginal groups and communities. Munro notes the growing success of the award, to the point where UQP publish all of the publishable manuscripts they receive. He also notes that one of the interesting aspects of the award is its geographic representation,

> The fact that it's a national award does create some political challenges with all the different regions represented, and those with greater access to publishing, like in the Eastern states. We find that the greatest number of entries come from the areas where there's fewer opportunities to get published.[420]

Recipients of the David Unaipon Award have been:
1998 – Ruth Hegarty *Is That You Ruthie?*
1997 – John Bodey *When Darkness Falls*
1996 – Steven McCarthy *Black Angels*
1995 – Edward Warrigal Anderson *Warrigal's Way*
1994 – Rosalie Medcraft and Valda Gee *The Sausage Tree*
1993 – John Muk Muk Burke *Bridge of Triangles*
1992 – Philip McLaren *Sweet Water, Stolen Land*
1991 – Bill Dodd *Broken Dreams*
1990 – Doris Pilkington *Caprice A Stockman's Daughter*
1989 - Graeme Dixon *Holocaust Island*

The award carries a $15,000 cash prize funded by the Queensland Government through the Ministry for the Arts, as well as a contract for publication through the UQP. The judging panel for 1997 consisted of Doris Pilkington, Sam Watson and Jackie Huggins, and in 1999 Huggins was replaced with author John Muk Muk Burke. The judges are all Aboriginal writers so, in the long run, the decision to publish lies with Aboriginal writers.

As the Award has grown and become one of the most prestigious literary prizes in Australia, it attracts manuscripts across genres and geography. A unique feature is that entries may be in English or the writers' own Aboriginal or Torres Strait Islander language, with bilingual texts equally acceptable.

Another bonus of the Award is that many manuscripts that are highly commended also receive an offer of publication through the Black Australian Writers' Series. Some of these works include Joe McGuiness' *Son of Aryandabu: My Fight For Aboriginal Rights* (1992), Mabel Edmund's *No Regret* (1992), Herb Wharton's *Unbranded* (1992), Lisa Bellear's *Dreaming in Urban Areas* (1996), Jeanie Bell's *Talking About Celia* (1997), Alexis Wright's *Plains of Promise* (1997), Melissa Lucashenko's *Steam Pigs* (1997) and Eve Fesl's *Conned* (1993).

Lisa Bellear talks about the opportunity the award provided to her, commenting,

> It gave me an opportunity to get a manuscript together, to get a CV on what I've published. I submitted my work on bright yellow paper to be noticed. I got a letter that didn't say I'd won the award but it gave me the option of being published anyway, and I took that option.

Melissa Lucashenko points out that while her first submission to the David Unaipon Award in 1991 was unsuccessful, the feedback she received made it all worthwhile, giving her the encouragement to write more, "I got a letter back, they sent responses to everyone and it said keep writing, it's worth keeping going, and that was just such a big thing for me. It was the most encouragement I got."

Jeanie Bell entered her unpublished manuscript *Talking About Celia* in the 1995 David Unaipon Award, and although she didn't win, the work was highly commended, and UQP made an offer to publish. As with all Award entrants, feedback is offered, and Bell notes, "it was really just good to get the feedback."

The Marrawarnging Award

In 1999 the Centre for Indigenous History and the Arts at the University of Western Australia (UWA) announced a new Indigenous writers' award known as the Marrawarnging Award with a $5000 prize cheque and a publishing contract with UWA Press. Unlike the Unaipon Award for unpublished authors, this new award was open to all Aboriginal and Torres Strait Islander peoples who may be published or unpublished writers.

Marrawarnging is a Nyoongah word meaning 'hands talking' and the award is open to book length works including novels, collections of stories or poems, individual and family oral history collections, histories, biographies and works for children. Entries are accepted in English, Aboriginal English or in bilingual text.

Entirely funded by UWA as part of the University's commitment to the advancement of Indigenous people, the Indigenous judging panel for the award comprises May O'Brien, Graeme Dixon and Sally Morgan.

The 1999 award went to Susan Kelly and Angus Wallan both of Western Australia for the children's book, Corroboree.

Patricia Weickhardts Award

The Patricia Weickhardts Award was created to honour the achievements of Aboriginal writers and was directly sponsored by Patricia Weickhardt. Worth $100 the award was administered by the Victorian Fellowship of Australian Writers (FAW) and recipients of the award include:

1991 – Richard Walley
1990 – Sam Watson
1989 – Lionel Fogarty
1989 – Sally Morgan
1987 – Eric Wilmot
1986 – Bob Merritt
1985 – David Unaipon
1984 – James Miller
1983 – Archie Weller (Special award to Sharelle McGuirk)
1981 – Hyllus Maris (Special Award to Karen Milward)
1980 – Jack Davis
1979 – Colin Johnson
1978 – Kevin Gilbert (Special Award to Noelene Lane)
1977 – Kath Walker (Special Award to Linda Walsh)
1976 – Dick Roughsey

FAW also gave Oodgeroo Noonuccal the Christopher Brennan Award in 1992 in acknowledgement of her contribution to poetry.

The Award ceased to exist when an unnamed 'Part-Aboriginal Committee member' said that Aboriginal writers were moving into the mainstream and it was now patronising to have a separate award.[421] But as Melissa Lucashenko points out, Aboriginal writers are more likely to submit their work to Aboriginal specific awards than mainstream ones, "Stuff like the Unaipon, specifically Indigenous things because people will put in for that, but won't put in for others."

Ruth Adeney Koori Award (RAKA)

The $10,000 RAKA award is administered by the University of Melbourne's Australian Centre and is one of Australia's most valuable awards for Aboriginal artists. The annual award is made available by Professor Emeritus Bernard Smith in memory of his late wife Kate Challis, who was known in her early days as Ruth Adeney. RAKA is an acronym for Ruth Adeney Koori Award.

Bernard Smith is a renowned art historian and writer, who donated a large sum of money to the Australian Centre to set up a fund to finance the award. Rhyll

Nance from the University of Melbourne says that the naming of the award is a really complex story:

> Bernard's first wife was adopted and known as Ruth Adeney —hence RAKA (Ruth Adeney Koori Award). At the age of about 18, she discovered that she was really Kate Challis. In very recent years, the family decided that the name Kate Challis should be incorporated into the title of the award, so we now have "The Kate Challis RAKA Award". Although not Indigenous herself, Kate was very interested in Aboriginal culture.[422]

The prize is awarded in a five-year cycle and each year a different area of artistic endeavour is rewarded—creative prose, drama, the visual arts, scriptwriting and poetry or music. When literary awards are involved, publishers who might wish to nominate writers are contacted. An entrant can nominate him / herself or be nominated by a community.

First awarded in 1991, RAKAs have recognised Aboriginal literature, drama, visual arts, script writing and poetry. In 1991, Bill Rosser won the RAKA for his book *Up Rode The Troopers: The Black Police in Queensland*; in 1992, Jack Davis for his play No Sugar; in 1993, Lin Onus for his sculptural installation *They Took The Children Away*; in 1994, Tracey Moffatt for her film script *Bedevil*; and in 1995, Kevin Gilbert (posthumously) for his collection of poems *Black From The Edge*.

Colin Johnson received the sixth award in 1996 for his introduction to Indigenous Australia entitled *Us Mob*. The winner in 1997 was John Harding for his play *Up The Road*, and in 1998 the prize was awarded to Brook Andrew for his digital photograph *Sexy and Dangerous*. The 1999 award went to Rima Tamou for his script for the short film, *Round Up*. John Muk Muk Burke won the 2000 award for his poetry collection *Night Song*. Both Colin Johnson and Roberta Sykes were nominated and short-listed for the 2000 award.

Criteria vary from year to year according to the category in which the award is being made. Nance says, "In general, the award is given to a person for a particular piece of work rather than a body of work, and it must have been published, produced or exhibited over the preceding five years."[423]

The judges also vary from year to year. There is normally a panel of four—two Indigenous members, two non-Indigenous members including someone from the donor family. The jury is chaired by the Director of the Australian Centre.

Other awards

The NSW Indigenous Arts Fellowship

Established in 1996 by the NSW Government in partnership with Sydney City Council, this Fellowship worth $15,000 is offered biennially to assist an Aboriginal or Torres Strait Islander artist to further the development of his or her career. The Fellowship is offered across artforms and it is expected that the specific project put forward by the applicant will result in artistic work of significant quality, and be of lasting benefit to the applicant's experience and professional development. The activities assisted may include further study or training, professional research or the undertaking of a particular arts project.[424]

The first award in 1996 went to visual artist Jingalu Melissa Craig and in 1998 it went to another visual artist, Brenda L Croft. Visual artist simply known as Rea was the 2000 Award winner. Margaret Minatel from the NSW Ministry for the Arts comments that because the award is relatively young,

> It is difficult to assess its impact... New fellowships generally take a while to gain profile in the community. A lot of this can depend on how enthusiastically the media pick it up as a story and more importantly the reputation it gets through word of mouth in both the Indigenous networks and the more general community.[425]

It is clear that there is still much to be done to supporting Aboriginal writers. The next two chapters will consider the experiences of Native writers in Canada and Maori writers in Aotearoa drawing comparisons and contrasts which will provide some suggestions for further support mechanisms for Aboriginal writers in Australia.

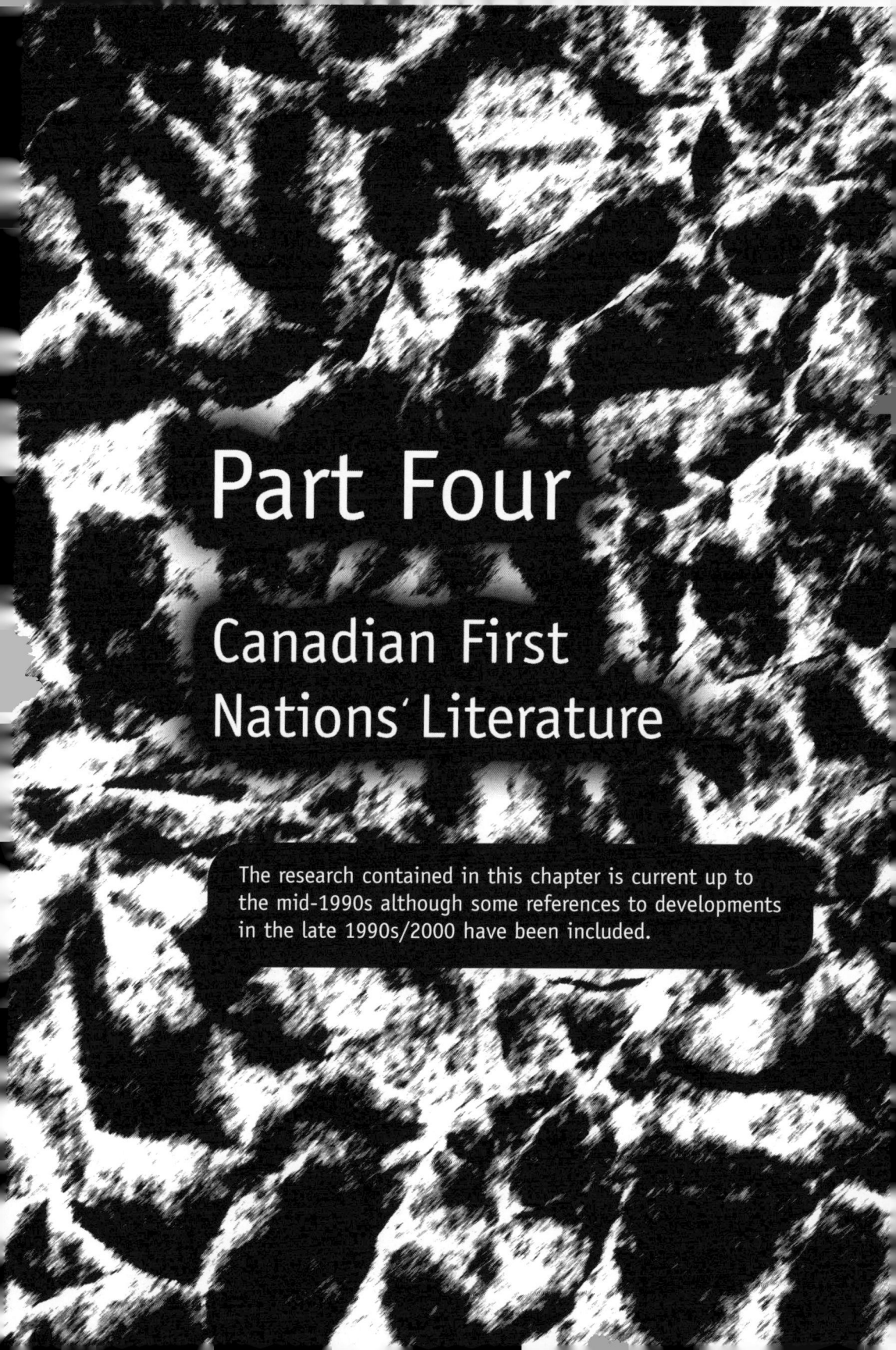

Part Four

Canadian First Nations' Literature

The research contained in this chapter is current up to the mid-1990s although some references to developments in the late 1990s/2000 have been included.

The following two chapters look closely at the similarities between the creative process engaged in by Aboriginal writers in Australia with those of First Nations' writers in Canada (including some mention of First Nations' American writers) and Moari writers in Aotearoa. The similarities stem from shared histories of invasion and colonisation including definitions of identity within and outside of Indigenous communities. These experiences in turn also impact upon the creative expressions of Indigenous writers.

I also discuss the striking differences between Aboriginal writers and publishers and those of Canada and Aotearoa. For example, the role and profile of the First Nations' writer is far more revered in Canada than that of the Aboriginal writer in Australia, in that the latter is generally still seeking rightful acknowledgement at festivals, on publishing lists and indeed, on library and book store bookshelves.

Another difference is the infrastructure in place for First Nations' writers in Canada. Canada appears to be much more supportive of creative and skills development than Australia. While Aboriginal writers can access writers grants through bodies like the Australia Council, there are no designated 'centres for learning' that focus on the skills that need to be developed if writers are to write well. Conversely the En'owkin International School of Writing in Penticton provides skills development through courses in creative writing facilitated by established First Nations' writers who work closely with students to assist them to find their own creative voice. This school is linked to Victoria University in British Columbia and is an example of what *could* also be done in Australia to support Aboriginal authorship. First Nations' people in Canada are also secure in the knowledge that there is a pool of treaty money that, if desired, can be used to finance publishing ventures. This kind of financing does not exist in Australia. Rather, Indigenous publishers compete alongside non-Indigenous publishers for government funding. That community support and advanced infrastructure for First Nation writers in Canada is much stronger than that available to Aboriginal writers in Australia could be a result of the fact that Canada was colonised almost 300 years prior to Australia. Canada has therefore had more time, and more recently treaty money, to develop provided mechanisms to support their Indigenous writers.

There are marked differences between the status of the Maori writer and that of the Aboriginal writer. The most obvious difference is that Maoris comprise a larger proportion of the New Zealand population than Aborigines do in Australia. The physical presence of Maori in society, their role in national politics, the education system and the media, supports their rightful positioning and profile in general society, and by association, this position is reflected in Maori writings. By way of contrast, Aboriginal writers often use their writing as a vehicle for asserting their rightful place not only as the First Peoples of Australia, but also as significant contributors to every aspect of Australian society.

Another key difference between the status of the Maori writer and the Aboriginal writer results from linguistic phenomena. While there was/is only one Maori language there are hundreds of Aboriginal Australian languages and dialects to be written and recorded, to then be read (where possible) by only small audiences. In context, this means that there is a much broader readership for Maori language work amongst Maori and Pakeha, than for Aboriginal works written in Indigenous dialects in and outside Australia.

Like many colonised nations, including Australia, there was a strong First Nations' literature in Canada before the arrival of the first Europeans. This was also an oral literature, used not only to pass on history, religion and laws but also to provide artistic expression and entertainment within communities. This literature also contributed to providing cultural identities for tribes and distinguished one from another.

Also similar to the Australian experience was the neglect and misrepresentation of First Nations' peoples in the written history of North America after colonisation. Many now see the emergence of contemporary First Nations' authors onto the literary scene in Canada as the major development in the literature of North America in the last three decades.

Canadian First Nations' Literature

George Copway was the first Canadian First Nations' writer to publish a book in English in 1847 with his autobiography, *The Life, History and Travels of Kah-ge-ga-gah-bowh*. The book became an instant success, was reprinted six times by the end of the first year and republished in London in 1850 under the title, *Recollections of a Fresh Life*. In 1850 Copway also wrote what he considered to be the first volume of Indian history written by an Indian, titled *The Traditional History and Characteristic Sketches of the Ojibwa Nation*. His success as a writer brought him international recognition, and tours of Europe lead him to write of these experiences in *Running Sketches of Men and Place in England, France, Germany, Belgium and Scotland* in 1851.

Pauline Johnson was another of the first First Nations' authors published in Canada with *The White Wampum* in 1895. After she died in 1913, almost six decades passed before Aboriginal authors reappeared on the Canadian literary scene. The politics of the late 1960s and early 1970s brought about a surge in Aboriginal literature. Like the works being penned by Australian Aboriginal writers at the time, the works being published in Canada were political in content and angry in tone.[426] Such works, also considered 'protest literature', included Howard Adams' *Prison of Grass: Canada From the Native Point of View* (1975), Howard Cardinal's *The Rebirth of Canada's Indians* (1977), Maria Campbell's *Half-Breed* (1973) and *We Are Metis* (1980) by Duke Redbird. Although these works were written in a mainstream literary style thanks to college and university educations, much of the writing was done by authors who were part of the residential school system (a system comparable to the boarding school system that many 'stolen' Aboriginal children in Australia were placed in).

The literary field saw publication of works by First Nations' authors fall in the late 1970s and early 1980s, and yet a distinct First Nations' literature did begin to appear using the traditional storytelling styles of earlier writing. It was soon replaced with new methods of expressing an Aboriginal voice, something that was termed by well-known First Nations' author Lee Maracle as a, "contemporary Aboriginal voice".[427]

Today, names that dominate the First Nations' literary scene in Canada include the first wave of writers as well as new contemporary writers: Jeannette Armstrong, Lee Maracle, Joy Harjo, Jordan Wheeler, Drew Hayden-Taylor, Howard Adams, Richard Van Camp and Maria Campbell.

Like the state and territory boundaries designed by the colonising government in Australia that cross Aboriginal tribal, clan and language boundaries, in Canada and America, some reserves cross the United States /Canadian border. For many First Nations' people this border does not reflect their own delineation of land.

Theytus Books staffer and occasional writer Florene Belmore says that while First Nations' writers don't recognise the imaginary line drawn between Canada and the United States, the content of some of the material between writers in the United States and those in Canada can show a difference in experience. This is a result of the fact that different methods of oppression were employed by the governments of the United States and Canada. Belmore also comments, "When they [writers] are writing about cultures, like Navajo, they are completely different to here. And while Cree is different to Mohawk, you are more familiar with it because you travel across Canada."[428]

While talking about First Nations' literature in Canada, then, I have also included authors like Joy Harjo and Thomas King, both from the United States, but who are heavily influential and recognised within Canada by both First Nations' and non-First Nations' peoples.

Similar to the Australian experience of the early 20th century, defining Aboriginality or 'Indianness' in Canada by blood-quantum or caste is very much a part of life today, with First Nations' peoples defined and categorised in many ways.

Indians of Canada call themselves Aboriginal, as well as 'First Nations'" and 'Native People'. There are also four categories of 'Natives' in Canada and they are known as Status Indians, non-status Indians, Metis and Inuit. Status Indians are defined by their admittance to a general registry, their affiliation with one of the 569 bands in Canada (membership is not automatic) and they come under the jurisdiction of the Indian Act. Status Indians have the right to live on a reserve.[429]

Non-status Indians are those who may never have possessed legal status because their ancestors were never included in a legal treaty agreement or who gave up their status in order to assume citizenship rights, the right to vote and buy property.[430] This relinquishment of rights was similar to Aboriginal people applying for exemption from the Aborigines Protection Act(s) in Australia.

Metis Indians are the children of mixed-Aboriginal and European relationships, and while excluded from the Indian Act are still regarded as Aboriginal. Finally, Inuit people have a special relationship with the Canadian government even though they have no special treaty arrangement and are not included under the Indian Act. They are different to other Aboriginal peoples as they immigrated recently into Canada and share the genetic pool of Asian populations such as the Siberian Chukchi.[431]

A 1999 article in *The Forgotten People: The National Voice of Off-Reserve Indian and Metis Peoples Throughout Canada* explains that, since 1874, the Indian Act has defined who is entitled to be registered as an Indian for the purposes of the Act:

> Since 1901 the Census of Canada has used Aboriginal ancestry, or origin, to determine the size of Canada's population. The descent ruling for tracing ancestry, and the name of Aboriginal groups to be included, however, have changed considerably over the years from one census to the next. This is a reflection of the fact that 'Aboriginality' has never been clearly defined by governments.
>
> The Constitution Act, 1982, Section 35(2) simply states: "In this Act, aboriginal★ peoples of Canada include the Indian, Metis and Inuit peoples of Canada". No mention is made of "Treaty Indians" or "Registered Indians" or "Non-Status Indians' or "North American Indians" or any other type of Indian.
>
> Neither is it mentioned whether an Aboriginal person is someone who identifies as being one, or is a person with Aboriginal ancestry, however that might be determined.[432]
>
> (★ Aboriginal is spelt with lower case 'a' within the Constitution)

The article goes on to explain that, other than 'Registered Indians' (otherwise known as 'Status Indians'), there was and there still is institutional definition of the Aboriginal peoples referred to in the Constitution. This has meant that each federal government department has developed a definition of an Aboriginal person to suit respective program and budgetary administration.[433]

Interestingly, while the 1901 Census in Canada defined an Indian as a person who is a member of a tribe—Cree, Chippewa, Mohawk, etc—the rule of descent to determine tribal membership was unclear. The 1911 Census then dropped tribal membership and replaced it with matrilineal descent as the determiner of an 'Indian', while the descent of the rest of the Canadian population was determined according to patrilineal lines.[434] Most First Nations' have matrilineal descent in their clan and traditional leadership systems, but not all.[435]

In contrast to the Census, though, Indian Acts from 1874 until recent times have used patrilineal descent to determine 'Indian status'. These Acts also provide for non-Indian women who married Indian men to automatically gain Indian status so that access to attendant rights and benefits, whether they had Indian ancestry or not, was a matter of course. Causing great controversy across Canada was the fact that if a Status Indian woman married a non-Indian man, she automatically lost the status and rights afforded to her as an 'Indian'.[436] The root of the controversy was the value laden [read sexist] belief that a woman automatically attains or is subsumed into the status of her husband.

The Congress of Aboriginal peoples in Ottawa and its predecessor, the Native Council of Canada, have, however, always used ancestry (both matrilineal and patrilineal) in defining an Aboriginal person, and have never discriminated against Aboriginal people living in Canada—regardless of their 'status'.[437]

Within their rules for entry, the North American Native Authors First Book Awards defines North American Native Writers as,

> Any writer who meets the following criteria: provable Native (American Indian, Aleut, Inuit or Metis) ancestry; self-identification as a 'Native writer', and recognition by the Native community to which they claim to belong.[438]

This is similar to the definition currently used by the Australian Federal Government and the Australia Council for the Arts to define Aboriginal Australians.

In discussing the Indian Act(s) and the damage they have done to Aboriginal identity, television and radio writer Bob Rock comments that over decades and centuries in Canada,

> The Indian Act has created a certain type of 'Indian Act Indian', that has been processed and groomed and prepared and brainwashed into becoming even more bureaucratic and more 'copies-in-triplicate' than their white overlords and masters. They had to become this way to survive, to get ahead, to feed their children and families, to access government monies, to hold down top Indian Act jobs. These 'Indian Act Indians', in many cases, pretty much lost any vestige of Indian in them in the process of surviving and learning to live and thrive in a 'white world'.[439]

The thoughts of author Mary Gloyne Byler on this issue are comparable to Jackie Huggins' comments about Aboriginal identity in the context of the Sally Morgan debate:[440]

> There is more to being an American Indian—Apache, Seneca, Hopi, or whatever tribe—than can be acquired through an act of will, a course of study, or discovering an Indian ancestry somewhere in the family tree. It is not an intellectual choice. In short, being Indian is growing up Indian: it is a way of life, a way of thinking and being. Shaped by their own life experiences, non-

Indians lack the feelings and insights essential to a valid representation of what it means to be an American Indian.[441]

Metis author Graham Scott Angus also talks about the discrimination from both the First Nations' and non-Native communities suffered by First Nations' peoples of mixed descent:

> A lot of the full-blooders look down their noses at those of us of mixed race. Well, the whites look down on us all: shaken, stirred or straight up. So I guess it's bully for us all then, eh? I might not look like an Indian, but I tell you, the blood runs awful thick in my veins. Besides, it's not the colour of my skin that matters. It's what I have in my heart, and the strength of my spirit, that's what makes me what I am.[442]

Taking into account the way the Canadian Government defines First Nations' peoples alongside how First Nations' peoples define themselves, we can consider whether or not Indigeneity impacts on the writing produced by First Nations' writers and whether it has created a First Nations' genre or not. Views vary on the issue of a First Nations' genre: some writers do not want to be 'ghettoised'; others believe that First Nations' writers actually create new genres relevant to their writing.

Greg Young-Ing, Managing Director of Theytus Books, is sure that novels are the strongest genre for First Nations' writers in terms of sales, because they are the books that become best-sellers.[443] Bob Rock says he would hate to think that First Nations' writers were limited on any frontier of writing, and that there are risks associated with lumping all writing into one 'genre' and calling this genre 'Aboriginal literature'.

Emma LaRocque on the other hand, says that First Nations' writers have been creating new genres in Canadian English literature, an occurrence that has been largely missed by readers and critics. She gives an early example:

> The more overt protest books of the 1970s often combined their sharp analyses of society with wit, humour, poetry, history, anthropology, and /or personal reflections. Authors turned to facts of biography to humanize the much dehumanized 'Indian'. Instead of being read as new genres, they were attacked as biased and parochial. Few bookstores, libraries or professors knew what to do with First Nations' writing that crossed or integrated well-defined genres, styles, or schools. First Nations' writing soon got thrown into one pot variously called 'First Nations' Literature' or 'First Nations' Studies'.[444]

Having said that, LaRocque acknowledges that while, "...Native literature has become a new genre...categorizing of literature on the basis of ethnicity, gender or politics also raises the spectre of ghettoisation."[445] This ghettoisation of First Nations' literature is what concerns LaRocque most because of its effect on First Nations' writers and writing,

> The lumping of our writing under the category 'Native' means that our discussion of issues and ideas that are universally applicable may not reach the general public…And what about Native writers who do not write about Native themes? What about Native women writers who do not write specifically or only about Native women, and so get excluded from 'women's writing' shelves?[446]

This compares with Aboriginal Australian writing being categorised as 'Australiana' and losing its potential broader marketing. There is however, the deeper issues of the stereotypical association of Aboriginal peoples with ghettoes.

Canada enjoys a large pool of anthologies of First Nations' writing due to the growing need for Aboriginal literary texts in the education system. The most well known anthology is *First People, First Voices* (1983) edited by non-Native Penny Petrone, although the first anthology was *I Am An Indian* published in 1969 and edited by non-Native Kent Goodman. This book included the work of such notable writers as Chief Dan George, Howard Adams and Duke Redbird. The first First Nations'-edited anthology appeared in 1984 with Beth Brant's *A Gathering of Spirit: a Collection by North American Indian Women*.

Just as Australian Aboriginal authors are concentrated in the mediums of autobiography and biography, so too are First Nations' authors. Maria Campbell's *Halfbreed* (1973) is undoubtedly the most well-known and widely read book, alongside Ruby Slipperjack's *Honour the Sun* (1987). The popularity of these books can be compared to that of Morgan's *My Place*, even though *Halfbreed* is far more confrontational than *My Place*. The acceptance of such a work in Canada occurs though because Native Americans were colonised 500 years ago (300 years before Aboriginal Australians), they have Treaty rights and higher socio-economic status, and more often hold positions of power in government. The role of First Nations' in society generally is much stronger and accepted than that of Aborigines in Australia. These factors contribute to the acceptance of First Nations' literature beyond the exotic notions of First Nations' peoples of the past and allows for wide reading of books on real political issues.

There is also a strong pool of fiction writers. Beatrice Culleton was the first First Nations' writer to attempt the novel with *In Search of April Raintree* (1983). Jeannette Armstrong's *Slash* (1985), was still in print in 1999. Other established fiction writers include Louise Erdrich (from the USA) Thomas King (whose *Medicine River* in 1990 was made into a television film), Lee Maracle and Richard Van Camp.

The short story form is also the preferred genre of many writers. *Achimoona* (1985) is a well known collection of ten short stories written as the result of a workshop conducted by Maria Campbell, and includes the work of Jordan Wheeler, author of the popular novella *Brothers in Arms* (1989). Thomas King also uses short stories to project his humour in *One Good Story, That One* (1993).

The largest development in First Nations' writing in Canada has been in the area of drama, with a growing number of First Nations' women writing for theatre. Maria Campbell, Margo Kane, Alanis King Odjig and others add to the list of men writing in the area, including Tomson Highway, whose plays *The Rez Sisters* (1988) and its sequel, *Dry Lips Oughta Move to Kapuskasing* (1990), both won awards and brought the author into international limelight.

Authors that have published in the areas of history, the social sciences, education and biography include Olive P. Dickason, Marlene Brant Castellano, George Sioui, Howard Adams, Anne Anderson (Cree linguist), Terry Lusty, Beth Brant, and Joseph Bruchac, to name just a few.

Editors Beverly Slapin and Doris Seale (from the USA), believe that poetry is also an important form of expression for First Nations' people as it is a way, "...of being able to make the words of an alien language speak for us."[447] Jeannette Armstrong, Kateri Akiwenzie-Damm and Daniel David Moses are some of those writers that have proved this to be true. First Nations' writer David Groulx comments that Aboriginal writers in Canada are drawn to poetry because, "It is a good fit with our oral cultures and more easily adaptable with an oral tradition than say the novel".[448] Because there are also many Aboriginal poets in Australia, Groulx's comment suggests that in the transition between oral and written expressive mediums, poetry is probably the first port of call in terms of being employed as a literary medium for the personification of cultural change.

And, as with Australian Aboriginal writing, oral histories are popular with First Nations' writers, with many of the works, such as, *Enough Is Enough, Aboriginal Women Speak Out* (1987) and *Our Grandmothers' Lives In Their Own Words* (1992). These works tell the stories of First Nations' women in their original voices.

While First Nations' writers are increasingly writing books for First Nations' children, when compared to the well-developed Aboriginal Australian children's list, this genre is as yet under-developed. Ethnic stereotyping also seems to be pervasive in the First Nations' books that are written for children. When compiling an annotated bibliography of children's books for First Nations' readers in 1987, Mary Gloyne Byler examined well over 600 books over a four year period, but rejected two out of three because the contents or illustrations were "conspicuously offensive".[449] A closer look at the remaining 200 or so books was also discouraging for Byler, who commented that the prevalence of more subtle stereotypes, misconceptions and clichés led to further rejections and the final outcome was that a 'good book' was one written by a First Nations' author. Byler commented,

> While non-Indian authors may produce well-written and entertaining children's books featuring American Indians, there is little in their stories that tells us much about American Indians. We do learn what non-Indians imagine Indians to be, or think they should be.[450]

161

Byler also commented that there were few children's books written by First Nations' authors, and suggested that this was a result of the lack of interest by publishers in promoting the work of First Nations' authors of children's books.[451] Subsequent to Byler's report though, the list of children's authors and books has grown. It now includes works by Freda Ahenakew (*How The Mouse Got Brown Teeth* [1988] and *How the Birch Tree Got Its Stripes* [1988]), Joseph McLelland (*The Birth of Nanabosho, Nanabosho Dances* and *Nanabosho Steals Fire* [1989]) and Thomas King (*A Coyote Columbus Story* [1992]).

Identity and Authenticity

With the various definitions of 'Indian' identity in mind, we can now consider what can and cannot be classified as First Nations' literature and the role of the First Nations' writer.

Defining writers by race was an issue for Kimberley M. Blaeser (from the USA), who spoke at the Returning the Gift Festival in July 1992. Blaeser discussed the distinction often made between 'Native Americans' and 'Poets'. In her view such distinctions implied that First Nations' American contributors to a magazine weren't also poets. She asked, "Why not use the title 'Native American Poets?'" adding that, "Clearly the mentality that makes a distinction between First Nations' Americans who are poets and real writers, between First Nations' Americans who teach at universities and real professors is to be resisted."[452]

While First Nations' writers themselves see their role as more than just that of the entertaining writer, many see themselves (as do their audiences) as spokespeople, activists, educators, ambassadors and story-tellers. As Sherman Alexie points out,

> We are more than just writers. We are (Native) storytellers. We are spokespeople. We are cultural ambassadors. We are politicians. We are activists. We are all of this simply by nature of what we do, without even wanting to be.[453]

The spiritual responsibility of the writer is further elaborated by Harold Littlebird who says,

> Our responsibility as writers is to keep that sacredness alive with story, with songs, with our legends, with our myths, to instil this into our own children so that they begin to have a sense of well-being and wholeness in terms of from where creative power comes.[454]

Lance Henson, (from the USA) sees the responsibility of the First Nations' writer as, "…make[ing] our literature reflect the true reality of being tribal people,"[455] while Joseph Bruchac, (also from the USA) writer and editor of a number of anthologies, comments that there is also the additional responsibility of returning the gift of writing to other First Nations' people. Bruchac goes on to say,

> The current popularity of Native American writing has resulted not only in many non-Indians jumping on the bandwagon and writing about Native people, but also in some writers who are not Indian passing themselves off as Natives.[456]

So what then is First Nations' literature? It is as clear that in Canada, as in Australia, Aboriginal literature is written by Aboriginal people. Bob Rock says that Aboriginal literature is, "Literature written by and about Aboriginals via their many and varied life experiences the world over." Kateri Akiwenzie-Damm comments that, "It is literature written by Aboriginal people who have some awareness of their Aboriginality."[457] But Blaeser—like Bellear and Wharton who question the definition of 'Aboriginal' Australian literature,[458] offers that, "[The thing that] makes writing Native American [is] the author's identity, the subject of the work, or the style and approach of the writing."[459]

Florene Belmore, former student of the En'owkin Centre, says that she would define First Nations' writing as a First Nations' person writing about their experience whether it be on a reserve or in the city—it could be a love story or in any genre. She says that one of the things she came up against as a student at the En'owkin Centre was, "Oh, it's not First Nations' enough, you have to put someone in there with braids and brown skin to make sure you identify who you're talking about. It can't be just Jim and Karen."

First Nations' literature is also seen by many as a way of rewriting history, and 'telling the truth'. This is also typical of the way in which many Aboriginal authors in Australia see their role in writing, rewriting the history books, and giving an authentic voice to the Aboriginal experience (however diverse), across a range of genres.

In terms of the First Nations' writer's role, Jeannette Armstrong comments,

> Our task as First Nations' writers is twofold. To examine the past and culturally affirm toward a new vision for all our people in the future arising out of the powerful and positive support structures that are inherent in the principles of cooperation...Lies need clarification, truth needs to be stated and resistance to oppression needs to be stated, without furthering division and participation in the same racist measures. This is the challenge that we rise to.[460]

Armstrong goes on to say that First Nations' literature is the writer's responsibility to their people, to their survival, to their creator:

> We see our literatures, our voice, as a mechanism of healing ourselves, as medicine to the societies, bringing the possibility of a better future, a more healthy future, not only for our children, but also the children of other people in the world.[461]

In the Foreword to *The Colour of Resistance*, Connie Fife writes,

> The act of literary creation and our oral past have merged into a medium through which we can pass on not only the truth of our history but the

moment in which we now exist. Our past, the present and the future come together through words that are 'living' from their first conception to the time when the reader finds her own meaning in them.[462]

Greg Young-Ing defines Aboriginal literature as an emerging body of literature by Aboriginal people in North America and beyond, that takes into account the different contemporary experience and the dualistic nature of the Aboriginal experience today, living in both the mainstream culture and the Aboriginal world:

> I think it's got a lot of characteristics that are different to European literature, a different spiritual base, a different body of characters and different body of knowledge and a different culture to draw upon. Literary techniques that Aboriginal writers use are often based on traditional techniques and Aboriginal cultures. It's a really interesting and vibrant body of literature and it's still being developed.

Lakota writer Kelly Morgan also identifies the healing process inherent in the publication and dissemination of First Nations' literature to a broad audience commenting, "There's some medicine that non-Natives don't want to swallow. There are reasons for medicine. I think there's a big sickness in the world literature that some of our writings can assuage, if not necessarily cure."[463]

LaRocque believes that to discuss First Nations' literature you need to deal with a number of issues including,

> Voicelessness, accessibility, stereotypes, appropriation, ghettoisation, as well as the linguistic, cultural, sexual, and colonial roots of experience and, therefore, of self-expression—all issues that bang at the door of conventional notions about Canada and about literature.[464]

But of defining First Nations' literature generally, she comments,

> [It] is protest literature in that it speaks to the processes of our colonisation: dispossession, objectification, marginalisation, and that constant struggle for cultural survival expressed in the movement for structural and psychological self-determination.[465]

Critic Penny Petrone agrees that defining First Nations' writing is, "Grounded in the political and social realities of life on Canada's reserves and in its urban centres, while also being rooted in oral tribal traditions."[466]

It is therefore important to consider the role identity plays in writing by First Nations' people. Akiwenzie-Damm believes that a writer writes best about what he/she knows and that there is "no truly 'objective' writer because one's beliefs and identity are reflected in one's writing."

So when considering First Nations' literature today and its place in Canadian and world literatures, writers themselves are positive in their view. Blaeser confidently states that First Nations' literature is a force to be reckoned with, having a distinct literary identity. She comments, "We have a place in world literature, recognised and unrecognised by the intellectual elite. May our place always be one of survival, of continuance and of revolution."[467]

Publisher and writer Kateri Akiwenzie-Damm thinks First Nations' writing is booming but admits that writers need more Indigenous publishers and First Nations' audiences. Similarly, Aboriginal Australian authors, also need to foster their own audiences. However, student Janine Willie is negative about the role and status of First Nations' literature today, commenting, "The odd First Nations' text does find its way on to university literature courses either in a Canadian literature course that seeks token representation or on post colonial courses — courses dealing with literature of 'the Other'".[468] This comment, though, emanates from the then contemporary post-structuralist theories in vogue in literary criticism.

Individual First Nations' writers have different inspirations and motivations for their writing, but many are driven by the desire to speak to, and for, their own Aboriginal nations. For example Akiwenzie-Damm wants to give voice to who she is as an Anishnaabe, while Rodger W. Ross is inspired by his own people, the Cree Nation commenting, "Within our culture there are many legends which I find fascinating, but there are also many recent historical stories which need to be told."[469] Blaeser also talks about the purpose of First Nations' writers:

> We can write a revolution. Filling our writing with the many voices from our tribal communities and families, according them status is one way of attempting to work for the continuance of family and community. Filling our writing with ceremony and song is more than a mere recording and it is more than pretty literature. It becomes an act of survival.[470]

Is there a First Nations' style?

Bob Rock feels there are many and varied 'Aboriginal styles' in Canada, rather than just one distinct one. Blaeser nevertheless believes that the distinctions that have been made regarding the style, method, themes and plots of Indigenous writing are for the most part legitimate. She comments,

> Native Americans have a distinct and important voice in American letters, a voice that speaks about what William Bevs calls 'homing in', a voice that speaks about natural cycles, spiritual connections, family, community and place. We are not content, however, with the kind of attention that says merely the writing by Indian people is unique in this or that way.[471]

Willie points out the different types of literatures created due to the effects of mixing of First Nations' and non-Native cultures, the result of oppression and colonisation commenting,

> It is pointless to argue that non-Native culture has had no impact on the writings of First Nations' people. Issues such as language, translation, education and the overarching influence of Western culture have played a role in the transformations from oral to written literatures. Therefore, these literatures can

be seen in varying degrees as being influenced by bicultural or multicultural experiences.[472]

Like Aboriginal writers in Australia, First Nations' writers in Canada often write from personal experience and therefore themes within genres can be similar. This is a result of a shared Aboriginal experience and perspective regardless of how diverse the particularities of the experiences are. Rock writes predominantly on Metis cultural issues because, he says, "It is what I am and it is what I know. And these Metis issues require my attention." Themes common in First Nations' American writing are similar to those of Australian Aboriginal writers. First Nations' literary journal *Gatherings Vol. III*, for example, has sections on "Identity", "Colonisation" and "Home".

The experience of being removed from their community and sent to residential schools has a strong presence in First Nations' literature in Canada. So too in Australia. Canadian works on this theme include Drew Hayden-Taylor's play, *Only Drunks and Children Tell The Truth*, which deals on one level with the 'scoop up' of First Nations' children that tore them from their families and placed them in non-Native homes.[473] Other works on the theme of 'stolen children' include Isabelle Knockwood's *Out of the Depths*, which not only documents the author's own 11 years at the Shubenacadie Residential school, but also includes the first-hand accounts of several other survivors of the school. *My Name Is Seepeetza* by Salish writer Shirley Sterling is another book on the theme of residential schooling. Semi-autobiographical, the story tells the tale of Martha Stone's years in a residential school in British Columbia, and includes the horrific beatings, psychological and sexual abuse, and the starvation diets that were part of school life there. As in Australia, the 'outing' of these experiences are profoundly healing and do much to compel the broader public into owning the true history of the oppression of Indigenous peoples.

The women's anthology, *Reinventing the Enemy's Language*,[474] edited by USA writers, Joy Harjo and Gloria Bird, includes 80 women writers from 50 Aboriginal nations in North America, and has as its central theme, the reclamation of individual voice and collective experience. This is both a personal and a political work and could be compared with the anthology *The Strength of Us As Women: Black Women Speak* (2000) compiled by Kerry Reed-Gilbert which includes the political and personal perspectives of 19 Aboriginal women from around Australia. LaRocque identifies common themes in First Nations' womens' writing. These include, "birthing, children, nurturing, sense of vulnerability, fear of violence, wife battering and sexual assault."[475]

Individual writers also have themes and issues relevant to their own personal experience. For example, as well as writing about love of family, of culture, of the earth, and of oneself, Kateri Akiwenzie-Damm writes erotica because, she says, "I believe that our sexuality, our expression of our sexuality and of our love for one another as Indigenous peoples has been degraded and repressed. Erotica is one way to reclaim that." As Damm says, even the most personal and gender-based experience of the First Nations' writer can become political: "I write about issues that affect me. I write about being a woman, being an Anishnaabe woman, being from a colonised people."

The experiences of women are very prevalent in First Nations' writing, but aside from gender issues, can First Nations' writing be easily detected? Young-Ing's experiences as a reader and editor is much the same as Sandra Phillip's experiences at UQP. Young's comments are in keeping with Phillip's comments in that he agrees that you can tell by just reading the first few pages of a manuscript whether or not it has been written by an Aboriginal person: "Certain nuances, a certain essence, you can just tell. In a very rare case it could be difficult to tell, but generally, it's just so distinct that you can just tell by reading a few pages."

First Nations' writers also believe strongly that there are differences between First Nations' and non-Native writing. Akiwenzie-Damm notes the differences in terms of content. She says there is a lot of non-Aboriginal writing about breaking free of one's family and community and going out into the larger world to 'make it'. This is in contrast to First Nations' writing which, "tends to be the opposite: it's about finding one's way home, about strengthening connections and understanding one's place in the world."

The issue of cultural stereotyping by non-Native writers was considered in the preparation of *How To Tell the Difference: A Checklist for Evaluating Children's Books for Anti-Indian Bias*. This book was developed by Beverly Slapin, Doris Seale and Rosemary Gonzales who identified that the realities of First Nations' lifestyles were almost completely unknown to outsiders. As a result it was often difficult if not impossible, for example, for 'outsiders' to evaluate the appropriateness of children's books about American Indians. For this reason, they compiled a list of criteria in the hope that it would make it easier for teachers, parents, librarians and students to choose non-racist and undistorted books about the lives and histories of Native people.[476] The set of criteria asks the reviewer to consider the following,

1) Look at picture books—In picture books is "E" for "Eskimo"? "I" for Indian? In counting books are "Indians" counted? Do "Indians" have ridiculous names like "Indian Two Feet" or "Little Chief"?

2) Look for stereotypes—Are First Nations' peoples portrayed as savages, or primitive crafts people, or simple tribal people, now extinct? or are First Nations' peoples shown as human beings, members of highly defined and complex societies? Are First Nations' cultures oversimplified and generalised? Are First Nations' peoples all one culture, one style?

3) Look for loaded words—Are there insulting overtones to the language in the book? Are racist adjectives used to refer to Indian people?

4) Look for tokenism—Are First Nations' peoples depicted as stereotypically alike, or do they just look like whites with brown tones—as opposed to being depicted as genuine individuals?

5) Look for distortion in history—Is there manipulation of words like 'victory', 'conquest', or 'massacre' to justify Euro-American conquest of the First Nations' homelands? Are First Nations' nations presented as being responsible for their own 'disappearance'? Is the United States government only 'trying to help'? Is history put in the proper perspective: the First Nations' struggle for self-determination and sovereignty against the Euro-American drive for conquest? Does the story encourage children to believe that First Nations' people accepted defeats passively? or does the story show the ways in which First Nations' peoples actively resisted the invaders?

6) Look at life-styles—Are First Nations' communities presented in a condescending manner? Are there paternalistic distinctions between 'them' and 'us'? or is the focus on respect for First Nations' peoples and understanding of the sophistication and complexity of their societies? Is there an ethnocentric Western focus on material objects, such as baskets, pottery, rugs? Or does the writer show any understanding of the relationship between material and non-material aspects of life?

7) Look at the dialogue—Do the people speak in either a sort of 'early jawbreaker' or in the oratorical style of the 'noble savage'? or do they use language with the accomplished or articulate skill of those who came from an oral tradition

8) Look for standards of success—Does it take 'white' standards for First Nations' peoples to get ahead? or are First Nations' values of hard work, sharing, honesty and courage seen as integral to growth and development?

9) Look at the role of women—Are women completely subservient to men? Do they do all the work, while the men loll around, waiting for the next hunt? or are women portrayed as the integral and respected part of First Nations' societies that they really are?

10) Look at the role of elders—Are elders treated as a dispensable burden upon their people to be abandoned in times of trouble or famine; querulous, petulant, demanding, nagging, irritating or boring? or are elders treated as the loved and valued custodians of a people's history, culture and life ways? Are they cherished in the words of the writer as they were and are in the reality of the lives of First Nations' people?

11) Look at the effects on a child's self image—Is there anything in the story that would embarrass or hurt a First Nations' child? or are there one or more positive role models with which a First Nations' child can identify?

12) Look at the author's and illustrator's background—Is the background of the author and illustrator devoid of the qualities that enable them to write about First Nations' people in an accurate, respectful manner? Is there an ethnocentric bias which leads to misrepresentations or oversights? or is there anything in the author's and illustrator's background that qualifies them to write about First Nations' peoples? Do their perspectives strengthen the work?[477]

This is a relevant checklist that could be adapted as criteria for measuring appropriate literature for young readers in Australia.

Audience

It is clear that in any writing the editorial process will consider the audience the work is written for. 'Audience' is as big an issue for First Nations' writers in Canada as it is for Aboriginal writers in Australia. Who am I writing for? and How do I encourage and foster a First Nations' audience who are traditionally an oral people? are questions that are as relevant to First Nations' writers as they are for Aboriginal writers in Australia.

Kateri Akiwenzie-Damm says she writes for other Indigenous people, but she isn't sure who actually reads what she writes, commenting that it is, "Probably far more white academics and students than I'd like to believe!" This experience is also common to Australia where Aboriginal writers write outside of a defined Aboriginal market. A broader audience than hitherto acknowledged are naturally attracted to and read Aboriginal authors.

Emma LaRocque also points out a number of issues relevant to audience as she acknowledges that in the 1970s she experienced and studied what she calls the 'Native voice/white audience dynamic'.[478] She comments,

> The interactions were often poignant. On another level, we were again rendered voiceless no matter how articulate we were. Apparently unable to understand or accept the truth of our experiences and perceptions, many white audiences, journalists, and critics resorted to racist techniques of psychologically labelling and blaming us. We were psychologised as 'bitter', which was equated with emotional incapacitation, and once thus dismissed we did not have to be taken seriously.
>
> We were branded as 'biased', as if whites were not!…
>
> Our anger, legitimate as it was and is, was exaggerated as 'militant' and used as an excuse not to hear us.[479]

LaRocque also comments that First Nations' readers and writers do not necessarily understand English words and phrases in the same context as non-Native peoples: each group has different associations with the same words. For example, LaRocque finds it difficult to accept terms such as, "savage, primitive, pagan, medicine man, shaman, warrior, squaw, red-skin, hostile, civilization, developed, progress, the national interest, bitter, angry, happy hunting grounds, brave, buck, red-man, chief, tribe or even Indian", as neutral language, and so LaRocque puts quotation marks around these words. She also prefers to use what she calls 'soul language' (her First Nations' language) but she is then faced with the basic problem of translating Cree words into English.[480]

On top of these issues, LaRocque points out another issue facing writers in the last twenty years: that of having to educate audiences before even beginning to communicate with them. She comments,

> Our energies have been derailed from purely creative pursuits. Many speakers and writers have been cornered into the hapless role of apologists, incessant (and very patient) explainers and overnight experts on all things Native.[481]

As in Australia, the key issues for First Nations' writers are, getting published and having works understood by mainstream audiences. Akiwenzie-Damm comments that trying to get poetry published, especially when one comes from outside the mainstream literary tradition, is hard:

> Sometimes people don't understand or even try to understand, they just don't get it! What might be carefully crafted work, drawing on a rich tradition of storytelling, songs, cultural knowledge and so on, seems empty to them apparently, because they don't get the references.

Willie says it is difficult enough for mainstream writers to make a living at their profession, but the First Nations' writer has many additional obstacles that s/he has to face in getting his/her materials published and sold. One frequent obstacle, as pointed out by Akiwenzie-Damm, is that the texts are often not understood by non-First Native readers. Although the language used by many First Nations' writers—English—is basically understood by non-Native readers, the symbols, allegories, spiritual associations, general lifestyles and world view in the text is often beyond the grasp of the non-Native readers unless they are willing and able to familiarise themselves with the culture of the First Nations' author.[482]

Bob Rock also points out that Aboriginal writers continue to write out against the social and cultural injustices. These are not popular topics for mainstream publishing houses, who are invariably run by 'white folks' and 'white' power brokers who don't want to hear about, "let alone publish 'our' wants, needs, desires, 'our truths', 'our histories'". Rock also believes that First Nations' writers mature later and realise successes later than white writers and that they face additional obstacles that are cultural, traditional and perceptual. He adds,

> We not only have to prove ourselves creatively, grammatically, and stylistically, but we often have to think and write and read in a 'foreign' language—'English'—and translate our stories and our thoughts into the language of the overarching and dominant society, that also happens to be the source of our repression, degradation, and attempted assimilation, if not down right cultural genocide.

As a self-defined 'half-breed' writer David Groulx says, "The half-breed voice is always in danger of being drowned out by the shouting of the dominant society", and that while "white writers get writers block, First Nations' writers get writers blockade" because of what is expected,

> You have to write about the past because in the colonial mind that is where Aboriginal people live, because that is where it is safe to keep them, or the white settler. I want to say I am here in the present. I guess this is a form of racism because I am a husband, a father, a son, a man. But all that seems to get published are what I call my 'Indian poems'.

Similar to the experience of many emerging Aboriginal writers in Australia, Young-Ing points out that in Canada too, some of the older Aboriginal writers are dealing with a self-confidence problem, something he believes is left over from the residential school system and colonisation in general. In contrast, the younger generation, says Young-Ing, don't have the self-confidence problem, but have a lot of anger ('there's good reasons for it') that can affect the writing of the author and their ability to get published in the mainstream.

There is in Canada, as there is in Australia, the continuing issue of non-Aboriginal people writing about Aboriginal society, culture and issues. Penny Petrone's *Native Literature in Canada: From the Oral Tradition to the Present* was the first critical study of First Nations' literature and was completed in 1990. This text is used by many universities, colleges and individuals wanting to get an overview of First Nations' literature in Canada. However, many First Nations' writers do not support Petrone's work. Tsawataineul student, Janine A. Willie, who completed a Masters Degree at York University in 1996 in, "Theorising First Nations' Literatures: Searching for Effective, Culturally Appropriate Ways to Read and Understand Native Literatures", comments that she finds mainstream criticism of First Nations' literatures marred by their inability to leave behind their, "Eurocentric assumptions".[483]

Young-Ing, who has been in the business for over ten years says that as a community of writers and publishers, First Nations' peoples are still struggling with the issue of non-Native writing about and for First Nations', and that while some non-Native writers have agreed to step aside or would be very careful in their dealing with Aboriginal subject matter, the main problem is that people have staked their careers on so-called 'Aboriginal Studies' (similar to the Reynolds, Rowleys, Berndts and Shoemaker's in Australian Aboriginal studies and history). Young-Ing adds,

> There's a lot of art historians, curators, Aboriginal Studies professors, and those who work in Indigenous law who have their career and all their training invested in this. It would be hard for them to turn around and start doing something else. Maybe in the next generation with cultural awareness happening, non-Aboriginal people that would have gone into those areas of study will do something else, and that won't be so much of a problem in years to come.

Editors Jeanne Perreault and Sylvia Vance who compiled *Writing the Circle: Native Women of Western Canada* said that,

> Although we are not Native, we felt then, as we do now, that anything we could do to lift the blanket of silence would be of value. We also knew that systemic racism and sexism in our society makes every stage of writing and publishing less accessible to Native women than it is to others.[484]

Because the editors' primary goal was to give voice to First Nations' women through the anthology they placed no restrictions or boundaries on content or forms the authors chose to use.

In terms of writing about First Nations' people and culture generally, Bob Rock believes non-Native writers can write whatever they like, because, "we live in a so-called free society." But he puts the onus on the Aboriginal readership to be intelligent and educated enough to realise what the 'non-Aboriginal writer writing about Aboriginal issues' is all about.

Kateri Akiwenzie-Damm continues the discussion saying that if a non-Native writer can be honest about their position as an outsider and yet still try to fully understand the issue, then maybe it's all right for them to write in the area. But she adds immediately that she thinks,

> It's an extremely difficult thing for a non-Aboriginal person to do well because not many have the knowledge of Aboriginal issues. Too many have a tendency to try to speak FOR Aboriginal people, and we are fully capable of speaking for ourselves so it's a bogus and condescending stance. I think it probably works best when they are writing to a non-Aboriginal audience to try to enlighten them on Aboriginal issues.

Blaeser also makes a pertinent point that reflects the inverted racism of some 'whites' writing in the area saying: "The racism lies, not in the claim to understand the identity and literature of another, but in the claim to understand it *better* than the spokesperson."[485]

Even with the arguments against non-Native writing in the area, Emma LaRocque points out that it is often the colonised peoples alone that "end up cleaning up the debris colonizers have left" and therefore end up doing all the writing to fight racism. In this sense, LaRocque rightly points out "Natives cannot be the only ones responsible for confronting racism and hate literature of this magnitude."[486]

Joy Asham Fedorick has devised a 'Self-Censorship Checklist'[487] for those contemplating using First Nations' stories in their writing. This list may be compared to Jackie Huggins' checklist for non-Aboriginal people considering writing about Aboriginal people and their culture.

Self-censorship Checklist

1) Am I doing this with permission, both before undertaking and before releasing completed artwork or writing?

2) Do I have consent of those affected?

3) Have I attempted to use "as near as... that man's words"?

4) Have I "given their dues to the folk I have described"?

5) Am I being humble? honest? responsible? caring? open minded and aware of my own filter screens?

6) Am I doing this to support the emergence of Aboriginal artists?

7) Am I art driven?

8) Am I courteous and fair?

The Disgruntling Negatives

1) Am I caricaturising instead of characterising and thus increasing negative stereotypes?

2) Am I commercially driven?

3) Am I reading my own cultural interpretation into what I perceive?

4) Am I failing to credit sources?

5) Are my intentions destructive?

6) Am I being arrogant? dishonest? untruthful? disrespectful?

First Nations' literature in the future

Kateri Akiwenzie-Damm sees the future of Aboriginal literature in international alliances, joint projects and market sharing saying, "If we can't find the audiences at home we have to reach out to other Indigenous peoples since they are the ones who will most likely be interested and who will better understand the work."

However, the academic arena is were Blaeser, Willie and Morgan see the future of First Nations' literature. Blaeser believes that First Nations' people will generally remain invisible in society and teaching in grade schools will not improve until Indian literature is studied as a legitimate literature in colleges.[488]

Willie sees the future of First Nations' literatures in the academic world as something that needs to be reconsidered and re-evaluated with significant input from First Nations' authors, teachers and scholars. She says: "With this input, I believe that First Nations' literature as an academic field of study can move beyond its colonised position of condescension to which it is currently relegated in the mainstream Canadian academic system.[489]

Kelly Morgan's thinking is in line with Willie's. She comments that the study of American Indian literature should be separate from the study of American literature because American Indian literature is both written specifically by American Indians, and is about American Indian people and their cultures.[490]

Joseph Bruchac sees the job of the First Nations' writer in the 21st century continuing to be a simple one, following the hard road of writing:

> Despite anger and sorrow, despite loss and pain, to write out of the spirit and the memory, to write out of the turmoil and the possibility, to know your heart and the heart of your people, to stand in that place and to write.[491]

Publishing

Gathering Strength, the 1996 Report of the Royal Commission into Aboriginal Peoples in Canada noted that while mainstream publishers, like those in Australia, have published numerous books *about* Aboriginal people, Aboriginal authors almost without exception, have been published by small, independent presses. It also stated that in major bookstores creative works by Aboriginal authors are usually found in the Aboriginal Studies section, not the literature section.[492]

The 1995 National Aboriginal Publishers' Conference was the first gathering of over 30 Aboriginal-controlled publishing operations in Canada. Featured presenters and workshop facilitators included Jeannette Armstrong, Maria Campbell, Darlene Speidel and Annais Allen (Aotearoa). Australian Aboriginal editors Rachel Bin Salleh and Sandra Phillips also attended representing Magabala Books.

In a support letter to Greg Young-Ing who was Coordinator of the Conference, Ovide Mercredi, National Chief of the Assembly of First Nations' in Ontario wrote,

> Aboriginal controlled publishing is an important entity as it increases cultural awareness among Aboriginals and non-Aboriginals as well as promotes Aboriginal perspectives. Your Conference will be a time for Aboriginal publishers to learn from each other and establish contacts.[493]

From that conference the Circle of Aboriginal Controlled Publishers was established.

The success and growth of First Nations' publishing in Canada has been due to the support and development of small presses across the country. These presses include Pemmican (Winnipeg, Manitoba), Theytus Books (Penticton, BC), Fifth House (Saskatoon, Saskatchewan), Women's Press (Toronto, Ontario), Seventh Generation Publishers (Toronto), Press Gang (Vancouver, BC), NeWest

(Edmonton, Alberta), Sister Vision (Toronto), William-Wallace (London, Ontario) and Coteau Books (Regina, Saskatchewan).

The Circle of Aboriginal Publishers has recently been superceded by the Aboriginal Book Publishers of Canada, a group that advocates on behalf of Aboriginal book publishing.

In 1980 **Theytus Books** established itself as the first publisher in Canada to be under Aboriginal ownership and control. The company is staffed by Aboriginal people and has published over 60 titles. After 20 years of operation, the company continues to carry out its mandate of producing quality literature presented from an Aboriginal perspective with the highest possible level of cultural authenticity and integrity.

Theytus' general philosophy has remained intact since its inception and is contained in the company's name. Theytus is a Salishan word which means, "preserving for the sake of handing down".[494] The name 'Theytus' was chosen to symbolise the goal of documenting Aboriginal cultures and world views through books. Beyond that, Theytus strives to play an active and important role in the development of Aboriginal literature through the promotion of Aboriginal authors. Theytus is also a member in good standing with the Association of British Columbia Book Publishers and the Association of Canadian Publishers.

In 1999 Theytus had two members on staff. Greg Young-Ing took over from founder Randy Fred in 1990 as the Managing Editor and, in 1999, design artist Florene Belmore was employed. The Press averages eight books per year and only publishes books by First Nations' authors. The authors they have published include well-known writers like Jeannette Armstrong, Drew Hayden Taylor, Jordan Wheeler, Dr Howard Adams and Maria Campbell.

Like Magabala Books and Aboriginal Studies Press, Theytus Books has an editorial committee that chooses which manuscripts the house will publish. On determining what to publish Young-Ing comments,

> We do turn away writing that is definitely worthy of publication, but we can only do a certain number of books each year so we have to send them back to the author, and sometimes if I have the time or if I think of it I will recommend some other publishers they might try, but then it's hard for new authors to get published.

Theytus have published in most genres including First Nations' Studies, fiction, children's, humour, non-fiction, anthologies, legal, political science, history, art, poetry, academic, and publish their own annual literary journal *Gatherings*.

Pemmican Publications was incorporated in October 1980 as a Metis publishing house. The purpose of the press is to provide opportunities for Metis and Aboriginal people to tell their own stories from their own perspectives.

Pemmican also publishes books by non-Aboriginal writers whose works are related to Metis and Aboriginal issues.[495]

Pemmican has established itself as a leading publisher of children's books, in addition to publishing fiction and non-fiction aimed at the general audience. The Press is committed to publishing books which depict Metis and Aboriginal cultures and lifestyles in a positive and accurate manner, and which address Metis and Aboriginal historical, social and contemporary issues.

Pemmican's books have earned numerous distinctions and in 1995 six Pemmican titles were chosen for inclusion on the list of "the best in Canadian children's books".[496]

Louise Erdrich, author of *The Bingo Palace* (HarperCollins, 1994) and *The Bee Queen* (Harper Perennial, 1993), says,

> The books available from Pemmican Publications are varied, fascinating and illuminating. Many of them are a must read for anyone who seeks to understand the historical and contemporary situations of those who settled the Plains and those who were here first.[497]

The Saskatchewan Indian Cultural Centre has published books by and about Aboriginal people of Canada since 1972. The Centre has provided authors with the opportunity to publish their works and also promote their art. They have published books and flash cards for learning in English, Cree, Dakota, Lakota, Dene, and Saulteaux, while also producing tapes, posters, CDs, CD Roms, maps, calendars and videos.

The books published in English are in the following areas: arts and crafts, biographies, dance, education, elders, environmental education, games, government, language issues, war veterans, story books, Cree traditional stories, Saulteaux traditional stories, Dene traditional stories, and Nakota traditional stories.[498]

Seventh Generation in Toronto was another small First Nations' publishing house that was the inspiration of a group of First Nations' organisations in the city who wanted to start a publishing house in eastern Canada, with the aim of supplementing the work of places like Theytus in the west. Florene Belmore says that Seventh Generation was incorporated as not-for-profit in the province of Ontario in March 1995 and started by training people in the industry, bringing people like Jeannette Armstrong in to run workshops, and sending people to the Banff Centre, which ran a publishing program at the time. Before Belmore moved to Theytus Books she worked as a volunteer with Seventh Generation and trained with Paul Sesequasis and worked with Beatrice Coulton (from Pemmican). Belmore worked in the office for a year before taking the business home and working as publishing assistant.

A small press, Seventh Generation co-published with Banff Press a dance project in 1997 and put out only one book of poetry in 1998. *Chinook Winds:*

Aboriginal Dance Project captured in book form the fusion of contemporary and traditional Aboriginal dance, documenting the creation and performance of the first dance piece to emerge from the Aboriginal Dance Program at the Banff Centre for the Arts in July 1996. The book included photographs, articles and interviews. In 1998 the press put out the anthology *A Shade of Spring: An Anthology of New Native Writers* which further demonstrated how they publish strictly on a project by project basis. Belmore says that when she was there the press received about six manuscripts, two recommended from Pemmican Publications because they were books of poetry. A couple of manuscripts were from people outside Toronto who had heard about the publishing house. Seventh Generation, however, is no longer in operation.

Kegedonce Press is a First Nations'-owned and operated publishing company based at Neyaashiinigmiing, the traditional territory of the Chippewas of Nawash First Nation. Kegendonce was set up in 1993 to publish and promote the work of Indigenous writers, and is committed to supporting the work of Indigenous artists, graphic illustrators, designers, editors, printers and others in all levels of production.[499]

Kegedonce strives to foster the creative cultural expression of Indigenous Peoples through the publication of well crafted books by supporting activities that promote Indigenous literary development.

In 1999 Kegedonce released a poetry collection by Joseph A. Dandurand, *Looking into the eyes of my forgotten dreams*, a collection of poetry by David Groulx and Al Hunter, and a collection of short fiction by Richard Van Camp. In addition to its publishing efforts, Kegedonce has also provided editorial advice and assistance to several writers as well as reviewing and providing comments on numerous manuscripts. Kegedonce takes the time to respond to these enquiries as a demonstration of their responsibility to support and develop the work of emerging writers along with providing opportunities to discover manuscripts worthy of publication.

Kegedonce is run by writer Kateri Akiwenzie-Damm and has an administrative assistant/editorial trainee, Renee Abram. The Press was a member of the Circle of Aboriginal Publishers and continues to network with other Aboriginal publishers. Even though this group no longer operates, Kegedonce remains firmly dedicated to networking with, supporting, and creating linkages with Indigenous publishers and this has resulted in ongoing contact with four international Indigenous publishers: Jukurrpa Books (Institute of Aboriginal Development Press) and Magabala Books in Australia, and Huia Publishers and Kupu Ao Publishers in Aotearoa.[500] In 2000, Kegedonce jointly published *Skins: an anthology of contemporary Indigenous writing*, with Jukurrpa Books.

The **Association of Book Publishers of British Columbia** (ABPBC) have a series of catalogues highlighting titles published in British Columbia (BC) which support the BC curriculum. These books range in scope from picture books to reference books, from fiction to non-fiction, covering kindergarten through grade 12.

In 1995 the ABPBC published a catalogue of First Nations' titles which support the BC curriculum. The catalogue uses a whalebone carving graphic to highlight books where First Nations' people are known to have been involved in their preparation—either as authors, artists, editors or publishers.[501]

Even though there are a number of First Nations' publishers in Canada, Bob Rock, who has written a short manuscript on the meeting of Metis Senator John B. Boucher and visiting South African President Nelson Mandela in 1998, says he is still having trouble locating a publisher for it because he says, "It is Metis in flavour and structure…because it threatens the status quo and because it strives to 'reveal' and 'unmask' the federal government of Canada". Because of the difficulty in finding a publisher for his manuscript Rock believes that Aboriginal people of the world need an international publishing house, "one that does not 'ghettoize' and try to 'screw financially'", and will publish works like his that are educational and emotionally charged.

On why mainstream publishers don't publish First Nations' work, Damm says: "They don't understand the work. They don't believe there is an audience. They don't want to take the risk. They don't want to invest in Aboriginal writers. It's a very bottom line, short term view." Writers that have been published by big houses include Richard Van Camp (Douglas & McIntyre) and USA writer, Lousie Erdrich (HarperCollins).

Belmore also says that it's the dollar that rules whether or not authors will get published and that mainstream publishers probably look at the statistic that says that only 3% of the population is First Nations' and that only First Nations' people are going to buy books about First Nations' people, "And they're thinking they [First Nations' people] don't read books or buy books."

Greg Young-Ing also points out that most books *about* Aboriginal people (by non-Aboriginal authors) are coming through mainstream publishers because there's only a few Aboriginal publishers doing a few books a year, and focus on First Nations' writers. And while there are mainstream publishers known for having First Nations' lists, no house has employed a full-time First Nations' editor, instead choosing to use the services of people like Young-Ing on an ad hoc basis for reading and critiquing manuscripts that have Aboriginal subject matter or are written by Aboriginal authors.

First Nations' writers are also fortunate to be able to contribute *Gatherings*, a literary journal of Indigenous people's writing in North America. It is compiled and published annually by the En'owkin Centre and Theytus Books Ltd on behalf of the En'owkin International School of Writing.

Editing

First Nations' writers have had both positive and negative experiences with the editorial process. For poet, song writer, short story writer and journalist Rodger W. Ross, working with editors resulted in differing outcomes, from providing a second opinion on the structure of his stories to having a story rearranged to 'fit their agenda'. Bob Rock prefers to edit his own work, particularly if the editor is white, because, "The 'white' editor is only (and can only) be interested in the 'form' of an Aboriginal's work and certainly not the 'substance'". In line with Rock's thinking, Blaeser asks,

> Since cultural values are clearly embodied in a people's literature, since different cultures have different aesthetic values, by whose standards should Native people's writing be evaluated — that of another culture, or that of their own? Is there a danger that inclusion in the canons can work to advance the designs of assimilation, and how do we prevent our artistic and cultural identities from being manhandled and subsumed in the established system?[502]

In putting together the *Writing the Circle* anthology, the non-Native editors Vance and Perrault followed conventional editorial policy, making grammar, spelling and punctuation consistent through the manuscript, while also working with individual authors to rework and rewrite pieces at an author's request. The editors add, though, that,

> Any substantial editorial changes we wanted to make were only made with the approval of the individual writers and, sometimes that was not given. One observed that if you changed the words you change the feelings; another wanted her story left alone, since it already had been 'improved' by a helpful school teacher. The author had rewritten the piece from scratch, reclaiming the flavour of her own words that had been lost in the revision. Yet another, who initially had given us editorial carte blanche, insisted that a section we had removed be put back in, since it explained to First Nations' people why she was making a certain argument. Because of the issue of appropriation or misuse of literary production, we wanted to make sure that the words of each writer would appear just as she wished them to.[503]

LaRocque noted in her Preface to the book that "several Native women have felt that white editorship of Native women's literature constitutes appropriation".[504] However, LaRocque argues,

> The editors of this anthology have not appropriated this literature; instead, they have facilitated its possibilities and transmission…If I thought appropriation was involved, I would have removed my materials. For the record, however, I would not have tried to stop the publishing process.[505]

LaRocque also adds that "Native writers, like all writers everywhere, must have access to and must avail themselves of good conscientious editing and editors" and that there must be a "distinction between editing as craft and editing as ideology".⁵⁰⁶ The main concern for LaRocque is the development in skill of the First Nations' writer, whether facilitated by either First Nations' or non-Native editor.

The reviewing or critiquing of First Nations' works is as problematic for First Nations' writers as it is for Aboriginal writers in Australia, highlighted by Willie who comments that Petrone's opinions of Ruby Slipperjack's *Honour the Sun* are a perfect example of the prevailing attitude of many influential critics. Petrone wrote, "The story rambles episodically, in the present tense. The narrative voice of the child does not preach or make sociological comment; there is no self-pity—just the straightforward telling of the story."⁵⁰⁷ Willie finds this critique disturbing, calling it 'self-assured ethnocentrism', suggesting that Petrone's reference to the text containing 'no self-pity' contains a strong Euro-Canadian racist assumption that all texts about First Nations' lifestyles are either 'poor us' or 'wannabe' white stories and perhaps illustrates the fact that if this were Petrone's story, she would naturally feel self pity.⁵⁰⁸ This is similar to the expectations reviewer Theresa Kuilboer had of Kenny Laughton's, *Not Quite Men, No Longer Boys*.⁵⁰⁹

First Nations' writer Doris Seale (Santee/Cree/French/English) wrote the poem "On Getting Published"⁵¹⁰ about the non-Native influence in the editorial and publishing processes:

Knowing better,
They took our words,
so carefully set
down
in a certain way
one beside another –
we were intent to say
exactly what we meant –
And rearranged them
to fit
some concept of the mind
some alien bent
from another place and time.

We are at home
And not at home
Where even our words
May be used
Against us

In the course of publishing First Nations' writers, Young-Ing found the need to develop a house-style for Theytus Books due to editorial issues pertaining specifically to writing by and/or about Aboriginal Peoples. Through the process of developing and establishing such a house style, Young-Ing also found a rationale for the development of a separate Aboriginal Style Guide, which he believes should be written sometime in the near future. Young-Ing submitted his style guide as part of completing his Master of Publishing at Simon Fraser University in April 1999. The primary purpose of the Theytus Books' House Style Guide and a general Aboriginal Style Guide are to provide guidelines that will firstly produce literature reflecting Aboriginal realities from Aboriginal Peoples' perspectives, and secondly assist writers to write truthfully and insightfully about Aboriginal Peoples, respecting Aboriginal cultural integrity.[511]

The proposed editorial guidelines Young-Ing puts forward include the need for publishers to work in partnership with Aboriginal Peoples and authors to ensure that Aboriginal material is expressed with the highest possible level of cultural authenticity. The guidelines also require avoiding using 'past tense' when writing about Aboriginal Peoples except when the author is writing about a past event or using a quote which uses past tense.

Distribution

The issues around marketing and distribution of Aboriginal works in Canada, are similar to those in Australia. Even the Report of the Royal Commission on Aboriginal Peoples in 1996 recognised that the emergence of a distinct Aboriginal literature, "had not been met with much openness by Canadian publishing houses and bookstores".[512]

In June 1999, Florene Belmore started at Theytus Books as the Office Operations Manager and, within that role, she was expected to improve sales volumes by developing a data base, targeting First Nations' communities and working more on marketing and promotions. On who was buying the books, she comments,

> From what I can tell a lot of the sales go to universities and they [Theytus Books] are also involved with the trade book fair. But within the trade industry the book stores have different representatives dealing with that, but part of my job will be to target First Nations' communities more and to increase those sales.

One of the largest booksellers of First Nations' books in Canada is Twin Trails Books and Music. After owner Karen Pheasant learned that even the largest book chains in Toronto only carried a small selection of books targeted to a First Nations' audience, she knew her store on the Wikwemikong Reserve had to be comprehensive.[513] Pheasant says that with the recent announcement of the Canadian government's apology and $350 million earmarked for healing and recovery, the demand for books on health and well-being has increased dramatically. She says she's had professionals, psychologists, lawyers and people in the medical profession go to her store and say, "Quick, give me one book that will tell me about working in a First Nations' community," which she admits can't be done, but notes that it's a pretty good start.[514] Many of the books at Twin Trails come straight from First Nations' Publishing houses like Theytus Books and Pemmican.

The North American Native Authors Catalogue (indexed by tribe, author and by title) specialises in work by United States American Indian poets, writers, historians, storytellers and performers (it also includes First Nations' writers from Canada). Produced by Greenfield Press in New York it offers more than 800 titles from over 90 different publishers. The publications range from novels and books of poetry to children's literature, historical analysis, journals and newspapers, sacred traditions and more. All books and tapes listed in the catalogue are authored or co-authored by people of First Nations' American ancestry, and the catalogue grew out of the Native American Distribution Project, which has been selling books at Northeastern Pow Wows, book fairs, and by direct mail since 1980.

The overall goal of the North American Native Authors Catalogue is to increase the distribution of creative work by First Nations' Writers, and to raise public awareness of the range, strength, and beauty of contemporary First Nations' American writing, research, storytelling and performance.[515]

The American Native Press Archives at the University of Arkansas are the world's largest archival collection of Native American newspapers and periodicals. Established in 1983 as a clearing house for information on American Indian and Alaskan Native newspapers and periodicals, the years that followed saw its mission changed to collecting and archiving the products of the Native press and materials related to press history.

Support Mechanisms for First Nations' Writers

There are a number of support mechanisms that give aspiring First Nations' writers practical and literary assistance in becoming published authors. Organisations that assist such emerging writers include: the Saskatchewan Indian Federated College, Regina; the Gabriel Dumont Institute of Native Studies and Applied Research, Saskatoon; Native Earth Performing Arts Inc., Toronto; De-be-jeh-mu-jig Theatre group, Maitoulin Island, Ontario; and the En'owkin International School of Writing, Penticton. Funding from federal and provincial governments for writers and publishers also supports the growth of the industry, as well as support from literary journals like Whetstone, (based in the Department of English, University of Alberta), that regularly has special issues that include contributions from First Nations' authors.

Funding through the Canada Council for the Arts

In March 1995, the Canada Council for the Arts, (equivalent to the Australia Council for the Arts), acknowledged the need to improve its support for Aboriginal arts and literature by establishing a First Peoples Secretariat and a First Peoples Committee to Advise the Council. It also adopted a series of objectives and initiatives intended to assist Aboriginal artists in new and traditional forms.[516]

The Canada Council for the Arts has a grant program for Aboriginal Literature: Written and Spoken. This program offers three types of grants, which provide project assistance for the creation, production and dissemination of Aboriginal written and spoken literature. The 'Grants to Individuals' are for Aboriginal writers and story-tellers, and the 'Project Grants to Publishers and Collectives' are for projects from Aboriginal-controlled publishing houses, periodicals and collectives. 'Infrastructure Grants to Publishers' were previously available to Aboriginal-controlled publishers who had shown their strategic importance at the national level in the creation, development and dissemination of Aboriginal literature. Aboriginal Peoples include Status, Non-Status, Metis and Inuit people.[517] This grant is, however, no longer available.

The program fosters long-term benefits for the creation, production and dissemination of Aboriginal written and spoken literature through support of capital purchases, professional development, social projects or infrastructure development by Aboriginal writers, publishers and story-tellers living in Canada.

The program also supports radio broadcasting initiatives that focus on both written and spoken literary arts. Priority is given to the projects that are not eligible for other Canada Council programs, and initiatives by established artists in genres that are new to them are encouraged. Established writers and storytellers are those who have been professionally published or have the recognition of their peers and/or community.

'Grants to Individuals' provide a maximum of $2500 each for emerging writers and storytellers, and a maximum of $5000 for established writers or storytellers and 'Project Grants to Publishers and Collectives' provide a maximum of $15,000.[518]

The Report of the Royal Commission into Aboriginal Peoples in 1996 welcomed the Canada Council's initiative to fund Aboriginal writers. It noted that much more needed to be done however, to provide an adequate and fair level of support for Aboriginal writers and publishers, because,

> Although Aboriginal languages and culture remain deeply rooted in the oral tradition, literary expression of the Aboriginal voices is vital to reaffirming the

identities of Aboriginal Peoples: first, because literature presents an authentic voice to the majority population in a medium with which it is familiar; and second, because it presents that same authentic voice and mirror for their identity to Aboriginal people themselves. To survive in the dominant culture, Aboriginal people are becoming more and more conversant with the literary tradition and the Aboriginal stereotypes with which it is replete. The dissemination of authentic Aboriginal voices is essential to educate Canadians about the rich heritage, knowledge and culture of Aboriginal peoples and to expose misrepresentation and misappropriation of Aboriginal identities.[519]

The En'owkin Centre

Established in 1979 by Seven Bands of the Okanagan Nation, the En'owkin Centre's mandate is to preserve, perpetuate and promote Okanagan knowledge through education. The centre is governed by the Okanagan Indian Educational Resources Society with a board comprised of representatives appointed from each Okanagan Band and off-reserve First Nations' controlled service organisations. Since 1983 the En'owkin Centre has been a registered Federal Charity and a Provincially recognised non-profit society.[520]

The Centre has recently relocated from downtown Penticton to the Okanagan reserve in Penticton, British Columbia, and the Centre also houses and works with Theytus Books.

The En'owkin Centre offers a variety of programs for First Nations' adults including: Race Relations Program, Okanagan Language Teacher Training, Historical Research and Community Development, College Prep/ABE, Qwilmist High School Completion, Environmental/Indigenous Keeper Program, School of Writing and Visual Arts, Educational Seminars and Workshops and Cultural and Environmental Research.

Aside from the other specialised programs available at the En'owkin Centre is the International School of Writing. In conjunction with the University of Victoria, it provides a two-year post-secondary certificate in Creative Writing. Courses focus on creative writing forms and techniques and also explore the way in which the unique cultural experiences of First Nations' peoples are reflected in literature. A team of established First Nations' writers work closely to assist students to find their own voice through the creative process.

All programs at En'owkin are designed to encompass principles grounded in service to the individual, the family, the community and the environment, flowing out of the Okanagan spiritual conviction of the sacredness and interconnection of all life.

Wordcraft Circle of First Nations' Writers and Storytellers

Largely focussing on writers from the USA, the Wordcraft Circle of First Nations' Writers and Storytellers produces the journal *Moccason Telegraph* and has a set of by-laws for members with a Code of Ethics which requires members to pledge they will,

> Actively support the vision of Wordcraft Circle of First Nations' Writers and Storytellers to ensure that the voices of First Nations' writers and storytellers—past, present and future—are heard through the world.[521]

For the first time since its founding in October 1992, Wordcraft Circle presented honours and awards to First Nations' and non-Native writers and storytellers in a wide variety of categories at the 1997 Returning the Gift Festival. Nominees for the honours and awards were screened by a Wordcraft Circle Honours and Awards Standing Committee which was chaired by Wordcraft Circle Mentor, Cheryl Savageau (Abenaki). Categories included: Wordcrafter of the Year, Writer of the Year, Mentor of the Year, Intern of the Year, Storyteller of the Year, Publisher of the Year and Literary Agent of the Year.

Returning the Gift Project

The Returning the Gift Foundation is an organisation based at the University of Oklahoma, which celebrates and draws attention to the accomplishments of contemporary North American First Nations' (American Indian, Aleut, Inuit and Metis) writers. The goals of the foundation include strengthening the role of First Nations' literatures in the literary canons, building coalitions of First Nations'-based literary organisations, encouraging First Nations' literary traditions and reaffirming First Nations' identity through contemporary literature with a strong emphasis on First Nations' youth.

The Returning the Gift project was born out of the first Returning the Gift Festival in 1992, held at University of Oklahoma at Norman. This was a large international event which drew First Nations' writers from throughout the upper Western Hemisphere, totalling over 500 First Nations' authors from the United States and Canada. The 1993 Festival, also held at the University of Oklahoma, drew writers from 17 U.S. states and Canada. The 1994 Festival was held at the Cape Fletter Resort, Neah Bay, Washington, and attendance at this conference was primarily from six states and three Canadian provinces, but First Nations' writers were present from across the continent. The En'owkin Centre hosted the 1996 Festival and in 1997 it was held at the Northeastern State University, Tahlequah, Oklahoma.

The Returning the Gift Festival offers an opportunity for writers throughout the continent to exchange information and network with other writers, with the opportunity to participate in panels and workshops relating to various genres. Evening readings and performances are included in the program.

Editors, book publishers and anthology editors are invited to have their publications, press catalogues or calls for submissions displayed at Returning the Gift. From the 1992 Returning the Gift conference, where encouraging First

Nations' American youth was one of the main goals, came the anthology *Reclaim the Visions* (Greenfield Press, 1996) edited by Lee Francis and Joseph Bruchac. This edited volume includes papers from the panel discussion of the conference as well as poetry and prose by American Indian students.

Since the first festival in 1992, more than 60 books have been published by writers who have attended Returning the Gift, and Bruchac believes many of those books were a direct result of contacts made at festivals.[522]

Aside from Returning the Gift Festivals, the activities of the project have also included an Outreach Program in 1991 and 1992, bringing First Nations' writers into First Nations' and non-Native secondary schools at different locations throughout North America. *A Directory of North American Native Writers* was also compiled and produced with the cooperation of the Smithsonian Institution in 1993 (but has not yet been updated). In 1992 Returning the Gift also awarded its first Lifetime Achievement Award to N. Scott Momaday, from the USA.

Support for the Project in the past has been received from The New York Times Foundation, The Bay Foundation, The Oklahoma Council for the Arts, The W.K. Kellogg Foundation and numerous private individuals.

North American First Nations' Authors First Book Awards

The Returning the Gift Project, in cooperation with The Greenfield Review Literary Centre present the North American First Nations' Authors First Book Awards, open to any North American First Nations' writer who has not yet published a first book. The winners of these awards, offered in prose (The Louis Littlecon Oliver Memorial Award) and poetry (The Diane Deborah Memorial Award), each received $500 and publication of their manuscript by a participating press. To date, no writers from Canada have won this award.

Aboriginal Voices Festival and Media Conference 1999

The Aboriginal Voices Festival and Media Conference was presented by *Aboriginal Voices* magazine in June 1999. First Nations' people from all over the Americas descended on the city of Toronto to celebrate Indigenous media, film, music and the performing arts.

The core of the festival was music and film, with musicians Joy Harjo and Poetic Justice, Jerry Alfred and the Medicine Beat, and Neil Young among others. Many of Alanis Obomsawin's films screened as part of the "Reel Aboriginal Film Festival", however literature was not represented on par with the other artforms. With six consecutive days and nights of the "Reel Aboriginal Film Festival" in the Studio Theatre, musical performances running on a number of stages consecutively, theatrical performances at least twice daily and a visual art exhibition open daily during the festival, it was disappointing to see a total of only two literary events on the program. They were a discussion between Richard Van Camp and Paul Martin and a Beat Poet Night with Joy Harjo, Daniel David Moses, Greg Scofield and Paul Martin.

The Aboriginal Media Conference, held at the University of Toronto on the first three days of the Aboriginal Voices Festival was also more directed at radio, television and film industries than literary ones. On the three day program there were only two sessions specifically related to publishing. "What's Happening in Aboriginal Publishing?" was an informative panel discussion with Greg Young-Ing, Darlene Speidel of the Saskatchewan Indian Cultural Centre publishing department, and Renee Abram from Kegedonce Press. Following the publishing panel was a session on "Aboriginal Editorial Practice" with Greg Young-Ing and Minnie Two Shoes, an editor with a US newspaper. This session was interactive as many freelance writers and would-be authors attended and received a summary of the style guide developed by Young-Ing. This raised discussion for the need of such a guide, but also the need for some possible inclusions and changes.

National Aboriginal Achievement Awards

The National Aboriginal Achievement Foundation organises the National Aboriginal Achievement Awards in Canada each year to pay tribute to talented and high-achieving Aboriginal people across the country, who are recognised for their individual accomplishments, while reflecting on the overall progress being made in strengthening Aboriginal communities, people and economies—an objective of the *Gathering Strength—Canada's Aboriginal Action Plan*.

Initiated in 1994, the only authors to receive awards so far are Maria Campbell and Howard Adams.

Other support

In the 1996 Report of the Royal Commission on Aboriginal People Gathering Strength, the section "Aboriginal Arts Council 3.6.19" recommended that,

> Federal, provisional, territorial and Aboriginal governments co-operate to establish and fund an Aboriginal Arts Council, with a minimum 20-year life span and an annual budget equivalent to five per cent of the Canada Council budget, to foster the revitalisation and development of Aboriginal arts and literature.[523]

As of March 2000 there had been no movement on this recommendation, although Greg Young-Ing who is a Member of the Canada Council Aboriginal Peoples Committee, commented that the Committee has been pushing the Canada Council to adopt the model of the Aboriginal and Torres Strait Islander Arts Board within the Australia Council for the Arts.[524] Richard Van Camp has replaced Young-Ing on this committee.

Lessons for Aboriginal publishing in Australia

There are many lessons for Australia to be gained from the First Nations' experience of publishing in Canada. Theytus Books, for example, exists on a skeleton staff of two and produces about the same amount of titles as Magabala Books each year, with less funding and better distribution across the country. Theytus have been far more effective in getting their materials on course guides at universities, but perhaps that is because they are publishing names like Jeannette Armstrong and Drew Hayden-Taylor while Magabala tends to publish more cultural and children's books than fiction and essays.

The support mechanisms afforded First Nations' writers are also what help to nurture and develop writers to the point of publication. Australia should work on the Returning the Gift model to ensure a writer's conference is held annually, establishing some momentum for writers. Writers and publishers would also benefit from the establishment of a writing school similar to the En'owkin Centre where students could learn and develop their skills in various forms of writing while getting an accredited degree.

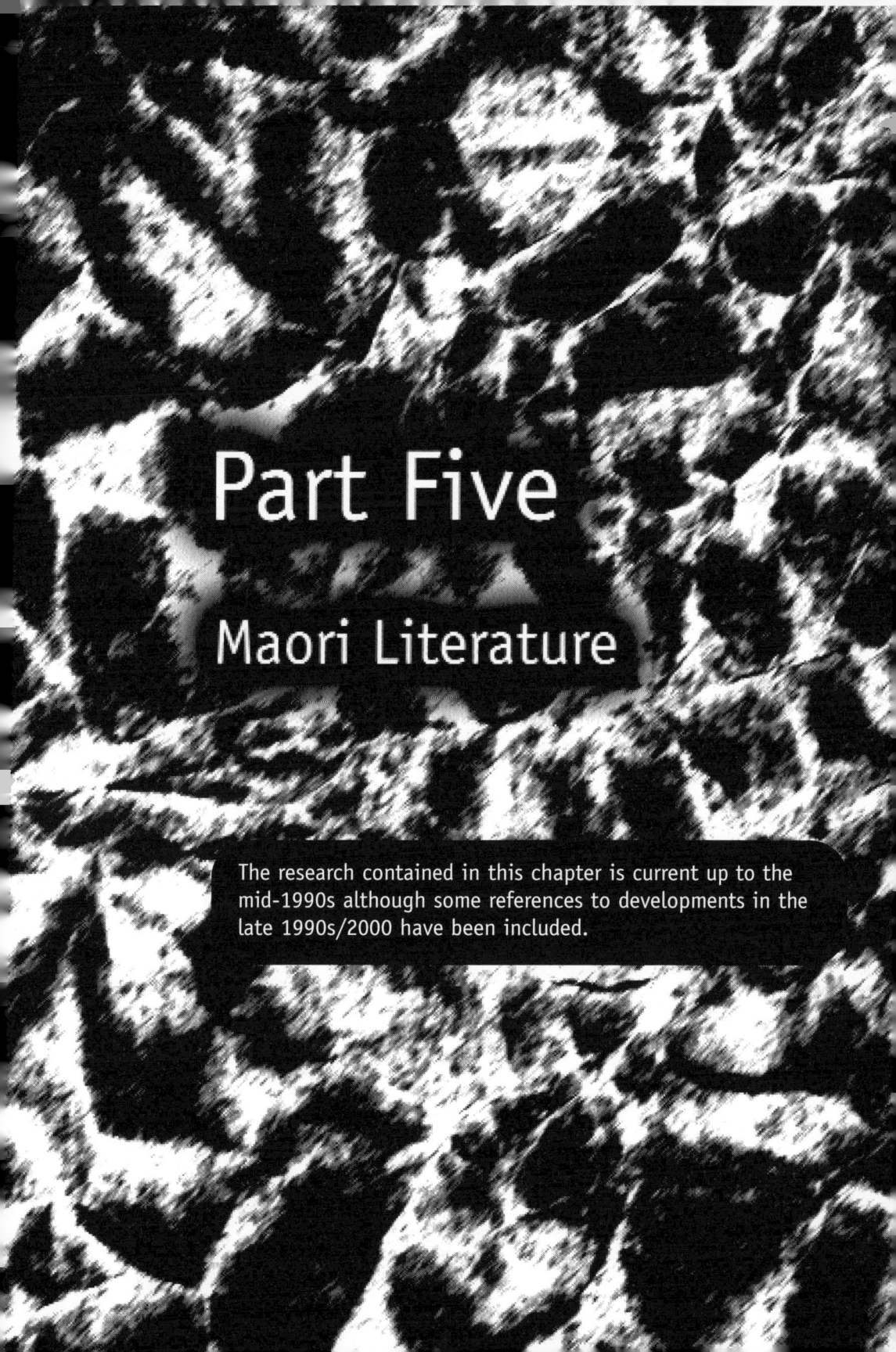

Part Five

Maori Literature

The research contained in this chapter is current up to the mid-1990s although some references to developments in the late 1990s/2000 have been included.

> *As Maori writers we share our dreams, passions, anger, humour, concerns, hopes and vision, showing the complexity that has become our world. Our role is to take our culture and our people with us into the future, looking back as we walk forward. For us, the past is not something that is behind us. It is before us, a long unbroken line of ancestors, to whom we are accountable. This is our implicit contract.*[525]

Like Australian Aborigines and First Nations' North Americans, the Maori had no written language or literature until colonisation. Oral expression was the form used to pass down traditions, legends, history and learning. Like Aboriginal stories and knowledge, the ownership of this tradition did not reside with an individual but was preserved communally. The oral tradition is still evident and important in written Maori literature today, and it is said,

> To speak of literature in Maori is to speak of the stylistic forms and subject matter of oral and literary traditions. Written texts of the traditional knowledge are regarded as a revered inheritance from the ancestors, but the oral form is arguably more important to Maori people.[526]

The Maori were presented with a transcription by missionaries of their spoken word into a written form in the early 1800s. These transcriptions were aimed at converting them to Christianity. There was a lot of material published in Maori by the Church and State that focussed on religious matters. Maori received the Bible, hymns, moral advice and more in their own language. This also happened in Australia. In Australia, as early as 1838, Lancelot Edward Threlkeld, missionary to the Aborigines at Ebenezer, Lake Macquarie, New South Wales, presented the Awabakal people with a translation of the 15th chapter of the Gospel according to St Luke.[527]

Robyn Bargh, Publisher at Huia in Wellington, explains how the role of Maori publishing has changed over time, saying they have come from a whole tradition of Maori publishers,

> As soon as missionaries hit this country, Maoris got much more interested in writing than they did in Christianity. The first books published in this country were published in Maori. Maori people owned printing presses in about the 1840s. And they learnt to read and write very early. The numbers don't even matter, it's just significant that it's being done in each community. Even in my family books were inherited by my great-great grandfather who went to school. I think we've always had a literature, whether it's oral or not, and when this new technology came along we just grasped it and got on with it.[528]

Bargh says Maori seized upon the idea of reading and writing and used the exciting new technology, adapting it for their own purposes. They published newspapers and printed books in their own language and several iwi (tribes) soon had a printing press of some description. Maori saw this as another way of preserving what people said and did, and as a way of trading ideas and information.

In contrast to the repression of Aboriginal languages in Australia, in Aotearoa an Act of Parliament was passed in 1987 declaring Maori an official language of Aotearoa and conferring the right to speak it in some legal contexts.[529]

In the 1940s organisations like the Progressive Publishing Society were founded to promote books dealing with Aotearoa or books by New Zealanders. The Society saw Maori as a group that needed such support, publishing *Maori Problems Today: A Short Survey*, by R.L. Meek (a Pakeha) in 1943.

From about the 1920s the publications by Maori almost ceased completely and only gained momentum again with the work of Witi Ihimaera in the 1960s. The publishing success of Maori writers and their history of publication by mainstream presses is very much comparable to that of Aboriginal Australia. Witi Ihimaera's first novel *Pounamu, Pounamu* published in 1972, was the first Maori novel, and if the work of Colin Johnson can be disregarded, then 1972 was also the year of the first Aboriginal novel, when Monica Clare brought her manuscript of *Karobran* to the FCAATSI office (it was published in 1978). Patricia Grace released the first collection of short stories Waiariki and Other Stories in 1975 and a children's book *The Kuia and the Spider* in 1981. And in 1964, the same year that Oodgeroo Noonuccal (then Kath Walker) released her first collection of poetry, *We Are Going*, the first collection of Maori poetry was published in the form of Hone Tuwhare's *No Ordinary Sun*.

Pakeha Margaret Orbell's anthology *Contemporary Maori Writing* (1970) is considered a pioneering work as it showcases the first generation of Maori writers to make use of literary forms in English. The anthology includes works by Hone Tuwhare, Witi Ihimaera, S.M. Mead and Patricia Grace. It was this anthology, along with Orbell's *Maori Poetry: An Introductory Anthology* (1974) and Barry Mitcalfe's *Poetry of the Maori* (1964) that opened up Maori writing to a non-Maori audience.[530]

The 1970s also saw the emergence of a group of active Maori writers and artists and the establishment of the Maori Artists' and Writers' Group who met annually. Prominent members of the group included Witi Ihimaera, Patricia Grace and Bruce Stewart.

The 1980s saw some significant developments with the 1985 *Penguin Book of New Zealand Verse* edited by Ian Wedde and Harvey McQueen including 33 Maori poets with their work in Maori and translated in English. Inclusion of examples of early waiata (songs) in sequence, before the European poets, was a significant statement by Penguin.

The same decade saw the Maori playwright and novelist simply referred as Renee, enjoy success with her trilogy *Wednesday to Come, Pass It On* and *Jeannie*

Once at major theatres in Aotearoa. Renee was considered to be one of Aotearoa's best playwrights.

Part of the process of reclaiming Maori identity over the past 20 years has involved far stronger tribal expression, and the treaty claims that are now being processed are returning much more power and resources to individual tribes so that they can administer their own affairs. One side effect of this has been to narrow the focus of a lot of Maori writers and activists so they are no longer speaking and behaving on behalf of all Maori so much as their own iwi, a priority for many Maori writers today. Penguin's publisher Geoff Walker points out that since the increase in iwi development people, including potential writers, have become more interested in studying law, for instance, and supporting community structures as their priority, rather than spending a year or two writing a novel for a Pakeha audience.[531]

It is clear that in Aotearoa, as in Australia and North America, Indigenous people who have the skills to write well are also those acting as lawyers, teachers and activists, busy working within their communities on a day-to-day basis, and unable to indulge the individual luxury of having a full-time writing career.

As well as being pioneers of Maori writing, both Patricia Grace and Witi Ihimaera also enjoy mainstream reputations as prolific writers, publishing consistently, selling well and acting as role models for other Maori writers—both emerging and established. Such success is evidenced by the numbers at their launches and their performances, says Walker, who is quick to add that, "Pakeha will never have the same community success."

Keri Hulme who won the Booker Prize in 1985 for *The Bone People* is another successful Maori writer, as is Alan Duff, author of the internationally acclaimed *Once Were Warriors* (1991). As opposed to Grace, Ihimaera and Hulme, though, Robyn Bargh feels Duff's work can be considered "populist rather than literary".

Bargh believes that in the 1990s Maori literature came into its own, and the release of works like Witi Ihimaera's story of coming out, *Nights In the Garden of Spain* (1995) illustrates the new heights Maori writers are reaching.

According to Geoff Walker, Maori literature is 'holding its own', even though he's getting fewer manuscripts sent to him at Penguin. Aside from the major names in Maori writing there are also many emerging writers who significantly contribute to the literary growth of Aotearoa. People like Robert Sullivan, Librarian at the University of Auckland, writes poetry about many different issues and topics, but nearly always related to Maori political issues. He has three published collections including *Jazz Waiata* (1990), *Pike Ake!* (1993) and *Star Waka* (1999).

Emerging writer Rawinia White (based in Hamilton) writes from the heart about her life because she's "wanting to make a difference".[532] Fellow writer Hinewirangi, who was first published when she was eight years old, sees writing as a way to work through anger and some of her work includes bilingual children's books.[533]

In the non-fiction area, Wena Harawira, based in Rotorua, is the author of a non-fiction work, *Kawa O Te Marae—A Guide For All Marae Visitors* (1996). Harawira started writing educational books with her sisters that she photocopied at her local total immersion language school. She is now in the process of putting together a set of seven books retelling some of the more common Maori myths and legends aimed at 8–10 year olds.

Maori playwrights include Briar Grace-Smith whose one-woman show *Nga Pou Wahine*, featured at the Sydney Opera House during the Festival of the Dreaming in 1997, and Phil Kawana, author of *Dead Jazz Guys* and winner of Huia's first short-story competition in 1995.

In terms of popular fiction, controversial writer Alan Duff has been criticised, largely from within the Maori community, for the work he has done as a Maori, in particular for his book *Once Were Warriors* which was later made into an internationally successful film. Duff, whose European father was 'educated' and 'rational', and whose Maori mother was 'uneducated' and 'volatile'[534], says of his novel, "I simply looked at the lives of a typical state house Maori family and portrayed them as they are. And it is not very nice".[535] But it was the imposing of his own life experience as the complete Maori experience that offended most critics of his work.

Perhaps annoyance stridently expressed by members of the Maori community at Duff's *Once Were Warriors* may have subsided had he not followed up with *Maori: The Crisis and the Challenge* (1993) where he questions why Maori don't take advantage of the educational opportunities afforded them? why Maori still listen to elders who are not qualified to lead? why they do not adopt the work ethic they see in Pakeha around them? and why they depend so much on government handouts? Harawira[536] and Walker both comment that Duff's work failed to comment effectively on the social and economic status of Maori, and was written to appease a Pakeha audience who already had such negative stereotypes of Maori.

In contrast to condemnation of his subject matter, Duff does receive praise for what is a distinct style of writing, which has been described as, "unmistakably Maori English, with its own rhythms, intonations and elisions."[537]

One of the differences between Aotearoa and Australia is in the involvement of non-Indigenous people writing in the area of Indigenous issues and culture. There are few Pakeha today that would dare to write books in the area of Maori affairs. It appears that this issue was dealt with some 12-15 years ago and that in the 1990s the few Pakeha who write in the area of Maori studies are generally those who have been approached by a particular iwi to write a biography or tribal history. In this case it is because some iwi prefer to have their tribal histories written by a completely neutral person rather than someone from another iwi who may well have been at war with them in the past.

This phenomenon is not duplicated in Australia where much of the area of Aboriginal studies is dominated by non-Aboriginal academics, historians and anthropologists. It is clear that while many non-Indigenous people have created careers out of researching and writing about Indigenous people in Australia, the time has come for them to move over, like the Pakeha of Aotearoa, and allow us to tell our stories, our way, providing books for the already existing market while creating new markets.

Identity and Authenticity

Unlike Aboriginal Australians who are estimated to make up 2.5% of the Australian population, or First Nations' peoples who make up perhaps 2-3% of the Canadian population, Maori make up some 14% of the general population in Aotearoa. Maoris are therefore a more visible part of the community, and by association have stronger support and power base within their own communities, and occupy more positions of political power in mainstream institutions.

Maori regard themselves as tangata whenua (people of the land) and taha Maori (Maori identity) is generally based on descent from the first peoples of Aotearoa.[538] Maoritanga (the values, traditions and culture of the Maori) is a component of Maori identity that incorporates racial elements as well as cultural features like language, religious beliefs and tribal identification.[539]

Maori identity pre-European contact was very similar to that of Aboriginal Australia where racial features such as skin colour and hair were not part of identification (although individuals would have skin names). Instead the Maori thought of themselves in terms of iwi (tribes) as did Aboriginal people across Australia. With the arrival of the Europeans, the Maori described the new strangers as Pakeha (white man) and themselves as Maori (normal or natural).[540]

The arrival and settlement of whites instituted definitions of Maori, which were then reinforced by a mainstream media. This is highlighted by James Ritchie's "Index of Maoriness" published in *The Making of a Maori* which sets as its criteria,

1) the degree of Maori blood someone has;

2) how many visits to a marae (courtyard in front of a meeting house) they make;
3) the use of a tohunga, or faith healer;
4) whether or not they use a Maori name;
5) whether or not they have fair conversational Maori;
6) whether or not Maori is used in home;
7) whether or not they can name their traditional canoe;
8) whether or not they can name their tribe and hapu (sub-tribe, descendants);
9) whether or not they can name meeting house;
10) whether or not they live in a pa (village/community).[541]

Ritchie's book was published in 1963 though, and perspectives in Aotearoa have changed with a move now towards Maori self-determination.[542]

A number of specific Maori movements emerged in the 19th century which aimed in part to secure Maori identity. One such movement was the Pai Marire Movement, a religious movement aimed at addressing and suppressing tribal jealousies in an effort to promote pan-Maoriness. Headed by the Prophet Te Ua Haumene, the movement was an alternative religious solution to the difficulties of enforced enculturation faced by the Maori in the 1860s. Te Ua's movement hoped to provide Maoris with, "a new Maori identity and a place in a nation becoming increasingly dominated by Pakeha".[543] People renounced their Christian names for their old Maori ones as a way of reclaiming their Maori identity.

Interestingly, the census of 1886 showed for the first time that the majority of Europeans living in Aotearoa had actually been born there, and so while previously 'New Zealand Native' generally meant a Maori, it soon became a term for New Zealand-born Pakeha too.[544] In the 1890s then, New Zealand Native Associations (for Pakeha) were established.[545] These 'Native Associations' were established for Pakeha who were 'Native' to Aotearoa and again forced Maori to establish an identity separately to the 'Native Pakeha' of Aotearoa.

Identification as a Maori can also be seen to have common links with the cultural expectations of Australian Aboriginal communities. For example, like Aborigines, Maori attend (and are expected to attend) the tangi (funeral) and the hui (gatherings or meetings), and this is seen as a method of preserving Maori identity.[546]

A study of Maori graduates in Aotearoa between 1967 and 1969 found that for Maori, cultural identity was not always based on identifiable cultural traits (like those found in James Ritchie's set of criteria), but as a function of birth, kin and tribal affiliation, so while a Maori might be accepted on merit in the Pakeha world, he was accepted by birth in the Maori world.[547] The survey also found that a Maori "can and often does identify with all Maoris". This would account for pan-Maoriness, and also allows for someone even with a trace of Maori blood to be accepted into Maori society.[548]

While older studies show a fear of assimilation of Maori into European ways, Brenda Tahi who was Manager of the Te Ohu Whakatupu (the Maori Policy Unit of the Ministry of Women's Affairs) in 1992 and 1993 says that the process of becoming bicultural (what some may call assimilated) was the choice of the Maori who "sought to understand Pakeha culture and language" in order "to trade with Pakeha, to obtain Pakeha technology, to take up the new religion and to take up new skills of Pakeha culture such as reading and writing for communication".[549] The problem with this interest in Pakeha culture, as pointed out by Tahi, is that nowadays many Maori are left with the fact that acculturation into the Pakeha world has left them devoid of their own culture.[550]

Because of the dynamics of Aotearoa society today, Tahi claims that "virtually all Maori are bicultural", with "Some cluster[ed] at the Maori end of the Maori-Pakeha spectrum in that they are culturally Maori in concept and practice, but frequently 'dip into' the Pakeha culture." Meanwhile, "Others string out along the spectrum to the other end inhabited by Maori often described as 'brown-skinned Pakeha'".[551] This reference to 'brown-skinned Pakeha' echoes references made to 'coconuts' (brown on the outside, white on the inside) in Aboriginal Australia, and 'apples' (red on the outside, white on the inside) in First Nations' North America.

It would appear today that far from being assimilated, the Maori of Aotearoa have been assertive in learning the processes and skills of modern and urban technology to further instil their cultural traits and identity through publishing. Considering that there is only one Maori language (that many Pakeha people also speak), the Maori are further advantaged by the interest in publication of works in their own language, as opposed to the minuscule market for works in community languages in both Australia and Canada.

Generally speaking then, Maori literature may be defined as works written by Maori. Publishers who rely on continually receiving manuscripts have broadened the definition to include works by and *about* Maori and collaborations between Pakeha and Maori. Most authors interviewed as part of research for my thesis were adamant, though, that Maori literature was work by Maori themselves, saying it was: "Any work written by Maori or who identify with being Maori,"[552] "Something written by a Maori who stands to say she's Maori,"[553] and, "Definitely writing by Maoris."[554]

Reina Whaitiri co-editor of *Te Pua*, a journal dedicated to publishing fiction and non-fiction by Maori women (because it provides somewhere for Maori women to be published without being critiqued or selected by males), says that defining Maori literature is a big debate, and a question she throws at her students at the University of Auckland. She herself says she would define it as "any work by Maori."[555]

In contrast, there are some writers like poet Robert Sullivan who believe, "There is no such thing as a Maori writer…By saying so, you are confining them to what they can write."[556] Marama Mihaka says she has always been careful not to use the word Maori in terms of her writing, being conscious of not having what she calls 'ethnic indicators' in her writing.[557] In this way Mihaka is clear that she will not create characters that fit stereotypes of Maori people, or place them in situations or environments that make them identifiably Maori.

Sid Mead who sits on one of the literary committees at Toi Maori says that "Maori writing must categorise itself as something different. Something that is more than being Maori by nationality".[558] His comments followed statements that contemporary Maori art, as opposed to traditional Maori art, was not authentic.

Comments by Pakeha working in the field of Maori literature and publishing also provided new definitions of Maori literature. For example Publisher Peter Janssen from Reed Books explained that a book on pig hunting by a Maori mightn't necessarily make it a Maori book, but a pig hunting book.[559] Janssen says he published a book on pig hunting by a first time Maori writer who was happy to be seen as a Maori writer but would be unhappy to be *only* seen as a Maori writer. And although Geoff Walker says that he generally defines Maori literature as work by a Maori author or literature written by Maori, he admits he would also include works that are collaborative works with Pakeha.

On the question of the post-colonialist nature of Maori writing, Albert Wendt, Samoan writer, teacher, editor, leader of creative writing groups and lecturer at the University of Auckland,[560] says that people might be surprised to find that the concept 'post-colonial' has been Indigenised, "to suit ourselves, to mean against/anti, around, through, out of. We can still be in a colonised position yet our literature is 'post-colonial' in that it analyses our colonised condition and answers and opposes the colonial literature about us, declaring our independence".[561] In this way, Maori and Samoan writing, emerges out of the experience of being colonised, or against or around colonialism. Wendt comments,

> If you take it this way then it makes sense so you can be in a colonial situation like Aborigines and Maori and look at the effects of colonialism on these people and it makes sense. It doesn't make sense if it just means 'after'… Even Edward Said who writes on the Middle-East doesn't reject the word but redefines it. It's like all these terms that we have to redefine to suit ourselves. It is appropriating colonisers' language to ourselves, we do it everyday, for example Maori English and Aboriginal English.

Wendt suggests the term could be changed to 'anti-colonial' or something similar.

Further on the concept of post-colonialism, academic and fiction writer Pita Rykis asks the question, "Where is the decolonisation process?", commenting that it annoys him that in some academic areas whole fields of Maori knowledge are captured by white academics (for example heritage and archeology).[562]

Interestingly, while Geoff Walker comments that, "People such as Witi Ihimaera and Patricia Grace would definitely describe themselves as post-colonial writers," Grace herself said of the question of defining Maori writing as post-colonial, "We can forget about the past when we are on equal footing."[563]

Is there a Maori style?

While some authors believe Maori writing has evolved and changed to the point where it is now difficult to tell whether a work is by a Maori or not, others aren't so convinced and believe that there is definitely a distinct style of Maori writing.

Mihaka believes that, "You do get social indicators that force people to assume that a work is written by a Maori because it reflects the socio-economic experience of being what is *perceived* in society to be Maori." Grace agrees there are indicators that will identify whether or not a manuscript is by a Maori writer or not,

> The content might be about Maori issues, but about different sorts of relationships than say Pakeha write about. Our relationships include community, inter-generation, grandparents etc, rather than the man/woman sexual relationship…Then there's the cliche, the tangi—the death ceremony pops up all over the place.

Wena Harawira comments that there are, "A lot of Maori bring back what they're writing about to themselves, quite often they personalise it. Makes it identifiable."

From a publisher's point of view, Robyn Bargh says that it mightn't be the style, but the accuracy of an experience being told. She comments,

> I can tell by what they describe, but I wouldn't like to have a test. In terms of style, it's not always different to Pakeha writing, but some writers have worked at being deliberately Maori in style [by using Maori identifiers mentioned above]—Api Taylor is one who is a more experienced writer who can play with style and language.

Geoff Walker says that most Maori writing is about Maori, and so that's stylistic. He also says that, 'Maori style' employs not only Maori words that are used by the Pakeha mainstream, but Maori words and codes that are generically used in Maori communities. The use of these words and codes are what Walker says give the writing a 'really distinctive voice'. Examples of such style would include the use of Maori names for characters, and using Maori and English inter-woven through the text as if the same language. This is comparable to the use of Aboriginal English in Indigenous Australian writing.

Patricia Grace has never thought of her work as being political, but says that if you are writing about people who haven't been written about before, then that is political—as they are usually people without power and who are struggling. She adds, "People recognise my style but I don't know what it is. I know what I like doing—my stories come from the character, not the plot. The story comes from the people. I work in a circular way, from the centre working out." Poet Hinewirangi says she breaks every writer's rule by writing the way she talks. This is also typical of the orally derived manner in which many Aboriginal writers in Australia choose to write, like Ruby Langford Ginibi and Lionel Fogarty.

Robert Sullivan, who calls himself a 'mongrel writer'—influenced by Aotearoa language poets, mainstream poets, multi-media, rap music and satire—says, "I don't want to be pigeonholed into just one style of writing."

Pita Rykis simply comments that there is, 'Heaps of difference' between Maori and Pakeha writing, explaining that even within Maori writing there is a spectrum. At one end there's what Rykis calls traditional writing and the other end has all the experience of what's happened in recent times using street talk, hip-hop, and borrowings from the American scene. He comments, "It's gone through a huge evolutionary process."

Mihaka notes technical differences as well as social ones saying there is a difference because Maori and Pakeha writers come from different histories, and Maoris tend to write passively: "See it's very rude in Maori, in our family, to talk actively."

Editor and Publisher Maarire Goodall believes that if he received a manuscript and didn't know the author, if it was a genuine piece of Maori writing he's quite sure he would recognise it commenting,

> I would see that they are describing the way I was when I was a child etc. …saying things and reacting in a way that I know that we do, and all these things are quite different to the way that Pakeha write…The voice of life experience is different, the way characters interact with each other.[564]

Goodall says Patricia Grace is writing in English but to him she's writing in Maori in the way she constructs stories, and that the stories she tells are Maori. While there can be considered to be a Maori style, there is no clear definition of what Maori literature is and it is also not easy to define what Maori are writing about. As Patricia Grace comments that, "We are Maori of the 90s, our writing must show that diversity."

Regardless of content and style, it appears that Maori writers are successful across all genres, with the big sellers like Patricia Grace, Keri Hulme, Witi

Ihimaera and Alan Duff in the area of fiction. It is hard to say whether or not there are any particular genres in which Maori are more likely to excel than others. Robyn Bargh of Huia comments that a lot of people would say that because Maori have an oral tradition they tend to be better at poetry—an argument also applied to Aboriginal poets. Bargh doesn't agree with this concept, though, saying,

> I feel sure we did have a poetry, a Maori literature where we used metaphor, alliteration, onomatopoeia and all those literary forms are used in Maori language and literature, but I think you can translate those just as easily into short stories.

Poet Robert Sullivan believes that Maoris have already excelled in the novel, because he sees it as a form of storytelling, but that poetry allows for more freedom in writing. He says, "You can say a lot of things in poetry that you can't say overtly. You can throw a lot more shit in poetry for example, in prose if you said in a sentence 'Kill a White' you could get in trouble."

There is also a move into drama/theatre/film as Maori have always been a very visual people, as have Aborigines. Ihimaera notes that most literature is now in the forms of theatre and dance which is much more subversive. Academic writer Pita Rykis adds, though, that you can't say,

> Because Maori have a close association with the oral that it's going to be a better play [than a Pakeha] because it's not necessarily going to be. I think Maori are just beginning to discover the power of 'oralcy' again and this is something I've been advocating for a long time...We've forgotten how powerful oral knowledge is, except for the recitation of genealogy which is a very powerful mechanism.

Pare Hopa, Associate Professor of Maori Studies at the University of Auckland, says that there is a movement away from conventional literature to playwriting, and that there are now a large number of Maori women (estimated 26) who make up a core of filmmakers in Aotearoa.[565]

Glenys Paraha, actor, filmmaker and visual artist supports the notion of writing for film saying it is still writing but it provides a venue for visual stories. She adds that, "Being on the film set is like being on the marae."[566]

It is clear that poetry is as difficult to get published in Aotearoa as it is in Australia, and Pita Rykis points out that it doesn't matter if you are Pakeha or Maori. Still there is a long list of published Maori poets including Alistair Te Ariki Campbell—who has published near 10 collections of poetry - Keri Hulme, Roma Potiki, Robert Sullivan, Apirana Taylor and Hone Tuwhare.

Geoff Walker at Penguin believes that Maori are writers of good fiction of a linear kind because it is like telling a yarn or story-telling. While Peter Janssen from Reed believes that children's non-fiction has a big strength.

Jane Collins, a journalist in the area of Maori affairs for many years, is putting together a book on bicultural Maori after discovering that there was very little written in recent times about mixed marriages, although a lot was written in the past.[567] She says it's about the 'cultural identity crisis'. Collins says there needs to be more understanding from the Maori perspective of what it is like to be from mixed marriages. This is in contrast to the experience of Aboriginal writing in Australia, where few writers are discussing the issues of the bicultural experience.

Author of short stories and self-publisher, Mihaka, adds that much of the writing available doesn't cover her experience living a middle-class life, from a mixed marriage, and growing up in the mainstream, and that's why she wanted to start writing, commenting, "It's like the missing piece of the jigsaw puzzle, the picture was incomplete."

Audience

To some extent issues of audience have been covered in the previous section. Nevertheless some specific comments deserve noting.

Maori writers are writing for different audiences although Collins comments, "You shouldn't write to anyone's expectations, write what's in the heart."

Robert Sullivan (like Herb Wharton) writes for the general population, while Patricia Grace says she's writing for anyone who'll read it, not wanting to limit her audience,

> Others say they write for Maori people, but I don't like to think of who the audience is because I think that's restrictive. I don't want to think about reviewers or anyone. But I don't think I'd keep writing if I didn't get good feedback from Maori people.

Wena Harawira aims her work at young people within the general population hoping to show the rich variety that is part of Maori culture to a lot of New Zealanders who don't know about it. She comments that there are probably more Japanese tourists that have visited the marae than Pakeha/European New Zealanders, proving that there is a huge audience to educate.

Publishing

Maori publishing in Aotearoa has developed in the past decade with the establishment of a number of Maori owned and controlled initiatives throughout the country. From large organisations like Huia in Wellington to community-based niche publishers like Te Reo Publications Ltd in Opononi, Maori works in both Te Reo (Maori) and English are being published across all genres.

Based in Wellington Huia began in 1991 as an independent publisher and in the first six years showed its willingness to publish works by and for Maori. In 1996 it published contemporary Maori plays for the first time, which will enable access to a wider audience as the book will be available in schools. Huia publish fiction, play scripts, picture books, Maori language readers, history and contemporary issues. They also provide a publishing service to clients who wish to produce books with a Maori focus. Their objective is to publish Maori writers as part of Aotearoa literature, and the common theme through all their work, in the words of the Maori publisher Robyn Bargh, is to convey Maori as, 'contemporary, active participants of society'. On the desire to set up Huia, Bargh comments,

> I could see that although we had Maori writers here like Witi and Patricia and Hone Tuwhare especially, those three who had been published for 30 years, were pretty much the only three. They forged the trail and I was really conscious they were the only ones. We didn't have a diversity, we had three writers representing all Maori experience. And so from reading these others I could see that we needed more to elevate our experience and to describe it.

So Bargh set up Huia with husband Brian with clear objectives in mind in regards to literature, Maori writers and Aotearoa literature. Having learned the Maori language at university, Bargh was also conscious that there was nothing for readers of both Maori and English.

Huia usually gets unsolicited manuscripts and selects some of those for publication. Bargh says she can often tell quickly if a manuscript has got any potential at all, and because of the focus of the Huia list on books of interest to Maori, the manuscripts that don't have anything to do with Maori automatically get a reject letter. In this way Bargh reinforces the concept of a Maori style including content laden with Maori issues and experiences.

Manuscripts at Huia go to one of the editors who does a quick assessment, and if it has got potential they do a more detailed critique. Huia is the only commercial publishing house that has an in-house Maori editor. Bargh herself will look at the manuscript if they're thinking of doing it, and says the process takes quite a while; if it's got potential it can take six months to a year. Once Huia have made the decision to publish the manuscript, to get it into print can take within a year if it doesn't need a lot of editing.

Huia are trying to develop a good fiction list because Bargh believes that fiction is the way that Maori are going to describe their lives:

> I see the development of Maori writers writing fiction will be more enduring, long-term, than non-fiction. Non-fiction often has a social context which ten years later is out of date. Good fiction can stand the test of time.

Huia have published many Maori authors, and some Pakeha authors in the non-fiction area including their most successful, James Ritchie, a well known commentator on Maori affairs and author of the non-fiction book *Becoming Bicultural* (1992). Written by a Pakeha for Pakeha the book follows the theme that Maori development is becoming more tribal and that Pakeha need to understand what that implies.⁵⁶⁸ The text is taught at the University of Waikato where Ritchie is Deputy Director of the Centre for Maori Studies.

Huia have a series for adults which includes fiction and non-fiction, and a picture-book series for children written in Maori, with an English edition. Bargh points out that other publishers tend to just do a Maori translation of their English, while Huia translate from Maori to English. Huia also do a series of readers for the 500 schools that are teaching some part of the curriculum in Maori.

In order to generate income to continue publishing books Huia also provides publishing as a service, providing layout and design for government agencies and community groups and producing annual reports and newsletters.

Bargh says of Huia's market that while there is an increasing number of Maori book buyers, the main people that buy the books today are probably liberal white people. Publishers' concerns regarding the marketing and distribution of books are based heavily on the minuscule readership in Aotearoa, particularly among Maori. Bargh points out that publishers are governed a lot by what book buyers say. She says, "The book buyers in the chains are very powerful. They have a fixed idea of what sells," so that anything other than stereotypical Maori would be perceived as not Maori, adding, "It doesn't even have to be radical, just different." Bargh gives an example of a book buying experience where the book buyer didn't understand the role of books in Maori and English,

> We did these children's books in Maori. The book buyer wants us to do bilingual ones and have Maori and English on the same page. She said that's what people want. I would claim that people who want that are probably Pakeha who don't read the Maori but it makes them feel bicultural to have the Maori there and they feel good. So far we've refused to do it, but possibly sales figures might have us move into that area.

Bargh admits that marketing is Huia's weakness because in the past they've focussed on production and put a lot of energy into design and typesetting. She says they still haven't got it right because the audience is Maori so they can't just use established mainstream networks. They are also in the process of setting up sales representatives, and Bargh is confident that, "You can grow a market," knowing that Maori people haven't got a history of buying books (because the books available haven't been relevant to them). She often hears from booksellers, "But Maoris don't come into my bookshop," to which she replies, "They won't come into your shop until you've got a whole section they can look at." Bargh also talks to a lot of Maori groups:

> We have to take ourselves to Maori to let them know we're here. And it's important that they know what we're doing, that they believe in what we're doing and that what we're doing represents what they want to have. It's a two way thing. I think in my position I should be inspiring people but I also feel that I should be doing what they want to happen.

Established in 1992, **Te Reo Publications Ltd** are based in Opononi and their publications give not just one Maori perspective, but many Maori perspectives. Te Reo Publications see their house as strongly community-based as opposed to publishing houses in the city where they can have a detached perspective. Founder and writer/editor Annais Allen comments,

> I think of Maori publishing as the voice of Maori people and in terms of Maori writers our business comes from a Maori base and philosophy. Where we are based is part of who we are as a publisher. Where we are is a strong Maori-based community, we work in the community and know what's happening here.[569]

However, both Allen and her partner Janine McVeagh (who is Pakeha) feel the financial pressures of not being in a major city where the funding bodies, government agencies and market are located. They continue to produce works though that are aimed at an 8-10 year old audience which are designed for and used in schools.

Allen says her idea of Maori publishing is not something based in cities:

> I think if I was based in Wellington and I tried to access some of the information and the stories of the Maori community it seems to me that I would find it a lot more difficult. My feeling about it is that I often perceive publishing as something that is city orientated and based and therefore out of touch when I think about Maori publishing. I know there are a lot of urban Maori as such, but from a starting point why not better than where I live, where I come, where there's a great resource of Maori people and Maori speakers, which is important for our organisation that publishes in particular in Te Reo. But because of the lack of Maori speakers I've really had to think about works in English. Whether it's in Te Reo or English it's about our own philosophical base as a company and how we approach and produce and edit stories.

But there is a problem in terms of Te Reo being recognised as serious publishers as well as being publishers who also want to be community-based. Allen comments,

> There is so much going on in terms of accessing stories and making ourselves accessible to the Maori community, but there's another part in terms of integrating into the mainstream so they will accept that we are a legitimate publishing house. I want legitimacy from our own people as a Maori publishing house, that I'm going to treat them well, that the stories are valued. If you are from a remote/rural and Maori area it's hard for people in the cities to conceive of you the right way or at all. The Department of Education and all the major players are in the city. The education market can ignore us because we're not present. They don't know us because they don't see us. In a way it's not even based on what you produce but where you are and who you know.

In 1997 they were only publishing works that were writing themselves i.e., the publisher's own works—and all Te Reo books have proved successful, usually selling as a set. The least successful book Te Reo has produced is in English, selling one of them to every two in Maori. Because many of the books are their own work Te Reo could be considered as a vanity press. In 1997 they published four collections by students they taught and a counting picture book in Maori and English by Julie Owen and Noelle Jakeman. The book continues to sell well, alongside small print runs of student collections published in 1998.

McVeagh explains that Te Reo's focus is on children's literature because both she and Allen think that to get a good foundation you need to begin where the language speaker begins and that's with children. She comments,

> If you instil that foundation of language and the love of books and of literacy and the love of learning then it will never go away, but you can't suddenly bring it in at a level as an adult. Our works have a very simple sentence structure so that it is accessible to the parent as well as the child, but the child has got to want to pick up the book. If the book is interesting, amusing, brightly coloured, well-produced, top-quality production then the statement is Te Reo Maori is as valuable, interesting, exciting [as Pakeha writing] so that anybody would want to take it off the shelf and read it.[570]

The types of manuscripts Te Reo have turned away include those written by Pakeha who use Maori words with no context, simply slotting Maori words into the story in an ad hoc fashion. McVeagh says they have also turned down someone who had good stories but was far too wordy and preachy. The author was given a long critique, and the publisher pointed out that people who write for them need to be up with the client, what children need and what they read.

Te Reo Publications Ltd also runs writing courses for Maori interested in putting their stories into print. These courses have been successful in terms of teaching people the processes involved in getting a story that is usually told as a yarn ready to be published. Many students have work published or accepted for publication by Huia, Learning Media, Reed and Scholastic as a result of doing the Te Reo writing course, which is now taught on-line as well. Students are both Pakeha and Moari.

Dr Maarire Goodall is the Maori entrepreneur behind **Aoraki Press** located at Oriental Bay, Wellington. Aoraki is basically a one-man private enterprise run by Goodall who calls himself a 'niche publisher', producing 'works by and about Maori' and distributing from home and Christchurch. He is proud to say that he already has over 2.5 million pages in print, and publishes mainly non-fiction works and some plays, based on the fact that Maori theatre has emerged quickly in Wellington, and the desire for theatre in the written word has grown substantially.

On setting up the press, Goodall says that once the opportunity was there for Maori to be published his business just flourished. He added,

> before too long people were shyly coming around to visit, bringing their manuscripts. For about the last five years it's been really embarrassing because I can only publish a few a year and it's embarrassing not doing some.

One of the problems Goodall acknowledges as a Maori publisher is what to do when a manuscript arrives from someone whose tribal background includes someone who was his own tribe's enemy. He says that as a publisher this can prove to be a difficult issue to deal with. (Such an issue hasn't appeared within the Australian Aboriginal publishing industry, although publishers in Aboriginal houses have to date been white. When management committees are responsible for approving manuscripts for publication it is possible that one may be blocked because of family politics outside the publishing house, however there is as yet no proof of that happening.)

Goodall explains that the Treaty of Waitangi is one of the major concerns for Maori, and that people hear about the public debates around the nation but to most Maori people in their ordinary lives their real concern is their local authority, and how the planning laws affect them and their farm land or extensions. He says of the book *Te Whakatau Kaupapa* (1990) on resources management, planning and local administration,

> This book became overnight the touchstone text for Maori people all over the country. We got people to discuss what they wanted the law to recognise and what concepts they wanted expressed. It took a lot of time and there were a lot of disagreements amongst us. As we produced successive drafts we took them back to the marae. Eventually we had a consensus and a Maori consensus is very difficult for the government to overturn and that's why the book is so powerful. Te Whakatau Kaupapa is about the Treaty of Waitangi and all the authors are Maori.

Aoraki didn't receive any financial assistance for the book because Goodall wanted to remain autonomous, feeling that if he took assistance it might affect the spirit of the book, saying, "It was important to do it entirely by ourselves." *Te Whakatau Kaupapa* has also become the official policy document for Canterbury Regional Council, which is responsible for the administration of the very powerful Resource Management Act in the Canterbury provincial region.

Because he runs such a small operation, Goodall says he can't pay wages or hire anybody, and it was computer technology that made it all possible. He took his portable computer to the marae and worked as he went along talking to people, typing almost verbatim what the old people were saying and tidying it up later.

In 1997, Aoraki had published 16 books including three plays by John Broughton and a play by Hone Kouka.

Mana Magazine is not a literary journal, but a glossy publication produced in Auckland and distributed nationally. It covers the Maori arts, education, sport, business, media, politics and is free from government funding. The print run is 17,000 with 10,000 of those sold through subscriptions and street sales. Gary Wilson, associate editor, says, "The strength of the operation will be in the involvement of predominantly Maori people with a balance of Pacific Islanders and Pakeha...There needs to be a reminder in the organisation of the balance of the community."[571] Mainstream publishers don't see the need to acknowledge that balance though.

Although Gary Wilson (who is Pakeha) says *Mana* provides a, "Maori voice through Maori eyes to reflect Maori life" he adds that as main editor of the magazine, "Inevitably the magazine reflects me and my judgments and that's not really what I want." He says he tries, "to encourage the Maori voice to be as strong as possible." Although *Mana* mightn't want to be seen to be catering to a Pakeha audience, the reality is that no Maori development can succeed unless there is mainstream support, so it must appeal to a Pakeha readership too. Wilson adds that, although a Maori magazine, *Mana*, "probably does it best to have some other element in it."

The magazine's style and writing needs to appeal to a range of readers, from those who have low literacy levels to those with high literacy levels like academics. Therefore there isn't a specific niche as the general community is their readership. *Mana Magazine* reads in conversational style, abandoning honorific titles like, "Sir". Wilson comments that people mightn't see *Mana Magazine* as 'real news' because people generally conceive the 'real news' as that which is shown by and dictated by mainstream media. What the mainstream might see as newsworthy, won't necessarily be so to Maoris.

For many years **Reed Publishing** has been Aotearoa's largest publisher of books on Maori subjects, a reflection of the interest of the founder of the company, A.H. Reed, and his nephew A.W. Reed. Some of the books currently in print have been available in their original or revised editions for more than 40 years. Peter Janssen, Publishing Manager of Reed comments,

> We have a long tradition of publishing Maori works and it is part of this company's culture...Reed are seen as neutral and has a profile as the main publisher of Maori works because we are not influenced by tribal differences.

As part of the company culture, Reed have developed a ceremony where newly released Maori books are blessed, acknowledging the ancestors and the book as a treasure.

Janssen says that Reed are committed to publishing works in Maori and have consciously developed their children's list, printing more Maori children's books than Pakeha. He says, "It is a commitment in terms of making money, money for our authors". With an extensive Aboriginal children's list in Australia, it could be assumed that publishers in Australia have a similar commitment to Aotearoa publishers. However, the reality is that there is a constant market for children's / juvenile literature because of the education sector. In terms of a commitment by publishers in Australia to make more money for their Aboriginal authors, while organisations like Magabala might have that commitment as one of their objectives, there is no proof that Aboriginal authors receive anything more than the standard 10% offered on most book contracts to authors generally.

Janssen comments that Reed doesn't generally get a lot of manuscripts from Maori writers, rather he has to approach them. Reed commission a significant number of tribal histories by dealing with particular tribes directly and letting people know what they are interested in. Reed also consider areas where there are gaps in tribal histories, and Janssen says, "We let people know we'd like to be approached and we wait for them." Reed are also in the practice of trying to find authors, and trying to encourage young authors.

Reed publishes a lot of emerging writers and is especially interested in encouraging more general Maori writing rather than academic writing. Janssen says that academic books just sit on academic shelves, but as a publisher he is interested in getting books into as many hands as possible.

Reed published the tribal history *Horouta* authored by Rongowhakaata Halbert in 1999, believed to be the largest in the last 30 years. The reason Reed were approached to publish the work is, Janssen believes, because "We are neutral and we can publish what they want. The book could go to a smaller house with Maori staff, but there are tribal differences." This reinforces the views and experiences of Goodall at Aoraki Press.

Janssen says Reed are sensitive to the audience they publish for and try to keep prices down commenting, "If the average mother isn't going to buy it, then we're not going to publish it. We need to publish books that are accessible, books that can be bought and read by ordinary Maori people." They use freelance Maori editors and the Maori Language Commission who check Maori language content.

Janssen says that it is easy for Reed to market Maori works for two reasons: firstly, they have a good reputation as a publisher of Maori works; and secondly they put more money into their Maori books to make them marketable. Reed books also often have two titles, one in English and one in Maori. But Janssen admits that books in Maori have a finite market, you sell a certain amount and then they stop.

Penguin Books based in Auckland publishes a number of the main fiction authors including Patricia Grace (for the last 15 years) and Witi Ihimaera

(*The Dream Swimmer: The Sequel to The Matriarch* was released by Penguin in 1997), as well as Apirana Taylor and Bruce Stewart.

Although Penguin have a commitment to Maori literature in terms of publishing works by Maori authors, Walker admits that they do not have it in a broader sense as they would need to be publishing many more books to be able to make a commitment to hiring full-time Maori editors, for instance. Having said that, Penguin do follow a specific process when producing Maori language works and, like Reed, send drafts to the Maori Language Commission. Penguin does not currently employ a Maori editor or language expert as the "establishment isn't large enough".

Currently Penguin are not publishing as much Maori fiction as they were or would like to be because they simply aren't receiving manuscripts. Walker says that Penguin turn away manuscripts that are not at the publishing stage or where the writing is not skilful enough, where the writer has not reached a level of technical competency, but they might keep it on if it's a really good story and take on a co-writer to go through the process with them.

Penguin's audience is the general community, acknowledging there are probably more Pakeha readers than Maori. Walker says that Maori books are not necessarily written for the Pakeha audience, and though authors don't necessarily change style, they are aware that Pakeha are reading them. Walker adds that Witi Ihimaera is an uncompromising writer, negotiating very little in the editing and publishing of his works.

As a mainstream publisher Walker finds that the process of editing Maori works takes three times longer than it does with non-Maori writing, sometimes having to negotiate face-to-face rather than in a letter or over the phone, as many Maori tend to operate through personal contact. Walker says that sometimes a wider group of people is involved in the face-to-face, because the issue is not between the publisher and author, but the author and a technical person.

One of the interesting things in Aotearoa is that **self-publishing** is not considered vanity publishing. Instead it is seen as a way of being in control of what people have written, and reaping a more financial reward than can be attained from being published by a publishing house.

One successful example is Marama Mihaka (Laurenson) who went into publishing with her husband Dun Mihaka, and together they wrote, edited, published and distributed the non-fiction book *Whakapohane* in 1989, reprinted it in 1990, and made a turn-over of $300,000 in two years for their business, Ruatara Publications. Mihaka says that her publishing process was actually, "the politics of independent resistance in a constructive way. We weren't collaborating with the Crown to ask what would be worth our saying."

In terms of marketing and distribution, Mihaka wrote to every library, school and institution in Aotearoa with a blurb sheet and an order form. She also sent two copies of the book to every library, which had a 90% success rate. The authors/publishers also did all the promotional work including the press, TV and radio saying it was successful because of Dun Mihaka's public profile as a well-known political activist.

While this was one case of a very successful and valuable self-publishing experience, there were a few authors like Robert Sullivan who said he would never self-publish because he feels he would lose his literary credibility.

In terms of improving the publishing process to make it more accessible to Maori writers, McVeagh believes going to a writing course like Te Reo's prepares people for the realities of the process. Pita Rykis comments, "The ultimate answer would be an Indigenous publishing house," possibly in the same style as Te Reo. It was obvious that he was unaware of the houses already in existence, possibly because they weren't located in Auckland, making real McVeagh and Allen's fears of being overlooked as small, community-based publishers.

Editing

With Huia Publishers and Te Reo Publications Ltd the only publishing houses with in-house Maori editors, it is obvious that issues of editorial control and processes are going to arise. But for the more established writers like Grace and Ihimaera, it is clear they have no issues at all with Pakeha editors working on their books.

For example, Patricia Grace says she's never had problems with editors, sending her work 'ready to go'. She says that if editors want to change something and she doesn't agree, then she won't change it. Grace, like many other successful writers, makes it sound a simple task, with all the rights and power in the hands of the author. In a similar vein, Ihimaera says that when his editors question something he responds in a way that they cannot challenge, by saying, "that might be how you look at it but from a Maori perspective…" Ihimaera says the editors usually say, "Oh well, all right then." It is without doubt, though, that both Grace and Ihimaera come from a position of power and control in the editorial process because of the power their names carry within the market.

Unlike Grace and Ihimaera, Robert Sullivan let the editors of his first book *Jazz Waiata* (Auckland University Press) do anything they wanted to it because he felt intimidated. With his second book, *Pike Ake! Poems 1990–1992* through the same press, though, he knew a bit more, getting advice from another author regarding the process and his rights as an author. Sullivan also contributed to the *Oxford Anthology of New Zealand Poetry* which didn't have a Maori editor, and he feels that the anthology misrepresented Maori poetry. He says he didn't feel comfortable telling the editors why he wanted certain poems pulled but would have, "Felt okay had it been a Maori editor, because a Maori editor would have understood."

Rawinia White was published in *New Women's Fiction* and she believes the editor was influenced by university academics who said that her work wasn't well written. White says they altered a phrase in her piece that she didn't agree with (a process she called 'academic wanking'), but when the piece "The Return" was reprinted in Witi Ihimaera's anthology, it was changed back to its original form.

Wena Harawira has experience working with both a magazine editor and a book publisher (on her guide for marae visitors *Kawa O Te Marae*). On working with Gary Wilson at *Mana Magazine* Harawira says that one of the things that always stuck in her mind was Wilson's insistence that the story have readability, capturing the reader's interest rather than causing them to wonder where the writer was coming from. When writing her book *Te Kawa O Te Marae* Harawira worked with the children's editor at Reed Books, describing the relationship as, "pretty good". Harawira says the editor admitted that she liked working with her because she got things done on deadline (an obvious hangover from Harawira's days of being a journalist). Harawira was told by her editor that some people did not like the constructive criticism she might want to give them, and they were difficult. Harawira comments about her experience,

> I was very conscious that I'm new to this business of writing children's books, and even with my mother's input [as a primary school teacher] I was conscious that if you want the story to be good then you have to take on board a lot of advice. It helped that she's a woman. And she's a mother so not only does she have that professional experience she's got that personal experience too.

Harawira says she never felt compromised by or disagreed with anything the editor suggested. She says that before changing any words the editor asked her why she had used them. Harawira says, "We had quite a good relationship and it's because she realised her lack of experience in regards to this whole Maori issue. We complemented each other."

Although Harawira had a positive experience she acknowledges there could be cultural issues between Maori writers and non-Maori editors. She says that non-Maori editors may not be able to pick out the mistakes in Maori names and places for example, or be able to make a judgment on whether something is factual. Harawira believes this practice is a reality with non-Maori editors, pointing out that some mainstream publishers don't have culturally sensitive editors working for them and so publish books "that trivialise a lot of Maori things". She cites the example of Don Stafford, who lives in Rotorua and has written extensively about the local tribe there. Stafford is well known and respected in both Maori and Pakeha circles, but Harawira says his book *People of the Land* is, "…just a bloody tourist brochure. His intention may be well-meaning but it's trivialised a lot of things that are culturally important to Maori."

Wiremu Kaa, Lecturer in Maori language at the University of Victoria in Wellington and author of a Maori version of the bible, says that instead of the 'proper way to write' being the way 'they say' it is, he'd rather determine the parameters of what he writes and how.[572]

On the other hand Sid Mead, author of *Landmarks*, a text book published by Victoria University Press in Wellington, comments that, "In spite of all the western education we've had, our writing levels have gone backwards…because students turn off Pakeha teachers, which make up most of the education system."

From a publisher's point of view, Robyn Bargh points out that Huia differs from mainstream publishers, who wouldn't touch a lot of the material Huia takes on because of the amount of work needed with the editorial process. She comments,

> A lot of the work that we publish requires lots of editing. In doing that we work a lot with the authors. I try as much as possible to make it an educational experience for them; we advise them about why we want to make the change, how they can do it next time. We do try and involve them as much as we can. We get the editor here to comment on the work and send it back and get the author to respond.

Te Reo Publishers Ltd follow a different process by allowing the writer to decide whether or not to accept the critique they give on a manuscript. Allen comments, "We won't change their words or what they are saying, we might suggest that it be said a different way though." Allen comments,

> A lot of our business is run on process rather than just result. Getting the editing process right, making sure all parties are happy with the way it runs. In some cases it was part of our funding agreement that a work be shown to the Maori Language Commission to check before it went to print. We sat down and explained this process to the author and why they had to do it and said we'd show him the work when it was returned from the Maori Language Commission.

It is clear that Te Reo have a very personal approach to editing, making suggestions, to-ing and fro-ing with the writer. They adopted the process of editing from the way Maori Learning Media functions. Maori Learning Media is the body responsible for developing and producing Maori language materials for the same 500 Maori medium schools that Huia publish for.

Te Reo also run a course teaching people how to write for children, and how to self-edit in the writing process, so that what comes through is exactly what they want to say. Allen is also aware of some Maori writers who have been upset with the editing they've received on manuscripts by mainstream publishers, saying, "They feel that the words have been changed, even changed into a different dialect and they're really touchy about that."

Goodall says he does not want to edit people, preferring that authors write simply what they want to write. He will then publish it the way they have written it. Of course this then leads to the question of quality control and the publication of 'bad writing'.

Geoff Walker says there are few issues he faces at Penguin with editing when the work is in English. He complements what Ihimaera and Grace have said above, commenting, "Pat and Witi are happy to be passed on to the best fiction editors. Issues arise when it's in Maori, but the work then gets passed on to the Maori Language Commission." In this way Walker suggests (as have Grace and Ihimaera) that there is little editorial negotiation or conflicts with the two big names, largely because their works are already refined to a point of being "publication ready" when they are submitted to the publisher.

Walker also points out that there are a number of Maori studies units at universities around Aotearoa with traditional experts that can analyse and review Maori writing. "They don't adopt the same criteria as English academics though, instead they measure the work in terms of its historical significance," he commented.

Reed Books uses freelance editorial staff where necessary on Maori books. Janssen says they also use Maori linguists (who also work for *Mana Magazine*) as well as using the Maori Language Commission for feedback and comment.

Editor Juliet Raven is a self-defined 'Maori Pakeha' (because she was tribally adopted by Maori parents about 20 yeas ago). Although her status is questioned by some Maori, she comments that in 1997 she is the only contract editor of Maori in Wellington, and used to contract to Maori Learning Media. Suggesting that she is 'A damned good editor', Raven says she has worked with Maori women revitalising old words to make new words for computer science, health and botany.[573] Raven says the most common issues that arise when editing a manuscript written by a Maori author are that, "Certain things shouldn't be put into the medium of writing…Sometimes we have stuff that is not going to transform into the written state, and that, in its oral form, doesn't translate, because it's a different ball game." In this way Raven suggests that some material is best left in the oral form and, at other times, "Maori writing is an area where the native speaker must be left to their own expression."

In terms of Pakeha editing Maori work, Raven says in her own defence that Pakeha can be used, but that they have got to be answerable to the Maori. She says, "We might have good editorial skills but they must be fed back to the Maori editorial team." But Gary Wilson of *Mana Magazine* asks the question, "When does the Pakeha help become an intrusion. They help provide the skills now but when will their help become an intrusion?"

Distribution and other issues

Some areas affecting distribution have already been canvassed under the section on publishing, but more detail on the issues involved are given below. Peter Janssen says the size of the country and market itself needs to be considered when defining where Maori literature is at today. With an estimated 500,000 Maori population, publishers need to make economic decisions which mean considering whether or not there is a school market, a general market, a Maori market, an interested Pakeha market and, significantly, a tourist market. He adds, "It's quite common for people to come to New Zealand and then come face to face with a culture that they previously might have thought was cute like say Hawaii, and they want to know more. And they buy a book." Different demands effect the growth of Maori literature too.

But while things might be developing on the publishing front, Witi Ihimaera says he still has to tell publishers what is right and what is wrong about cover design and marketing. He comments,

> We get sick and tired of having to interpret. They don't understand when they put something totally inappropriate on the cover or their time constraints stop them from doing what's right. So you are constantly always engaged with these issues.

In terms of Maori authors having to compromise in order to get things into print, Pita Rykis says that it's an absolute reality, "because the market defines what's publishable." And Poet Hinewirangi says that while she thinks a lot of people compromise so their work is publishable, it is more important for her to be empowered and so doesn't negotiate with publishers, instead giving them the ultimatum: "Either print it as is or not at all. Publish it like I want it or don't bother—I don't compromise."

Marama Mihaka is also uncompromising saying, "I wouldn't compromise at all. I would accept literary advice but I would not accept any advice that would change the meaning or the whole point I was trying to make."

Peter Janssen says authors at Reed do not have to compromise, but all writing has to have a market. He says Maori authors generally comments,

> This is the level of editing we want, and we say fine. This is how we want it to come out, we want you to back it, publish it and use your marketing muscle, but quite frankly we don't want you to be editorially involved apart from correcting grammar. We don't have a problem with that. And they would maybe feel uncomfortable going to someone else, particularly people involved at that level from other tribal areas.

Reviewing

In terms of reviews of Maori writing (in Maori and English), there is some feeling that Maori writing is not being understood by some non-Maori reviewers, while Maori reviewers themselves are not necessarily reviewing the works based on their literary merits. Marama Mihaka says there were two areas of consideration when it came to reviewing the books she and her husband published: the 'political pot' (what the work said politically) and the 'Maori pot' (what the work said about and for Maori). She says the 'literary pot' and how well it worked as a piece of literature was only considered after the other things when the books were reviewed.

Robert Sullivan commented that, "The *New Zealander* [newspaper] reviewer treated me with kid gloves, probably because I'm Maori," while a visiting British academic commented that the content of Sullivan's work was "not poetic".

Gary Wilson says that unfortunately some language reviews and awards are done by Maori but that they are too sympathetic and not critical enough on a literary basis. He pointed out that something cannot be good enough just because it's Maori, and that there needs to be someone criticizing its worth, whoever that is.

In terms of issues faced by Maori writers, from a publisher's perspective Geoff Walker says Maoris sometimes feel insecure about writing solo, especially young writers who choose to write for theatre and music where they can collaborate and workshop as a group on a script or song, making the writer one of a team of actors and production people. He says that a lot of Maori don't have the confidence when it comes to the written word and both young and older people benefit from the work-shopping process.

Robyn Bargh agrees saying that when Huia ran the short story competition, they found that a lot of Maori people were writing, but the level of technical skill needed developing, and so the following year Huia ran workshops called "Technical Skills For Creative Writing". Bargh assumed the participants had the creativity and the ideas of what they wanted to write about and knew how to write to a certain standard, but what Huia wanted was to provide some technical skills of how to develop their writing.

Support mechanisms

Like Australia and Canada, there are some appropriate support mechanisms afforded Maori writers in Aotearoa including government funding, the Huia Short Story Competition and writers workshops.

Government Funding to Literature as an artform

Toi Maori Aotearoa (Maori Arts New Zealand) is a Maori arts organisation that is an advocacy agency for Maori arts, established under the old Queen Elizabeth II Arts Council structure, with the support of Creative New Zealand through Te Waka Toi (the Council for Maori and South Pacific Arts) who provide funding for Maori arts

Creative New Zealand funded Toi Maori to set up as an independent organisation and developed a Trust. Creative New Zealand now provides them with a budget for operating costs as well as project funding through granting rounds. Toi Maori make applications to Creative New Zealand who get the majority of their funding from the Lotteries Office. Participants who attended the 1997 Festival of the Dreaming in Sydney were funded through the Lotteries Office. Toi Maori aims to move away from Creative New Zealand funding and seek private sponsorship in the future.

All of the Committees that make up the charitable Trust present a powerful face for Maori art, its preservation, development, promotion and participation. The objectives of the Trust include,

- to promote, preserve and develop Maori art;
- to promote and implement Maori art projects;
- to promote and develop cultural exchange opportunities with other Indigenous cultures;
- to promote and develop Maori art interests and concerns in the political, corporate and local government arenas;
- to promote and assist in the development of policy advice on all Maori artforms;
- to promote and develop the wairua (spirit) and general education of the beneficiaries.[574]

Toi Maori provide services to all of the national Maori artform committees and their projects, including other Maori artform organisations with a national focus who wish to join the Trust. These services include:[575]

- administrative services;
- a resource base for nga Toi Maori (the arts of the Maori);
- development and promotion of nga Toi Maori both internationally and nationally;
- development and promotion of cultural exchange;
- providing a national support base for nga Toi Maori.

The Trust represents eight of the national Maori artform committees that existed within the original Te Waka Toi structure. There are eight committees, two of which are devoted to literature,

- Te Hunga Taunaki Kaituhi Maori—Maori literature in the Maori language
- Te Ha—Maori literature in English

Both these committees play important roles in the development of Maori literature and provide a national focus for that development to take place. The other committees are for weaving, waka, dance and drama, music, customs and traditions, and visual arts.

Te Hunga Taunaki Kaituhi Maori have been responsible for the publishing of books written in the Maori language. They have played a major role in assisting writers in Maori by holding workshops in different regions and providing expert guidance to prospective Maori authors. Without the assistance of this committee many written Maori projects would not have been completed. This committee includes amongst its kaupapa (philosophy) the provision of a 'vehicle' for the writing and publication of original writing in Te Reo and establishment of a wananga (the learning environment) to promote writing in Te Reo.[576]

Te Ha lists among its long term goals[577]:
- to have a self-sustaining Maori publishing industry;
- to see a significant, measurable increase in the number of Maori writers;
- to have works published, widely distributed and adequately promoted;
- to ensure total quality management of works published by Maori writers;
- the establishment of a Maori writing and publishing school.

Te Ha have held writers forums to promote Maori writers, assisted writers to attend international conferences overseas, initiated the development of a database for Maori writers, and sponsored literary awards for Maori writers.

Toi Maori and literature

About $30,000 – $60,000 per annum goes to literature through Toi Maori.[578] Visual and performing arts get the majority of the funding because they are oriented towards greater audiences and there's more people in performance than writing. Eric Tamepo of Toi Maori Aotearoa comments that, "The writers always seem to be the ones that come out last." For example, while they have had visual arts and basket weaving exchanges and exhibitions in America and Australia, similar projects haven't happened with writers.

Toi Maori mostly invite writers to Aotearoa. They invited First Nations' American writers to the International Festival of the Arts in 1996, and Aboriginal writer Phillip McLaren to the first Toi Maori Festival in Rotorua in early 1997.

Tamepo says that the more prominent writers like Patricia Grace, Keri Hulme and Witi Ihimaera are the only ones acknowledged and given credibility, "They are the nucleus of the more well-known writers." He says the literature committee Te Hunga Taunaki Kaituhi Maori looks at educating Maoris who wish to write, running workshops for writers to write in Maori, offering services to edit scripts and advise on getting published. Te Ha looks at writers who write in English (across all genres) and who run workshops. Tamepo notes they are also looking at providing opportunities for writers to go overseas for international experiences.

In terms of funding, Witi Ihimaera says that Maori writers are obviously disadvantaged when it comes to the application process of funding bodies unless they are well known to those involved in the selection. Only those writers with established public profiles are likely to be funded, which is not the case for emerging Aboriginal writers in Australia who often receive one-off funding for developing and/or researching manuscripts. The credibility of Aboriginal writers comes in the form of support letters from community organisations and individuals who support the particular concept or writing project proposed by the individual writer, and a committee funds the applications according to merit and criterion that include support.

Huia Short Story Awards

Another support mechanism for Maori writers is the Huia short-story competition run every two years with successful stories appearing in a Huia anthology. There is a $3,000 computer as a prize in each of the following categories:

1) Toi Aotearoa Award for best short story for adults in Maori by a Maori writer;
2) Te Puni Kokiri Award for best short story for children in Maori by a Maori writer;
3) Telecom Award for best short story in English by a previously published Maori writer;
4) GP Print Award for best short story in English by an unpublished author.

The first competition was in 1995 and attracted 300 entries, sixty of them in Maori. Bargh says the purpose of the competition is to create more Maori literature in the long run, while also aiming to increase the number of books in print for Maori adult readers because, "Not many books that have been published in Maori are for adults. Ninety-nine per cent are for children, so this was a way of changing that."

Workshops

To overcome the technical writing issues facing Maori writers, Te Reo run a writing program that aims to provide a course of study that enables students to develop awareness of children's literature in general, including particularly those books in Maori or from a Maori perspective, and to give them the skills to create saleable material of their own, whether in Maori or English.

In terms of issues writers faced when wanting to get published McVeagh says there is a general lack of knowledge about the whole process, and particularly for Maori people because it's not something that's thought of as a possibility. Annais Allen adds that it is clear that most people don't have any understanding of the process of writing and re-writing and using drafts.

Lessons for Aboriginal Publishing In Australia

There are a number of lessons that can be learned from the Maori publishing experience. Firstly, that it should be the responsibility of publishers to provide some nurturing of writers to assist in the development of writers as individuals, which would in turn assist the industry as a whole. Such nurturing or support would come by way of writing courses and workshops as well as writing competitions like the Huia Short Story competition. While UQP and UWA currently sponsor writers' awards, they are both for manuscript length works, and many emerging writers are far from that level.

The success of Marama Mihaka's self-publishing experience is also an inspiration and model from which Aboriginal authors could work if complete control of a published work is the desire of the writer. Her marketing and distribution strategy is also something that Aboriginal publishers in Australia could adopt as they currently appear to fail their authors in appropriate marketing and reasonable distribution.

Appendix A
Catalogue of Aboriginal Literature

For the purpose of developing a catalogue of Aboriginal literature, I have included only those works that are written by Aboriginal people, or collaborative works between Aboriginal and non-Aboriginal people. The catalogue is not comprehensive but ongoing. The categories are:

1. **Aboriginal studies**
    a) Aboriginal culture
    b) History and oral history
    c) Others—social commentary, literary criticism, profiles etc other works not included in this research, but which would classify as works of Aboriginal culture include books on bush foods, art, women's studies, encyclopaedias, language dictionaries, regional studies, land rights, education and media studies.
2. **Anthology**
3. **Autobiography**
4. **Biography**
5. **Children's stories**
6. **Fiction**
7. **Plays and Scripts**
8. **Poetry**

1. Aboriginal Studies

a) Aboriginal Culture

Ahern, Amanda & the Mornington Island Elders, *Paint Up*, UQP, St Lucia, 2001.

Crugnale, Jordan ed., *Footprints Across Our Land,* Magabala Books, Broome, 1995.

Kimberley Language Resource Centre and authors, *Moola Bulla: in the shadow of the Mountain*, Magabala Books, Broome, 1996.

Lands, Merrilee, *Traditional food of the Dampier Peninsula and Broome*, Magabala Books, Broome, 1996.

Lester, Yami, *Learning from the Land,* IAD Press, Alice Springs. 1990.

Lowe, Pat (NA) and Jimmy Pike, *Jilji: Life in the Great Sandy Desert,* Magabala Books, Broome, 1990.

Mowaljarlai, David and Jutta Malnic, *Yorro Yorro, Spirit of the Kimberley,* Magabala Books, Broome, 1993 /2001.

Mowaljarlai, David, *Visions of Mowanjum: Aboriginal Writing from the Kimberley,* Rigby, Adelaide, 1980.

Mutitjulu Community and Lynn Baker, *Mingkiri*, IAD Press, Alice Springs, 1995.

Nangan, Joe, *Joe Nangan's Dreaming: Aboriginal Legends of the North-West*, T. Nelson, West Melbourne, 1976.

Noonuccal, Oodgeroo, *The Spirit of Australia*, Golden Press, Silverwater, 1989.

—— *Australian Legends and Landscapes*, Random House, Sydney, 1990.

—— *Australia's Unwritten History: More Legends of Our Land*, Harcourt Brace Jovanovich, Sydney, 1992.

Skipper, Peter & Pompy Siddon, *Kungkala-Firesticks*, Summer Institute of Linguistics. Australian Aboriginal Branch, Berrimah, NT, 1973.

—— *Yawartarlu piyirn tarapinya = Thrown By A Horse*, Summer Institute of Linguistics, Australian Aboriginal Branch, Darwin, 1975.

—— *Purlumanu parayanany piyirntu =The Bullock Riders*, Summer Institute of Linguistics. Australian Aboriginal Branch, Darwin, 1974

—— *Wangkiwarnti yiljimgajangkawarnti=Stories of life in the desert,* Summer Institute of Linguistics. Australian Aboriginal Branch, Darwin, 1979.

—— *Nganpayi pujman = The Bushman*. Summer Institute of Linguistics. Australian Aboriginal Branch, Darwin, 1978.

—— *Yawartalu Piyin tarapinya,* Summer Institute of Linguistics, Australian Aboriginal Branch, Berrimah, 1973.

Stevens, Peter, Nelson Hughes and the Gurama Elders Group, Guruma Story, IAD Prress, Alice Springs, 2001.

Tjapaltjarri, (Kevin Morris), *Tjakumanu tjuta yirrititja*, Papunya Literature Production Centre, Alice Springs, 1982.

—— *Catching Brumbies: a story*, NT Department of Education, Darwin, 1983.

—— *Pungkupayitarra: a story,* Papunya Literature Production Centre, Alice Springs, 1983.

—— *Wati kutja mamu mirrintanu: a story*, Papunya Literature Production Centre, Alice Springs, 1983.

—— *Wati kukaku yankukitja: a story*, Papunya Literature Production Centre, Alice Springs, 1983.

—— *Kukawiyaya nyinanyi: a story,* Papunya Literature Production Centre, Alice Springs, 1983.

—— *Ikunytjinya: a story,* Papunya Literature Production Centre, Alice Springs, 1983.

—— *Yara pangkalangutjarra: a story,* Papunya Literature Production Centre, Alice Springs, 1983.

—— *Haasts Bluff ikuntjinya ngankirritjanya: a story,* Papunya Literature Production Centre, Alice Springs, 1983.

—— *Tji-lpi kutju katja kutjarra,* Papunya Literature Production Centre, Alice Springs, 1984.

—— *Rodeo,* Papunya Literature Production Centre, Alice Springs. 1985.

—— *Yara mulyatanku puluka mantjintja*, Papunya Literature Production Centre, Alice Springs, 1985.

Ula kutjarra yankupayi, Papunya Literature Production Centre, Alice Springs, 1985.

—— *Wati kutju maluku anu na anytjangka,* Papunya Literature Production Centre, Alice Springs, 1985.

—— *Napangatinyapilku maniwiyangka nyinapayi,* Papunya Literature Production Centre, Alice Springs, 1988.

—— *Ula tjangayitjarra,* Papunya Literature Production Centre, Alice Springs, 1988.

Tulo, Gordon, *Mibi Aboriginal tales from Queensland's Endeavour River,* ANU Press, Canberra, 1980.

Trezise, Percy, *Rock Art of South East Cape York,* AIAS, Canberra, 1971.

Unaipon, David, *Native Legends,* Hunkins, Ellis and King, Adelaide, c1920

—— *Aborignal Legends.* Hunkins, Ellis and King, Adelaide, 1921.

—— *Australian Aborigines,* Aborigines Friends Association, Adelaide, 1928.

b) History and oral history

Alherramp-areny — *Angkety Arelh-kenh: Womens stories from Laramba,* IAD Press, Alice Springs, 200.

Bell, Desmond ed., *Aborigines in Defence of Australia,* ANU Press, Sydney, 1991.

Bray, George, & Kenny Laughton eds, *Aboriginal Ex-Servicemen of Central Australia,* IAD Press, Alice Springs, 1995.

Chryssides, Helen *Local Heroes,* Collins Dove, North Blackburn, 1993.

Hall, Bob, *Fighters From The Fringe: Aborigines and Torres Strait Islanders Recall the Second World War,* Aboriginal Studies Press, 1995.

Jackomos, Al and Derek Fowell, *Forgotten Heroes: Aborigines at War from the Somme to Vietnam.* Victoria Press, South Melbourne, 1993.

Japaljarri, Dinny, *Long Time, Olden Time: Aboriginal accounts of Northern Territory history,* IAD Press, Alice Springs, 1993.

Kartinyeri, Doreen, *Ngarrindjeri Anzacs,* SA Museum and Raukkan Council, Adelaide, 1996.

Koch, Grace ed., translations by Harold Koch, *Kaytetye Country: an Aboriginal history of the Barrow Creek area,* IAD Press, Alice Springs, 1993.

Lowe, D, *Forgotten Rebels: Black Australians Who Fought Back,* Permanent Press, Melbourne, 1994.

Marshall, Paul, *Raparapa,* Magabala Books, Broome, 1988.

Matthews, Janet, *The Opal that Turned Into fire,* Magabala Books, Broome, 1994.

McPhee, Jack & Patrick Konigsberg, *Bee Hill River Man: Kanulangu-Bidi,* Magabala Books, Broome, 1994.

Munro, Morndi, as told to Mary Anne Jebb, *Emarara: man from Merara,* Magabala Books, Broome, 199.

Neidjie, Bill, *Story About Feeling, Aboriginal Australia,* Magabala Books, Broome, 1989.

Pepper, Phillip and Tess D. Araugo, *You Are What You Make Yourself To Be: the story of a Victorian Aboriginal Family 1842-1980,* Hyland House, South Yarra, 1980.

—— *The Kurnai of Gippsland,* Hyland House, South Yarra, 1985.

Rockman, Napaljarri Peggy and Lee Cataldi, *Warlpiri Dreamings and Histories,* HarperCollins, San Francisco, 1994.

Roe, Paddy and Steven Muecke, *Gularabulu: Stories from West Kimberley,* Fremantle Arts Centre Press, South Fremantle, 1983.

Rosser, Bill, *Up Rode the Troopers: The Black Police in Queensland,* UQP. St Lucia. 1990.

—— *This Is Palm Island,* AIAS, Canberra, 1978.

—— *Return to Palm Island,* Aboriginal Studies Press, Canberra, 1994.

Taylor, Alf, *Long Time Now,* Magabala Books, Broome, 2001.

Trezise, Percy, *Dream Road: A Journey of Discovery,* Allen and Unwin, St Leonards, 1993.

Vaarzon-Morel, Petronella ed, *Warlpiri Women's Voices, Warlpiri karnta karnta-kurlangu yimi, Our Lives, Our History.* IAD Press, Alice Springs, 1995.

Wharton, Herb ed., *Cattle Camp: Murri Drovers and Their Stories,* UQP. St Lucia, 1994.

Merlan, Francesca as told to, *Big River Country: stories from Elsey Station,* IAD Press, Alice Springs, 1996.

Miller, James, *Koori, A Will To Win*; Survival and Triumph of Black Australia, Angus & Robertson, Sydney, 1985.

Williams, Edna Tantjingu and Eileen Wani Wingfield, *Down the hole,* IAD Press, Alice Springs, 2000.

Wositzky, Jan as told to by Wardaman storyteller Yidumduma Bill Harney, *Born Under a Paperbark Tree: A Man's Life,* ABC Books, Sydney, 1996.

Wright, Alexis, *Grog War,* Magabala Books, Broome, 1997.

Zagar, Cilka, *Goodbye Riverbank: The Barwon-Namoi People Tell their story,* Magabala Books, Broome, 2000.

c) Other

Bennett, Roger ed & Bob Hodge, *Aboriginal Writing Today. Papers from 1st National Conference of Aboriginal writers,* AIAS, Canberra, 1985.

Buchanan, Cheryl, *We Have Bugger All!: the Kulaluk story of Cheryl Buchanan,* Race Relations Dept of Australian Union of Students, Carlton, 1974.

—— *Responding to Custody Levels,* AGPS, Canberra, 1994.

Coolwell, Wayne, *My Kind of People,* UQP, St. Lucia, 1993.

Heiss, Anita, *Sacred Cows,* Magabala Books, Broome, 1996.

Fesl, Eve Mumewa D., *Conned: A Koori Perspective,* UQP, St Lucia, 1993.

Gilbert, Kevin, *Because a White Man'll Never Do It,* Angus and Robertson, Sydney, 1973.

—— *Living Black: Blacks Talk to Kevin Gilbert,* Penguin, Melbourne, 1977.

—— *Aboriginal Sovereignty: Justice, the Law and Land,* Burrambinga Books, Canberra, 1987.

Huggins, Jackie, *Sister Girl: The Writings of Aboriginal Activist and Historian,* UQP, St. Lucia, 1998.

Jones, Elsie, *Paakantji alphabet book,* Disadvantaged Country Area Programme, Western Readers Committee. Dubbo, 1981.

Moreton-Robertson, Aileen, *Talkin' up to the White Woman: Indigenous Women and Feminism,* UQP, St Lucia, 2000.

Trezise, Percy, *The Last Days of Wilderness,* Collins, Sydney, 1975.

—— *Quinkan Country, adventures in search of Aboriginal Cave Paintings in Cape York,* Reed, Sydney, 1969.

Willmot, Eric, *Social Development in Northern Australia: and the Effects of Social Institutions,* University of Northern Territory Planning Authority, Darwin, 1982

—— *Future Pathways: Equity or Isolation,* University of New England, Armidale, 1988.

2. Anthologies

Akiwenzie-Damm, Kateri and Josie Douglas, *skins: contemporary indigenous writing,* Jukurrpa Books/Kegedonce Press, Alice Spring/Canada, 2000.

Bin-Sallik, Mary Ann, *Aboriginal Women By Degrees: Their stories of the journey towards academic achievement,* UQP, St. Lucia, 2000.

Bin Salleh, Rachel, ed., *Holding Up The Sky: Aboriginal Women Speak,* Magabala Books, Broome, 1999.

Bowden R. & B. Bunbury, *Being Aboriginal,* ABC Enterprises, Crows Nest, 1990.

Brewster, Anne, Angeline O'Neill & Rosemary van den Berg, *Those Who Remain Will Always Remember: An Anthology of Aboriginal Writing,* Fremantle Arts Centre Press, Fremantle, 2000.

Gallagher, Nan, *A Story To Tell: The Working Lives of 10 Aboriginal Australians,* Cambridge University Press, Melbourne, 1992.

Davis, Jack, Stephen Muecke, Mudrooroo and Adam Shoemaker eds, *Paperbark: A Collection of Black Australian Writings,* UQP. St Lucia. 1990.

Davis, Kerry ed., *Across Country: Stories from Aboriginal Australia,* ABC Books, Sydney, 1998.

Douglas, Josie, compiled by, *Untreated,* IAD Press, Alice Springs, 2001.

Heiss, Anita(ed), *Life in Gadigal Country,* Gadigal Information Service, Sydney, 2002.

Kapetas, Jan Teagle, Ivy Dodd, Valmae Dalgetty Walley, Fiona Stafford & Jay Walley, *From Our Hearts: an anthology of new Aboriginal writing from southwest Western Australia,* Kadadjiny Mia Walyalup Writers, South Fremantle, 2000.

Pascoe, Bruce, *Aboriginal Short Stories,* Pascoe Publishing, Apollo Bay, 1990.

Reed-Gilbert, Kerry ed., *Message Stick: Contemporary Aboriginal Writing,* IAD Press, Alice Springs, 1997.

—— *The Strength Of Us As Women: Black Women Speak,* Ginninderra Press, Canberra, 2000.

Sabbioni, Jennifer, Kay Schaffer & Sidionie Smith, *Indigenous Australian Voices: A Reader,* Rutgers University Press, New Jersey. 1998

Weller, Archie & C. Glass, *Us Fellas: An Anthology of Aboriginal Writing,* Artlook Books, Perth, 1987.

Wright, Alexis ed., *Take Power,* IAD Press, Alice Springs, 1998.

3. Autobiography

Anderson, Barbara, *Think Before You Judge,* B. Anderson, Frankston, 1994.

Bohemia, Jack and Bill McGregor, *Nyibayarri: Kimberley Tracker,* Aboriginal Studies Press, Canberra, 1995.

Bropho, Robert, *Fringedweller,* APCOL, Sydney, 1980.

Camfoo, Tex & Nelly, *Love Against the Law: The autobiographies of Tex and Nelly Camfoo,* recorded and edited by Gillian Cowlishaw, Aboriginal Studies Press, Canberra, 2000.

Chesson, Keith, *Jack Davis: a life-story,* Dent, Melbourne, 1988.

Cohen, Bill, *To My Delight: The Autobiography of Bill Cohen, a Grandson of the Gumbangarri,* Aboriginal Studies Press, Canberra, 1987.

Crawford, Evelyn, *Over My Tracks: A Remarkable Life: as told to Chris Walsh,* Penguin Books, Ringwood, 1993.

Crugnale, Jordan compiled by, *Footprints Across Our Land: Short Sories by Senior Western Desert Women,* Magabala Books, Broome, 1995.

Davis, Jack, *A Boy's Life,* Magabala Books, Broome, 1991, 2000.

Dodd, Bill, *Broken Dreams,* UQP, St. Lucia, 1992.

Edmund, Mabel, *No Regrets,* UQP, St. Lucia, 1992.

Goolagong-Cawley, Evonne & Jarret, Phil, *Home!: The Evonne Goolagong story,* Simon & Schuster, 1993

Gaffney, Ellie, *Somebody Now: The Autobiography of Ellie Gaffney, A Woman of Torres Strait,* Aboriginal Studies Press, Canberra, 1989.

Hamilton, Jean, *Just Lovely.* McKenzie, Coonamble, 1989.

Harrison, (Bill) Shorty, *All Hearts Bleed The Same: Reflections, Recollections and Memories, an Autobiography,* B. Harrison, Nowra, 1994.

Hegarty, Ruth, *Is That You Ruthie?,* UQP, St. Lucia, 1999.

Holt, Albert, *Forcibly Removed,* Magabala Books, Broome, 2001

Huggins, Rita and Jackie Huggins, *Auntie Rita,* Aboriginal Studies Press, Canberra, 1994.

Kennedy, Marnie, *Born a Half-Caste,* Aboriginal Studies Press, Canberra, 1985.

King, Wayne, *Black Hours.* Angus & Robertson, Pymble, 1996.

Langford Ginibi, Ruby, *My Bundjalung People,* UQP, St. Lucia, 1994.

—— *Don't Take Your Love To Town.* Penguin, Ringwood, 1988.

—— *Real Deadly.* Angus and Robertson, Sydney, 1992.

—— *Haunted By The Past,* Allen & Unwin, St. Leonard's, 1999.

Lennon, Jessie, *And I Always Been Moving!: The Early Life of Jessie Lennon,* Jessie Lennon & Michelle Maddigan, Coober Pedy, 1996.

—— *I'm The One That Know This Country: the story of Jessie Lennon and Coober Pedy,* Aboriginal Studies Press, Canberra, 2000.

Lester, Yami, *Yami: The autobiography of Yami Lester,* IAD Press Press, Alice Springs, 1993.

Lovett-Gardiner, Aunty Iris, *Lady of the Lake: Aunty Iris's Story,* Koori Heritage Trust, Melbourne, 1997.

Mallett, Molly, *My Past Their Future, Stories from Cape Barren Island,* Blubber Head Press, Sandy Bay, 2001.

McDonald, Connie Nungulla, *When You Grow Up,* Magabala Books, Broome, 1996.

McGuinness, Joe, *Son of Alyandabu: My Fight for Aboriginal Rights,* UQP, St. Lucia, 1991.

Medcraft, Rosalie and Gee, Valda, *The Sausage Tree,* UQP, St Lucia, 1995.

Morgan, Eileen, *The Calling of the Spirits,* Aboriginal Studies Press, Canberra, 1995.

Morgan, Sally, *My Place,* Fremantle Arts Centre Press. Fremantle, 1987.

Neidjie, Bill, *Kakadu Man: Bill Neidjie,* ed by Stephen Davis & Allan Fox, Mybrood, Queanbeyan, 1985.

Noonuccal, Oodgeroo, *Stradbroke Dreamtime,* Angus & Robertson, Sydney, 1972.

Perkins, Charles, *A Bastard Like Me,* Ure Smith, Sydney, 1975.

Perry, Colleen Shirley, *Mum Shirl: an autobiography,* 1981.

Pring, Adele, ed., *Women of the Centre.* Pascoe Publishing, Apollo Bay, 1990.

Roughsey, Dick, *Moon and Rainbow: The Autobiography of an Aboriginal,* Rigby, Adelaide, 1977.

Rubuntja, IAD Press, Alice Springs, 2002.

Saunders, Keith, *Learning the Ropes,* Aboriginal Studies Press, Canberra, 1992.

Smith, Ollie & Diana Plater, *Raging Partners: two worlds one friendship,* Magabala Books, Broome, 2000.

Simon, Ella, *Through My Eyes,* Rigby, Adelaide, 1978.

Somerville, Margaret, Marie Dundas, May Mead, Janet Robinson and Maureen Sulter, *The Sun Dancin': People and Place in Coonabarabran,* Aboriginal Studies Press, Canberra, 1994.

Sullivan, Jack, *Banggaiyerri: the story of Jack Sullivan,* AIAS, Canberra, 1983.

Taylor, Alf, *Long Time Now,* Magabala Books, Broome, 2001.

Tucker, Margaret, *If Everyone Cared,* Ure Smith, Sydney, 1977

Walgar, Monty, as told to Cloud Shabalah, *Jinangga: On My Tracks,* Magabala Books, Broome, 1999.

Walker, Della, *Me and You: The Life Story of Della Walker as told to Tina Coutts,* Aboriginal Studies Press, Canberra, 1989.

Williams, Magdelene, with Pat Torres, *This Is My Word,* Magabala Books, Broome, 1999.

Unaipon, David, *My Life Story,* Aboriginal Friends Association, Adelaide, 1954.

Ward, Glenyse, *Wandering Girl,* Magabala Books, Broome, 1987.

—— *Unna You Fullas,* Magabala Books, Broome, 1991.

West, Ida, *Pride Against Prejudice: Reminiscences of a Tasmanian Aborigine,* Aboriginal Studies Press, Canberra, 1984.

Wharton, Herb, *Where Ya' Been Mate?* UQP, St. Lucia, 1996.

Woodrow, Marjorie, *One of the Lost Generation*, M. Woodrow, Eight Mile Plains, 1990.

4. Biography

Anderson, Warrigal, *Warrigal's Way,* UQP, St Lucia, 1996.

Beeson, Margaret J, ed, *Some Aboriginal Women Pathfinders: Their Difficulties and their Achievements*, National Women's Christian Temperance Union of Australia, Adelaide, 1980.

Bell, Jeanie, *Talking About Celia,* UQP, St Lucia, 1997.

Burgoyne, Iris Yumadoo Kochallalya, *The Mirning: We are the Whales,* Magabala Books, Broome 2000.

Coe, Mary, *Windradyne: A Wiradjuri Koori,* Aboriginal Studies Press, Canberra, 1986.

Corrigan, Florence, as told to Loreen Brehaut, *Miles of Post and Wire,* Magabala Books, Broome, 1998.

Edmund, Mabel, *Hello Johnny!: stories of my Aboriginal and South Sea Islander Family,* Central QLD University Press, Rockhampton, 1996.

Loos, Noel, & Mabo, Koiki, *Edward Koikoi Mabo: His Life and Struggle for Land Rights,* UQP, St. Lucia, 1996.

Nannup A, L Marsh & S. Kinnane, *When The Pelican Laughed*. Fremantle Arts Centre Press, Fremantle, 1992.

Marshall, Paul ed *Raparapa,* Magabala Books, Broome, 1988.

Matthew, Janet with Jimmy Barker, *The Two Worlds of Jimmie Barker: The Life of an Australian Aboriginal,* Aboriginal Studies Press, Canberra, 1977.

McKellar, Hazel, *Woman From No Where,* as told to Kerry McCallum, Magabala Books, Broome, 2000.

Moran, Rod, *Icon of the North: The Legend of Tom Gray,* Access Press, Northbridge, 1995.

Morgan, Sally, *Wanamurraganya, The Story of Jack McPhee,* Fremantle Arts Centre Press, Fremantle, 1989.

—— *Arthur Corunna's Story,* Fremantle Arts Centre Press, Fremantle, 1990.

—— *Mother and Daughter: the story of daisy and Gladys Corunna*, Fremantle Arts Centre Press, Fremantle, 1990.

—— *Sally's Story,* Fremantle Arts Centre Press. Fremantle. 1990.

Pederson, Howard & Banjo Woorunumurra, *Jandamarra and the Bunuba Resistance,* Magabala Books, Broome, 1995.

Rosser, Bill, *Dreamtime Nightmares: Biographies of Aborigines Under the QLD Act*. AIAS, Canberra, 1985.

Roughsey, Elsie & Virginia Huffer, *The Sweetness of the Fig: Aboriginal women in transition*, UNSW Press, Sydney, 1980.

—— *An Aboriginal Mother Tells of the Old and The New,* McPhee Gribble, Penguin Books. Fiztroy, 1984.

van den Berg, Rosemary, *No Options, No Choice! The Moore River Experience,* Magabala Books, Broome, 1994.

Wilmot, Eric, *Pumulwuy: The Rainbow Warrior,* Weldons, McMahons Point, 1987.

Wilson, Graham J, *Pilbara Bushman: the Life Experience of W. Dunn,* Hesperian Press, Victoria Park, 1989.

5. Children's stories / juvenile literature

Abdulla, Ian, *As I Grow Older,* Omnibus Books. Norwood, 1993.

—— *Tucker,* Omnibus Books, Norwood, 1994.

—— *As I Grew Older: The Life and Times of a Numga Growing Up Along the River Murray,* Omnibus Books, Norwood, 1993.

Adams, Jeannie, *Going for Oysters,* Omnibus Books, Norwood, 1991.

—— *Pigs and Honey,* Omnibus Books, Adelaide, 1989.

Arrernte Curriculum Project, *Unte Nthenharenye? (Where do you come from?)* IAD Press, Alice Springs, 1993.

Bin Saad, Sermsah, *The Best Little Knitter in the West*, Illustrated by Samantha Cook, Magabala Books, Broome, 2000.

Boddington, Ross, *The Budura Story,* Magabala Books, Broome, 1996.

Boney, Maria, *Biggie-Billa The Porcupine*, Disadvantaged Country Area Programme, Western reader Committee, Dubbo, 1980

Borinelli, Martha, *How Nurn The Snake Got The Poison,* AERU, Leederville, 1992.

Burton, Daphne Punytjina, *Kupi Kupi and the Girl*, Illustrated by Carolyn Windy, Magabala Books, Broome, 2000.

Byno, J and D. Wright, *Mundaguddah and Warwai,* Disadvantaged Country Area Programme, Western Reader Committee, Dubbo, 1980.

Cameron, Olly, *Emu Hunting,* Harcourt Brace Jovanovich, Sydney, c1987.

Cairns, Sylvia, *Uncle Willie McKenzie's Legends of the Goundirs*, Jacaranda Press, Milton, 1967.

Charles, Mary Carmel, *Winin, Why the Emu Cannot Fly,* Magabala Books, Broome, 1993.

Chi, Jimmy, *Broome Songwriters*, Hodja Educational Resources Cooperative, Richmond, 1985.

Cruse, Beryl, Rebecca Kirby, Liddy Stewart and Steven Thomas, *Bittangabee Tribe: An Aboriginal Story from Coastal NSW,* Aboriginal Studies Press, Canberra, 1994.

Daley, Lucy, *Dirrangun,* HarperCollins, Pymble, 1997.

Edwards, Yvonne, Brenda Day and Tjitji Tjuta, *Going for Kalta: Hunting for sleepy lizards at Yalata,* IAD Press, Alice Springs, 1997.

Fogarty, Lionel, *Booyooburra: A Story of the Wakka Murri,* Hyland House, South Melbourne, 1993.

Furber, G, *Kake Artepe Mwernelhentye Atherre, The Siamese Twins,* IAD Press, Alice Springs. 1993.

Gadja, Michael & Wanyarra, Roy Banning, *Bulurru Storywater,* M. Quinn, Kuranda, 1990.

Gela, Anne Abednego, *Gelam, The Man from Moa,* Magabala Books, Broome, 1993.

Gilbert, Kevin, *Me and Mary Kangaroo,* Viking, Ringwood, 1994.

Greene, Gracie, Tramacchi Joe, Gill, Lucille, *Tjarany Roughtail, The Dreaming of the Roughtail Lizard and other Stories told by the Kukatja,* Magabala Books, Broome, 1992.

Heffernan, M. *The Crawling Baby Boy,* IAD Press, Alice Springs, 1990.

—— *The Snake's Tree Apmwe-kenhe arne,* IAD Press Press, Alice Springs, 1993.

Jarl, Moonie, *The Legends of Moonie Jarl,* Jacaranda Press, Milton, 1964.

Jones, Elsie, *The Galah and the frill neck lizard,* Disadvantaged Country Area Programme, Western Reader Committee, Wilcannia, 1978.

—— *The Story of the Falling Star,* Aboriginal Studies Press, Canberra, 1989.

Lowe, Pat & Jimmy Pike, *Desert Dog,* Magabala Books, Broome, 1997.

—— *Yinti- Desert Child,* Magabala Books, Broome, 1992.

—— *The Girl With No Name,* Puffin, Ringwood, 1994.

—— *Desert Cowboy,* Magabala Books, Broome, 2000.

Lurda, Johnny, *The Lost Pup,* Harcourt Brace Jovanovich, Sydney, 1987.

Meeks, AR, *Enora and the Black Crane.* Ashton Scholastic, Sydney, 1991.

—— *Our Land Our People,* NSWLALC, Liverpool, 1991.

Miller, Olga, *Fraser Island Legends,* Jacaranda Press, Milton, 1993.

—— *Legends of Fraser Island,* Reigby Heinemann, Port Melbourne, 1994.

Morgan, Sally, *Little Piggies,* Femantle Arts Centre Press, Fremantle, 1991.

—— *The Flying Emu and other Australian stories,* Viking, Ringwood, 1992.

—— *Hurry Up, Oscar!,* Puffin Books, Ringwood, 1993.

—— *Dan's Grandpa,* Sandcasltle, South Fremantle, 1996.

—— *Just A Little Brown Dog,* Fremantle Arts Centre Press, Fremantle, 1997.

—— *Pet Problem,* Fremantle Arts Centre Press, Fremantle, 1994.

—— *In Your Dreams,* Sandcastle Books, South Fremantle, 1997.

McRobbie, Narelle, *BIP: The Snapping Bungaroo,* Magabala Books, Broome, 1990.

—— *Who's That Jumbun in the Log,* Magabala Books, Broome.

Mumbulla, Percy, *The Whalers,* HarperCollins, Pymble, 1996.

—— *Minah: A Poem in Four Parts,* HarperCollins, Pymble, 1995.

Noonuccal, Oodgeroo, *Legends of Our Land,* Harcourt Brace Jordan, Marrickville, 1990.

—— *Rainbow Serpent,* AGPS, Canberra, 1988.

O'Brien, May, *Wunambi The Water Snake,* Aboriginal Studies Press, Canberra, 1991.

—— *The Legend of the Seven Sisters,* Aboriginal Studies Press, Canberra. 1990.

—— *Badadu Stories,* Sandcastle, Fremantle, 1994.

—— *Why The Emu Can't Fly,* Fremantle Arts Centre Press, Fremantle, 1992.

—— *How Crows Became Black,* Fremantle Arts Centre Press, Fremantle, 1992.

—— *The Kangaroos Who Wanted To Become People,* Fremantle Arts Centre Press, Fremantle, 1992.

—— *Barn-Barn Barlala: The Bush Trickster,* Fremantle Arts Centre Press, Fremantle, 1992.

Pilawuk, Markotic, Rosemary, and Forest Ray, *The Arguing Edibles,* Magabala Books, Broome, 1992.

Porter, James, *Piya,* Hodder & Stoughton, Sydney, 1990.

Poulter, Jim, *Majorie's Magic Mook Mook,* Red Hen Press, Melbourne, 1989.

—— *The Secret of the Dreaming: The Story of Why the Land is Sacred and Man Must be its Caretaker,* Red Hen Press, Melbourne, 1988.

Richards, June Wulkutjukurr, *Eagle's Nest: Warlawurra Manngutjarra,* Magabala Books, Broome, 1997.

Roughsey, Dick, *The Giant Devil Dingo,* Collins, Sydney, 1973.

—— *The Rainbow Serpent,* Collins, Sydney, 1975.

Roughsey, Dick & Percy Tresize, *The Quinkins,* Collins, Sydney, 1978.

—— *Banana Bird and the Snake Men,* Collins, Sydney, 1980.

—— *Turramulli the Giant Quinkin,* Collins, Sydney, 1982.

—— *The Magic Firesticks,* Collins, Sydney, 1983.

—— *Gidja,* Collins, Sydney, 1984.

—— *The Flying Fox Warriors,* Collins, Sydney, 1985.

Roughsey, Elsie, *The Turkey and the Emu,* Harcourt Brace Jovanovich Group, Sydney, 1978.

Sheppard, Nancy, *Alitj in Dreamland: An Aboriginal Version of Lewis Carroll's Alice in Wonderland,* Simon & Schuster, East Roseville, 1992.

Soloman, Selena, *Dabu, The Baby Dugong-Kazi Dhangal,* Magabala Books, Broome, 1997.

Timbery, Laddie, *Timbery Tales: children's stories from the dawn of time,* L. Timbery, NSW. 1994.

Torres, Pat, *Jalygurr, Aussie Animal Rhymes,* Magabala Books, Broome. 1987.

—— *The Story of Crow, a Nyul, Nyul Story,* Magabala Books, Broome, 1987.

Trezise, Percy, *Peopling of Australia,* William Collins, Sydney, 1987.

—— *Quinkin Mountain,* Angus & Robertson, Pymble, 1995.

—— *The Owl People,* Collins, Sydney, 1987.

—— *Black Duck & Water Rat,* Collins Australia in association with Anne Ingram Press, Sydney, 1988.

—— *The Cave Painters,* Collins Australia in association with Anne Ingram Press, Sydney, 1988.

—— *Ngalculli, the Red Kangaroo,* Collins, Sydney, 1986.

—— *Lasca & her Pups,* William Collins, North Ryde, 1990.

—— *Mungoon-gali, the giant goanna,* Collins, Angus & Robertson, North Ryde, 1991.

—— *Nungadin and Willijen,* Angus & Robertson, Pymble, 1992.

—— *Children of the Great Lake,* Angus & Robertson, Pymble, 1992.

Utemorrah, Daisy, *Do Not Go Around the Edges,* Magabala Books, Broome, 1990.

—— *Moonglue,* Magabala Books, Broome, 1993.

Walker, Kath, *Father Sky and Mother Earth,* Jacaranda Wiley, Milton, 1981.

Watson, Maureen, *Kaiyu's Waiting: an Aboriginal story,* Hodja Educational Resource Cooperative, Richmond, 1984.

Western Regional Aboriginal Land Council, *The Story of the Falling Star,* Aboriginal Studies Press, Canberra, 1989.

Wright, Doreen, *King Clyde of Brewarrina,* Development & Advisory Publications. Dubbo, 1991.

6. Fiction

Bodey, John, *When Darkness Falls,* UQP, St. Lucia, 2000.

Burke, John Muk Muk, *Bridge of Triangles,* UQP, St Lucia, 1994.

Clare, Monica, *Karobran: The Story of an Aboriginal Girl*, Alternative Publishing, Chippendale, 1978.

Cleven, Vivienne, *Bitin' Back*, UQP, St Lucia, 2001.

Laughton, Kenny, *Not Quite Men, No Longer Boys*, IAD Press, Alice Springs, 2000.

Lucashenko, Melissa, *Steam Pigs,* UQP, St Lucia, 1997.

—— *Killing Darcy,* UQP, St Lucia, 1998.

—— *Hard Yards,* UQP, St. Lucia, 1999.

—— *Too Flash,* IAD Press, Alice Springs, 2002.

Martin, Angela, *Beyond Duck River,* Hodder Hedline, Sydney, 2000.

McLaren, Philip, *Sweet Water—Stolen Land*, UQP, St Lucia, 1993 / Magabala Books, Broome, 2001.

—— *Scream Black Murder,* Harper Collins, Sydney, 1995 / Magabala Books, Broome, 2001.

—— *There'll Be New Dreams,* Magabala Books, Broome, 2001.

Pascoe, Bruce, *A Corner Full of Characters*, Blackstone Press, Malacoota. 1981

—— *Night Animals,* Penguin, Ringwood, 1986.

—— *Fox,* McPhee Gribble / Penguin, Ringwood, 1988.

—— *Ruby Eyed Coucal*, Magabala Books, Broome, 1996.

—— *Shark,* Magabala Books, Broome, 1999.

—— *Earth,* Magabala Books, Broome, 2001.

Pilkington, Doris and Nugi Garimara, *Caprice: A Stockman's Daughter*, UQP, St Lucia, 1991.

—— *Follow The Rabbit-Proof Fence,* UQP, St. Lucia, 1996.

—— *Under the Windamarra Tree*, St Lucia, 2002.

Pugh, Derek and the Sunshine Girls, *Tammy Damulkurra,* Aboriginal Studies Press, Canberra, 1995.

Scott, Kim, *True Country,* Fremantle Arts Centre Press, South Fremantle, WA. 1993.

—— *Benang: From The Heart,* Fremantle Arts Centre Press, Fremantle, 1999.

Watson, Sam, *Kadaitcha Sung.* Penguin, Ringwood, 1990.

Weare, Romayne, *Malanbarra Midja,* Magabala Books, Broome, 1997.

Wharton, Herb, *Unbranded,* UQP, St Lucia, 1992.

—— *Where Ya' Been Mate,* UQP, St Lucia, 1996.

Wilkes, Richard, *Bulmurn: A Swan River Noongar,* UWA Press, Nedlands, 1994.

Willmot, Eric, *Below The Line,* 1991

Wright, Alexis, *Plains of Promise,* UQP. St Lucia, QLD. 1997.

7. Plays and Scripts

Bennett, Roger, *Funerals and Circuses,* Currency Press, Sydney, 1995.

—— *Up The Ladder,* Playlab Press, Brisbane, 1997.

Chi, Jimmy and the Kuckles, *Bran Nue Dae,* Currency Press, Sydney, 1991.

Davis, Jack, *Kullark and The Dreamers, No Sugar,* Currency Press, Sydney, 1983.

—— *No Sugar,* Currency Press, Sydney, 1986.

—— *In Our Town,* Currency Press, Sydney. 1992.

—— ed. *Plays from Black Australia,* Currency Press, Sydney, 1989.

—— *Barungin (Smell the Wind),* Currency Press, Sydney, 1989.

—— *Honeyspot,* Currency Press, Sydney, 1987.

—— *Moorli and the Leprechaun: A Play for Children,* Currency Press, Sydney, 1994.

Enoch, Wesley & Deborah Mailman, *The Seven Stages of Grieving,* Playlab Press, Brisbane, 1997.

Gilbert, Kevin, *The Cherry Pickers: the first written Aboriginal play,* Burrambinga Books, Canberra, c1988.

Harding, John, *Up The Road,* Currency Press, Sydney, 1997.

Harrison, Jane, *Stolen,* Currency Press, Sydney, 1998.

Johnson, Eva, "What do they call Me?, *In Australian Gay and Lesbian Plays,* ed. Bruce Parr, Currency Press, Sydney, 1996.

Maris, Hyllus and Borg, Sonia, *Women of the Sun,* Currency Press, Sydney, 1983.

Merritt, Robert J, *The Cake Man,* Currency Press, Sydney, 1978.

Walley, Richard, *Coordah,* Currency Press, Sydney, 1987.

8. Poetry

Bellear, Lisa, *Dreaming In Urban Areas,* UQP, St Lucia, 1996.

Bennett, Roger ed., *Voices from the Heart: Contemporary Aboriginal poetry from Central Australia,* IAD Press Press. Alice Springs. 1995.

Bil Bil, Marjorie, *It Just Lies There From The Beginning: Aboriginal Stories and Poems from the Top End,* IAD Press Press, Alice Springs, 1995.

Brusnahan, Margaret, *Raukkan and Other Poems,* Magabala Books, Broome, 1992.

Buchanan, Michelle, *Consuming Reality,* Cheryl Buchanan, Coominya, 1998.

Burke, John Muk Muk, *Night Song and Other Poems,* NTU Press, Darwin, 1999.

Canning, Ken (Burraga Gutya), *Ngali Ngalga (let's talk): poetry,* Breakout Press, Sydney, c1990.

Cassady, Coralie, *Poetic Perspective,* Coral Cassady, 2001.

Davis, Jack, *Black Life,* UQP. St Lucia. 1992.

—— *The First: Born and other poems,* Angus and Robertson, Sydney, 1970.

—— *Jagardoo: poems from Aboriginal Australia,* Methuen of Australia, Sydney, 1978.

—— *John Pat and other poems,* Dent, Melbourne, 1988.

Dixon, Graeme, *Holocaust Island,* UQP, St Lucia, 1992.

Dixon, RMW and Martin Duwell, *The Honey-Ant Men's Love Song and other Aboriginal song poems,* UQP, St Lucia, 1990.

Dixon RMW & Koch, Grace, eds, *Dyirbal Song Poetry,* UQP, St. Lucia, 1996.

Dodd, Bill, *Just Billy,* Cheryl Buchanan, Comminya, 1988.

Duroux, Mary, *Dirge for Hidden Art.* Heritage Publishing, Moruya, 1992.

Everett, Jimmy, *The Spirit of Kuti Kina: Tasmanian Aboriginal Poetry,* Eumarrah Publications, Hobart, 1990.

Fesl, Eve, ed. *Koori Poems from the Heart,* Koori Research Centre, La Trobe University, VIC, 1991.

Fischer, Cec, *Flag of Unity,* C. Fischer, Brisbane, 1993.

—— *Unity Now,* Perfection Press, Booval, 1991.

Fogarty, Lionel George & Cheryl Buchanan, *Kargun,* Cheryl Buchanan, North Brisbane, 1980.

Fogarty, Lionel George, *Yoogum, Yoogum,* Penguin Books. Ringwood, 1982.

—— *Ngutji,* Cheryl Buchanan, Spring Hill, 1984.

—— *Jagera,* Cheryl Buchanan, Coominya, 1990.

—— *New and Selected Poems: Munaldjali, Mutuerjaraera,* Hyland House, South Yarra, 1995.

Gilbert, Kevin, *End of Dream-Time,* Island Press, Sydney, 1971.

—— *People Are Legends: Aboriginal poems,* UQP, St Lucia, 1978.

—— *Black From The Edge,* Hyland House, South Yarra, 1994.

—— *The Blackside: People are legends and other poems,* Hyland House, South Yarra, 1990.

—— *Child's Dreaming.* Hyland House, South Yarra, 1992.

Gilbert, Kevin (ed), *Inside Black Australia: an anthology of Aboriginal poetry,* Penguin, Ringwood, 1988.

Harding, John, *Little Black Book of Poems.* Dynamo House, VIC, 1994.

Imlah, Cherie, *The Dark Side: poems,* Jiggi Publishing, Goolmangar, 1990.

Maffi-Williams, Lorraine, *Spirit Song: a collection of Aboriginal poetry,* Omnibus Books, Norwood, 1993.

Moreton, Romaine *The Callused Stick of Wanting,* R. Moreton. St Peters, 1995.

Newlin, Norm, *My Worimi Love Song Dreaming,* N.Newlin, Sydney, 1996.

Noonuccal, Oodgeroo, *Kath Walker in China,* Jacaranda Press, Milton, 1988.

Reed-Gilbert, Kerry, *Black Woman, Black Life,* Wakefield Press, Kent Town, 1996.

Talkin About Country, Kuracca Communications, Canberra, 2002.

Robinson, Roland, *The Nearest the Whiteman Gets: Aboriginal Narratives & Poems of New South Wales,* Hale & Iremonger, Sydney, 1989.

Taylor, Alf, *Singer Songwriter,* Magabala Books, Broome, 1992

—— *Winds,* Magabala Books, Broome, 1994.

van Moolenbroek, Lesley, *Collected Works,* Cheryl Buchanan, Comminya, 1984.

Walker, Kath, *We Are Goin: poems,* Jacaranda Press, Brisbane, 1964.

—— *The Dawn is at Hand: poems,* Jacaranda Press, Milton, 1966

—— *My People: a Kath Walker Collection,* Jacaranda Press, Milton, 1970.

Walker, Robbie, *Up Not Down Mate! Thoughts from a Prison Cell,* Linda Walker and family, South Australia, 1987.

Watson, Maureen, *Stepping Out,* Amurriwal, Brisbane, 1994.

Watson, Samuel Wagan, *Itinerant Blues,* UQP, St Lucia, 2002.

—— *Of Muse, Meadnering and Midnight,* UQP, St Lucia, 2002.

Williams, Joy, *Blackberry's Child,* Breakout Press, Sydney. 1991.

APPENDIX B
Select Bibliography of First Nations' Literature in Canada

Anthologies

Armstrong, Jeannette & Damm, Kateri eds, *Gatherings VII,* Theytus Books, Penticton, 1996.

Batisse, Ken George, *Native Sons,* Highway Bookshop, Cobalt, Ontario, 1977.

Belmore, Florene, Gatherings XI: *Flight Scape: a multi-directional collection of Indigenous creative works,* Theytus Books, Penticton, 200.

Belmore, Florene, & Eric Ostrowidzki, *Gatherings XII, Transformation,* Theytus Books, Penticton, 2001.

Brancewicz, Jan ed., *Who Put Custer's Bloomers on the Pony?: A Collection of Native Words,* Bearpaw Publishing, Manitoba, 1998.

Brant, Beth ed., *A Gathering of Spirit: A Collection by North American Indian Women,* Firebrand Books, Ithaca, 1984.

Bruchac, James & Francis, Lee eds, *Reclaiming the Vision,* The Greenfield Review Press, New York, c1996.

Cuthand, Beth & George, William *Gatherings V,* Theytus Books, Penticton, 1995

Day, David & Marilyn Bowering eds, *Many Voices: An Anthology of Contemporary Canadian Indian Poetry,* J.J. Douglas, Vancouver, 1977.

Dolan, Marlena ed., *Just Talking Amongst Ourselves: Voices of Our Youth Volume 1 & 2,* Theytus Books, Penticton, 1994.

Fiddler, Don ed., *Gatherings Volume IV,* Theytus Books, Penticton, 1993.

Fife, Connie ed., *The Colour of Resistance: A Contemporary Collection of Writing by Aboriginal Women,* Sister Vision, Toronto, 1993.

Grant, Agnes ed., *Our Bit Of Truth: An Anthology of Canadian Native Writing* Pemmican Publications, Winnipeg, c1990.

Harjo, Joy & Gloria Bird eds, *Reinventing the Enemy's Language: Contemporary Native Women's Writings of North America,* W.W. Norton, New York, c1987.

Hodgeson, Heather ed., *Seventh Generation: Contemporary Native Writing,* Theytus Books, Penticton, 1989.

Jaine, Linda & Drew Hayden-Taylor eds, *Voices: Being Native in Canada,* University of Saskachewn Extension Division, Saskatoon, 1992.

Jaine, Linda & Don Fiddler eds, *Gatherings VI,* Theytus Books, Penticton, 1995

Joe, Rita & Lesley Choyce eds, *The Mi'kmaq Anthology,* Pottersfield Press, Lawrencetown Beach, c1997.

Joy, Joyce ed., *Gatherings VIII,* Theytus Books, Penticton, 1997.

King, Thomas ed., *All My Relations: An Anthology of Contemporary Canadian Native Fiction,* McLellan & Stewart, Toronto, 1990.

Maki, Joel ed., *Steal My Rage: New Native Voices,* Douglas & McIntyre, Vancouver, 1995.

—— *Let The Drums Be Your Heart: New Native Voices,* Douglas & McIntyre, Vancouver, 1996.

Moses, Daniel David & Goldie, Terry eds, *An Anthology of Canadian Literature in English Revised Edition,* Oxford University Press, Toronto, 1998.

Mowat, William & Christine eds, *Native Peoples in Canadian Literature,* Macmillan, Toronto, c1975.

Perreault, Jeanne & Sylvia Vance eds, *Writing the Circle: Native Women of Western Canada, An Anthology,* NeWest Publications, Edmonton. 1993

Petrone, Penny ed., *First People, First Voices,* University of Toronto, Toronto, 1983.

Roman, Trish Fox ed., *Voices Under One Sky: Contemporary Native Literature: Reflections in Fiction and Non-Fiction,* Nelson Canada, Ontario, 1994

Spirit Within Our Dreams: Stories, Poetry and Visual Art, by a collective of Wichiwakan Meegwetch, The Institute, Stony Mountain, Manitoba, 1994.

Usmiani, Reante (project coordinator), *Kelusultiek: Original Women's Voices of Atlantic Canada,* Institute for the Study of Women, Mount Saint Vincent University, Halifax. 1994

Waubageshig, Don Mills ed., *The Only Good Indian: Essays by Canadian Indians,* New Press, Ontario. 1974

Young-Ing, Greg ed., *Gatherings Volume II,* Theytus Books, Penticton, 1991

—— *Gatherings Volume III,* Theytus Books, Penticton, 1992.

—— *Gatherings Volume IX,* Theytus Books, Penticton, 1998.

Young-Ing, Greg & Florene Blemore, *Gatherings X: A Restrospective of the First Decade,* Theytus Books, Penticton, 1999.

Autobiographies

Anahero, *Devil in Deer Skins: My Life With Grey Owl,* New Press, Toronto, 1972.

Brant, Beth, *Writing as Witness: Essay and Talk,* Women's Press, Toronto, 1994.

Brass, Eleonor, *I Walk in Two Worlds,* Glenbrow Museum, Calgary, 1987.

Calihoo, Robert & Hunter, Robert, *Occupied Canada: A Young White Man Discovers His Unsuspected Past,* McLelland & Stewart, Toronto, 1991.

Campbell, Maria, *Halfbreed,* Goodread Biographies, Halifax, 1973.

Copway, George, *The Life, History and Travels of Kah-ge-ga-gah-bowh(George Copway),* J. Harmstead, Philadelphia, 1847.

—— *Running Sketches of Men and Places in England, France, Germany, Belgium and Scotland,* J.C. Riker, New York, 1851.

Davidson, Florence, *During My Time,* University of Washington, Seattle, Vancouver. 1982.

Dion, Joseph, *My Tribe The Crees,* Glenbrow Museum, Calgary, 1979.

Evans, Augusta, *The Days of Augusta,* J.J. Douglas, Vancouver, 1973.

French, Alice, *My Name Is Masak,* Peguis Publishers, Winnipeg, c1976.

—— *The Restless Nomad,* Pemmican Publications, Winnipeg. 1992.

Gros-Louis, Max, *First Among Huron,* Harvest House, Montreal, 1973.

Green, Alma, *Forbidden Voice: Reflections of a Mohawk Indian,* Green Dragon Press, Toronto, 1997.

Metayer, Manrile ed., *I, Nuligak,* Simon & Schuster, Richmond Hill, Ontario, 1966.

Jacobs, Peter, *Journal of Reverend Peter Jacobs,* Carlton & Phillips, New York, 1855.

Joe, Rita, *Song of Rita: Autobiography of a Mi'kmaq Poet,* Ragweed Press, Prince Edward Island, 1996.

Johnston, Basil H., *Indian School Days,* Key Porter Books, Toronto. 1988.

Jones, Chief Charles, *Queesto: Pacheenacht Chief by Birthright,* Theytus, Nanaimo, BC, 1981.

Jones, Rev. Peter, *Life and Journals of Kah-ke-wa-quo-na-by,* A. Green, Toronto, 1860.

Knockwood, Isabella, *Out of the Depths,* Roseway Publishing, Lockeport, NS, 1992.

Maracle, Brian, *Back on the Rez: Finding the Way Home,* Viking, Toronto, 1996.

Maracle, Lee, *I Am Woman: A Native Perspective on Sociology and Feminism,* Press Gang Publishers, Vancouver, 1988.

—— *Bobbi Lee: Indian Rebel: Struggles of a Native Canadian Woman,* Women's Press, Toronto, 1996.

Marchessault, Jovette, *Like A Child of the Earth,* Talon Books, Vancouver, 1988.

—— Jovette, *Mother of the Grass,* Talon Books, Vancouver, 1989.

Mountain Horse, Mike, *My People The Bloods,* Glenbrow-Alberta Institute, Calgary, 1979.

Pennier, Henry, *Chiefly Indian: The Warm and Witty Story of a British Columbia Half-Breed Logger,* Graydonald Graphics, West Vancouver, 1972.

Sewid, James, *Guests Never Leave Hungry,* Yale University Press, New Haven, 1969.

Testo, John, *Trapping Is My Life,* P. Marton Associates, Toronto, 1970.

Thrasher, Anthony Apakark, *Thrasher: Skid Row Eskimo,* Griffin Houe, Toronto, 1976.

Tyman, James, *Inside Out: an Autobiography by a Native Canadian,* Fifth House, Saskatoon, 1989.

Biographies

Grant, Agnes, *James McKay: A Metis Builder of Canada,* Pemmican Publications, Winnipeg, c1994.

Kennedy, Dan, *Recollections of an Assinibione Chief,* McLelland & Stewart, Toronto, 1972.

Pelletier, Wilfred, *No Foreign Land: the Biography of a North American Indian,* McLelland & Stewart, Toronto, 1976.

Redksy, James, *Great Leader of the Ojibway: Mis-quona-queb,* McLelland & Stewart, Toronto, 1972.

Children's

Ahenakew, Freda, *How the Mouse got Brown Teeth,* Fifth House, Saskatoon, 1988.

—— *How The Birth Tree Got It's Stripes,* Fifth House, Saskatoon, 1988.

Armstrong, Jeannette, *Enwhisteekwa — Walk in Water,* Theytus Books, Penticton, 1982.

—— *Neekna and Chemai,* Theytus Books, Penticton, 1984.

Ballantyne, Evelyne, *The Aboriginal AplhaBet for Children,* illustrations by J. Marlene Ross and Noah Head, Pemmican Publications Inc, Winnipeg, 2002.

Bruchac, Joseph, *Turkey Brother and other tales: Iroquois Folk Stories,* Crossing Press, Trumasburg, New York, c1975.

Campbell, Maria (ill. by Sherry Farrell Rocette), *Stories of the Road Allowance People,* Theytus Books, Penticton, 1995.

Capek, Peggy, *Mirrna and the Marmots,* Theytus Books, Penticton, 1984.

Carriere, Ken, *The Bulrush Helps the Pond,* Gabriel Dumont Institute, Saskatoon, 2002.

Chartrand, Jane, *How the Eagle Got His White Head,* illustrations by Zaawaazit Mkwa Tsun, Pemmican Publications Inc, Winnipeg, 2002.

Condon, Penny, *Changes,* Gabriel Dumont Institute, Saskatoon, 2002.

—— *My Family,* Gabriel Dumont Institute, Saskatoon, 2002.

Culleton, Beatrice, *Spirit of the White Bison,* Pemmican Publications, Winnipeg, 1985.

——Unusual Friendships — *A little black cat and a little white rat,* illustrations by Rebecca Belmore, Theytus Books, Penticton, 2002.

Cuthand, Beth, *The Little Duck,* Theytus, Penticton, 1999.

Delaronde, Deborah L, *Flour Sack Flora,* illustrations by Gary Chartrand, Pemmican Publications Inc, Winnipeg, 2002.

Eigenbrod, Renate & Jo-Ann Episkenew, *Creating Community,* Theytus Books, Penticton, 2002.

Flett, Leanne & Lee Maracle, *Gatherings — Volume 13: Reconciliation: Elders as Knowledge Keepers,* Theytus Books, Penticton, 2002

King, Thomas, *A Coyote Columbus Story,* Douglas & McIntyre, Toronto, 1992.

—— *Coyote Sings to the Moon,* Key Porter Kids, Toronto, 1998.

LaDuke, Winona, *The Winona LaDuke Reader: A Collection of Essential Writings,* Theytus Books, Penticton, 2002.

Marchand, Barb, *How Turtle Set the Animals Free: An Okanagan Legend,* Theytus Books, Penticton, 1991.

Marchand, Barb, *How Food Was Given: An Okanagan Legend,* Theytus Books, Penticton, 1991.

Marchand, Barb, *How Names Were Given: An Okanagan Legend,* Theytus Books, Penticton, 1991.

—— illustrator, *Kou-Skelowh/We are the people: A trilogy of Okanagan legends,* Theytus Books, Penticton, 200.

McLellan, Joseph, *The Birth of Nanabosho, Nanabosho dances,* Pemmican Publications, Winnipeg, 1989.

—— *Nanabosho Steals Fire,* Pemmican Publications, Winnipeg, 1990.

Mosionier, Beatrice (illustrated by Terry Gallagher), *Christopher's Folly,* Pemmican Publications, Winnipeg. 1996

Murray, Bonnie, *Li Minoush*, illustrations by Sheldon Dawson, translation by Rita Flamand, Pemmican Publications Inc, Winnipeg, 2002.

Plain, Ferguson, *Rolly's Bear*, Pemmican Publications, Winnipeg, 1996.

―― *Grandfather Drum*, Pemmican Publications, Winnipeg, c1994.

―― *The Little White Cabin*, Pemmican Publications, Winnipeg, 1992.

―― *Eagle Feather*, Pemmican Publications, Winnipeg, c1989.

―― *Amikoonse*, Pemmican Publications, Winnipeg, c1993.

Wheeler, Jordan, *Just A Walk*, Theytus Books, Penticton, 1993.

―― *Chuck in the City*, illustrated by Bill Cohen, Theytus Books, Penticton, 2000.

Wheeler, Bernelda, *A Friend Called Chum*, Pemmican Publications, Winnipeg, 1984.

―― *I Can't Have Bannock, But The Beaver Has A Dam*, Pemmican Publications, Winnipeg, 1984.

―― *Where Did You Get Your Moccasins?* Pemmican Publications, Winnipeg, 1986.

White, Elle, *Kwulasulwut: Stories from the Coast Salish*, Theytus Books, Penticton, 1992.

―― *Kwukasukwut II*, illustrated by Bill Cohen, Theytus Books, Penticton, 1997.

Fiction

Armstrong, Jeannette, *Slash*, Theytus Books, Penticton, 1985.

―― *Whispering in Shadows*, Theytus Books, Penticton, 1999.

Joan Crate, *Breathing Water*, NeWest, Edmonton, 1990.

Culleton, Beatrice, *In Search of April Raintree*, Pemmican Publications, Winnipeg, 1983.

Erdrich, Louise, *Love Medicine*, HarperPerennial, New York, 1993.

―― *The Bingo Palace*, HarperCollins, New York, c1994.

―― *Tracks*, Harper and Row, New York, 1989.

―― *Tales of Burning Love*, Flamingo, London, 1997.

Forbes, Jack, *Red Blood*, Theytus Books, Penticton, 1997.

Highway, Thompson, *Kiss of the Fur Queen*, Doubleday Toronto, 1998.

Keon, Orville, *Thunderbirds of the Ottawa*, Highway Bookshop, Cobalt Ontario, 1977.

King, Thomas, *Medicine River*, Viking, Markham, Ontario, 1990.

―― *Green Grass, Running Water*, HarperCollins, Toronto, 1993.

Maracle, Lee, *Ravensong*, Press Gang Publishers, Vancouver, 1993.

―― *Sundogs*, Theytus Books, Penticton, 1992.

Marchessault, Jovette, *Like a Child of the Earth*, Talon Books, Vancouver, 1975.

―― *White Pebbles in the Dark Forests*, Talon Books, Vancouver, 1990.

Mosionier, Beatrice Culleton, *In the Shadow of Evil*, Theytus Books, Penticton, 2000.

Simon, Lorne, *Stones and Switches*, Theytus Books, Penticton, 1994.

Slipperjack, Ruby, *Honour the Sun*, Pemmican Publications, Winnipeg, 1987.

―― *Silent Words*, Fifth House, Saskatoon, 1992.

—— *Weesquachak and the Lost Ones,* Theytus Books, Penticton, 2000.

Smith, Barbara, *Renewal: Book II - Teoni's Giveaway,* Theytus Books, Penticton, 1986.

Sterling, Shirley, *My Name Is Seepeetza,* Douglas & McIntyre, Vancouver, c1992.

Van Camp, Richard, *The Lesser Blessed,* Douglas & McIntyre, Vancouver. 1996.

—— *Angel Wing Splash Pattern,* Kegedonce Press, Ontario, 2002.

Walters, Eric, *War of the Eagles,* Orca Book Publishers, Victoria, BC, 1998.

Wheeler, Jordan, *Brothers In Arms,* Pemmican Publications, Winnipeg, 1989.

William, Gerry, *The Black Ship: Book One of Enid Blue Starbreaks,* Theytus Books, Penticton, 1994.

Non-Fiction including Native Studies/histories/oral histories

Acoose, Janice, *Iskwewak--kah'ki yaw ni wahkomakanak: Neither Indian Princesses Nor Easy Squaws,* Women's Press, Toronto, 1995.

Adams, Dr. Howard *Prison of Grass: Canada from the Native Point of View,* Fifth House, Saskatoon, 1975.

—— *A Tortured People: The Politics of Colonisation,* Theytus Books, Penticton, 1999.

Ahenakew, Freda, *Our Grandmothers' Lives as Told in Their Own Words,* Fifth House, Saskatoon, 1992.

Armstrong, Jeannette ed., *Looking At The Words of Our People: First Nations' Analysis of Literature,* Theytus Books, Penticton, 1993.

Armstrong, Jeanette, Delphine Derickson, Lee Maracle & Greg Young-Ing eds, *We Get Our Living Like Milk From the Land,* Theytus Books, Penticton, 1994.

Barkwell, Lawrence J, Leah Dorion and Darren Fontaine, *Metis Legacy,* Pemmican Publications Inc, Winnipeg, 2002.

Beaver, George, *Mohawk Reporter: The Sic Nations Columns of George Beaver,* Iroquois Publishing, Ontario, 1997.

Brant, Beth *I'll Sing 'til the Day I Die: conversations with Tyendinaga Elders,* McGilligan Books, Toronto, 1995.

Cardinal, Harold, *The Rebirth of Canada's Indians,* Hurtig, Edmonton, c1977.

—— *The Unjust Society: The Tragedy of Canada's Indians,* M.G. Hurtig, Edmonton, 1969.

Chinook Winds: Aboriginal Dance Project, 7th Generation Books, Vancouver, 1997.

Chitze, Miranda ed., *Mukwa Geezis: Resource Guide to Aboriginal Literature in Canada,* Wabanoong Multimedia Publications, Toronto, 1997.

Cohen, Bill, ed., *Stories and Images of What The Horse Has Done For Us: An Illustrated History of Okanagan Ranching and Rodeo,* 1998.

Chrisjohn, Roland & Young, Sherri with Michael Maraun, *The Circle Game: Shadows and Substance in the Indian Residential School Experience in Canada,* Theytus Books, Penticton, 1997.

Copway, George, *The Traditional History and Characteristic Sketches of the Ojibwa Nation,* C. Gilpin, London, 1850.

Goodleaf, Donna, *Entering the Warzone: A Mohawk Perspective on Resisting Invasions,* Theytus Books, Penticton, 1995.

Goodtrack, Kim Soo, *The ABCs of Our Spiritual Connection,* Theytus, Penticton, 1994.

Harpelle, Alix, *My Children Are My Reward: The Life of Elsie Spence*, Pemmican Publications Inc, Winnipeg, 2002.

Hill, Barbara-Helen, *Shaking the Rattle: Healing the Trauma of Colonization,* Theytus Books, Penticton. 1996.

Jack, Agnes, *Behind Closed Doors: Stories from the Kamloops Indian Residential School,* Theytus Books, Penticton, 2001.

Knight, Rolf, *Indians At Work: An Informal History of Native Labour in British Columbia 1858 - 1930,* New Start Books, Vancouver, 1996.

Maracle, Brian, *Crazy Water: Native Voices on Addiction and Recovery,* Viking, Toronto, 1993.

Marsden, Rasunah, *Crisp Blue Edges: Indigenous Creative Non-Fiction,* Theytus Books, Penticton, 2000.

Monture-Angus, Patricia, *Thunder In My Soul: A Mohawk Woman Speaks,* Fernwood Publishers, Halifax, NS, 1993.

Pelletier, Emile, *A Social History of the Mannitoba Metis,* Mannitoba Metis Federation Press, Winnipeg, 1977.

Ruffo, Armond Garnet et, *(Ad)dressing our Words: Aboriginal Perspectives on Aboriginal Literatures,* Theytus Books, Penticton, 2001.

Rustige, Rona, *Tyendinaga Tales,* McGillis University Press, Kingston, Ontario, 1998.

Sam, Lillian ed, *Nak'azdil t'enne Yahulduk/Nak'azdli Elders Speak,* Theytus Books, Penticton, 2001.

Silman, Janet, *Enough is Enough: Aboriginal Women Speak Out,* Women's Press, Toronto, 1987.

Spielman, Roger, *"You're So Fat!:" Exploring Ojibwe Discourse,* University of Toronto Press, Toronto, 1998.

Taylor, Drew Hayden, *Funny, You Don't Look Like One,* Theytus Books, Penticton, 1998.

―― *Further Adventures of a Blue-Eyed Ojibway: Funny, You Don't Look Like One Two,* Theytus Books, Penticton, 2001.

―― *Furious Observations of a Blue-Eyed Ojibway: Funny, You Don't Look Like One Two Three,* Theytus Books, Penticton 2002.

Troupe, Cheryl, *Expressing Our Heritage: Metis Artistic Designs,* Gabriel Dumont Institute, Saskatoon, 2002.

Venne, Sharon Helen, *Our Elders Understand Our Rights: Evolving International Law Regarding Indigenous Peoples,* Theytus Books, Penticton, 1999.

Yaghulaanas, Michael Nicol, *A Tale of Two Shamans,* Theytus Books, Penticton, 2001.

Poetry

Abel, Ben, *Okanagan Indian Poems & Short Stories,* Highway Bookshop, Cobalt, Ontario, 1974.

────── *Wisdom of Okanagan Poetry,* Highway Bookshop, Cobalt, Ontario, 1977.

Armstrong, Jeannette, *Breath Tracks,* Theytus Books, Penticton, 1991.

Baker, Marie Annharte, *Being On The Moon,* Polestar Press, Winlaw, BC, 1990.

────── *Coyote Columbus Cafe,* Moonprint Press, Winnipeg, 1994.

Chester, Bruce, *Paper Radio,* Theytus Books, Penticton, 1986.

Crate, Joan, *Pale As Real Ladies: Poems for Pauline Johnson,* Brick Books, Ilderton, Ontario, 1989.

Cuthand, Beth, *Voices In The Waterfall,* Theytus Books, Penticton, 1982.

────── *Horse Dance To Emerald Mountain,* Lazara Publications, Vancouver, 1987.

Damm, Kateri, *My Heart is a Stray Bullet,* Kegedonce Press, Ontario, 1993.

Dandurand, Joseph A., *Burning for the Dead & Scratching for the Poor,* Rez Press, Ft Langley, BC, 1995.

────── *Looking Into the Eyes of My Forgotten Dreams,* Kegedonce Press, Ontario, 1998.

Halfe, Louise, *Bear Bones and Feathers,* Coteau Books, Regina, 1994.

────── *Blue Marrow,* McLelland & Stewart, Toronto, 1998.

Hunter, Al, *Spirit Horses,* Kegedonce Press, Ontario, 2002.

Kenny, George, *Indians Don't Cry,* Chimbo Publications, Toronto, 1977.

Maracle, Lee, *Bent Box,* Theytus Books, Penticton, 2000.

Mercredi, Duncan, *Spirit of the Wolf,* Pemmican Publications, Winnipeg, 1991.

Moses, Daniel David, *Delicate Bodies,* Blewointment Press, Vancouver, 1980.

────── *The White Line,* Fifth House, Saskatoon, 1990.

Ruffo, Armand Garnet, *Opening In The Sky,* Theytus Books, Penticton, 1994.

────── *Grey Owl,* Coteau Books, Regina, 1996.

George, Chief Dan, *My Heart Soars,* Hancock House, Surrey, BC, 1989.

────── *My Spirit Soars,* Hancock House, Surrey, BC, 1982.

Groulx, David A., *Night In The Exude,* Tyro Publications, Sault Ste Marie, 1997.

────── *The Long Dance,* Kegedonce Press, Ontario, 1999.

Joe, Rita, *Poems of Rita Joe,* Abanaki Press, Halifax, 1978.

────── *Lnu & Indians Were Called,* Ragweed Press, Prince Edward Island, 1991.

────── *Song of Eskasoni: More Poems of Rita Joe,* Ragweed Press, Prince Edward Island, 1988.

Johnson, Pauline E., *The White Wampum,* Copp, Clarke, Toronto, 1895.

────── *Canadian Born,* G.N. Morang, Toronto, 1903.

────── *The Moccasin Maker,* William Briggs, Toronto, 1913.

────── *The Shagganappi,* William Briggs, Toronto, 1913.

────── *Flint & Feather,* Musson Book Company, Toronto, 1913.

Keon, Wayne, *Sweetgrass II,* Mercury Press, Stratford, Ontario, 1990.

────── *My Sweet Maize,* Mercury Press, Stratford, Ontario, 1997.

────── *Storm Dancer,* Mercury Press, Stratford, Ontario, 1993.

Lawrence, Mary, *In Spirit And Song,* Highway Bookshop, Cobalt, Ontario, 1992.

MacLeod, Heather, *My Flesh Is The Sound of Rain,* Coteau Books, Reina, 1998.

Mecredi, Duncan, *Dreams of Wolf In The City,* Pemmican Publications, Winnipeg, 1992.

—— *Spirit of Wolf in the City: Raise Your Voice,* Pemmican Publications, Winnipeg, c1992.

—— *Duke of Windsor: Wolf Sings The Blues*, Pemmican Publications, Winnipeg, 1997.

—— *Wolf and Shadows,* Pemmican Publications, Winnipeg, 1995.

Martin, Michael J. Paul, *She Said Sometimes She Hears Things*, 7th Generation, Toronto, 1997.

Robinson, Michael, *The Freedom of Silence,* Waapoone Publications, & Promotions, Moonbeam, Ontario, 1987.

—— *Touching The Serpents Tail,* Martin House Publications, Keene, Ontario, 1992.

—— *The Earth And The Dancing Man,* Martin House Publications, Keene, Ontario, 1991.

Scofield, Gregory, *The Gathering,* Polestar Book Publishers, Vancouver, 1993.

—— *Native Canadian,* Polestar Book Publishers, Vancouver, 1996.

—— *Love Medicine & One Song,* Polestar Book Publishers, Vancouver, 1997.

Stamp, Sarin, *There Is My People,* Gray's Publishing, Sidney, BC, 1970.

Young-Ing, Greg, *The Random Flow of Blood and Flowers,* Ekstasis Editions, Victoria, BC, 1996.

Plays

Clements, Marie, Greg Daniels & Margo Kane, *DraMetis: Three Metis Plays*, Theytus Books, Penticton, 2001.

Highway, Thompson, *The Rez Sisters*, Fifth House, Saskatoon, 1998.

—— *Dry Lips Oughta Move to Kapuskasing*, Fifth House, Saskatoon, 1989.

Marchessault, Jovette, Saga of the Wet Hens: A Play, Talon Books, Vancouver, 1983.

Mercredi, Monringstar & MacNally, Darren, Fort Chipewyan Homecoming, Lerner Publishers, Minneapolis, 1998.

Mojica, Monique, *Princess Pocohantas and the Blue Spots*, 1991.

Highway, Thompson, *The Rez Sisters,* Fifth House, Saskatton, 1988.

—— *Dry Lips Oughta Move to Kapuskasing,* Fifth House, Saskatoon, 1989.

Marchessault, Jovette, *Saga of the Wet Hens: a play*, Talon Books, Vancouver, 1983.

Mercredi, Monringstar & MacNally, Darren, *Fort Chipewyan Homecoming,* Lerner Publishers, Minneapolis, 1998.

Mojica, Monique, *Princess Pocohantas and the Blue Spots*, 1991.

Moses, Daniel David, *Coyote City*, Williams-Wallace, Stratford, Ontario, 1990.

—— *Indian Medicine Shows,* Excile Editions, Toronto, 1995.

—— *Almighty Voice and His Wife,* PUC Play Service, Toronto, 1996.

Taylor, Drew Hayden, *Someday,* Fifth House, Saskatoon, 1993.

—— *Toronto At Dreamer's Rock / Education Is Our Right,* Fifth House, Saskatoon, 1990.

—— The Bootlegger Blues, Fifth House, Saskatoon, 1991.
Waboose, Jan Bourdeau, *Morning on the Lake,* Kids Can Press, Toronto, 1998.

Short Stories

Brant, Beth, *Food and Spirits,* Press Gang Publishers, Vancouver, 1991.
—— *Mohawk Trail,* Firebrand, Ithaca, New York, 1985.
Drew Hayden Taylor, *Fearless Warriors,* Talon Books, Burnaby, 1998.
Ipellie, Alootook, *Arctic Dreams & Nightmares,* Theytus Books, Penticton, 1993.
Basil Johnston, *Moose Meat & Wild Rice,* McLelland & Stewart, Toronto, 1978.
Thomas King, *That One Good Story, That One,* Harper Perennial, Toronto, 1993.
Maracle, Lee, *Sojourner's Truth,* Press Gang Publishers, Vancouver, 1990.

Books on Native literature and writers by non-Native authors

Petrone, Penny, *Native Literature in Canada: From the Oral Tradition to the Present,* Oxford University Press, Toronto, 1990.

Dorothy Ryder & Helen Rogers, *Indian-Inuit Authors: An Annotated Bibliography,* Information Canada, Ottawa, 1974.

Witalec, Janet ed., *Native North American Literature: Biographical and Critical Information on Native Writers and Orators From the United States and Canada From Historical Times to the Present*, Gale Research, Toronto. 1994.

APPENDIX C
Select Bibliogrpahy of Maori Literature

Anthologies

Ko nga pikitia na Caroline Down, *Nga Pakiwaitara ma nga tamariri*, Huia, Wellington, 1998.

Ihimaera, Witi (ed), *Te Ao Marama: Contemporary Maori Writing* 5 Volumes, Reed Books, Auckland, 1992-1996.

Ihimaera, Witi & Long, D.S., *Into the World of Light: an anthology of Maori writing*. Heinemann, Auckland, 1982.

Te Awekotuku, Ngahuia (ed), *Mana Wahine Maori: Selected Writings on Maori Women's Art, Culture and Politics*, New Women's Press, Auckland, 1991.

Autobiography/biography

Campbell, Alistair, *Island to Island*, Whitcoulls, Christchurch, 1984.

Duff, Alan, *Alan Duff's Maori Heroes*, Random House, Auckland, 2000.

—— *Out of the Mist and Steam: a memoir*, Tandem Press, Auckland, 1999.

Ihimaera, Witi (ed), *Growing Up Maori*, Tandem Press, Auckland, 1998.

Paki-Titi, Rora, *Rangimarie: Recollections of Her Life*, Huia Publishers, Wellington, 1998.

Phillis, Te Onehou, *Eruera Manuera*, Huia Publishers, Wellington, 2001.

Children's Books / picture books

Allen, Annais & Janine McVeagh, *I Tenei Ra*, Te Reo, Opononi, 1992.

—— *It's Saturday Today*, Te Reo, Opononi, 1992.

Clarke, mere, *Whirikoki and his Seal*, illustrations by Manu Smith, Huia Publishers, Wellington 1997.

Grace, Patricia, *The Kuia and the Spider*, Penguin, Auckland, 1981.

—— *Wahine Toa*, Collins, Auckland, 1984.

—— *Watercress Tuna and the Children of Champion Street* 1985.

—— *The Trolley*, Puffin Books, Auckland, 1994.

Harawira, Wena, *Te Kouame te pepe = Grandpa and the baby*, Network Communications, Wellington, 1985.

—— *Hangi*, Reed, Auckland, 1997.

Hyland, Queenie Rikihana, *The Creation*, Reed, Auckland, 1998.

—— *Kopuwai the Monster*, Reed, Auckland, 1998.

Mason, Te Haumihiata, *Tiakiwai*, illustrations by Trina Wirihana, Huia Publishers, Wellington, 2002.

Mataira, Katerina Te Heikoko, *Rangi and His Dinosaurs*, illustrations by Ali Teo, Huia Publishers, Wellington, 1998.

Reedy, Mokena Potae, *Te Mura a Tangaroa*, Huia Publishers, Wellington, 2000.

Tamehana, Esther, *He Kahurere / Roimata's Cloak* Huia, Wellington, 1995.

—— *Sandman / He Tangata Kirikiri,* Huia, Wellington, 1997.

Whakaahua, Nga Kupa, *Rapu Kai Moana,* Te Reo Publications, Waimamaku, 1991.

Young, Hepora, *Hinemoa and Tutanekai: A Maori Legend,* Huia, Wellington, 1995.

Fiction

Baker, Chris, *Kokopu Dreams,* Huia Publishers, Wellington, 2001.

Baker, Pat, *Behind the Tattooed Face.* Queen Charlotte Sound, Cathy, 1975.

Campbell, Alistair, *Sidewinder,* Reed, Auckland, 1991

—— *Fantasy With Witches,* Hazard Press, Christchurch, 1998.

—— *The Frigate Bird,* Heinemann Reed, Auckland, 1989.

Duff, Alan, *Once Were Warriors,* UQP, St. Lucia, 1991.

—— *One Night Out Stealing,* UQP, St. Lucia, 1992.

—— *State Ward,* Vintage, Auckland, 1994.

—— *Both Sides of the Moon,* Vintage, Auckland, 1998.

—— *What Becomes of the Broken Hearted,* Vintage, Auckland, 1996.

Charman-Love, Lindsay, *Top Hat and Taiaha and other stories,* Huia Publishers, Wellington, 2001.

Grace, Patricia, *Potiki,* Women's Press, London, 1986.

—— *Mutuwhenua= The Moon Sleeps,* Livenire, London, 1978.

—— *Cousins,* Women's Press, London, 1993.

Hulme, Keri, *The Bone People: A Novel,* Spiral in association with Hodder & Staughton, Auckland, c1983.

—— *Te Kaihau - The Windeater,* UQP, St. Lucia, 1986.

—— *Stone Fish,* Huia Publishers, Wellington, 2001.

Ihimaera, Witi, *Tangi,* Heinemann, London, 1973.

—— *The Matriarch,* Heinemann, Auckland, 1986.

—— *The Dream Swimmer: The Sequel to the Matriarch,* Penguin, Auckland, 1997.

—— *Nights in the Garden of Spain,* Secker & Warbug, Auckland, 1995.

—— *Pounamu, Pounamu,* Heinemann, Auckland, 1972.

—— *The Whale Rider,* Heinemann, Auckland, 1987.

—— *Whanau,* Heinemann, Auckland, 1974.

—— *Kingfisher Come Home: The Complete Maori Stories of Witi Ihimaera,* Reed, Auckland, 1995.

O'Leary, Michael, *Unlevel Crossings,* Huia Publishers, Wellington, 2001.

Reedy, Mokena Potae Reedy, *Te Whenua Kauruki,* Huia Publishers, Wellington 2001.

Shaw, Tom, *Longfin.* Shaw Books, Auckland, 1983.

Taylor, Apirana, *He Tanga Aroha,* Huia, Wellington, 1993.

Myths and Legends

Campbell, Alistair (illustrated by Robin White), *Maori Legends: some myths and legends of the Maori people*, Seven Seas Publishing, Wellington, 1969.

Kanawa, Kiri Te, *Land of the Long White Cloud,* Pavilion Books, 1989.

Non-fiction

Anderson, Atholl, *Te Puoho's Last Raid,* Otago Heritage Books, Denedin, 1986.

Duff, Alan, *Maori: The Crisis and the Challenge,* HarperCollins, Auckland, 1993.

Garven, P, Nepia, M., Ashwell, H., *Te Whakatau Kaupap o Murihiku,* Aoraki Press, Wellington, 1987.

Goodall, Anake, *Ko Waitaki te Awa, ka Roimata na Aoraki i riringi,* Aoraki Press, Wellington, 1992.

Goodall, M & Griffiths, G., *Maori Dunedin,* Otago Hertiage Books, Denedin, 1980.

Grace, Patricia, *Wahine Toa: Women of Maori Myth*, Viking Pacific, Auckland, c1984.

Grace, Patricia, Irihapeti Ramsden & Jonathan Dennis stories told to, *The Silent Migration*, Huia Publishers, Wellington, 2001

Harawira, Wena, *Te Kawa te o Marae: A Guide for all Marae Visitors,* Reed, Auckland, 1997.

Ihimaera, Witi ed, *Kaupapa New Zealand, Vision Aotearoa*, Bridget Williams Books, Wellington, 1994.

Karetu, Timoto, *Haka,* Reed Books, Auckland, 1993.

Mead, Hirini Moko, *An Introduction to Tikanga Maori*, Huia Publishers, Wellington, 2002.

Orbell, Margaret, *Contemporary Maori Writing,* Reed, Wellington, 1970.

Rei, Tania, *Moari Women and the Vote*, Huia Publishers, Wellington, 1993.

Ricketts, Harry, *Talking About Ourselves—12 NZ Poets in Conversation with Harry Ricketts,* Mallinson Rendel, Wellington, 1986.

Royal, Te Ahukaramu Charles Royal, *Kati au knoei: A Collection of Songs from Ngati Toarangatira and ngati Raukawa*, Huia Publishers, Wellington, 1994.

Tau, T , Goodall, A, Palmer, D. , Tau, R., *Te Whakatau Kaupapa,* Aoraki Press, Wellington, 1990.

Walker, Ranginui, *Struggle Without End,* Penguin, Auckland, 1990.

Plays

Broughton, John, *Te Hokinga Mai (The Return Home),* Aoraki Press, Wellington, 1998.

—— *Nga Puke (The Hills)*, Aoraki Press, Wellington, 1992.

—— *Michael James Manaia*, Dept. of Preventive and Social Medicine, University of Otago, Dunedin, 1994.

Dansey, Harry, *Te Raukura - The Feathers of the Albatross,* Longman Paul, Auckland, 1974.

Fransen, Willy Craig, Taku Waimarie, Huia Publishers, Wellington, 1997.

Garrett, Simon, ed., *He Reo Hou: Five Plays by Maori Playwrights,* Playmarket, Wellington, 1991.

Grace-Smith, Briar, *Nga Pou Wahine,* Huia, Wellington, 1997.

—— *Purapurawhetu*, Huia Publishers, Wellington, 1999.

Ihimaera, Witi, *Woman Far Walking*, Huia Publishers, Wellington, 2000.

Kouka, Hone, *Waiora: te ukaip o - the homeland: a play,* Huia, Wellington, 1997.

—— *Mauri Tu: a short play*, Wellington: Aoraki Press, Wellington, 1992.

Kouka, Hone (ed), *Ta matou mangai = Our own voice,* Victoria University Press, Wellington, 1994.

Owen, Rena, *Te Awa i Tahutu: Daddy's Girl,* 1991.

Poetry

Campbell, Alistair, *Mine Eyes Dazzle: Poems 1947-1949,* Pegasus Press, Chirstchurch, 1956.

—— *Sanctuary of Spirits: Poems,* Wai-te-ata Press, Wellington, 1963.

—— *Wild Honey,* Oxford University Press, London, 1964.

—— *Blue Rain: Poems,* Wai-te-ata Press, Wellington, 1967.

—— *Kapiti: Selected Poems 1947-1971,* Pegasus Press, Christchurch, 1972.

—— *Dreams, Yellow Lions,* Alistair Taylor, Martinborough, 1975.

—— *The Dark Lord of Savaiki,* Te Kotare Press, Pukerua Bay, 1980.

—— *Collected Poems 1947-1981,* Alistair Taylor, Martinborough, 1981.

—— *Soul Traps: A Lyric Sequence,* Te Kotare Press, Pukerua Bay, 1985.

—— *Stone Rain: The Polynesian Strain,* Hazard Press, Christchurch, 1992.

—— *Death and the Tagua,* Wai-te-ata Press, Wellington, 1995.

—— *Gallipoli and Other Poems,* Wai-te-ata Press, Wellington, 1999.

—— *The Happy Summer,* Price Milburn, Wellington, 1975.

—— *Pocket Collected Poems,* Hazard Press, Christchurch, 1996.

Faith, Rangi, *Rivers Without Eels*, Huia Publishers, Wellington, 2001.

Hulme, Keri, *The Silences Between (Moeraki Conversations),* Auckland University Press/Oxford University Press, Auckland, 1982.

—— *Strands*, Hale and Iremonger, Auckland, 1992.

—— *Lost Possessions,* Victoria University Press, Wellington, 1985.

Potiki, Roma, *Stones in her Mouth: Poems,* IWA Associates, Auckland, 1992.

—— *Shaking the Tree*, Steele Roberts, Wellington, 1998.

Sullivan, Robert, *Jazz Waiata,*. Auckland University Press, Auckland, 1990.

—— *Piki Ake! Poems 1990-92,* Auckland University Press, Auckland, 1993.

—— *Star Waka,* Auckland University Press, Auckland, 1999.

Taylor, Apirana, *Eyes of the Ruru,* Voice Press, Wellington, 1979.

Tuwhare, Hone, *No Ordinary Sun,* Blackwood and Janet Paul, Auckland, 1964.

—— *Come Rain Hail,* Uni of Otago, Dunedin, 1970.

—— *Sap-Wood and Milk,* Caveman Press, Dunedin, 1975.

—— *Something Nothing,* Caveman Press, Dunedin, 1974

—— *Making a Fist of It: poems and short stories,* Jackstraw Press, Dunedin, 1978.

—— *Selected Poems,* McIndoe, Dunedin, 1980.

—— *Year of the Dog: Poems New and Selected,* McIndoe, Dunedin, 1982.

—— *Mihi: Collected Poems,* Penguin Books, Auckland, 1987.

—— *Short Back and Sideways: Poems and Prose,* Godwit Press, Auckland, 1992

—— *Deep River Talk: Collected Poems,* Godwit Press, Auckland, 1993.

—— *Shape-shifter,* Steele Roberts, Wellington, c1997.

Short Stories

Huia Short Stories, Huia Publishers, Wellington, 1995.

Huia Short Stories, Huia Publishers, Wellington, 1997.

Huia Short Stories 3, Huia Publishers, Wellington, 1999.

Huia Short Stories 4: Contemporary Maori Fiction, Huia Publishers, Wellington, 2001.

Grace, Patricia, *Waiariki and Other Stories,* Penguin Books, Auckland, 1975.

—— *The Sky People.* Penguin, Auckland, 1994.

—— *The Dream Sleepers and Other Stories,* Penguin, Auckland, 1980.

—— *Short Stories: Selections,* Penguin, Auckland, 1991.

—— *Collected Stories,* Penguin, Auckland, 1980.

—— *Electric City and Other Stories.* Penguin, Auckland, 1989.

Ihimaera, Witi, *The New Net Goes Fishing,* Heinemann, Auckland, 1977.

—— *Dear Miss Mansfield: A Tribute to Kathleen Mansfield Beauchamp,* Viking, Auckland, 1989.

Kawana, Phil, *Dead Jazz Guys: and other stories,* Huia, Wellington, 1997.

—— *Attack of the Skunk People,* Huia, Wellington, 1999.

Taylor, Apirana, *He Rau Aroha: A Hundred Leaves of Love,* Penguin, Auckland, 1986.

—— *Ki te Ao: New Stories,* Penguin, Auckland, 1990.

End Notes

Chapter One

[1] Laurie, Victoria, "Identity Crisis", *Australian Magazine* July 20-21, 1996, p.30. In this article Johnson's sister Betty claims that after some research she was elated to discover that her father's origins were mixed Negro or Creole and that on their mother's side they were directly descended from the first white child born in 1829 on the shores of the Swan River colony in Western Australia.

[2] Kelly, Susan, "The Outsider", *HQ*, May - June 1996, p.49.

[3] Durack, Mary, Foreword, *Wildcat Falling*, Angus & Robertson, Sydney, 1965, pp.xvi-xvii.

[4] Fogarty, Lesley, "Mogwi-Djan National Indigenous Writers and Playwrights Conference and Workshop Report", 1996, p.16.

[5] Jopson, Debra, "Destroy Books: Black Group", *Sydney Morning Herald,* 25 March 1997, p.5.

[6] Perrett, Bill, "Questions of Identity, *The Sunday Age*, 17 August 1997, p.7.

[7] Sue Abbey, email to the author, 18 August 2000.

[8] Little, Lorna & Little, Tom, "The Mudrooroo Dilemma", *Westerly,* vol. 41, no. 3, Spring, 1996, p.7.

[9] Dixon, Graeme, "The Mudrooroo Dilemma", *Westerly,* vol. 41, no. 3, Spring 1996, p.5.

[10] ibid., p.6.

[11] Little & Little, op.cit., p.7.

[12] ibid., p.8.

[13] Mudrooroo, "Tell Them You're Indian", *Race Matters: Indigenous Australians and "Our" Society,* ed. G. Cowlishaw & B. Morris, Aboriginal Studies Press, Canberra, 1997, p.262.

[14] ibid., p.266. Johnson does the same thing in *Writing from The Fringe*, shifting between a genetic and a social (communal) sense of Aboriginality.

[15] Eggington, Robert in "Novelist Defends His Black Identity", *Weekend Australian,* 5 April 1997, p.3.

[16] ibid.

[17] ibid.

[18] van den Berg, Rosemary, "Intellectual Property Rights for Aboriginal People", A paper given at the Utrecht Conference, Holland, October 4, 1997. Published in *The Strength of Us As Women: Black Women Speak*, Ginninderra Press, Canberra, 2000, p.77.

[19] Shapcott, Thomas, "The disturbing journey of Mudrooroo", *The Age (VIC),* 27 July 1996, p.9.

[20] Faust, Beatrice, "Races Are Easy to Lose", *Weekend Australian,* 2-4 August 1996, p.25.

[21] Ginibi, Ruby Langford, Letter to the Editor, "The Right to be a Koori Writer", *The Australian,* 7 August, 1996, p.12.

[22] Rachel Bin Salleh, email to the author, 29 March 2000. All other quotes from Bin Salleh in this chapter are from this source unless otherwise indicated.

[23] Faust, op.cit., p.25.

[24] ibid.

[25] One example is the Museum of Contemporary Arts' "Word on Sunday Series 25", August - September 1998 promotional flyer that states "Distinguished Aboriginal writer and activist". Promotional material for *Snake Dancing* also states: "From her appointment to the *Nation Review* as Australia's first Aboriginal columnist", on-line at: http://www.australias.org/sykes/sd.html.

[26] Newfong, John A. ed., "Birds Both Black and Beautiful", *Identity,* vol. 1, no. 6, November, 1972, pp.32-33.

[27] Slattery, Luke, "Sykes Is Not Aboriginal, Says the One Who Knows Best... Her Mum", *The Weekend Australian,* October 24 - 25, 1998, p.11.

[28] Marsh, John, "Clan Casts Out the Snake Woman", http://www.smh.au//news/9810/17/text/pageone4.html

[29] Meade, Kevin, "Activist Had Black View of Racist World", *The Weekend Australian,* October 24 - 25, 1998, p.11.

[30] ibid.

[31] ibid.

[32] Anne Coombs writes in "A Life Told Too Soon" that "The mystery of her father's identity continues", *Sydney Morning Herald,* 12 September 1998. p.8s.

[33] Sandra Phillips quoted in Willa McDonald's, "Tricky Business: Whites On Black Territory" *Australian Author,* vol. 29, no. 1, Autumn 1997, p.13.

[34] Huggins in McDonald, op.cit., p.13.

[35] ibid.

[36] Jackie Huggins, personal interview, 10 December 1997. All other quotes from Huggins in this chapter are from this source unless otherwise indicated.

[37] Kenny Laughton, email to the author, 17 October 1998. All other quotes from Laughton in this chapter are from this source unless otherwise indicated.

[38] Robert Bropho, personal interview, 4 March 1998.

[39] Wright, Alexis, "Breaking Taboos", a paper given at the Tasmanian Readers' and Writers' Festival, September 1998.

[40] Cathie Craigie, personal interview, 9 October 1997. All other quotes from Craigie in this chapter are from this source unless otherwise indicated.

[41] Rosemary van den Berg, email to the author, 12 August 1999. All other quotes from van den Berg in this chapter are from this source unless otherwise indicated.

[42] Morris in McDonald, op.cit., p.12.

[43] ibid.

[44] Macartney, Frederick, *Australian Literary Essays,* Angus and Robertson, Sydney, 1957, p.112.

[45] Langford Ginibi, Ruby, "My Mob, My Self", *The Strength Of Us As Women Speak: Black Women Speak,* Ginninderra Press, Canberra, 2000, p.17.

[46] Wright, Alexis, "Language and Empire", a paper presented to the Brisbane Writers' Festival, 7 September 1997.

[47] Morrissey, Di, "Letter to the Editor", *Australian Author,* vol. 26, no. 3, Spring 1994, p.7.

[48] Wheatley, Nadia, "Black and White Writing: The Issues", *Australian Author,* vol. 26, no. 3, Spring 1994, p.22.

[49] ibid., p.23.

[50] Rhydwen, Mari, *Writing on the Backs of Blacks: Voice, Literacy and Community in Kriol Fieldwork,* UQP, St. Lucia, 1996, pp.vii-viii.

[51] Huggins, Jackie, "Respect V Political Correctness", *Australian Author,* vol. 26, no. 3, Spring 1994, p.12.

⁵² Ray Coffey, email to the author, 12 August 1999. All other quotes from Coffey in this chapter are from this source unless otherwise indicated.

⁵³ Milne, Geoffrey, "The Other Side of the Story: Multicultural Drama in Australia", *Meanjin*, vol. 53, no. 3, Spring 1994, p.495.

⁵⁴ ibid.,p.502.

⁵⁵ Gordon Francis is a non-Aboriginal playwright. His play *God's Best Country* was originally workshopped during the Western Australian Theatre Company's 1985 Playwrights Workshop and published by Currency Press in 1987.

⁵⁶ Milne, op.cit., p.502

⁵⁷ ibid.

Chapter Two

⁵⁸ Jaimes, M. Annette, *The State of Native America: Genocide, Colonisation and Resistance*, South End Press, Boston, 1992, p.127.

⁵⁹ cited in Lippman, Lorna, *Generations of Resistance: Aborigines Demand Justice*, 2nd edition. Longman Cheshire, Melbourne, 1991, p.29.

⁶⁰ Fesl, Eve D., "How the English Language is Used to Put Koories Down, Deny Us Rights, Or Is Employed as a Political Tool Against Us", Monash University - Rev.6/89, a paper distributed at the "Our Words-Our Ways" National Aboriginal and Torres Strait Islander Writers' Workshop 1992.

⁶¹ Birch, Tony, "'Real Aborigines' - Colonial Attempts to Re-Imagine and Re-Create the Identities of Aboriginal People", *Ulitarra*, no .4, 1993, p.13.

⁶² ibid., p.19.

⁶³ Langton, Marcia, *Well I Heard It On The Radio And I Saw It On The Television*, Australian Film Commission, Sydney, 1993, pp.28-29.

⁶⁴ ibid., p.33.

⁶⁵ ibid., pp.34-35.

⁶⁶ Green, Nellie, "Chasing an Identity, An Aboriginal perspective on Aboriginality", *The Strength Of Us As Women: Black Women Speak*, Ginninderra Press, Canberra, 2000, p.47.

⁶⁷ ibid., p.51.

⁶⁸ Langford Ginibi, Ruby, "My Mob, My Self", *The Strength Of Us As Women: Black Women Speak*, Ginninderra Press, Canberra, 2000, p.19.

⁶⁹ Kurtzer, Sonja, "'Wandering Girl': Who Defines Authenticity in Aboriginal Literature?", *Southerly*, vol. 58, no. 2, Winter 1998, p.20.

⁷⁰ ibid., p.21.

⁷¹ cited in Lippman, op.cit., p.88.

⁷² *Australia Council 1998 Grants Handbook*, Australia Council, Strawberry Hills, Sydney. 1998. p.15.

⁷³ "Jim Davidson interviews Kath Walker", *Meanjin*, vol. 36, no .4, December 1977, p.434.

⁷⁴ Noongar is a word used by Aboriginal people of the south west of Western Australia to describe themselves, their language and their culture. McCarron uses this spelling of the community which she comes from. Other spellings include Nyoongah and Nyoongar.

⁷⁵ McCarron, Robyn, "Noongar Language and Literature", *Span*, vol.1, no. 36, October 1993, p.274.

⁷⁶ Dodson, Michael, "The Wentworth Lecture - The End in the Beginning: Re(de)fining Aboriginality", *Australian Aboriginal Studies*, no. 1, 1994, p.3.

[77] Jeanie Bell, personal interview, 15 January 1998. All other quotes from Bell in this chapter are from this source unless otherwise indicated.

[78] Bruce Pascoe, responses to questionnaire, 22 November 1997. All other quotes from Pascoe in this chapter are from this source unless otherwise indicated.

[79] Kerry Reed-Gilbert, responses to questionnaire, 28 September 1997. All other quotes from Gilbert on this chapter are from this source unless otherwise indicated.

[80] Cathy Craigie, personal interview, 9 October 1997. All other quotes from Craigie in this chapter are from this source unless otherwise indicated.

[81] Kenny Laughton, email to the author, 17 October 1998. All other quotes from Laughton in this chapter are from this source unless otherwise indicated.

[82] Rosemary van den Berg, email to the author, 9 August 1999. All other quotes from van den Berg in this chapter are from this source unless otherwise indicated.

[83] Melissa Lucashenko, personal interview, 30 January 1998. All other quotes from Lucashenko in this chapter are from this source unless otherwise indicated.

[84] In her article "In the Public Interest" *Weekend Australian*, October 24-25, 1998, Sykes reacts to criticism of assuming an Aboriginal identity and adopting the snake as her totem. Throughout she refers to "the Black community", "other Blacks" as opposed to "the Aboriginal community" and "other Aborigines."

[85] McCarron, op.cit.p. 281. This is also highlighted in the anthology *Those Who Remain Will Always Remember*, Fremantle Arts Centre Press, Fremantle, 2000.

Chapter Three

[86] *Report on Strategies for the Further Development of the National Aboriginal and Torres Strait Islander Arts and Cultural Industry: Main Report*. A Report to ATSIC by Arts Training Northern Territory. ATSIC, Canberra, 1994, p.255.

[87] van Toorn, Penny, "Early Aboriginal Writing and the Discipline of Literary Studies", *Meanjin*, no. 4, 1996, p.754.

[88] ibid.

[89] Muecke, Stephen, "Always Already Writing", *Reading the Country: Introduction to Nomadology*, Krim Benterrak, Stephen Muecke & Padde Roe, Fremantle Arts Centre Press, Fremantle, 1984, p.61.

[90] ibid., p.63.

[91] ibid., p.62.

[92] Biddle, Jennifer, "Dot, Circle, Difference: Translating Central Desert Paintings", *Cartographies: Poststructuralism and the Mapping of Bodies and Spaces,* Diprose, R & Ferrell, R. Allen & Unwin, Sydney, 1991, p. 28. Unfortunately, Biddle is more concerned with what defines bilingualism in her discussion, than the actual expression being presented in visual, Warlpiri and English forms.

Regardless of how many Europeans speak, or rather don't speak Warlpiri, Biddle is off-base in her reading of what has been described as a "bilingual dreaming book", failing to see that in this context the artists and owners of the intellectual property of the stories have been generous in allowing their stories to be told for three audiences. Biddle however is more concerned with the translations of Warlpiri stories (and indeed every reproduction of Central Desert Arts), highlighting that her academic training leads her to focus heavily on a linear analysis of how these paintings are translated and by whom, rather than what these paintings are saying and by whom.

[93] Wright, Judith, "The Writer As Activist", *Born of the Conquerors: Selected Essays,* Aboriginal Studies Press, Canberra, 1991, p.132.

[94] ibid.

[95] Jackie Huggins, personal interview, 10 December 1997. All other quotes from Huggins in this chapter are from this source unless otherwise indicated.

[96] Jeanie Bell, personal interview, 15 January 1998. All other quotes from Bell in this chapter are from this source unless otherwise indicated.

[97] Wright, Alexis, "Language & Empire: The Empires Of The East Have Crumbled Into Dust, But The English Language Remains", a paper presented at the Brisbane Writers' Festival, 7 September 1997.

[98] Lisa Bellear, personal interview, 5 June 1997. All other quotes from Bellear in this chapter are from this source unless otherwise indicated.

[99] Cathie Craigie, personal interview, 9 October 1997. All other quotes from Craigie in this chapter are from this source unless otherwise indicated.

[100] Melissa Lucashenko, personal interview, 30 January 1998. All other quotes from Lucashenko in this chapter are from this source unless otherwise indicated.

[101] Longley, Kateryna Olijnyk, "Directions", *Australian Book Review*, no. 131, June 1991, p.30.

[102] Sandra Phillips, personal interview, 5 June 1997. All other quotes from Phillips in this chapter are from this source unless otherwise indicated.

[103] Herb Wharton, personal interview, 10 December 1997. All other quotes from Wharton in this chapter from this source unless otherwise indicated.

[104] Leon Carmen on *A Current Affair*, cited in Debra Jopson's article, "Writing Wrongs", *Sydney Morning Herald*, 15 March 1997, p.38.

[105] Arthur, J.M. *Aboriginal English: A Cultural Study*, Oxford University Press, Melbourne, 1996, p.235.

[106] Term coined by Ruby Langford Ginibi.

[107] Kenny Laughton, e-mail to the author, 17 October 1998. All other quotes from Laughton in this chapter are from this source unless otherwise indicated.

[108] Wright, Alexis, "Language and Empire", op.cit.

[109] ibid.

[110] Roe, Paddy and Stephen Muecke, *Gularabulu: Stories of the Kimberley*, Fremantle Arts Centre Press, Fremantle, 1983, p.iv.

[111] ibid., p.vi.

[112] ibid., p.67.

[113] Alf Taylor, "The Wool Pickers", *Across Country*, ABC Books, Sydney. 1998, p.187.

[114] Langford Ginibi, Ruby, *The Strength of Us As Women*, op.cit., p.18.

[115] Mudrooroo, *Us Mob: History, Culture, Struggle: An Introduction to Indigenous Australia*, Angus & Robertson, Sydney, 1995, p.94.

[116] Johnson, Colin, *Writing from the Fringe: A Study of Modern Aboriginal Literature*, Hyland House, South Yarra, 1990, p.6.

[117] ibid., p.143.

[118] Moran, Rod, "About Books: Aboriginal Literary Voices", *National Library of Australia News*, vol. 2, no. 2, November 1991, p.10.

[119] Kerry Reed-Gilbert, response to questionaire, 28 September 1997. All other quotes form Reed-Gilbert in this chapter are from this source unless otherwise indicated.

[120] Rosemary van den Berg e-mail to the author, 12 August 1999. All other quotes from van den Berg in this chapter are from this source unless otherwise indicated.

[121] John Muk Muk Burke, personal interview, 12 March 1998.

[122] Graham, Mary, "Indigenous Writing and Editing", APA Residential Editorial Program Report 1999, pp.27-28.

[123] Ravenscroft, Alison, "Politics of Exposure: An Interview with Alexis Wright", *Meridian*, vol. 17, no.1, 1998, p.76.

[124] Douglas, Josie & Bowman, Marg, "New Publisher for Black Poetry", *Five Bells*, vol. 4, no. 6, July 1997, p.9.

[125] Arens, Werner, "The Image of Australia in Australian Poetry", *Australian Papers: Yugoslavia, Europe and Australia*, ed. by Mirko Jurak, Faculty of Arts and Science, Edvard Kardelj University of Ljubljana, 1983, p.229.

[126] ibid., p.229

[127] Johnson, *Writing from the Fringe*, op.cit., p.28.

[128] Lisa Bellear on ABC Radio National's "Women Out Loud", 19 March 1997.

[129] Langford Ginibi, Ruby, *The Strength of Us As Women*, op.cit., p.17.

[130] ibid., p.18.

[131] Mudrooroo, *Us Mob*, op.cit., p.178.

[132] ibid.

[133] Huggins, Jackie, *Sister Girl*, UQP, St. Lucia, 1998, p.11.

[134] ibid., p.51.

[135] Wright, Alexis, "Language and Empire", op.cit.

[136] Wright, Alexis, "Breaking Taboos" a paper given at the Tasmanian Writers' and Readers' Festival, September 1998.

[137] Ravenscroft, op.cit. p.75

[138] Chesson, Keith, *Jack Davis: A life story*, Dent, Melbourne, 1988, p.197.

[139] Brisbane, Katherine, "The Future in Black and White: Aboriginality in Recent Australian Drama", published in Currency Press -The Performing Arts Publisher catalogue.

[140] ibid.

[141] "Lionel Fogarty talks to Philip Mead" *Jacket Magazine*, http://www.jacketmagazine.com/01/fogartyiv.html

[142] McRobbie, Narelle, *Who's That Jumbun in the Log*, Magabala Books, Broome, 1996, p.30.

[143] Kerry Davies Publishing Services, *Register of Editorial Services 1998*, Society of Editors (NSW)

[144] An anthology written for American tertiary students and published by Rutgers University Press, New Jersey, 1998.

[145] Sam Cook, email to the author, 2 October 1999.

[146] Ravenscroft, op.cit., p.78.

[147] Ray Coffey, email to the author, 12 August 1999. All other quotes from Coffey in this chapter are from this source unless otherwise indicated.

[148] Langford Ginibi, *The Strength Of Us As Women*, op.cit. p.19.

[149] Pascoe, Bruce, "Land, Life, Literature", presented at the 1998 Spring Writing Festival, Sydney. September 13, 1998.

[150] ibid.

[151] Ashcroft, W.D, Gareth Griffiths & Helen Tiffin, *The Empire Writes Back: Theory and Practice in Post-Colonial Literatures*, Routledge, London. 1989. p.2

[152] ibid., p.11.

[153] Trees, Kathryn, "Postcolonialism: Yet Another Colonial Strategy?", *Span*, vol. 1, no. 36, 1993, pp.264-265.

[154] Albert Wendt, personal interview, 12 June 1997.

[155] Jackie Huggins, personal interview, 10 December 1997. The MP referred to by Huggins is Pauline Hanson of the One Nation Party.

[156] Brewster, Anne, *Literary Formations: Post-colonialism, Nationalism, Globalism,* Melbourne University Press, 1995, p.19.

[157] ibid.

[158] Muecke, Stephen, *Textual Spaces: Aboriginality and Cultural Studies.* UNSW Press, Kensington, 1992, p.10.

[159] Albert Wendt, personal interview, 12 June 1997.

Chapter Four

[160] Mann, Maria, "Magabala Books: The Politics of Design", *Artlink,* vol. 17, no.1, 1997, p.37.

[161] Rose, Michael ed., *For the Record: 160 Years of Aboriginal Print Journalism*, Allen & Unwin, St. Leonards, 1996, p. 2.

[162] ibid., p.3.

[163] ibid., p.22.

[164] ibid.

[165] ibid., p.46.

[166] ibid.

[167] ibid., p.68.

[168] ibid., p.88.

[169] ibid., p.106.

[170] ibid., p.126.

[171] *Koori Mail* promotional flyer distributed at the Aboriginal Arts and Culture Conference, Armidale. March 2000.

[172] ibid.

[173] McDonald, Willa, "Tricky Business: Whites on Black Territory", *Australian Author,* vol. 29, no.1, Autumn 1997, p.14.

[174] Lisa Bellear, personal interview, 5 June 1997. All other quotes from Bellear in this chapter are from this source unless otherwise indicated.

[175] "IAD Press", *ABC of Indigenous Publishing* catalogue, 1997, p.6.

[176] Simon MacDonald, personal interview, 10 September 1999. All other quotes from MacDonald in this chapter are from this source unless otherwise indicated.

[177] Rule, Rosemary, "Publishing in Broome", *Editions*, vol. 1, no. 1, August 1989, p.7.

[178] ibid., p.6.

[179] *Magabala Books Catalogue*, February 1993.

[180] *Magabala's Publishing Policy,* Magabala Books, 1996.

[181] Rule, op.cit., p.6.

[182] "APA Residential Editorial Program 1999 Report", p.17.

[183] *Magabala's Publishing Policy*, op.cit.

[184] "Magabala Books", *ABC of Indigenous Publishing Catalogue,* 1997, p.10.

[185] Jose, Nicholas, "Pearls of Wisdom", *The Australian Way,* October 1996, p.62.

[186] Sims, Bruce, "Bruce Sims: Transition", *Publishing Studies,* 1997, p.35.

[187] ibid.

[188] Rachel Bin Salleh, letter to the author, 24 October 1996.

[189] Sam Cook, email to the author, 2 October 1999. All other quotes from Cook in this chapter are from this source unless otherwise indicated.

[190] Mann, op.cit., p.36.

[191] ibid., p.37.

[192] *Report on Strategies for the Further Development of the National Aboriginal and Torres Strait Islander Arts and Cultural Industry: Main Report.* A Report to ATSIC by Arts Training Northern Territory. ATSIC, Canberra, 1994, p.281.

[193] *Annual Report 1996-97,* Australian Institute of Aboriginal and Torres Strait Islander Studies, Canberra, p.15.

[194] *Aboriginal Studies Press 1999–2000 Catalogue*, p.3.

[195] ibid.

[196] *Annual Report 1998–99*, Australian Institute of Aboriginal and Torres Strait Islander Studies, Canberra, p.30.

[197] Cormick, Craig, "Change of Direction", *The Canberra Times,* 15 March 1997.

[198] Kenny Laughton, email to the author, 17 October 1997. All other quotes from Laughton in this chapter are from this source unless otherwise indicated.

[199] Shoemaker, Adam, "Who Should Control Aboriginal Writing?", *Australian Book Review*, May 1983, p.21.

[200] ibid.

[201] Johnson, Colin, "The Growth of Aboriginal Literature", *Social Alternatives,* vol. 7, no. 1, March 1988, p.53.

[202] "APA Residential Editorial Program 1999 Report", p.17.

[203] ibid.

[204] Kerry Reed-Gilbert, response to questionnaire, 28 September 1997.

[205] Betti, Leeroy, "Writer Turns Back Pages", *The West Australian,* 7 March 1998, p.42.

[206] Ray Coffey, email to the author, 12 August 1999. All other quotes from Coffey in this chapter are from this source unless otherwise indicated.

[207] Muecke, Stephen, "Aboriginal Literature and the Repressive Hypothesis", *Southerly*, vol. 48, no. 4, December 1988, p.413.

[208] ibid.

[209] ibid.cit., p 412.

[210] Biographical details, *Ruby-eyed Coucal,* Magabala Books, Broome, 1996.

[211] Pascoe, Bruce ed., "Editorial", *Aboriginal Short Stories,* Pascoe Publishing, Apollo Bay, 1990, p.i.

[212] Pascoe, Bruce, "Bruce Pascoe & Lyn Harwood, Editors of *Australian Short Stories*", *Ulitarra,* no. 5, 1994, p.118.

[213] Biographical details for Pascoe in *Fox* (McPhee Gribble) in 1988 simply state "He now lives at Cape Otway with his family". In 1996, his biographical details in *Ruby-Eyed Coucal* (Magabala) were amended to say "...Cape Otway in Victoria where he is a proud member of the Wathaurong Aboriginal Co-operative".

[214] Pascoe Publishing, aside from *Australian Short Stories,* also published with the assistance of the Australia Council, *Wathaurong: Too Bloody Strong - Stories of Life Journeys of People From Wathaurong,* edited by Pascoe and released in 1997. In his Foreward Pascoe states, "These stories reflect the spirit and pride of our community and were compiled as a result of a project instituted by the Wathaurong Co-operative in 1994-96", p.6.

[215] Sue Abbey, email to the author, 18 August 2000.

[216] Sandra Phillips on ABC Radio National, "Women Out Loud", 19 March 1997.

[217] Wu, Anthea, Acquittal Report to the Literature Fund of the Australia Council for "Strategic Initiative: Professional Development / Training or Indigenous Editors 1998" Grant.

[218] ibid.

[219] Anthea Wu, email to the author, 1 October 1999.

[220] *Report on Strategies for the Further Development of the National Aboriginal and Torres Strait Islander Arts and Cultural Industry: Main Report,* op.cit., p.284.

[221] ibid.

[222] Michael Schoo, personal conversation, 21 August 2000. All other quotes from Schoo in this chapter are from this source unless otherwise indicated.

[223] *Black and White Australia,* Currency Press: The Performing Arts Publisher, catalogue, p.1

[224] Katherine Brisbane, letter to the author, 18 August 2000.

[225] ibid.

Chapter Five

[226] Jeanie Bell, personal interview, 12 January 1998 and Lisa Bellear, personal interview, 5 June 1997.

[227] Arms, Jane, "A Report to the Australia Council on the Training of Senior Literary Editors and a Proposed Scheme for the Training of Indigenous Editors", Adelaide, November 1997, p.21.

[228] Sandra Phillips, personal interview, 5 June 1997. All other quotes from Phillips in this chapter are from this source unless otherwise indicated.

[229] Josie Douglas, personal interview, 10 September 1999. All other quotes from Douglas in this chapter are from this source unless otherwise indicated.

[230] Rachel Bin Salleh, email to the author, 29 March 2000. All other quotes from Bin Salleh in this chapter are from this source unless otherwise indicated.

[231] Mann, Maria, "Magabala Books: The Politics of Design", *Artlink,* vol.17, no.1, 1997, p.37.

[232] Sam Cook, email to the author, 2 October 1999.

[233] Kenny Laughton, email to the author, 17 October 1998. All other quotes from Laughton in this chapter are from this source unless otherwise indicated.

[234] Ray Coffey, email to the author, 12 August 1999. All other quotes from Coffey in this chapter are from this source unless otherwise indicated.

[235] Mudrooroo, "Being Published from the Fringe", *Australian Author*, vol. 26, no. 3, Spring 1994, p.16.

[236] Josie Douglas, email to the author, 10 August 2000.

[237] ibid.

[238] Sue Abbey, email to the author, 18 August 2000.

[239] Rule, Rosemary, "Publishing in Broome", *Editions*, vol. 1, no.1, August 1989, p.6.

[240] Brisbane, Katherine, "The Future in Black and White: Aboriginality in Recent Australian Drama" a paper presented at IDEA '95 - 2nd World Congress of Drama / Theatre Education, *Currency Press: The Performing Arts Publisher. Black and White Australia*, catalogue.

[241] Bruce Pascoe, response to questionnaire, 22 November 1997. All other quotes from Pascoe in the chapter will come from this source unless otherwise indicated.

[242] Jeanie Bell, personal interview, 15 January 1998. All other quotes from Bell in the chapter will come form this source unless otherwise indicated. An example of other books written about FCAATSI include Faith Bandler's *Turning the Tide: a personal history of FCAATSI* [1989].

[243] Lisa Bellear, personal interview, 5 June 1997. All other quotes from Bellear in this chapter will come from this source unless otherwise indicated.

[244] Melissa Lucashenko, personal interview, 30 January 1998. All other quotes from Lucashenko in this chapter will come from this source unless otherwise indicated.

[245] Jackie Huggins, personal interview, 10 December 1997. All other quotes from Huggins in this chapter will come from this source unless otherwise indicated.

[246] Kerry Reed-Gilbert, response to questionnaire, 28 September 1997.

[247] Herb Wharton, personal interview, 10 December 1997.

[248] John Muk Muk Burke, personal interview, 12 March 1998

[249] For legal reasons and at the request of Ginibi, the editor of *Don't Take Your Love To Town* will simply be referred to as Susan.

[250] Ruby Langford Ginibi, personal interview, 29 February 2000. All other quotes from Ginibi in this chapter are from this source unless otherwise indicated.

[251] Langford Ginibi, Ruby, "My Mob, My Self", *The Strength Of Us As Women: Black Women Speak*, op. cit., p.20.

[252] ibid., p.18.

[253] Arts Training Northern Territory, op.cit., p.263.

[254] Arms, op.cit., p.21.

[255] ibid.

[256] ibid., p.27.

[257] "APA Residential Editorial Program Report 1999", op.cit., p.26.

[258] ibid., p.11.

[259] ibid., p.17.

[260] ibid, p.26.

[261] ibid., p.27.

[262] ibid., p.30.

[263] Mudrooroo, op.cit., p.17.

Chapter Six

[264] Janke, Terri, "Protecting Australian Indigenous Arts and Cultural Expression: A Matter of Legislative Reform or Cultural Policy?", *Culture and Policy,* vol. 7, no. 3, 1996, p.14.

[265] Section 359(2) *Copyright Act 1968,* cited in Janke, Terri, *Our Culture: Our Future: The Report on Australian Indigenous Cultural and Intellectual Property Rights*, Michael Frankel & Co., Sydney, 1998, p.31.

[266] Section 98(1) & (2) and Section 22(4) *Copyright Act 1968* cited in Janke, ibid., p.32.

[267] *Walter vs Lane* [1900] AC 539 cited in Janke, *Our Culture, Our Future,* op.cit., p.53.

[268] ibid.

[269] Torres, Pat, "Interested in Writing About Indigenous Australians?", *Australian Author,* vol. 26, no. 3, Spring 1994, p.24.

[270] ibid., p.25.

[271] Terri Janke, letter to the author, 13 April 2000.

[272] "APA Residential Editorial Program 1999 Report", p.26.

[273] ibid., p.22.

[274] ibid.

[275] Wheatley, Nadia, "Black and White Writing: The Issues", *Australian Author*, vol. 26, no. 3, Spring 1994, p.22.

[276] Janke, *Our Culture, Our Future,* op.cit., p.xxix.

[277] ibid.

[278] Terri Janke, letter to the author, 13 April 2000.

[279] Arts Training Northern Territory, op.cit., pp.273-274.

[280] ibid.

[281] Janke, *Culture and Policy*, op.cit., p.18.

[282] Arts Training Northern Territory, op.cit., p.273.

[283] Janke, *Our Culture: Our Future* , op.cit., p.xvii.

[284] ibid.

[285] ibid.

[286] ibid., p.21.

[287] ibid., p.23.

[288] ibid., p.39

[289] ibid., p.55.

[290] Mann, Maria, "Magabala Books: The Politics of Design", *Artlink*, vol. 17, no.1, 1997, p.37.

[291] Wu, Anthea, "Report on Preparation for Indigenous Writers' Series", University of Western Australia Press, September 1998.

[292] Anthea Wu, email to the author, 1 October 1999.

[293] Rachel Bin Salleh, email to the author, 29 March 2000.

End Notes

Chapter Seven

[294] A survey by the Cultural Strategies Working Group in 1995 found that 38.4% of the population visited libraries while only 26.9% attended pop music concerts and 22.3% visited art galleries. See Chapter Six for more detail.

[295] Sandra Phillips on "Not Another Koori Show", 3NCR. 5 June 1998. The Australian Reconciliation Convention took place from 26 to 28 May 1997 at the Melbourne Convention and Exhibition Centre with the theme of "Renewal of the Nation". There were 32 workshop sessions and 160 prominent Indigenous and non-Indigenous speakers, but as Phillips pointed out, no Indigenous writers were on the arts panel.

[296] Lisa Bellear, personal interview, 5 June 1997. All other quotes from Bellear in this chapter are from this source unless otherwise indicated.

[297] Sandra Phillips, personal interview, 5 June 1997. All other quotes from Phillips in this chapter are from this source unless otherwise indicated.

[298] Jeanie Bell, personal interview, 15 January 1998.

[299] Melissa Lucashenko, personal interview, 30 January 1998.

[300] Cathy Craigie, personal interview, 9 October 1997. All other quotes from Craigie in this chapter are from this source unless otherwise indicated.

[301] Ray Coffey, email to the author, 11 August 2000. All other quotes from Coffey in this chapter are from this osurce unless otherwise indicated.

[302] Simon MacDonald, email to the author, 11 August 2000. All other quotes from McDonald in this chatper are from this osurce unless otherwise indicated.

[303] Kenny Laughton, email to the author, 17 October 1998. All other quotes from Laughton in this chapter are from this source unless otherwise indicated.

[304] Spender, Lynne, *Australian Author,* vol. 26, no. 3, Spring 1994, p.10.

[305] Jackie Huggins, personal interview, 10 December 1997. All other quotes from Huggins in this chapter are from this source unless otherwise indicated.

[306] Sam Cook, email to the author, 2 October 1999. All other quotes from Cook in this chapter are from this source unless otherwise indicated.

[307] Rachel Bin Salleh, email to the author, 29 March 2000. All other quotes from Bin Salleh in this chapter are from this source unless otherwise indicated.

[308] *Report of Strategies for the Further Development of the National Aboriginal and Torres Strait Islander Arts and Cultural Industry: Main Report.* A report to ATSIC from Arts Training Northern Territory. ATSIC, Canberra, 1994, p.269.

[309] ibid.

[310] ibid.

[311] ibid.

[312] Simon MacDonald personal interview, 10 September 1999. All other quotes from MacDonald in this chapter are from this source unless otherwise indicated.

[313] In 1999, the Australian Society of Authors estimate that the average Australian author generates $3000 per annum from their writing made up of royalties, performance and workshop fees.

[314] Lydia Miller, letter to the author, 8 September 1997.

[315] Irina Dunn, personal interview, 30 September 1997. All other quotes from Dunn in this chapter are from this source unless otherwise indicated.

[316] *Blackbooks 1996 Catalogue*, p.1.

[317] Wright, Judith, *Born of the Conquerors: Selected Essays by Judith Wright*, Aboriginal Studies Press, Canberra, 1991, p.91.

[318] Wright, Alexis, "Language and Empire", a paper presented at the Brisbane Writers' Festival, 7 September 1997.

[319] Nelson, Emmanuel S, "Struggle for a Black Aesthetic: Critical Theory in Contemporary Aboriginal Australia", *Australian Studies*, no. 6, November 1992, p.32.

[320] Beston, John, "The Aboriginal Poets in English: Kath Walker, Jack Davis and Kevin Gilbert", *Meanjin*, no. 36, December 1977, p.459.

[321] Nelson, op.cit., p.33.

[322] Johnson, Colin, "The Growth of Aboriginal Literature", *Social Alternatives*, vol. 7, no. 1, March 1988, p.54.

[323] Wright, Judith, op.cit., p.92.

[324] Anderson, Ian, Letter, *Australian Book Review*, no.150, May 1993, p.4.

[325] Shoemaker, Adam, "A Bridge Too Far", *Australian Book Review*, no. 166, November 1994, p.17.

[326] ibid.

[327] John Muk Muk Burke, personal interview, 12 March 1998.

[328] Danaher, P.A., "Reviews and Booknotes", *Idiom 23*, vol. 7, no. 2, Nov-Dec. 1994, p.119.

[329] ibid., p.120.

[330] Liverani, Mary Rose, "From Outside, Without Insight", *Weekend Australian Review*, 28-29 March 1992, p.rev6.

[331] Langford Ginibi, Ruby, "A Koori's Lesson in Dispossession", *Weekend Australian Review*, 2-3 May 1992, p.rev6.

[332] Watego, Cliff, "Being Done To Again", *Social Alternatives*, vol. 7, 1988, p.34.

[333] Kuilboer, Theresa , "Life and laughs in hell: Vietnam vet's powerful story", *Sunday Territorian* 6 June 1999, p.17.

[334] Langton, Marcia, "*Well I Heard It On the Radio And I Saw It On The Television...*", Australian Film Commission, Sydney, 1993, p.29.

[335] Kurtzer, Sonja, "'Wandering Girl': Who Defines Authenticity in Aboriginal Literature?", *Southerly*, vol. 58, no. 2, Winter 1998, p.22.

[336] ibid., p.27.

[337] Huggins, Jackie, "Always Was Always Will Be", *Australian Historical Studies*, vol. 25, no. 100, April 1993, p.460.

[338] ibid., p.461.

[339] ibid., p.463.

[340] Cathy Craigie, personal interview, 9 October 1997. All other quotes from Craigie in this book are from this source unless otherwise indicated. One could, of course, argue that this may have been a deliberate oversight by Morgan in a desire to respect her grandmother's personal history.

[341] Narogin, Mudrooroo, *Writing from the Fringe: A Study of Modern Aboriginal Literature*, Hyland House, Melbourne, 1990, p.149.

[342] Herb Wharton, personal interview, 10 December 1997. All other quotes from Wharton in this chapter are from this source unless otherwise indicated.

[343] Rosemary van den Berg, email to the author, 9 August 1999. All other quotes from van den Berg in this chapter are from this source unless otherwise indicated.

Chapter Eight

[344] *Report on Strategies for the Further Development of the National Aboriginal and Torres Strait Islander Arts and Cultural Industry: Main Report.* A report to ATSIC by Arts Training Northern Territory. ATSIC, Canberra, 1994. p.271.

[345] *Australia Council Grants 1998 Handbook*, Australia Council, Strawberry Hills, 1998. p.2.

[346] *Writers Have Their Say*, Australia Council for the Arts, Sydney, 1999.

[347] *Policy for the Promotion and Support of Indigenous Arts and Cultural Activity in New South Wales*, NSW Ministry for the Arts, Sydney, March 2000.

[348] ibid.

[349] *Program of Assistance Handbook 2001*, Arts Queensland, Brisbane, 2000, p.6.

[350] Di Spencer, email to author, 10 August 2000.

[351] ibid.

[352] Sam Cook, email to the author, 18 August 2000.

[353] "ArtsWA Aboriginal Arts Policy", Final Draft, August 2000.

[354] ibid.

[355] ibid.

[356] *National Indigenous Arts Advocacy Association Vision Statement*

[357] Richard Walley, Chair of ATSIAB speaking at the Festival of Pacific Arts, Western Samoa, September 1996.

[358] cited in Narogin, Mudrooro, *Writing From the Fringe: A Study of Modern Aboriginal Literature*, Hyland House, South Yarra, 1990, p.94.

[359] Chesson, Keith *Jack Davis: A Life Story*, op.cit., p.209.

[360] Irina Dunn, personal interview, 30 September 1997. All other quotes from Dunn in this chapter are from this source unless otherwise indicated.

[361] Christine McKenzie, email to the author, 12 August 2000.

[362] Marian Devitt, letter to the author, 11 February 1999. All other quotes from Devitt in this chapter are from this source unless otherwise indicated.

[363] Terri Anne Whitebeach, letter to the author, 28 February 1999.

[364] "Writer in Community Project", QWC Final Acquittal 1997, p.1.

[365] "Strategic Initiatives, Indigenous Writers' Mentorship - Queensland 1998-99".

[366] Susan Hayes, letter to the author, 10 February 1999. All other quotes from Hayes in this chapter are from this source unless otherwise indicated.

[367] Anne-Marie Britton, email to the author, 10 August 2000.

[368] Lynne Spender, personal interview, 2 October 1997. All other quotes from Spender in this chapter are from this source unless otherwise indicated.

[369] Arts Training Northern Territory, op.cit., p.285.

[370] "Aims of the Indigenous Portfolio", Australia Society of Authors, Sydney, 1998.

[371] Whitebeach, Terri Anne, "Interim Report: Culturally Appropriate Professional Training Opportunities for Central Australian Indigenous Writers".

[372] Whitebeach, Terri Anne, "Second Report: Culturally Appropriate Professional Training Opportunities for Central Australian Indigenous Writers", September 1997.

[373] Batchelor College is a specialist tertiary institution providing accredited TAFE and Vocational education and training and other education programs for Aboriginal and Torres Strait Islander people. Approximately 85% of students come from remote Indigenous communities in the Northern Territory where the majority of people speak English as a second or foreign language.

[374] Whitebeach, Terri Anne, "Third Report: Culturally Appropriate Training Opportunities for Central Australian Indigenous Writers".

[375] Whitebeach, Terri Anne, "5th & Final Project Report 1998: Culturally Appropriate Training Opportunities for Central Australian Indigenous Writers".

[376] Arts Training Northern Territory, op.cit., pp.279-280.

[377] ibid., p.280.

[378] Simon MacDonald, personal interview, 10 September 1999.

[379] Phillips, Sandra, "White Noise and Fuzzy Hazy Stuff", *QWC News*, February 1999, p.13.

[380] ibid.

[381] Josie Douglas, personal interview, 10 September 1999.

Chapter Nine

[382] Alexis Wright, email to the author, 12 July 1999. All other quotes from Wright in this chapter will be from this source unless otherwise indicated.

[383] Lisa Bellear, personal interview, 5 June 1997. All other quotes from Bellear in this chapter are from this source unless otherwise indicated.

[384] Meredith Curnow, email to the author, 25 May 1999.

[385] Meredith Curnow, email to the author, 19 July 2000.

[386] Margaret Burke, email to the author, 14 July 1999.

[387] ibid.

[388] Barry Gamba, letter to the author, 21 November 1995.

[389] Catherine Sheedy, letter to the author, 22 June 1999.

[390] The *Age* Melbourne Writers' Festival organisers were contacted for purposes of finding out the history of Indigenous involvement in the Festival but no information was forthcoming.

[391] The *Age* Melbourne Writers' Festival 1998 program.

[392] The 1999 Festival of Perth Writers' Festival Events program.

[393] Tim Thorne, letter to the author, 28 May 1999.

[394] Starke, Ruth, *Writers, Readers, Rebels: Upfront and Backstage at Australia's Top Literary Festival*, Wakefield Press, Kent Town, 1998, p.76.

[395] Rose Wight, letter to the author, 28 May 1999

[396] Judy Pearce, letter to the author, 4 June 1999

[397] Jill Eddington, email to the author, 22 August 2000.

[398] Irina Dunn, personal interview, 30 September 1997. All other quotes from Dunn in the chapter are from this source unless otherwise indicated.

[399] Walbira Watts, email to the author, 11 March 2000. All other quotes from Watts in this chapter are from this source unless otherwise indicated.

[400] Watego, Cliff, "Backgrounds to Aboriginal Literature", *Connections — Essays on Black Literatures*, ed by Emmanuel S. Nelson, Aboriginal Studies Press, Canberra, 1988, p.18.

[401] Cathy Craigie, personal interview, 9 October 1997. All other quotes from Craigie in this chapter are from this source unless otherwise indicated.

[402] Jeanie Bell, personal interview, 15 January 1998. All other quotes from Bell in this chapter are from this source unless otherwise indicated.

[403] Jonah Jones, letter to the author, 5 June 1996.

[404] Rhoda Roberts, letter to the author, 4 June 1997.

[405] Kerry Reed-Gilbert, response to questionnaire, 28 September 1997.

[406] Sandra Phillips, personal interview, 5 June 1997. All other quotes from Phillips in this chapter are from this source unless otherwise indicated.

[407] Grace, Patricia, "Which Way Tellem Story", a paper presented at the Festival of the Dreaming, 22 September 1997.

[408] "Report on the Planning and Staging the Festival of Pacific Arts, Townsville, Australia, 14-27 August, 1988", Festival of Pacific Arts Ltd, 1989.

[409] Phillips, Sandra, statement to participants at "Our Words - Our Ways" Writers' Workshop 1992.

[411] Terri Anne Whitebeach, email to the author, 21 July 2000.

[411] Fogarty, Lesley, " Report on Mogwi-Djan: National Indigenous Writers' and Playwrights' Conference and Workshops", p.3.

[412] ibid.

[413] Phillips, Sandra, "Mogwi Djan" Editorial, *QWC Newsletter*, June 1996, p.6.

[414] ibid., p.7.

[415] ibid.

[416] ibid.

[417] Melissa Lucashenko, personal interview, 30 January 1998. All other quotes from Lucashenko in this chapter are from this source unless otherwise indicated.

[418] Arts Training Northern Territory, op.cit., p. 281.

[419] Craig Munro, personal interview, 1994.

[420] Ibid.

[421] Adrian Peniston-Bird, conversation with, 25 November 1997.

[422] Rhyll Nance, email to the author, 19 May 1999.

[423] ibid.

[424] 1997/98 NSW Ministry for the Arts—Fellowships, Scholarships and Awards Guidelines, NSW Arts Advisory Council, p.12.

[425] Margaret Minatel, email to the author, 20 July 1999.

Part 4

[426] *Gathering Strength*. 1996 Report of the Royal Commission into Aboriginal Peoples, Canada, Volume 3 p.640

[427] *Gathering Strength,* op.cit. p.640.

[428] Florene Belmore, personal interview, 11 June 1999. All other quotes from Belmore in this chapter are from this source unless otherwise indicated.

[429] Fleras, Augie, & Jean Leonard Elliott, *The Nations Within: Aboriginal - State Relations in Canada, the United States and New Zealand,* Oxford University Press, Toronto, 1992, p.14.

[430] ibid.

[431] ibid.

[432] Aboriginal Population…Who Decides? *The Forgotten People: The National Voice of Off-Reserve Indian and Metis Peoples Throughout Canada,* vol. 1, no. 1, March 1999, p. 3.

[433] ibid.

[434] ibid.

[435] Greg Young-Ing, email to the author, 13 March 2000.

[436] "Aboriginal Population...Who Decides?", op.cit. p.3

[437] ibid., p.4.

[438] North American Native Authors First Book Awards promotional flyer with "Rules", En'owkin Centre, Penticton, BC.

[439] Bob Rock, email to the author, 15 July 1999. All other quotes from Rock in this chapter are from this source unless otherwise indicated.

[440] See Huggins' comments on p.31 of thesis.

[441] Byler, Mary Gloyne, "American Indian Authors for Young Readers: An Annotated Bibliography", *Through Indian Eyes - The Native Experience in Books for Children,* Beverly Slapin & Doris Seale, New Society Publishers, Philadelphia, 1987, p.289.

[442] Angus, Graham Scott, "Change Is Upon Us, So Call Me a Dreamer", *Let the Drums Be Your Heart: New Native Voices,* Joel T. Maki ed., Douglas & McIntyre, Vancouver, 1996, p.103.

[443] Greg Young-Ing, personal interview, 17 June 1999. All other quotes from Young-Ing in this chapter are from this source unless otherwise indicated.

[444] LaRocque, Emma, Preface or "Here Are Our Voices - Who Will Hear?, *Writing the Circle - Native Women of Western Canada: An Anthology,* Jeanne Perreault & Sylvia Vance eds, NeWest Publishers, Edmonton, 1990, p. xviii.

[445] ibid.

[446] ibid.

[447] Slapin, Beverly & Seale, Doris eds, *Through Indian Eyes - The Native Experience on Books for Children,* New Society Publishers, Philadelphia, 1987, p.32.

[448] David Groulx, email to the author, 10 August 1999. All other quotes from Groulx in this chapter are from this source unless otherwise indicated.

[449] Byler, op.cit., p.289.

[450] ibid.

[451] ibid.

[452] Blaeser, Kimberley M., "Entering the Canons: Our Place in World Literature", *Akwe:kon Journal: A Journal of Indigenous Issues,* Spring 1993, p.35.

[453] Alexie, Sherman, "Who Said What", *Aboriginal Voices,* vol. 6, no. 3, May - June 1999, p. 54.

[454] Francis, Lee & Bruchac, James, *Reclaiming the Vision: Past, Present and Future: Native Voices for the 8th Generation,* Greenfield Press Review, 1996, p.15.

[455] ibid., p.30.

[456] ibid., p.xvi.

[457] Kateri Damm, email to the author, 14 July 1999. All other quotes from Damm in this chapter are from this source unless otherwise indicated.

[458] See p.37 of thesis for Bellear's comments and p.38 for Wharton's comments.

[459] Blaeser, op.cit., p.37.

[460] Armstrong, Jeanette, "The Disempowerment of First North American Native Peoples and Empowerment Through Their Writing", *Gatherings Vol. I,* Theytus Books, Penticton, BC, 1990, p.145.

[461] Francis & Bruchac, op.cit., p.33.

[462] Fife, Connie ed., *The Colour of Resistance - A Contemporary Collection of Writing by Aboriginal Women*, Sister Vision Press, Toronto, 1993, p.i.

[463] Francis & Bruchac, op.cit., p.32.

[464] LaRocque, op.cit., p.xv.

[465] ibid., p.xviii.

[466] Petrone, Penny, *Native Literature in Canada: From the Oral Tradition to the Present,* Oxford University Press, Toronto, 1990, p.vii.

[467] Blaeser, op.cit., p.37.

[468] Willie, Janine A., "On Theorising Native Literatures: Searching for Effective, Culturally Appropriate Ways To Read and Understand Native Literatures", York University, Ontario, 1996, p.6. Unpublished thesis.

[469] Rodger W. Ross, email to the author, 20 July 1999. All other quotes from Ross in this chapter are from this source unless otherwise indicated.

[470] Blaeser, op.cit., p.37.

[471] ibid., p.36.

[472] Willie, op.cit., p.2.

[473] "Reviews", *Aboriginal Voices*, vol. 5, no. 3. May - June 1998, p.52.

[474] Harjo, Joy, & Bird, Gloria, *Reinventing the Enemy's Language: Contemporary Native Women's Writings from North America,* W.W. Norton, New York, c1987.

[475] LaRocque, op.cit., p.xxviii.

[476] Slapin, Beverly, Doris Seale & Rosemary Gonzales, *How to Tell the Difference: A Checklist for Evaluating Children's Books for Anti-Indian Bias,* New Society Publishers, Gabriola Island, BC, 1992, p.1

[477] ibid., pp.7-28.

[478] LaRocque, op.cit., p.xvi.

[479] ibid., pp.xvi-xvii.

[480] ibid., p.xxi.

[481] ibid., p.xxii.

[482] Willie, op.cit., p.3.

[483] ibid., p.iv.

[484] Perreault, Jeanne & Sylvia Vance, *Writing the Circle - Native Women of Western Canada: An Anthology*, NeWest Publishers, Edmonton, 1990, p.xii.

[485] Blaeser, op.cit., p.37.

[486] LaRocque, op.cit., p.xxv.

[487] Fedorick, Joy Asham, "Fencepost Sitting", *Give Back: First Nations' Perspective on Cultural Practice*, Gallerie Publications, Vancouver, 1992, p.40.

[488] Blaeser, op.cit., p.36.

[489] Willie, op.cit., p.v.

[490] Francis and Bruchac, op.cit., p.30.

[491] ibid., p.xvii.

[492] *Gathering Strength*, op.cit., p.641.

[493] Ovide Mecredi, letter to Greg Young-Ing, 31 July 1995. En'owkin Centre, Penticton, BC.

[494] *Theytus Books Ltd Catalogue, Fall '95 and Spring '96.*

[495] *Pemmican Publications 1996 Catalogue.*

[496] ibid.

[497] *Pemmican Publications 1996 Catalogue.*

[498] Saskatchewan Indian Cultural Centre Product / Price List.

[499] *Kegedonce Press* Promotional flyer distributed at the Aboriginal Voices Conference, Toronto, 1999.

[500] ibid.

[501] *First Nations': A Catalogue of B.C. Books for B.C. Schools*, ABPBC, Vancouver, B.C., 1995.

[502] Blaeser, op.cit., p.37.

[503] Perreault and Vance, op.cit., p.xiv.

[504] LaRocque, op.cit., p.xxiv.

[505] ibid.

[506] ibid.

[507] Petrone, op.cit., p.142.

[508] Willie, op.cit., p.4.

[509] See comments by Kuilboer on p.118 of this thesis.

[510] Seale, Doris, "On Getting Published", *The Colour of Resistance - A Contemporary Collection of Writing by Aboriginal Women,* Connie Fife ed., Sister Vision Press, Toronto, 1993, p.88.

[511] Young-Ing, Greg, "Understanding Peoples on Their Own Terms: A Rationale and Proposal for An Aboriginal Style Guide", submitted in the Master of Publishing, Simon Fraser University, Vancouver, 1999. Unpublished thesis.

[512] *Gathering Strength*, op.cit., p.641.

[513] "Books Abound at Twin Trails", *Aboriginal Voices*, May - June 1998. vol. 5, no. 3, p.52.

[514] ibid.

[515] *North American Native Authors Catalogue,* 1998 The Greenfield Review Press, p.1.

[516] *Gathering Strength*, op.cit., p.641.

[517] *The Canada Council for the Arts, Grants Program Information Booklet.*

[518] ibid.

[519] *Gathering Strength,* op.cit., pp.641-642.

[520] En'owkin Centre "Collaborating Our Creative Future" promotional brochure.

[521] "Wordcraft Circle Bylaws", *Moccasin Telegraph*, vol. 5, no. 4, Aug.-Oct.1997, p.15.

[522] Francis & Bruchac, op.cit., p.xvi.

[523] *Gathering Strength,* op.cit., p.644.

[524] Greg Young-Ing, email to the author, 13 March 2000.

Part 5

[525] Witi Ihimaera, in conversaton, 1 August, 2002.

[526] McRae, Jane, "Maori Literature: A Survey", *The Oxford History of New Zealand Literature in English,* Terry Sturm ed., Oxford University Press, Auckland, 1991. p.2.

[527] See Australian Reminiscences & Papers of L.E. Threlkeld Missionary to the Aborigines 1824-1859 Edited by Neil Gunson, Vol1, Australian Aboriginal Studies No 40, Australian Institute of Aboriginal Studies, Canberra, 1974.

[528] Robyn Bargh, personal interview, 24 June 1997. All other quotes from Bargh in this chapter are from this source unless otherwise indicated.

[529] McRae, op.cit., p.2.

[530] Evans, Patrick, *The Penguin History of New Zealand Literature,* Penguin, Auckland, 1990, p.219.

[531] Geoff Walker, personal interview, 9 June 1997. All other quotes from Walker in this chapter are from this source unless otherwise indicated.

[532] Rawinia White, personal interview, 19 June 1997. All other quotes in this chapter by White are from this source unless otherwise indicated.

[533] Hinewirangi, personal interview, 19 June 1997. All other quotes from Hinewirangi in this chapter are from this source unless otherwise indicated.

[534] Thompson, Christine, "Alan Duff: The Book, The Film, The Interview", *Meanjin*, vol. 54, no. 1, 1995, p.6.

[535] *Metro Magazine,* July 1991, p.39.

[536] Wena Harawira, personal interview, 16 June 1997. All other quotes from Harawira in this chapter are from this source unless otherwise stated.

[537] Bellette, Tony, "Warriors", *Island* , no. 48, Spring 1991, p.39.

[538] Walker, R.J., "Maori Identity", *Culture and Identity in New Zealand*, David Novitz and Bill Willmott eds, G.P.Books, Wellington. 1989, p.35.

[539] ibid.

[540] Sinclair, K., *A History of New Zealand,* Penguin, Harmondsworth, 1960, p.14.

[541] Ritchie, James, *The Making of a Maori,* AH & AW Reed, Wellington, 1963, p.39.

[542] Robyn Bargh, email to the author, 30 July 2000.

[543] Clark, Paul, *Hauhau: The Pai Marire Search For Maori Identity,* Auckland University Press / Oxford University Press, Auckland, 1975, p.x.

[544] Sinclair, Keith, *The Native Born: The Origins of New Zealand Nationalism*, Massey University, Palmerston North, NZ, 1986, p.2.

[545] ibid.

[546] Meek, R.L., *Mauri Problems Today: A Short Survey*, Progressive Publishing Society, Wellington, 1943, p.35. Although this source is from 1943 there is continuing validity of the points made.

[547] Fitzgerald, Thomas, K., *Education and Identity: A Study of the New Zealand Maori Graduate,* New Zealand Council for Educational Research, Wellington, 1977, p.62.

[548] ibid.

[549] Tahi, Brenda, "Biculturalism: The Model of Te Ohu Whakatupu", *Justice and Identity: Antipodean Practices*, Margaret Wilson and Anna Yeatman eds. Bridget Williams Books Ltd, Wellington, 1995, p.62.

[550] ibid.

[551] ibid., p.64

[552] Witi Ihimaera, personal interview, 12 June 1997. All other quotes from Ihimaera in this chapter are from this source unless otherwise indicated.

[553] Hinewirangi, personal interview, 19 June 1997.

[554] Rawinia White, personal interview, 19 June 1997.

[555] Reina Whaitiri, personal interview, 12 June 1997.

[556] Robert Sullivan, personal interview, 10 June 1997. All other quotes from Sullivan in this chapter are from this source unless otherwise indicated.

[557] Marama Mihaka, personal interview, 24 June 1997. All other quotes from Mihaka in this chapter are from this source unless otherwise indicated.

[558] Sid Mead, personal interview, 24 June 1997.

[559] Peter Janssen, personal interview, 11 June 1997. All other quotes from Janssen in this chapter are from this source unless otherwise indicated.

[560] Wendt's own publications begin with *Sons for the Return Home* (1973) and continue through five other novels (two made into films), two books of short stories and two poetry collections. He has taught in Fiji and Samoa.

[561] Albert Wendt, personal interview, 12 June 1997. All other quotes from Wendt in this chapter are from this source unless otherwise indicated.

[562] Pita Rykis, personal interview, 11 June 1997. All other quotes from Rykis in this chapter are from this source unless otherwise indicated.

[563] Patricia Grace, personal interview, 22 June 1997. All other quotes from Grace in this chapter are from this source unless otherwise indicated.

[564] Dr. Maarire Goodall, personal interview, 23 June 1997. All other quotes from Goodall in this chapter are from this source unless otherwise indicated.

[565] Pare Hope, personal interview, 11 June 1997.

[566] Glenys Paraha, personal interview, 11 June 1997.

[567] Jane Collins, personal interview, 26 June 1997. All other quotes from Collins in this chapter are from this source unless otherwise indicated.

[568] Ritchie, James, *Becoming Bicultural,* Huia Publishers, Wellington, 1992. Promotional material on book jacket.

[569] Annais Allen, personal interview, 14 June 1997. All other quotes from Allen in this chapter are from this source unless otherwise indicated.

[570] Janine McVeagh, personal interview, 14 June 1997. All other quotes from McVeagh in this chapter are from this source unless otherwise indicated.

[571] Gary Wilson, personal interview, 10 June 1997. All other quotes from Wilson in this chapter are from this source unless otherwise indicated.

[572] Wiramu Kaa, personal interview, 26 June 1997

[573] Juliet Raven, personal interview, 26 June 1997. All other quotes from Raven in this chapter are from this source unless otherwise indicated.

[574] "Toi Maori Aotearoa (Maori Arts New Zealand) Mission Statement" brochure, p.4

[575] ibid., p.7.

[576] ibid., p.2.

[577] ibid., p.3.

[578] Eric Tamepo, personal interview, 25 June 1997. All other quotes from Tamepo in this chapter are from this source unless otherwise indicated.

Bibliography

Personal Interviews

Allen, Annais, personal interview, 14 June 1997
Bargh, Robyn, personal interview, 24 June 1997
Bell, Jeanie, personal interview, 15 January 1998
Bellear, Lisa, personal interview, 5 June 1997
Bropho, Robert, personal interview, 4 March 1998
Burke, John Muk Muk, personal interview, 12 March 1998
Belmore, Florene, personal interview, 11 June 1999
Collins, Jane, personal interview, 26 June 1997
Craigie, Cathy, personal interview, 9 October 1997
Douglas, Josie, personal interview, 10 September 1999
Dunn, Irina, personal interview, 30 September 1997
Goodall, Dr. Maarire, personal interview, 23 June 1997
Grace, Patricia, personal interview, 22 June 1997
Harawira, Wena, personal interview, 16 June 1997
Hinewirangi, personal interview, 19 June 1997
Hope, Pare, personal interview, 11 June 1997
Huggins, Jackie, personal interview, 10 December 1997
Ihimaera, Witi, personal interview, 12 June 1997
Jansen, Peter, personal interview, 11 June 1997
Kaa, Wiramu, personal interview, 26 June 1997
Langford Ginibi, Ruby, personal interview, 29 February 2000
Lucashenko, Melissa, personal interview, 30 January 1998
MacDonald, Simon, personal interview, 10 September 1999
McVeagh, Janine, personal interview, 14 June 199
Mead, Sid, personal interview, 24 June 1997
Mihaka, Marama, personal interview, 24 June 1997
Munro, Craig, personal interview, 1994
Paraha, Glenys, personal interview, 11 June 1997
Peniston-Bird, Adrian, conversation with, 25 November 1997
Phillips, Sandra, personal interview, 5 June 1997
Raven, Juliet personal interview, 26 June 1997
Rykis, Pita, personal interview, 11 June 1997
Schoo, Michael, conversation with, 21 August 2000
Spender, Lynn, personal interview, 2 October 1997
Sullivan, Robert, personal interview, 10 June 1997

Tamepo, Eric, personal interview, 25 June 1997
Walker, Geoff, personal interview, 9 June 1997
Wendt, Albert, personal interview, 12 June 1997
Whaitiri, Reina, personal interview, 12 June 1997
Wharton, Herb, personal interview, 10 December 1997
White, Rawinia, personal interview, 19 June 1997
Wilson, Gary, personal interview, 10 June 1997
Young-Ing, Greg, personal interview, 17 June 1999

Emails to the author

Abbey, Sue, email to the author, 18 August 2000
Bargh, Robyn, email to the author, 30 July 2000
Bin Salleh, Rachel, email to the author, 29 March 2000
Britton, Anne-Marie, email tot he author, 10 August 2000
Burke, Margaret, email to the author, 14 July 1999
Coffey, Ray, email to the author, 12 August 1999
Coffey, Ray, email to the author, 11 August 2000
Cook, Sam, email to the author, 2 October 1999
Cook, Sam, email to the author, 18 August 2000
Curnow, Meredith, email to the author, 25 May 1999
Curnow, Meredith, email to the author, 19 July 2000
Damm, Kateri, email to the author, 14 July 1999
Douglas, Josie, email to the author, 10 August 2000
Eddington, Jill, email to the author, 22 August 2000
Groulx, David, email to the author, 10 August 1999
Laughton, Kenny, email to the author, 17 October 1998
MacDonald, Simon, email to the author, 11 August 2000
McKenzie, Christine, email to the author, 12 August 2000
Minatel, Margaret, email to the author, 20 July 1999
Nance, Rhyll, email to the author, 19 May 1999
Rock, Bob, email to the author, 15 July 1999
Ross, Rodger W., email to the author, 20 July 1999
Spencer, Di, email to the author, 12 August 2000
Thorne, Tim, email to the author, 28 May 1999
van den Berg, Rosemary, email to the author, 9 August 1999
Watts, Walbira, email to the author, 11 March 2000
Whitebeach, Terri Anne, email to the author, 21 July 2000
Wright, Alexis, email to the author, 12 July 1999
Wu, Anthea, email to the author, 1 October 1999
Young-Ing, Greg, email to the author, 13 March 2000

Letters to the author

Bin Salleh, Rachel, letter to the author, 24 October 1996

Brisbane, Katherine, letter to the author, 18 August 2000

Devitt, Marian, letter to the author, 11 February 1999

Gamba, Barry, letter to the author, 21 November 1995

Hayes, Susan, letter to the author, 10 February 1999

Janke, Terri, letter to the author, 13 April 2000

Jones, Jonah, letter to the author, 5 June 1996

Miller, Lydia, letter to the author, 8 September 1997

Pearce, Judy, letter to the author, 4 June 1999

Ruhfus, Margaret, letter to the author, 4 May 1997

Roberts, Rhoda, letter to the author, 4 June 1997

Sheedy, Catherine, letter to the author, 22 June 1999

Thorne, Tim, letter to the author, 28 May 1999

Whitebeach, Terri Anne, letter to the author, 28 February 1999

Wight, Rose, letter to the author, 28 May 1999

Written responses to interview schedule

Pascoe, Bruce, response to questionnaire, 22 November 1997

Reed-Gilbert, Kerry, response to questionnaire, 28 September 1997

Books

Arthur, J.M., *Aboriginal English: A Cultural Study,* Oxford University Press, Melbourne, 1996.

Australia Council 1998 Grants Handbook, Australia Council, Strawberry Hills, Sydney, 1998.

Ashcroft, W.D., Gareth Griffiths & Helen Tiffin, *The Empire Writes Back: Theory and Practice in Post-Colonial Literatures*, Routledge, London, 1989.

Barterrak, Krim, Stephen Muecke & Padde Roe, *Reading the Country: Introduction to Nomadology*, Fremantle Arts Centre Press, Fremantle, 1984.

Brewster, Anne, *Literary Formations: Post-colonialism, Nationalism, Globalism*, Melbourne University Press, Melbourne, 1995.

Brewster, Anne, Angela O'Neill & Rosemary van den Berg eds, *Those Who Remain Will Always Remember: An Anthology of Aboriginal Writing,* Fremantle Arts Centre Press, Fremantle, 2000.

Cowlishaw, G. & B. Morris, eds, *Race Matters: Indigenous Australians and "Our" Society*, Aboriginal Studies Press, Canberra, 1997.

Chesson, Keith, *Jack Davis: A Life Story*, Dent, Melbourne, 1988.

Clark, Paul, *Hauhau: the Pai Marire Search for Maori Identity*, Auckland University Press, Auckland, 1975.

Davis, Kerry ed., *Across Country*, ABC Books, Sydney, 1998.

Diprose, R. & R. Ferrell, eds, *Cartographies: Poststructuralism and the Mapping of Bodies and Spaces,* Allen & Unwin, Sydney, 1991.

Evans, Patrick, *The Penguin History of New Zealand Literature,* Penguin, Auckland, 1990.

Fife, Connie, ed., *The Colour of Resistance—A Contemporary Collection of Writing by Aboriginal Women*. Sister Vision Press, Toronto, 1993.

Fitzgerald, Thomas K., *Education and Identity: A Study of the New Zealand Maori Graduate*, New Zealand Council for Educational Research, Wellington, 1977.

Fleras, Augie & Jean Leonard Elliott, *The Nations Within: Aboriginal-State Relations in Canada, the United States and New Zealand*, Oxford University Press, Toronto, 1992.

Francis, Lee & Bruchac, James, *Reclaiming the Vision: Past, Present and Future. Native Voices for the 8th Generation*, Greenfield Press, New York, 1996.

Give Back: First Nations' Perspective on Cultural Practice, Gallerie Publications, Vancouver, 1992.

Harjo, Joy & Gloria Bird, *Reinventing the Enemy's Language: Contemporary Native Women's Writings from North America*, W.W. Norton, New York, c1987.

Hodges, Bob & Jack, Davis, *Aboriginal Writing Today: Papers from the First National Conference of Aboriginal Writers Held in Perth, WA in 1983*. Australian Institute of Aboriginal Studies, Canberra, 1985.

Huggins, Jackie, *Sister Girl*, UQP, St. Lucia, 1998.

Jaimes, M. Annette, *The State of Native America: Genocide, Colonisation and Resistance*, South End Press, Boston, 1992.

Jurak, Mirko ed., *Australian Papers: Yugoslavia, Europe and Australia*, Faculty of Arts and Science, Edvard Kardelj University of Ljubljana, 1983.

Langton, Marcia, *"Well I Heard It On The Radio And I Saw It On The Television..."*, Australian Film Commission, Sydney, 1993

Lippman, Lorna, *Generations of Resistance: Aborigines Demand Justice*, 2nd edition, Longman Cheshire, Melbourne, 1991.

Macartney, Frederick, *Australian Literary Essays*, Angus and Robertson, Sydney, 1957.

Maki, Joel T. ed., *Let the Drums Be Your Heart: New Native Voices*, Douglas & McIntyre, Vancouver, 1996.

McRobbie, Narelle, *Who's That Jumbun In The Log*, Magabala Books, Broome, 1996.

Meek, R.L., *Mauri Problems Today: A Short Survey*, Progressive Publishing Society, Wellington, 1943.

Morgan, Sally, *My Place*, Fremantle Arts Centre Press, Fremantle, 1987.

Muecke, Stephen, *Textual Spaces: Aboriginality and Cultural Studies*, UNSW Press, Kensington, 1992.

Mudrooroo, *Us Mob: History, Culture, Struggle: An Introduction to Indigenous Australia*, Angus & Robertson, Sydney, 1995.

Narrogin, Mudrooro, *Writing from the Fringe: A Study of Modern Aboriginal Literature*, Hyland House, South Yarra, 1990.

Nelson, Emmanuel S. ed., *Connections—Essays on Black Literatures*, Aboriginal Studies Press, Canberra, 1988.

Novits, David & Bill Willmott, eds, *Culture and Identity in New Zealand*, G.P. Books, Wellington, 1989.

Pascoe, Bruce, *Fox*, McPhee Gribble, 1988.

Pascoe, Bruce, *Wathaurong: Too Bloody Strong: Stories of Life Journeys of People from Wathaurong*, Pascoe Publishing, Apollo Bay, 1997

Perreault, Jeanne & Sylvia Vance, *Writing the Circle: Native Women of Western Canada: An Anthology*, NeWest Publishers, Edmonton, 1990.

Petrone, Penny, *Native Literature in Canada: From the Oral Tradition to the Present*, Oxford University Press, Toronto, 1990.

Program of Assistance Handbook 2001, Arts QLD, Brisbane, 2000.

Reed-Gilbert, Kerry, ed., *The Strength of Us As Women: Black Women Speak*. Ginninderra Press, Canberra, 2000.

Rhydwen, Mari, *Writing on the Backs of Blacks: Voice, Literacy and Community in Kriol Fieldwork*, UQP, St. Lucia, 1996.

Ritchie, James, *The Making of a Maori*, AH & AW Reed, Wellington, 1963.

Roe, Paddy & Stephen Muecke, *Gularabulu: Stories of the Kimberley*, Fremantle Arts Centre Press, Fremantle, 1983.

Rose, Micheal ed., *For the Record: 160 Years of Aboriginal Print Journalism*, Allen and Unwin, St. Leonards, 1996.

Slapin, Beverly & Doris Seale eds., *Through Indian Eyes - The Native Experience on Books for Children*, New Society Publishers, Philadelphia, 1987.

Slapin, Beverly, Doris Seale & Rosemary Gonzales, *How To Tell the Difference: A Checklist for Evaluating Children's Books for Anti-Indian Bias*, New Society Publishers, Gabriola Island, BC, 1992.

Sinclair, K., *A History of New Zealand*, Penguin, Harmondsworth, 1960.

Starke, Ruth, *Writers, Readers, Rebels: Upfront and Backstage at Australia's Top Literary Festival*, Wakefeld Press, Kent Town, 1998.

Sturme, Terry ed., *The Oxford History of New Zealand Literature in English*, Oxford University Press, Auckland, 1991.

Wedde, Ian & Harvey McQueen, *The Penguin Book of New Zealand Verse*, Penguin, Auckland, 1985.

Wilson, Margaret & Anna Yeatman eds, *Justice and Identity: Antipodean Practices*, Bridget Williams Books, Wellington, 1995.

Wright, Judith, *Born of the Conquerors: Selected Essays*, Aboriginal Studies Press, Canberra, 1991.

Chapters in Books

Angus, Graham Scott, "Change Is Upon Us, So Call Me a Dreamer", *Let the Drums Be Your Heart: New Native Voices*, ed. Joel T. Maki, Douglas & McIntyre, Vancouver, 1996.

Arens, Werner, "The Image of Australia in Australian Poetry", *Australian Papers: Yugoslavia, Europe and Australia*, ed. Mirko Jurak, Faculty of Arts and Science, Edvard Kardelj University of Ljubljana, 1983.

Biddle, Jennifer, "Dot, Circle, Difference: Translating Central Desert Paintings", *Cartographies: Poststructuralism and the Mapping of Bodies and Spaces*, ed. R. Diprose & R Ferrell, Allen & Unwin, Sydney 1991.

Byler, Mary Gloyne, "American Indian Authors for Young Readers: An Annotated Bibliography", *Through Indian Eyes—The Native Experience in Books for Children*, ed. Beverly Slapin & Doris Seale, New Society Publishers, Philadelphia, 1987.

Durack, Mary, "Foreward", *Wildcat Falling*, Angus and Robertson, Sydney, 1965.

Fedorick, Joy Asham, "Fencepost Sitting", *Give Back: First Nations' Perspective on Cultural Practice*, Gallerie Publications, Vancouver, 1992.

Green, Nellie, "Chasing an Identity: An Aboriginal Perspective of Aboriginality", *The Strength of Us As Women: Black Women Speak,* ed. Kerry Reed-Gilbert, Ginninderra Press, Canberra, 2000.

Langford Ginibi, Ruby, "My Mob, My Self", *The Strength of Us As Women: Black Women Speak,* ed. Kerry Reed-Gilbert, Ginninderra Press, ACT, 2000

LaRocque, Emma, "Here Our Voices—Who Will Hear?", *Writing the Circle—Native Women of Western Canada: An Anthology,* ed. Jeanne Perrault & Sylvia Vance, NeWest Publishers, Edmonton, 1990.

McRae, Jane, "Maori Literature: A Survey", *The Oxford History of New Zealand Literature in English,* ed. Terry Sturme, Oxford University Press, Auckland, 1991

Mudrooroo, "Tell Them You're Indian", *Race Matters: Indigenous Australians and "Our" Society*, ed. Cowlishaw and Morris, Aboriginal Studies Press, Canberra, 1997.

Seale, Doris, "On Getting Published", *The Colour of Resistance: A Contemporary Collection of Writing by Aboriginal Women*, ed. Connie Fife, Sister Vision Press, Toronto, 1993.

Tahi, Brenda, "Biculturalism: The Model of Te Ohu Whakatupu, *Justice and Identity: Antipodean Practices*, ed. Margaret Wilson & Anna Yeatman, Bridget Williams Books Ltd, Wellington, 1995.

Taylor, Alf, "The Wool Pickers", *Across Country*, ed. Kerry Davis, ABC Books, Sydney, 1998.

van den Berg, Rosemary, "Intellectual Property Rights for Aboriginal People",
The Strength of Us As Women: Black Women Speak, ed. Kerry Reed-Gilbert, Ginninderra Press, Canberra, 2000.

Walker, R.J., "Maori Identity", *Culture and Identity in New Zealand*, ed. David Novitz & Bill Willmott, G.P.Books, Wellington, 1989.

Watego, Cliff, "Backgrounds to Aboriginal Literature", *Connections—Essays on Black Literatures*, ed. Emmanuel S. Nelson, Aboriginal Studies Press, Canberra, 1998.

Articles in journals

"Aboriginal Population... Who Decides?", *The Forgotten People: The National Voice of Off-Reserve Indian and Metis peoples Throughout Canada*, vol. 1, no. 1, March 1999, pp.3-4.

Alexie, Sherman "Who Said What", *Aboriginal Voices*, vol. 6, no. 3, May-June, 1999, p.54.

Anderson, Ian, "Letter", *Australian Book Review*, no. 150, May 1993, p.4.

Armstrong, Jeannette, "The Disempowerment of First North American Native
Peoples and Empowerment Through Their Writing", *Gatherings Vol. 1,* Thetyus Books, Penticton, BC, 1990, pp.141.147.

Attwood, Bain, "Portrait of an Aboriginal as an Artist: Sally Morgan and the Construction of Aboriginality", *Australian Historical Studies*, vol. 25, no. 99, October 1992, pp.302-309.

Australian Author: Journal of the Australian Society of Authors, vol. 26, no. 3, Spring 1994.

Bellette, Tony, "Warriors", *Island*, no. 48, Spring 1991, p.39.

Beston, John, "The Aboriginal Poets in English: Kath Walker, Jack Davis and Kevin Gilbert", *Meanjin*, no. 36, December 1977, p.446-461.

Betti, Leeroy, "Writer Turns Back Pages", *The West Australian,* 7 March 1998, p.42.

Birch, Tony, "Half Caste", *Australian Historical Studies*, vol. 25, no. 100, April 1993, p.458.

——— "'Real Aborigines' - Colonial Attempts to Re-Imagine and Re-Create the Identities of Aboriginal People", *Ulitarra*, no. 4, 1993, pp.15-21.

Blaeser, Kimberly M., "Entering the Canons: Our Place in World Literature", *Akwe:kon Journal: A Journal of Indigenous Issues*, Spring 1993, pp.35-37.

"Books Abound at Twin Trails", *Aboriginal Voices*, vol. 5, no. 3, May-June, 1998, p.52.

Brisbane, Katherine, "The Future in Black and White: Aboriginality in Recent Australian Drama" a paper presented at IDEA '95 - 2nd World Congress of Drama / Theatre Education, *Currency Press —The Performing Arts Publisher catalogue.*

Coombs, Anne, "A Life Told Too Soon", *Sydney Morning Herald*, 12 September 1998, p.8s.

Cormick, Craig, "Change of Direction", *The Canberra Times,* 15 March 1997.

Danaher, P.A., "Reviews and Booknotes", *Idiom 23*, vol. 7, no. 2, Nov.-Dec. 1994, pp.119-120.

Dixon, Graeme, "The Mudrooroo Dilemma", *Westerly*, vol. 41, no. 3, Spring 1996, pp.5-7.

Dodson, Michael, "The Wentworth Lecture- The End in the Beginning: Re(de)fining Aboriginality", *Australian Aboriginal Studies*, no. 1, 1994, p.2-13.

Douglas, Josie & Bowman, Marg, "New Publisher for Black Poetry", *Five Bells*, vol. 4, no. 6, July 1997, p.9.

Faust, Beatrice, "Races Are Easy to Lose", *Weekend Australian*, 2-4 August 1996, p.25.

Huggins, Jackie, "Respect V Political Correctness", *Australian Author*, vol. 26, no. 3, Spring 1994, p.12.

—— "Always Was Always Will Be", *Australian Historical Studies*, vol. 25, no. 100, April 1993, pp.459-462.

Ihimaera, Witi, "Why I Write", *World Literature Written in English*, no. 14, 1974, pp.117-118.

Janke, Terri, "Protecting Australian Indigenous Arts and Cultural Expression: A Matter of Legislative Reform or Cultural Policy?", *Culture and Policy*, vol. 7, no. 3. 1996, pp.13-18.

"Jim Davidson Interviews Kath Walker", *Meanjin*, vol. 36, no. 4, December 1977, pp.428-441.

Johnson, Colin, "The Growth of Aboriginal Literature", *Social Alternatives*, vol. 7, no. 1, March 1988, pp.53-54.

Jopson, Debra, "Writing Wrongs", *Sydney Morning Herald*, 15 March 1997, p.38.

—— "Destory Books: Black Group", *Sydney Morning Herald*, 25 March 1997, p.5.

Jose, Nicholas, "Pearls of Wisdom", *The Australian Way*, October 1996, p.6.

Kelly, Susan, "The Outsider", *HQ*, May-June 1996, p.49.

Kuilboer, Theresa, "Life and Laughs in Hell: Vietnam Vet's Powerful Story", *Sunday Territorian*, 6 June 1999, p.17.

Kurtzer, Sonja, "'Wandering Girl' : Who Defines Authenticity in Aboriginal Literature?", *Southerly*, vol. 58, no. 2, Winter 1998, pp.20-29.

Langford Ginibi, Ruby, "A Kooris' Lesson in Dispossession", *Weekend Australian Review*, 2–3 May 1992, p.rev6.

Langford Ginibi, Ruby, "The Right to be a Koori Writer", *The Australian,* 7th August, 1996, p.12.

Laurie, Victoria, "Identity Crisis", *Australian Magazine*, July 20-21 1996, pp.28–32.

Little, Lorna & Little, Tom, "The Mudrooroo Dilemma", *Westerly*, vol. 41, no. 3, Spring 1996, pp.5-7.

Liverani, Mary Rose, "From Outside, Without Insight", *Weekend Australian Review,* 28 - 29 March 1992, p.rev6.

Longley, Kateryna Olijnyk, "Directions", *Australian Book Review*, no. 131, June 1991, pp.30-31.

McCarron, Robyn, "Noongar Language and Literature", *Span*, vol. 1, no. 36, October 1993, pp.274-281.

McDonald, Willa, "Tricky Business: Whites On Black Territory", *Australian Author*, vol. 29, no.1, Autumn 1997, pp.12-14.

Mabelson, Roger, "Better Stats on Culture", *Smarts*, no. 5, March 1996, p.7.

Mann, Maria, "Magabala Books: The Politics of Design", *Artlink*, vol. 17, no. 1, 1997, pp.36-37.

Meade, Kevin, "Activist Had Black View of Racist World", *The Weekend Australian*, October 24-25, 1998, p.11.

Metro Magazine, July 1991, p.39.

Milne, Geoffrey, "The Other Side of the Story: Multicultural Drama in Australia", *Meanjin*, vol. 53, no. 3, Spring 1994, pp.495-503.

Moran, Rod, "About Books: Aboriginal Literary Voices", *National Library of Australia News*, vol. 2, no. 2, November 1991, p.10.

Morrissey, Di, "Letter to the Editor", *Australian Author*, vol. 26, no. 3, Spring 1994, p.7.

Mudrooroo, "Being Published from the Fringe", *Australian Author*, vol. 26, no. 3, Spring 1994, p.16.

Muecke, Stephen, "Aboriginal Literature and the Repressive Hypothesis", *Southerly,* vol. 48, no. 4, December 1988, pp.405-418.

Nelson, Emmanuel S, "Struggle for a Black Aesthetic: Critical Theory In Contemporary Aboriginal Australia", *Australian Studies*, no. 6, November 1992, pp.29-37.

Newfong, John A. ed, "Birds Both Black and Beautiful", *Identity*, vol. 1, no. 6, November 1972, pp.30-33.

Novelist Defends His Black Identity", *Weekend Australian*, 5 April 1997. Pascoe, Bruce, "Editorial", *Aboriginal Short Stories,* Pascoe Publishing, Apollo Bay, 1990, p.i.

Pascoe, Bruce & Lyn Harwood, "Bruce Pascoe and Lyn Harwood, Editors of *Australian Short Stories*", *Ulitarra,* no. 5, 1994, p.118.

Perrett, Bill, "Questions of Identity", *The Sunday Age*, 17 August 1997, p.7.

Phillips, Sandra, "Mogwi-Djan" Editorial, *QWC News*, June 1996, pp.6-7.

—— "White Noise and Fuzzy Hazy Stuff, *QWC News,* February 1999, p.13.

Ravens-Croft, Alison, "Politics of Exposure: An Interview With Alexis Wright", *Meridian*, vol. 17, no. 1, 1998, pp.76-78.

"Reviews", *Aboriginal Voices*, vol. 5, no. 3, May-June 1998, p.52.

Rule, Rosemary, "Publishing in Broome", *Editions*, vol. 1, no.1, August 1989, pp.6-7.

Shapcott, Thomas, "The Disturbing Journey of Mudrooroo", *The Age* (VIC), 27 July 1996, p.9.

Shoemaker, Adam, "A Bridge Too Far", *Australian Book Review*, no. 166, November 1994, p.17.

—— "Who Should Control Aboriginal Writing?", *Australian Book Review*, May 1983, p.21.

Sims, Bruce, "Bruce Sims: Transition", *Publishing Studies*, 1997, p.35.

Sinclair, Keith, *The Native Born: The Origins of New Zealand Nationalism* Massey University, Palmerston North, NZ, 1986, p.2.

Slattery, Luke, "Sykes Is Not Aboriginal, Says The One Who Knows Best. Her Mum", *The Weekend Australian*, October 24-25, 1998, p.11.

Spender, Lynne, *Australian Author*, vol. 26, no. 3, Spring 1994, p.10.

Sykes, Bobbi, "Black Australians, Aboriginal Australians, Aborigines", *Filmnews*, April 1978, p.5.

Thompson, Christine, "Alan Duff: The Book, The Film, The Interview", *Meanjin*, vol. 54, no. 1, 1995, p.6.

Torres, Pat, "Interested in Writing About Indigenous Australians?", *Australian Author*, vol. 26, no. 3, Spring 1994, pp.24-25.

Trees, Kathryn, "Postcolonialism: Yet Another Colonial Strategy?", *Span*, vol. 1, no. 36, 1993, pp.264-272.

van Toorn, Penny, "Early Aboriginal Writing and the Discipline of Literary Studies", *Meanjin*, no. 4, 1996, pp.754-765.

Watego, Cliff, "Being Done To Again", *Social Alternatives*, vol. 7, 1988, p.34.

Weller, Archie, "Portrayal of Aboriginal Men in Literature", *Social Alternatives*, vol. 7, no. 1, 1988, pp.55-57.

Wheately, Nadia, "Black and White Writing: The Issues", *Australian Author*, vol. 26, no. 3, Spring 1994, pp.22-23.

Wordcraft Circle Bylaws", *Moccasin Telegraph*, vol. 5, no. 4, Aug/Sept /Oct 1997, p.15.

Other

Aboriginal and Torres Strait Islander Protocols for Libraries, Archives and Information Services, http://www.ntu.edu.au/library/protocol.html

Marsh, John, "Clan Casts Out the Snake Woman", http://www.smh.au//news/9810/17/text/pageone4.html

Lionel Fogarty talks to Philip Mead", *Jacket Magazine*, http://www.jacket.zip.com.au/jacket01/fogartyiv/html

Roberta Sykes promotional site: http://www.australias.org/sykes/sd.html

Unpublished Theses

Willie, Janine A., "On Theorising Native Literatures: Searching for Effective, Cultural Appropriate Ways To Read and Understand Native Literatures", York University, North York, Ontario, 1996.

Young-Ing, Greg , "Understanding Peoples on Their Own Terms: A Rationale and Proposal for An Aboriginal Style Guide", Simon Fraser University, Vancouver, 1999.

Reports

"Australian Publishers Association Residential Editorial Program Report 1999".

Arms, Jane, "A Report to the Australia Council on the Training of Senior Literary Editors and a Proposed Scheme for the Training of Indigenous Editors", Adelaide, November 1997.

Annual Report 1996-97 Australian Institute of Aboriginal and Torres Strait Islander Studies, Canberra.

Annual Report 1998-99, Australian Institute of Aboriginal and Torres Strait Islander Studies, Canberra.

Fogarty, Lesley, "Report on Mogwi-Djan: National Indigenous Writers and Playwrights Conference and Workshop", 1996.

Gathering Strength, 1996 Report of the Royal Commission into Aboriginal Peoples, Canada. Volume 3.

Janke, Terri, *Our Culture: Our Future- The Report on Australian Indigenous Cultural and Intellectual Property Rights* , Michael Frankel & Co., Sydney, 1998.

NSW Ministry for the Arts Annual Report 1998 - 99. "Report on Planning and Staging the Festival of Pacific Arts, Townsville, Australia, 14–27 August, 1988", Festival of Pacific Arts Ltd, 1989.

Report on Strategies for the Further Development of the National Aboriginal and Torres Strait Islander Arts and Cultural Industry: Main Report. A Report to ATSIC by Arts Training Northern Territory, ATSIC, Canberra, 1994.

"Strategic Initiatives, Indigenous Writers' Mentorship - Queensland 1998-99", QLD Writers' Centre, Brisbane.

Whitebeach, Terri Anne, "Interim Report: Culturally Appropriate Professional Training for Indigenous Writers".

—— "Second Report: Culturally Appropriate Professional Training Opportunities for Central Australian Indigenous Writers", September 1997.

—— "Third Report: Culturally Appropriate Training Opportunities for Central Australian Indigenous Writers".

—— "5th and Final Project Report 1998: Culturally Appropriate Training Opportunities or Central Australian Indigenous Writers".

"Writer in Community Project", QLD Writers' Centre Final Acquittal to the Australia Council, 1997.

Wu, Anthea, "Report on Preparation for Indigenous Writers' Series", UWA Press, September 1998.

——"Acquittal Report to the Literature Fund of the Australia Council for "Strategic Initiative: Professional Development / Training or Indigenous Editors 1998".

Programs

The Age Melbourne Writers' Festival 1998 program.

The 1999 Festival of Perth Writers Festival Events program.

Pamphlets/Catalogues

1997/98 NSW Ministry for the Arts -Fellowships, Scholarships and Awards Guidelines issued by the NSW Arts Advisory Council.

ABC Of Indigenous Publishing catalogue 1997.

Aboriginal Studies Press 1999-2000 catalogue.

Black and White Australia, Currency Press: The Performing Arts Publisher catalogue.

Blackbooks 1996 catalogue.

Canada Council for the Arts, Grants Program Information booklet.

En'owkin Centre, "Collaborating Our Creative Future", promotional brochure.

First Nations': A Catalogue of BC Books fr BC Schools, ABPBC, Vancouver, BC. 1995.

Kegedonce Press Promotional flyer.

Koori Mail promotional flyer distributed at the Aboriginal Arts and Culture Conference, Armidale, March 2000.

Magabala Books February 1983 catalogue.

Magabala Publishing Policy, Magabala Books, Broome, 1996.

National Indigenous Arts Advocacy Association Vision Statement, NIAAA, Sydney, 2000.

North American Native Authors Catalogue, 1998 The Greenfield Review Press, New York.

North American Native Authors First Book Awards with "Rules", promotional flyer, En'owkin Centre, Penticton, BC.

Pemmican Publications 1996 catalogue.

Policy for the Promotion and Support of Indigenous Cultural Activity in New South Wales, NSW Ministry for the Arts, Sydney, March 2000.

Register of Editorial Services 1998, Society of Editors (NSW).

Saskatchewan Indian Cultural Centre Product / Price List.

Theytus Books Ltd Catalogue Fall '95 and Spring '96.

Toi Maori Aotearoa (Maori Arts New Zealand) Mission Statement brochure.

University of Queensland Press Black Australian Writers Series publicity pamphlet.

Writers Have Their Say, Australia Council 1999.

The Circle of Aboriginal Controlled Publishers flyer, En'owkin Centre, Penticton, BC.

Conference papers (unpublished)

Grace, Patricia, "Which Way Tellem Story", presented at the Festival of the Dreaming, 22 September 1997

Pascoe, Bruce, "Land, Life, Literature", presented at 1998 Spring Writing Festival, Sydney, 13 September 1998.

Wright, Alexis, "Language and Empire: The Empires of the East Have Crumbled Into Dust, But the English Language Remains", presented at the Brisbane Writers' Festival, 7 September 1997.

—— "Breaking Taboos", presented at the Tasmanian Readers' and Writers Festival, September 1998.

Radio Transcripts

ABC Radio National, "Women Out Loud", 19 March 1997.

3NCR, "Not Another Koori Show", 5 June 1998.

Manuscripts

"Aims of the Indigenous Portfolio", Australian Society of Authors, Sydney, 1998.

"ArtsWA Aboriginal Arts Policy", Final Draft, August 2000.

Fesl, Eve D. "How the English Language is Used to Put Koories Down, Deny Us Rights, Or Is Employed as a Political Tool Against Us", Monash University—Rev.6/89.

Letter from Ovide Mecredi to Greg Young-Ing, 31 July 1995, En'owkin Centre, Penticton, BC.

Sandra Phillips "Statement to Participants" at "Our Words - Our Ways" National Aboriginal and Torres Strait Islander Writers' Workshop, Victoria, 1992.

Index

A.I.M., 49
Abbey, Sue, 61, 67, 72, 73, 145
ABC of Indigenous Publishing, 98
Abo Call, 48–9
Aboriginal Advancement League, 49
Aboriginal and Torres Strait Islander Arts Board (ATSIAB), 79–80, 106–7, 111, 123, 141, 142
Aboriginal and Torres Strait Islander Commission (ATSIC), 52, 86, 109, 123
Aboriginal and Torres Strait Islander Handbook, 66
Aboriginal and Torres Strait Islander Writers' and Playwrights' Conference (Brisbane, 1996), 4–5, 102, 111, 114, 143–5
Aboriginal Arts Board, 111
Aboriginal Arts Committee, 4, 142
Aboriginal Book Publishers of Canada, 175
Aboriginal designers, *see* Indigenous designers
Aboriginal editors, *see* Indigenous editors
Aboriginal English, 12, 28–9, 30–3, 34, 75, 197
   'coconuts', 196
   editors on, 67–8, 69–70
Aboriginal Independent Newspaper, 50
'Aboriginal Label of Authenticity', 18, 83
Aboriginal Media Conference (Toronto, 1999), 187
Aboriginal Mythology, 4–5
The Aboriginal or Flinders Island Chronicle, 48
Aboriginal organisations, 109–12, 184–6
Aboriginal Publications Foundation, 111–12
Aboriginal publishing houses, *see* Indigenous publishing houses
Aboriginal reviewers, 100
Aboriginal Studies Press, 51, 56–7, 140
   copyright/royalty arrangements, 84, 97
   editing, 77–8
   marketing and distribution, 93, 98
Aboriginal style, *see* style
Aboriginal Tourist and Economic Development Association, 49
Aboriginal Voices Festival and Media Conference (Toronto, 1999), 186–7
Aboriginal voices magazine, 186
Aboriginal Women's Arts Festival (Adelaide, 1984), 39
Aboriginal Writers and Playwrights Conference (Brisbane, 1996), 4–5, 102, 111, 114, 143–5
Aboriginal Writers' Conferences, 57–8, 112, 142
Aboriginal Writers, Oral Literature and Dramatists Association, 4, 58, 112
Aboriginal Writing Today, 112
Aboriginality, 2–10, 17–24, 27, 41–3
   Tasmania, 108
   see also identity

Aborigines Progressive Association, 48–9
Abram, Renee, 177, 187
academic books, 37–8, 95, 173
   see also history
academics, 10, 84, 198
acceptance, 4–7, 9–10, 20, 22
Achimoona, 160
Across Country, 12, 21, 41
ACT Writers' Centre, 118
Adams, Howard, 155, 156, 160, 175, 187
Adamson, Robert, 72
Adelaide, Debra, 136
Adelaide Writers' Week, 132–3
Adeney, Ruth, 150–1
adolescents, *see* youth literature
advisory and support organisations, 109–21, 182–6, 215–19
The Age Melbourne Writers' Festival, 131–2
Ahenakew, Freda, 162
A.I.M., 49
Akiwenzie-Damm, Kateri, 111, 161, 177
   on Aboriginal identity, 163, 164, 165
   on audience, 169
   on publishing poetry, 170
   on writing, 163, 164, 165, 166–7, 173: by non-Native writers, 172
Alchuringa, 49
Alexie, Sherman, 162
Allen, Annais, 174, 204, 212
Allen and Unwin, 76, 98, 101
America, *see* North American First Nations' peoples
American Native Press Archives, 182
Anderson, Ian, 100
Anderson, Warrigal, 130, 131, 148
Andrew, Brook, 151
Angus, Graham Scott, 159
Angus and Robertson, 75, 101
anthologies, 12, 34, 115, 166, 177, 224–5
   Canadian First Nations', 160, 166, 172, 177, 179–80, 235–6
   Maori, 191, 210–11, 245
Anu, Helen, 111
Aoraki Press, 205–6, 213
Aotearoa, *see* Maori
APA Residential Editorial Program, 54, 58, 80–1, 84–5
appropriation of culture and voice, 2–16, 87
   see also literary fraud
Arens, Werner, 35
Arms, Jane, 79–80

Armstrong, Jeanette, 156, 160, 161, 174, 175, 176
    on writing, 163
arts, *see* plays and playwrights; visual arts and design
Arts Queensland, 108
Arts South Australia, 109
Arts Tasmania, 108
Arts Training Northern Territory Report, 79, 94–5
Arts WA, 108–9
Arts Yarn Up, 141
ArtsACT, 109
assimilation, 17–18, 196
Association of Book Publishers of British Columbia, 175, 177–8
Association of Canadian Publishers, 175
ATSIC, 52, 86, 109, 123
Auckland University Press, 210
audience, 90–2, 93, 94, 97–8
    Aotearoa, 191, 192, 201, 203, 208, 209, 217
    Canada, 165, 169–73, 178
    influence of critics and reviewers, 101
    My Place, 102
    see also education market
audiotapes, 83, 84
Auntie Rita, 36, 77–8, 93, 103
Australia, 2–152
Australia Council for the Arts, 96, 97, 106–7, 115, 144
    Aboriginal and Torres Islander Arts Board (ATSIAB), 79–80, 106–7, 111, 123, 141
    Aboriginal Arts Committee, 4, 142
    Community Cultural Development Fund, 117–18, 121
    definition of Aboriginality, 20
    Literature Fund, 62, 80, 121
    organisational support, 52, 62, 109, 111, 114, 119
    training: of editors, 80; report, 66
Australia First Movement, 49
The Australian Abo Call, 48–9
Australian Author, 119
Australian Bicentennial Authority, 53
Australian Book Review, 100
Australian Capital Territory Writers' Centre, 118
Australian Centre, 150
Australian Excellence in Educational Publishing Award, 146
Australian Heritage Commission, 147
Australian Institute of Aboriginal and Torres Strait Islander Studies, 56
Australian Literary Essays, 13
Australian Multicultural Children's Book Award, 40
Australian Publishers Association Residential Editorial Program, 54, 58, 80–1, 84–5
Australian Short Stories, 60–1

Australian Society of Authors, 110, 118–21
Australians for Native Title, 119
authenticity, 2–16, 18, 83
    Aotearoa, 194–8
    Canada, 162–5
    see also literary fraud
authors' tours, 39, 96, 116–7, 155
authorship, 2–46
    Canadian First Nations' peoples, 155–74
    Maori, 190–201
    see also book catalogues; Indigenous Cultural and Intellectual Property rights
autobiography, 34–6, 37, 42, 95, 225–7
    Canadian First Nations', 155, 160, 166, 236–7
    Maori, 245
    My Place, 101–4
Awabakal people, 190
awards, 10, 40, 54, 64, 146–52
    Aotearoa, 192, 193, 215, 218
    Canada, 158, 161, 176, 185, 186

Banff Centre for the Arts, 176, 177
Banff Press, 176–7
Bangarra Performance Theatre, 130
Bann, Getano, 124
Barclay, Peter, 134
Bargh, Robyn, 192, 198, 215
    on editing, 212
    on genres, 200, 202, 218
    on publishing, 190, 202, 203
Barkly Arts, 116
Barlow, Annette, 76
Batchelor College for Indigenous Tertiary Education, 116, 122, 123, 143
BAWS, 5, 28, 37, 61, 67, 104, 149
Bay Foundation, 186
Bayet, Fabienne, 41
Beaton, Hilary, 117
Becoming Bicultural, 202–3
Bedevil, 151
Bell, Jeanie, 61, 149
    on Aboriginal identity, 41
    editorial experiences, 73
    literary festivals, 91, 130, 139
    marketing and distribution experiences, 91–2
    on writing, 22, 26, 32, 41
Bell, Sharenne, 108
Bellear, Lisa, 73, 114, 117

conferences and workshops, 145, 146
editorial experiences
at literary festivals, 129, 130, 131, 132
on literary festivals, 127
on marketing and distribution, 91, 104
on publishing, 51
on writing, 26–7, 36: post-colonial, 44
Belmore, Florene, 156, 163, 175, 176, 177, 181
Benang: From the Heart, 147
Bennell, Eddie, 112
Bennelong, 25
Bennett, Roger, 39, 64
Bermagui Festival of Words, 138–9
Beston, John, 99
Bevs, William, 165
Bibby, Peter, 72
Biddle, Jennifer, 25
Bil Bil, Marjorie, 52
Bin Salleh, Rachel, 54–5, 63, 66, 69–70
conferences and workshops, 80, 174
on copyright ownership, 88
on editing, 71, 78–9, 94
on marketing and distribution, 94, 95–6
on publishing, 57, 59
support for Colin Johnson, 8
biography, 35, 36, 42, 95, 227–8
Canadian First Nations', 160, 166, 237
Maori, 245
see also autobiography
Birch, Tony, 18
Bird, Gloria, 166
Birri-gubba people, 9–10
Black Action, 49
Black Angels, 148
Black Australian Writers Series (BAWS), 5, 28, 37, 61, 67, 104, 149
'Black Australians', 23–4
Black Books award, 54
Black from the Edge, 128, 151
Black in Focus, 40–1
Black Knight, 49
Black Liberation, 49
Black Mary, 57, 140
Black News Service, 49
'Black Power' tone, 49
Black Woman, Black Life, 41, 73, 135
Black Women's Action Committee, 49

Black Women's Writers' Conference (Brisbane, 1993), 119, 143
Blackbooks, 98, 114, 119, 120, 128, 142
Blaeser, Kimberley M., 162, 163, 164–5, 172, 173, 179
bloodlines (descent), 6–7, 17–18, 20, 21, 22
    Canadian First Nation peoples, 157–9
    Maori, 194, 195–6
Bodey, John, 148
The Bone People, 192
Bonney, Chris, 110
book catalogues, 90, 98–9, 114
    Canada, 178, 182
book jackets, 91
book launches, 53, 114, 131, 135, 143, 145
    Sydney Writers' Festival, 128, 129, 130
    Woodford Folk Festival, 91, 137
Booker Prize, 192
booksellers, *see* marketing and distribution
Booyooburra, 40
Borghino, Jose, 110
Born of the Conquerors, 99
Bostock, Gerry, 127, 128, 142
Bostock, Lester, 142
Bowles, Blanche, 55–6
Bowman, Marg, 35, 74, 80
Box The Pony, 130
Boyle, Josie, 132
Bran Nue Dae, 39–40, 64, 146
Brant, Beth, 160
Brewster, Anne, 46
Bridge of Triangles, 74, 100–1, 116, 148
Briggs, Ronald, 128
Brisbane, Katherine, 39–40, 64, 72
Brisbane Writers' Festival, 21, 130–1
Britain, 53
broadcasting, 64, 107, 110–11, 144
    Canada, 160, 183, 187
Broken Dreams, 148
Bropho, Robert, 12
Brothers in Arms, 160
Broughton, John, 206
Bruchac, Joseph, 162–3, 174, 186
Brune, Thomas, 48
Brusnahan, Margaret, 117
Buchanan, Cheryl, 131
Buchanan, Michelle, 145
Budsoar Ltd, 50

Bulmurn, 62
Bundjalung Tribal Society, 50
Bunjum Aboriginal Co-operative, 50
Bunuba people, 84
Burke, John Muk Muk, 38, 61
    awards, 148, 151
    editorial experiences, 74
    reviews, 100–1
    workshops, 116
    on writing, 33
Burke, Margaret, 128
Burrup, Eddie, 83, 87
Buyinbin, 50
Byler, Mary Gloyne, 158–9, 161–2
Byron Bay Writers' Festival, 133–5

Callinan, Peter, 116
The Callused Stock of Wanting, 135
Camfoo, Nelly, 84
Camfoo, Tex, 84
Campbell, Alistair Te Ariki, 200
Campbell, Maria, 156, 160, 161, 174, 175, 187
Canada Council for the Arts, 183–4, 187
Canadian First Nations' peoples, 111, 154–88, 235–44
Canberra Word Festival, 133
Canning, Ken (Burraga Gutya), 129, 136
Canterbury Regional Council, 206
Caprice, 148
Cardinal, Howard, 155
Carey, Gabrielle, 136
Carmen, Leon (Koomatrie, Wanda), 2, 28, 72, 87, 128, 136
Carmody, Kev, 130
Carr, Bob, 107–8
Carriage, Owen, 50
Carriage, Sue, 50
caste, *see* bloodlines
Castlemaine Festival, 114
catalogues, *see* book catalogues
categorisation, 95–6, 159–60, 162
    see also genres
CDEPs, 121
Central Land Council, 96
Centre for Blackbooks, 98, 114, 119, 120, 128, 142
Centre for Indigenous History and the Art, 149
Challis, Kate, 150–1
Charlton, Kerry, 130

The Cherry Pickers, 137
Chesson, Keith, 112
Chesson, Marlene, 112
Chi, Jimmy, 26, 64, 146
Children's Book of the Year Award, 40, 146
children's literature, 11, 40–1, 107, 122, 143, 228–31
    awards, 40, 146, 149
    Canadian First Nations', 161–2, 167–9, 176, 237–9
    Jukurrpa Books, 52, 177
    Maori, 191, 193, 200, 203, 207–8, 218, 245–6: training courses, 212, 219
    print runs, 92
    see also education market
Chinook Winds, 176–7
Christopher Brennan Award, 150
Churinga, 49
cinema, *see* films
Circle of Aboriginal Controlled Publishers, 174, 175, 177
Clare, Monica, 2, 191
Coe, Mary, 36
Coffey, Ray, 62
    on editing, 70–1
    on marketing and distribution, 92, 93, 94
    on publishing, 59
    on writers and writing, 15, 42, 62
collaborative works, 84–5
Collins, Jane, 201
Collins Imprint, 75
The Colour of Resistance, 163–4
colonisation, 43–6
Community Cultural Development Fund, 117–18, 121
Community Development Employment Programs, 121
community life, 21, 22
"Companionship", 138
Condon, Matt, 129
conferences, 116, 141–5
    Aboriginal and Torres Strait Islander Writers' and Playwrights' Conference (Brisbane, 1996), 4–5, 102, 111, 114, 143–5
    Canada, 174, 185–7
    National Aboriginal and Torres Strait Islander Women Writers' Conference (Brisbane, 1993), 119, 143
    National Conferences of Aboriginal Writers, 57–8, 112, 142
    see also literary festivals; workshops and seminars
Congress of Aboriginal Peoples, 158
Conned, 149
Contemporary Koori Woman, 129
Contemporary Maori Writing, 191
contracts, 88, 118

Cook, Sam, 55, 63, 108–9
   on editing, 70
   on intellectual property rights, 87
   on marketing and distribution, 94
   on publishing, 48, 59
   on writing, 41
Coolbaroo League, 49
Coolwell, Wayne, 131
Copway, George, 155
copyright, *see* Indigenous Cultural and Intellectual Property rights
Copyright Agency Limited, 85
Copyright Council, 86
Corroboree, 149
Coulton, Beatrice, 176
Council for Maori and South Pacific Arts, 216
Cowlishaw, Gillian, 84
Craig, Jingula Melissa, 152
Craigie, Cathy, 39, 111, 113–14
   on Aboriginal identity, 22
   conferences and workshops, 143, 146
   literary festivals, 127, 128, 135, 137, 139, 140
   on marketing and distribution, 92
   on post-colonial, 45
   on writing, 22, 27, 34: Morgan's *My Place*, 104; whites about blacks, 12
Crawford, Evelyn, 133
creation/Dreaming stories, 11, 13, 31, 45, 85, 95
   Maori, 247
Creative New Zealand, 216
crime writing, 129, 131, 136
critics, *see* reviewers and critics
Croft, Brenda I., 152
cross cultural titles, 93, 96
cross-cultural training, 62–3
Culleton, Beatrice, 160
Cultural Industries Statistics Working Group, 109
cultural maintenance/revival, 51–2
Cultural Ministers' Council, 109
cultural property, *see* Indigenous Cultural and Intellectual Property rights
cultural tourism, 95, 201
Culturally Appropriate Professional Training Opportunities for Centre Australia Indigenous Writers project, 121–3
culturally inappropriate treatment, *see* appropriation of culture and voice
Cunningham, Sophie, 76
Curnow, Meredith, 127, 129
Currency Press, 64
curriculum material, *see* education market

Daily Telegraph, 25
Danaher, P.A., 100–1
dance, 39, 130, 131, 132, 137, 141
    Canada, 176–7
    support and advisory organisations, 110, 112
Dandurand, Joseph A., 177
David Unaipon Award, 34, 73, 104, 131, 147–9
    judging panel, 4, 5, 61, 148
Davis, Jack, 2, 27, 35, 39, 64, 111–12
    awards, 150, 151
    Identity, 50, 60, 111
    literary festivals, 132
    reviews, 99
    on theatre, 39
    University of Queensland Press (UQP) and, 61, 148
Davis, Kerry, 12, 41
Day, Marele, 131
deceptive conduct, 87
    see also literary fraud
definitions of Aboriginality, 17–21, 27, 156–8, 194–6
definitions of Aboriginal literature, 22–8, 34, 162–5, 196–8
descent, *see* bloodlines
design, *see* visual arts and design
Devaney, Jim, 59
Devitt, Marian, 115
Diane Deborah Memorial Award, 186
dictionaries, 51–2, 53
A Directory of North American Native Writers, 186
distribution, *see* marketing and distribution
Dixon, Graeme, 6, 104, 148, 149
Do Not Go Around the Edges, 40
Dodd, Bill, 148
Dodson, Mick, 21, 60
Doherty, Anne, 137
Dominican Sisters of Eastern Australia, 129
Don't Take Your Love to Town, 8, 36, 74–5, 146
Douglas, Josie, 35, 51, 68–9, 123
    on editing, 71
    training, 80
    on training, 124–5
drama, *see* plays and playwrights
Dreaming in Urban Areas, 73, 91, 131
Dreaming stories, 11, 13, 31, 45, 85, 95
Dry Lips Oughta Move to Kapuskasing, 161
Duff, Alan, 192, 193

Duke, Tony, 142
Dumbartung Aboriginal Corporation, 9
Dunkle, Margaret, 40–1
Dunn, Irina, 98, 113, 135, 136
Durack, Elizabeth, 83, 87
Durack, Mary, 4, 60
duration of copyright, 86

Eddington, Jill, 135
editing, 58, 60–1, 63, 66–82, 122, 131, 145
    Aotearoa, 202, 208, 209, 210–13, 214
    Canada, 160, 178, 179–81, 187
    see also Indigenous editors
editorial training, 67, 78–82
Edmund, Mabel, 131, 149
education market, 36, 62, 94, 96, 116–17
    Aotearoa, 204, 204–5, 212
    awards, 146
    North America, 173–4, 178, 186
    see also children's literature; university market
Egert, Irene, 130
Eggington, Robert, 7
Encyclopaedia of Aboriginal Australia, 57, 77
enemies, tribal, 206
English, *see* Aboriginal English: Maori English
Enoch, Wesley, 39, 117, 130, 135
Enough is Enough, Aboriginal Women Speak Out, 161
En'owkin Centre, 163, 178, 184, 185, 188
En'owkin International School of Writing, 154, 178, 182, 184
Erdrich, Louise, 160, 176
erotica, 136, 166–7
essays, 37
Ethnic Communities Council of NSW, 129
ethnographic writing, 14
Eurocentrism of reviewers, 99, 101, 171, 180
Eva Pownall Award for Information Books, 146
Evans, Audrey, 124
Evans, Ray, 11
Everett, Jimmy, 132

FACP, *see* Fremantle Arts Centre Press
family politics, 206
Faust, Beatrice, 7, 9
Fedorick, Joy Asham, 173
fellowships, 75, 106, 151–2
    see also awards

feminism, 37, 46
Ferguson, William, 48–9
Fesl, Eve, 17–18, 142, 149
Festival of Pacific Arts, 141
Festival of the Dreaming (Sydney, 1997), 97, 111, 139–41, 193, 216
festivals, *see* literary festivals
fiction, 38, 52, 64, 231–2
    Canadian First Nations', 160, 177, 239–40
    Maori, 191, 193, 196, 199–200, 208–9, 246
Fife, Connie, 163–4
Fiji, 130
film scripts, 128, 151, 200
films, 130, 186, 200
    copyright ownership, 83, 84
    made from books, 143–4, 160, 193
financing, *see* funding
First Nations' peoples, *see* North American First Nations' peoples
First People, First Voices, 160
Flinders Island, 48
Fogarty, Lesley, 144
Fogarty, Lionel, 16, 28, 64
    awards, 150
    conferences and workshops, 142, 145
    literary festivals, 128, 130, 137, 140
    on writing, 40
Foley, Denis, 145
Follow the Rabbit Proof Fence, 143–4
For the Record: 160 Years of Aboriginal Print Journalism, 48
Forde, HE Mrs Leneen, 131
The Forgotten People, 157
Fox, Judith, 129
Francis, Gordon, 15–16
Francis, Lee, 186
fraud, *see* literary fraud
Fred, Randy, 175
Freebury, Julia, 9
Fremantle Arts Centre Press (FACP), 42, 59, 62, 98
    marketing, 94, 95
    print runs, 92, 93
    see also Coffey, Ray
Frost, Lucy, 133
funding, 75, 106–9, 116, 118, 121
    Aotearoa, 216–18
    Canada, 154, 182–4
    editorial training, 79–80
    Institute of Aboriginal Development (IAD) Press, 52
    see also Australia Council for the Arts

Gadigal Information Service (GIS), 110–11, 120, 141
Gadigal Writers' Group, 111, 139
Gamba, Barry, 129
A Gathering of Spirit, 160
Gathering Strength, 174, 181, 183–4, 187
Gatherings, 166, 175, 178
Gee, Valda, 148
genres, 35–41, 67, 95, 107, 220–49
    Canadian First Nations', 159–62, 166–7, 235–44
    Maori, 191–3, 199–200, 245–9
    whites writing on blacks, 10–11
George, Chief Dan, 160
Gilbert, Kevin, 2, 35, 64, 72
    awards, 146, 150, 151
    literary festivals, 128, 132, 137, 140
    print journalism, 49, 50
Gilbert, Ruth, 66, 69
Ginsberg, Allen, 133
God's Best Country, 15–16
Going for Kalta, 52–3, 146
Gonzales, Rosemary, 167
Good, Francis, 115
Goodall, Heather, 10, 139
Goodall, Dr Maarire, 199, 205–6, 213
Goodman, Kent, 160
Government funding, *see* funding
Grace, Patricia, 140–1, 191, 192, 208, 218
    editing and, 210, 213
    on writing, 198, 199, 201
Grace-Smith, Briar, 111, 193
Graham, John, 131
Graham, Mary, 33–4, 80, 124
grants, *see* funding
The Great Forgetting, 57
Green, Nellie, 19
Greenfield Press, 182
Greenfield Review Literary Centre, 186
Griffiths, Lorraine, 132
Grosvenor, Rhonda, 146
Groulx, David, 161, 171, 177
Gularabulu, 25, 30–1, 62
Gunjies, 57
Gutya, Burraga, 129, 136

Halbert, Rongowhakaata, 208
Hale & Iremonger, 98
half-caste, *see* bloodlines
Halfbreed, 160
Hamm, Treahna, 147
Hampton, Denella, 52
Handbook for Central Australian Indigenous Writers, 115
Hannigan, Robyn, 119
Harawira, Wena, 193, 198, 201, 211
Harding, John, 64, 132, 151
Harjo, Joy, 156, 166, 187
Harmony, 49
HarperCollins, 93
Harrison, Jane, 64
Harwood, Lyn, 60
Haunted by the Past, 76
Havnen, Peg, 115
Hawke, Bob, 53
Hayden-Taylor, Drew, 156, 166, 175
Hayes, Susan, 117
Hayward, Bevan, 57
Headline, Hodder, 130
Heath, John, 133
Hegarty, Ruth, 137, 145, 148
'heir letters', 85
Heiss, Anita M., 41, 96–7, 107, 110, 111, 117, 119, 120
    literary festivals, 128–9, 130, 131, 133–5, 136, 137, 138–40, 141
    reviewer, 100
    workshops, 146
Hello, Johnny, 131
Henson, Lance, 162
Higgins, Simon, 131
Highway, Thomson, 161
Hinewirangi, 193, 199, 214
history, 10, 11–13, 36–7, 42, 151, 222–3
    Aotearoa, 208, 211
    Canada, 155, 240–1
    see also biography; oral literature
History Fellowship, 75
Hodge, Bob, 112
Hodge, Dino, 115
Holding Up the Sky, 34, 69
Holocaust Island, 6, 104, 148
Holt, Albert, 124
Honour the Sun, 160, 180
Hookey, Gordon, 130

Hopa, Pare, 200
Horouta, 208
Horton, David, 57
Hosking, Dianne, 57
house styles, 34–5, 180–1, 187
How To Tell the Difference, 167–9
Huggins, Jackie, 40, 57, 119, 148
    on Aboriginal identity, 21
    Auntie Rita, 36, 77–8, 93, 103
    on autobiography, 35–6
    conferences and workshops, 142, 143, 145
    editorial experiences, 73, 77–8
    literary festivals, 21, 128, 131, 137
    on marketing and distribution, 93
    on post-colonial, 44
    on reviewers, 99
    Sister Girl, 37, 73
    on writing, 25, 32: by non-Aboriginal people, 11, 15
Huggins, Rita, 36, 77, 78, 103, 137
Huia Publishers, 177, 201–3, 210, 212
    Short Story Awards, 193, 218
    workshops, 215
    see also Bargh, Robyn
Hulme, Keri, 192, 200, 218
Human Rights Awards for Literature, 146
Hunt, Harold, 41
Hunter, Al, 177
Hunter, Ruby, 128, 131
Hyland House, 5, 64, 98

I Am An Indian, 160
IAD Press, *see* Institute of Aboriginal Development Press
identity, 2–24, 27, 41–6
    Australian Society of Authors membership, 118–19
    Canadian First Nations' peoples, 156–9, 162–5
    family politics, 206
    Maori, 192, 194–8, 206
    Tasmania, 108
Identity magazine, 9, 50, 60, 111
Ihimaera, Witi, 191, 192, 198, 208–9, 211, 218
    editing and, 210, 213
    on marketing and distribution, 214
    on writing, 200
illustrations, 55, 57, 143
    artwork, 110
In Search of April Raintree, 160

income, 107, 118
"Index of Maoriness", 194–5
Indian Acts (Canada), 156–7, 158
Indigenous Arts Fund, 107
Indigenous Australian Voices, 41, 145
Indigenous Cultural and Intellectual Property (copyright) rights, 83–8, 121
    advisory organisations, 110, 118
        Tasmania, 108
Indigenous designers, 57, 175
    see also Cook, Sam
Indigenous editors, 66–70, 78–82, 160, 210
    see also Bin Salleh, Rachel; Douglas, Josie; non-Aboriginal editors; Phillips, Sandra; Young-Ing, Greg
Indigenous languages, 87
    Australia Council consumer information, 107
    Canadian First Nations', 170, 176
    dictionaries, 51–2, 53
    Nyoongah, 39
    see also Aboriginal English; Maori language
Indigenous organisations, 109–12, 184–6
Indigenous publishing houses, 51–7
    Canadian First Nations', 174–6, 178, 183
    Maori, 201–8, 210, 212–13, 219
    see also Aboriginal Studies Press; Huia Publishers; Institute of Aboriginal Development Press: Magabala Books
Indigenous reviewers, 100, 215
Indigenous Writers' Conference (Northern Territory, 1995), 143
Indigenous Writers' Symposium, 145
Inner-City Education Centre, 66
Innes, Carol, 143
Institute of Aboriginal Development, 52, 116
Institute of Aboriginal Development (IAD) Press, 51–3, 63, 68, 106, 177
    copyright, 85–6
    editing, 72, 74
    marketing and distribution, 53, 95, 96, 98
    training, 80, 122, 123
    see also Douglas, Josie; MacDonald, Simon
intellectual property, *see* Indigenous Cultural and Intellectual Property rights
International Festival of the Arts (1996), 217
Inuit people, 157, 158
Is That You Ruthie?, 148

Jacaranda Press, 132
jackets, 91
Jackson, Melissa, 128
Jakeman, Noelle, 205

Jandamarra and the Bunuba Resistance, 84
Janke, Terri, 83, 84, 85, 86–7
Janke, Toni, 143
Janson, Julie, 57, 140
Janssen, Peter, 197, 200, 207–8, 213, 214
Jazz Waiata, 210
Jeannie Once, 191–2
Jebb, Mary Ann, 63
Jimbidie, Irene, 63
Jinangga, 34–5
Johnson, Colin (Mudrooroo), 3–8, 43, 59–60, 148
    awards, 5, 150
    on editors, 71, 81
    on genres, 35, 37
    literary festivals, 130
    on literary standards, 31, 99
    on *My Place*, 104
    on oral literature, 31
Johnson, Darlene, 130
Johnson, Eva, 39, 128, 132, 142
Johnson, Pauline, 155
Jones, Jonah, 139–40
journalism, 25, 48–51
judgment of standards, *see* literary standards
Jukurrpa Books, 52, 177

Kaa, Wiremu, 212
Kaino, Tazuko, 63
Kane, Margo, 161
Kapu, 111
Karobran, 191
Kawa O Te Marae, 211
Kawana, Phil, 193
Kegedonce Press, 177
Kelen, Steve, 118
Kelly, Phillip, 115
Kelly, Susan, 149
Kerr-Wilson, Barbara, 145
Kibble Literary Award, 10
Kimberley Aboriginal Law and Cultural Centre, 53
Kimberley Cross Cultural Training, 63
King, Thomas, 156, 160, 162
Kinnane, Stephen, 62, 132, 133
Kjar, Barbie, 115
Knight, Olive, 63
Knockwood, Isabelle, 166

Kooemba Jdarra Indigenous Performing Arts Group, 39, 131, 143
Koolmatrie, Wanda, *see* Carmen, Leon
Koori-Bina, 49
Koori Love, 39
Koori Mail, 50, 97
Koori Radio, 110–11
Koori Readings, 137
Koorier, 49
Kouka, Hone, 206
Kriol, 28–9, 70
    see also Aboriginal English
Kuckles, 64, 146
The Kuia and the Spider, 191
Kuilboer, Theresa, 101
Kum Sing, Kathy, 142
Kupu Ao Publishers, 177
Kuri-Ngai Partners, 129
Kurrachee Co-operative Society, 50
Kurtzer, Sonja, 20, 102–3
Kuruwarri: Yuendumum Doors, 25

Label of Authenticity, 18, 83
Land of the Golden Clouds, 95–6
Land Window, 131
Landmarks, 212
Lands, Merrilee, 54
Lane, Noelene, 150
Langford Ginibi, Ruby, 8, 146
    on Aboriginal identity, 19–20, 42
    editorial experiences, 74–6
    literary festivals, 130, 133, 135
    reviews, 101
    on writing, 13, 31, 36–7
Langton, Marcia, 19, 57, 102
language, 11–12, 28–35, 60
    academic books, 38
    Canadian First Nations' writers, 170–1
    Mana Magazine, 207
    Maori writers, 193, 198–9
    non-Aboriginal editors and, 67, 179
    see also Indigenous languages
LaRocque, Emma, 159, 164, 166, 169–70, 172, 179–80
Latona, Peter, 138
Laughton, Kenny, 52, 74, 130, 146
    on Aboriginal identity, 23, 42
    on editors, 70, 74

    on marketing and promotion, 93, 104
    on publishing, 57, 58–9
    reviews, 101
    on writing, 29, 33, 42, 45: whites about black, 11
launches, *see* book launches
Laurenson, Marama, *see* Mihaka, Marama
Lee, Penelope, 57
legends, *see* creation/Dreaming stories
Leichhardt Council, 129
Lester, Yami, 52
libraries, 90
The Life, History and Travels of Kah-ge-ga-gah-bowh, 155
literacy, 25, 121, 122, 190–1
literary festivals, 91, 114, 119, 121, 126–41
    Aotearoa, 217
    Canada, 162, 185, 186–7
    Festival of the Dreaming, 97, 111, 139–41, 193, 216
    Spring Writing Festival, 42–3, 97–8, 111, 113, 135–6
    United States, 162, 185
literary fraud, 2, 83, 87, 131, 136
    Morgan, Marlo, 13–14, 15, 87, 93
    see also Carmen, Leon
literary standards, 26–7, 31, 99, 213, 215
    see also reviewers and critics
Literature Fund, 62, 80, 121
Little, Lorna, 6
Little, Tom, 6, 59, 63
Littlebird, Harold, 162
Liverani, Mary Rose, 101
Living Black, 146
'Living Ghost', 30–1
Longley, Kateryna Olijnyk, 27
looking into the eyes of my forgotten dreams, 177
Louis Littlecon Oliver Memorial Award, 186
Love, Owen, 39, 143, 146
Love Against the Law, 84
Lowe, Pat, 128
Lucashenko, Melissa, 38, 41, 61, 117, 124
    on Aboriginal identity, 23, 26
    awards, 131, 146, 149
    on awards, 149, 150
    conferences and workshops, 80, 144–5
    on editing, 73, 81
    literary festivals, 111, 129, 131, 132, 135
    on marketing and distribution, 92
    reviewer, 100
    on writing, 26, 32, 45

Lukin-Amundsen, Judith, 124

Macartney, Frederick, 13
McCarron, Robyn, 21, 23
McCarthy, Steven, 38, 148
McCorquordale, John, 19
McDermott, Vi, 130
McDonald, Connie Nungulla, 103, 119, 128
MacDonald, Simon, 52–3, 60, 92–3, 96, 122
McGee-Sippel, Lorraine, 136, 137
McGuiness, Joe, 149
McGuirk, Sharelle, 150
McKenzie, Christine, 114
Mackerras, Lindsay, 57
McLaren, Philip, 129, 130, 135, 136, 148, 217
McLelland, Joseph, 162
McLeod, Pauline, 141
McMillan, Andrew, 143
McQueen, Harvey, 191
McRobbie, Narelle, 40
McVeagh, Janine, 146, 204, 205, 210, 219
Magabala Books, 53–6, 63, 64, 67, 119, 188
    copyright/royalties arrangements, 84
    editing, 69, 72
    house style, 34–5
    international contacts, 174, 177
    marketing and distribution, 94, 95, 98
    support for Sydney Writers' Festival, 128
Mailman, Deborah, 39
mainstream awards, 40, 146–7, 192
mainstream publishing, 5, 57–65, 73, 76, 98, 132
    Aotearoa, 191, 192, 208–9, 213
    Canada, 170, 174, 178
    contracts, 88
    training Aboriginal editors through, 81–2
    United Kingdom, 53
    see also Fremantle Arts Centre Press; University of Queensland Press
mainstream support and advisory organisations, 113–21, 183–4, 215–18
Mainstreet Community Theatre Company, 143
The Making of a Maori, 194–5
Malaney Folk Festival, 91, 136
Mana Magazine, 207, 211, 213
Maori, 177, 190–219, 245–9
    at Australian events, 111, 130, 135–6, 140, 146
    at Canadian events, 174

Maori: The Crisis and the Challenge, 193
Maori Artists' and Writers' Group, 191
Maori Arts New Zealand, 216–18
Maori editors, 210
Maori English, 193, 196, 197, 198–9
Maori language, 196, 198–9, 202
    editing and, 212, 213
    works published in, 191, 203, 204–5, 212, 217, 218
Maori Language Commission, 208, 209
Maori Poetry, 191
Maori Problems Today, 191
Maori reviewers, 215
Maracle, Lee, 156, 160
Maris, Hyllus, 150
marketing and distribution, 53, 90–9
    Aotearoa, 203, 208, 210, 214
    Canada, 181–2
Marrawarnging Award, 149
Marshall-Stoneking, Billy, 74
Martin, Paul, 187
Martiniello, Jennifer, 16, 138
Master Classes for Aboriginal writers (1998), 111, 120, 146
Maza, Bob, 142, 143, 146
MC Media & Associates, 107
Mead, Sid, 191, 197, 212
Medcraft, Rosalie, 148
Medicine River, 160
Meek, R.L., 191
Melbourne Writers' Festival, 131–2
mentoring, 117, 121, 122, 124–5
    Canada, 185
Mercredi, Ovide, 174
Merritt, Robert J., 39, 64, 150
Metis Indians, 157, 158, 159, 166, 176, 178
Mihaka, Don, 209, 210
Mihaka, Marama, 209–10, 219
    on reviewing, 215
    on writing, 197, 198, 199, 201, 214
Miles Franklin Award, 147
Miller, James, 150
Miller, Lydia, 97, 128
Milne, Geoffrey, 15–16
Milroy, David, 143
Milward, Karen, 150
Minatel, Margaret, 152
misleading and deceptive conduct, 87

missionaries, 190
Mitcalfe, Barry, 191
Mitchell, Pauline, 146
Moccason Telegraph, 184–5
Moffat, Tracey, 151
Mogwi-Djan National Indigenous Writers and Playwrights Conference and Workshop
    (Brisbane, 1996), 4–5, 102, 111, 114, 143–5
Momaday, N. Scott, 186
moral rights, 86–7
Moran, Rod, 31
Moreton, Romaine, 16, 135
Moreton-Robinson, Aileen, 37
Morgan, Eileen, 138
Morgan, Kelly, 164, 174
Morgan, Marlo, 13–14, 15, 87, 93
Morgan, Sally, 3, 27, 62, 63, 101–4, 149
    awards, 150
    Johnson's criticism of, 4–5, 104
Morris, Christine, 13
Morris, Donna, 146
Morrissey, Di, 13–14
Mosely, Eileen, 122
Moses, Daniel David, 173, 187
'Mudrooroo', 3
'The Mudrooroo Dilemma', 6
Muecke, Stephen, 10, 25, 30–1, 45, 59–60
Multicultural Arts Network, 143
multimedia, 107, 118
Munduwalawala, Ginger Riley, 147
Munro, Craig, 147–8
Murdoch University, 112
Murray, Les, 136
Murri Time, 39
Museum and Art Gallery of the Northern Territory, 147
music, 111, 137, 141, 186
musical theatre, 39–40, 64, 146
Mutant Message Down Under, 13–14, 15, 87, 93
My Bundjalung People, 75–6
My Name is Seepeetza, 166
My Own Sweet Time, *see* Carmen, Leon
My Place, *see* Morgan, Sally
myths, *see* creation/Dreaming stories

N.Q. Messagestick, 50
names, 3–4, 195
Nance, Rhyll, 150–1
Nangun, Butcher Joc, 62

Nannup, Alice, 62
Narogin, Mudrooroo, *see* Johnson, Colin
National Aboriginal Achievement Awards, 187
National Aboriginal and Torres Strait Islander Art Award, 147
National Aboriginal and Torres Strait Islander Playwrights Conference, 144
National Aboriginal and Torres Strait Islander Women Writers' Conference (Brisbane, 1993), 119, 143
National Aboriginal Publishers' Conference (1995), 174
National Aboriginal Theatre Foundation, 49
National Aboriginal Writers' Conferences, 57–8, 112, 142
National Aboriginal Writers' Workshop, 142
National Black Playwrights Conference, 39
National Conference of Aboriginal Writers, 57–8, 112, 142
National Heritage Art Award, 147
National Indigenous Arts Advocacy Association, 83, 109–10
National Indigenous Times, 50
Native American Distribution Project, 182
Native Americans, *see* North American First Nations' peoples
Native Council of Canada, 91, 158
Native Legends, 25
Native Literature in Canada, 171
native title, 119
'Native voice/white audience dynamic', 169
Nelson, Emmanuel S., 99
New South Wales Indigenous Arts Fellowship, 151–2
New South Wales Ministry for the Arts, 75, 107–8, 152
New South Wales Writers' Centre, 111, 113–14
    Spring Writing Festival, 42–3, 97–8, 111, 113, 135–6
New Women's Fiction, 211
New York Times Foundation, 186
New Zealand, *see* Maori
New Zealand Lotteries Office, 216
New Zealand Native Associations, 195
Newfong, John A., 9, 50
Newlin, Norm, 16, 129, 136
newspapers, 25, 48–51, 190
Nga Pou Wahine, 193
Nicholson, Barbara, 128, 137
Night Song, 151
Nights In the Garden of Spain, 192
Ninu, Yaaltje, 122
Nita B. Kibble award, 146
No Option! No Choice!, 128
No Ordinary Sun, 191
No Regret, 149
No Shame, 39, 143

No Sugar, 151
non-Aboriginal editors, 70–2, 160
    Abbey, Sue, 61, 67, 72, 73, 145
    Aotearoa, 191, 210–13
    Bowman, Marg, 35, 74, 80
    Canada, 172, 179–80
non-Aboriginal writers, 2–16, 121
    Aotearoa, 194, 205
    Canada, 171–3, 178, 244
non-fiction, 35–8, 220–4
    Canadian First Nations', 161, 240–1
    Maori, 193, 200, 202–3, 206, 247
    print runs, 92
    see also biography; history
non-status Indians, 157
Noongar community, 23
Noonuccal, Oodgeroo (Kath Walker), 2, 35, 59, 61, 150, 191
    on identity, 20
    literary festivals, 128, 132, 140
    name, 3, 138
    reviews of, 99
    University of Queensland Press (UQP) and, 61, 148
North American First Nations' Authors First Book Awards, 186
North American First Nations' peoples, 87, 111, 140, 154–88, 235–44
    'apples', 196
    see also United States
North American Native Authors Catalogue, 182
North American Native Authors First Book Awards, 158
Northeastern State University, 185
Northern Rivers Writers' Centre, 133
Northern Territory Department of the Arts and Museums, 121
Northern Territory Museum and Art Galley, 147
Northern Territory Writers' Centre, 115–16
Not Quite Men, No Longer Boys, 74, 101, 130
novels, *see* fiction
N.Q. Messagestick, 50
NSW, *see* New South Wales
Nungera Co-operative, 50
Nyoongar people, 6, 7, 9, 39, 59
    Aboriginal Independent Newspaper, 50

O'Brien, May, 40, 62, 149
Odjig, Alanis King, 161
Okanagan Nation, 184
Oklahoma Council for the Arts, 186
"On Getting Published", 180

Once Were Warriors, 192, 193
One Good Story, That One, 160
Only Drunks and Children Tell The Truth, 166
Onus, Lin, 147, 151
'Oodgeroo', 3
oral literature/tradition (storytelling), 28–31, 33–4, 45, 107, 222–3
    artwork as, 25
    Canadian First Nations', 161, 183–5
    cultural and intellectual property rights, 83–9, 121
    literary festivals, 129, 132, 137, 141
    Maori, 111, 190, 200
    support and advisory organisations, 112, 115
    theatrical opportunities, 39
    training, 115, 121, 122
Orbell, Margaret, 191
organisations, 109–21, 182–6, 215–19
    see also publishing and publishers
O'Shane, Pat, 128
Our Culture: Our Future, 83
Our Grandmothers' Lives In Their Own Words, 161
"Our Words—Our Ways": National Aboriginal and Torres Strait Islander Writers' Workshop, 142
Out of the Depths, 166
Owen, Julie, 205
ownership of copyright, 83–8
Oxford Anthology of New Zealand Poetry, 210–11

Pacific Book Exhibition, 141
Pacific Highway Boo Blooz, 7
Page, Geoff, 57
Pai Marire Movement, 195
Palawa writing, 114–15
Palm Island, 49
Palmer, Kingsley, 57
pan-Aboriginality, 21
pan-Maoriness, 195–6
Paperbark, 148
Paperbark Literature program, 97–8, 139
Paraha, Glenys, 200
part-Aboriginal, *see* bloodlines
Pascoe, Bruce, 41, 60–1, 72
    on Aboriginal identity, 22, 42–3
    literary festivals, 42–3, 129
    on post-colonial, 46
    reviewer, 100
    workshops, 146

Pascoe Publishing, 60–1
Pass It On, 191–2
paternalism of reviewers, 99
Paterson, Rachel, 9
Patricia Weickhardts Award, 150
Patten, John, 48–9
pay, 107, 118
Pearce, Judy, 133
Pearson, Noel, 60
Pederson, Howard, 84
Pemmican Publications, 175–6
Penguin, 91, 104, 191, 192, 208–9, 213
    see also Walker, Geoff
Penguin Book of New Zealand Verse, 191
People of the Land, 211
performing arts, *see* dance; plays and playwrights
Perkins, Rachel, 130
Perreault, Jeanne, 172, 179
Perth Writers' Festival, 132
Petrone, Penny, 160, 164, 171, 180
Pheasant, Kareen, 181–2
Phillips, Sandra, 61, 66–8, 119, 124, 143
    conferences and workshops, 142, 144, 145, 174
    on David Unaipon Award, 147
    literary festivals, 130, 140
    on marketing and distribution, 91, 92
    on publishing, 51
    writers on, 72–3
    on writing, 27–8, 44, 67–8, 32: by non-Aboriginal people, 10–11, 34
photographs, 84, 151
picture books, *see* children's literature; visual arts and design
Pike, Jimmy, 128
Pike Ake!, 210
Pilkington, Doris, 38, 143–4, 146, 148
Plains of Promise, 38, 149
Playlab Press, 39
plays and playwrights, 39–40, 57, 64, 139, 141, 232
    awards, 151
    Canadian First Nations', 161, 166, 243–4
    film scripts, 128, 151, 200
    Maori, 191–2, 193, 200, 201–2, 205, 206, 247–8
    Mogwi-Djan National Indigenous Writers and Playwrights Conference and Workshop (Brisbane, 1996), 4–5, 102, 111, 114, 143–5
    radio-plays, 111
    reviewers, 15–16
    support and advisory organisations, 111, 112, 114, 117

Plummer, Rosemary, 122
poetry, 35, 36, 64, 107, 232–4
    Aboriginal Studies Press, 57
    awards, 150, 151, 161, 186
    Canadian First Nations', 161, 170, 176, 177, 180, 186, 241–3
    editors, 67
    language used in, 32
    literary festivals, 129, 130, 132, 138
    Maori, 191, 192, 200, 210–11, 248–9
    print runs, 92
    reviewers, 99
    support and advisory organisations, 111, 114
Poetry of the Maori, 191
The Poets' Union, 129
post-colonial literature, 43–6, 165, 197–8
Potiki, Roma, 200
Pounamu, Pounamu, 191
press releases, 97
print journalism, 25, 48–51, 190
    Aotearoa, 207, 211
print runs, 53, 91, 92–3, 207
Prior, Doris, 9
Progressive Publishing Society, 191
promotion, *see* marketing and distribution
Proof of Aboriginality form, 18
Prospect Media, 98
Pryor, Boori, 114, 129, 132, 135
pseudonyms, 3–4
publisher contracts, 88, 118
publishing and publishers, 16, 23, 25, 48–65
    Aotearoa, 177, 190–1, 196, 201–10
    Canada, 170, 174–8, 183, 187, 188
    copyright/royalties arrangements, 84, 97
    see also Indigenous publishing houses; mainstream publishing houses; marketing and distribution
Purcell, Leah, 130
Pusacker, Jenny, 131

Queensland Folk Federation, 136
Queensland Ministry for the Arts, 148
Queensland Writers' Centre, 116–17, 124

"Rabbit Proof Fence", 143–4
Race Matters, 6–7
Racism, Representation and Photography, 66
radio broadcasting, 107, 110–11, 183, 187

radio-plays, 111
Radio Skid Row, 110
Raven, Juliet, 213
Ravenscroft, Alison, 34, 77–8, 145
Rea, 152
readership, 90–152, 181–7, 215–19
   see also audience; marketing and distribution
reading lists, *see* education market
Real Deadly, 75, 101
Realist Writer, 138
Reclaim the Visions, 186
recognition of authors, 106–25
Recollections of a Fresh Life, 155
reconciliation, 92, 137
recording oral literature, *see* transcription
Redbird, Duke, 155, 160
Reed, A.H., 207
Reed, A.W., 207
Reed-Gilbert, Kerry, 16, 111, 118, 119, 166
  on Aboriginal identity, 22, 41
  conferences and workshops, 143, 146
  editorial experiences, 73
  literary festivals, 111, 129, 135, 136, 137, 140
  on publishing, 58
  on writing, 32, 41
Reed Publishing, 197, 207–8, 213, 211, 214
region, identification with, 21
Registered (Status) Indians, 156, 157, 158, 159
Reinventing the Enemy's Language, 166
Renee, 191–2
Report on Strategies for the Further Development of the National Aboriginal and Torres Strait Islander Arts and Cultural Industry, 55–6, 106, 123, 146
"The Return", 211
Returning the Gift Festival, 162, 185
Returning the Gift Project, 185–6, 188
review copies, 97
reviewers and critics, 15–16, 99–101
    Aotearoa, 213, 215
    Canada, 171, 180
The Rez Sisters, 161
Rhydwen, Mari, 14
rights, *see* Indigenous Cultural and Intellectual Property rights
Riki, Jean, 130
Riley, Sally, 130
Ritchie, James, 194–5, 202–3
Roach, Archie, 128

Robinson, G.A., 48
Rock, Bob
    on Aboriginal identity, 158, 166
    on editing, 179
    on publishing, 178
    on writing, 159, 163, 165, 166, 170–1: by non-Native people, 172
Roe, Paddy, 25, 30–1, 62
Rose, Debbie, 137
Rose, Michael, 48, 49
Ross, Rodger W., 165, 179
Rosser, Bill, 49, 151
Roughsey, Dick, 150
Round Up, 151
Royal Commission into Aboriginal Peoples in Canada, 174, 181, 183–4, 187
royalties, 83, 84–6, 96, 97
    see also Indigenous Cultural and Intellectual Property rights
Ruatara Publications, 209–10
Running Sketches of Men and Place in England, France, Germany, Belgium and Scotland, 155
Russell, Garrett, 131
Ruth Adeney Koori Award, 5, 150–1
Rykis, Pita, 198, 199, 200, 210, 214

Sabbioni, Jennifer, 145
Sacred Cows, 96
Samoan writing, 197
Saskatchewan Indian Cultural Centre, 176
Saunders, Keith, 128
The Sausage Tree, 148
Savageau, Cheryl, 185
SBS *Bookshow*, 145
Schaffer, Kay, 145
Schnierer, Stephen, 135
Schoo, Michael, 64
school texts, *see* education market
science fiction/fantasy, 95–6
Scofield, Greg, 187
Scott, Kim, 62, 128, 132, 133, 147
Scott, Rosie, 136
script writing, *see* plays and playwrights
Seale, Doris, 161, 167, 180
'Self-Censorship Checklist', 173
self-publishing, 16, 93, 96–7, 209–10, 219
selling, *see* marketing and distribution; reviewers and critics
seminars, *see* workshops and seminars
Sesequasis, Paul, 176
The 7 Stages of Grieving, 39

Seventh Generation, 176–7
Sexy and Dangerous, 151
A Shade of Spring, 177
Shapcott, Thomas, 7
Shea, Agnes, 133
Shoemaker, Adam, 100
Shorelines—Bermagui Festival of Words, 138–9
short stories, 60–1, 40, 41, 129
    Canadian First Nations', 160, 244
    Maori, 191, 193, 218, 249
Sims, Bruce, 55, 81, 84–5, 88
"Singing and Talking Up Loud", 111
Sister Girl, 37, 73
Skins, 177
Slapin, Beverly, 161, 167
Slash, 160
Slater, Janice, 41
Slipperjack, Ruby, 160, 180
Smallwood, Associate Professor Gracelyn, 10
Smith, Bernard, 150–1
Smith, Fiona, 111
Smith, Rosie, 146
Smithsonian Institution, 186
Smoke Signal, 49
Snake Cradle, 10
Son of Aryandabu, 149
Speidel, Darlene, 174, 187
Spender, Lynne, 93, 118–120
Spinifex Press, 98
spiritual characters, 11
spirituality, appropriation of, 87
Spring Poetry Festival (ACT, 1998), 138
Spring Writing Festival, 42–3, 97–8, 111, 113, 135–6
Stafford, Don, 211
standards, *see* literary standards
State Library of NSW, 97, 127, 137
state policies and funding, 75, 107–8, 121
Status Indians, 156, 157, 158, 159
Steam Pigs, 73, 131, 146, 149
Sterling, Shirley, 166
Stewart, Bruce, 191, 209
Stolen, 64
'stolen children' theme, 36, 39, 64, 122, 128, 129, 131
    Canada, 166
    visual arts, 151
Stone, Martha, 166

storytelling, *see* oral literature
The Strength of Us As Women, 166
style, 6, 28–35
    Canadian First Nation writing, 155–6, 165–73, 180–1, 187
    Maori writing, 198-201
    see also editing; language
Sullivan, Robert, 192, 201
    on editing, 210–11
    on reviewing, 215
    on self-publishing, 210
    on writing, 197, 199, 200
A Summer Readers' Feast (Sydney, 1998), 137–8
Sunshine Club, 39
support and advisory organisations, 109–21, 182–6, 215–19
Sweet Water, Stolen Land, 148
Sydney City Council, 151
Sydney Writers' Festival, 119, 127–30
Sykes, Roberta, 3, 5, 8–10, 23, 128, 131
    awards, 10, 151
Syron, Byron, 128

Tahi, Brenda, 196
Take Power, 96, 127
Talkin' Up to the White Woman, 37
Talking About Celia, 73, 91–2, 149
Tamepo, Eric, 217, 218
Tamou, Rima, 151
Tangentyere Council, 122
tapes, 83, 84
Tasdance, 132
Tasmanian Arts Advisory Board, 108
Tasmanian Department of Education and Community Development, 114–15
Tasmanian Poetry Festival, 132
Tasmanian Writers' Centre, 114–15
Taylor, Alf, 31, 41, 132
Taylor, Apirana, 200, 209
Taylor, Ben, 132
Taylor, Russ, 57
Te Ha, 217
Te Hunga Tannaki Kaitushi Maori, 217
Te Hunga Taunaki Kaituhi Maori, 218
Te Kawa O Te Marae, 211
Te Pua, 196
Te Reo Publications Ltd, 204–5, 210, 212, 219
Te Ua Haumene, 195
Te Waka Toi, 216

Te Whakatau Kaupapa, 206
television, 64, 107, 144, 160
Tell Them You're Indian, 6–7
theatre, 130
    see also dance; plays and playwrights
themes, 4, 37, 166–7, 170
    see also genres; 'stolen children' theme
They Took The Children Away, 151
Theytus Books, 175, 180–1, 184, 188
Thompson, Frank, 57
Thompson, Nick, 57
Thompson, Tom, 75
Thorne, Tim, 132
Threlkeld, Lancelot Edward, 190
time, 45
Tjindarella, 39
Toi Maori Aotearoa, 216–18
Toi Maori Festival (1997), 217
Toia, Eva, 146
Token Koori, 96–7
Toomath, Alma, 112
Torres, Pat, 40, 119
    conferences, 143, 145
    literary festivals, 130, 141
    on copyright and royalties, 84, 86
    on workshops, 146
tourism, 95, 201
tours, 39, 96, 116–7, 155
Tovey, Noel, 130
Trade Practices Act 1974, 87
The Traditional History of Characteristics of the Ojibwa Nation, 155
traditional stories, *see* oral literature
training, 62–3, 115, 121–5
    Aotearoa, 205, 210, 212
    Batchelor College, 116, 122, 123, 143
    Canada, 154, 176, 184
    about copyright, 86
    for editors, 67, 78–82
    see also mentoring; workshops and seminars
Tranby Aboriginal College, 128, 129
Tranby Cooperative for Aborigines Ltd, 142
transcription, 29–30, 115, 121, 190
    cultural and intellectual rights, 83, 84
Treaty of Waitangi, 206
Trees, Kathryn, 43–4
tribal enemies, 206

True Country, 128
Tsiolkos, Christos, 129
Tuwai, Lili, 130
Tuwhare, Hone, 191, 200, 202
Twin Trails Books and Music, 181–2
Two Rivers, 115
Two Shoes, Minnie, 187
The Two Worlds of Jimmy Barker, 57

Unaipon, David, 2, 25, 128, 150
    see also David Unaipon Award
Unbranded, 74, 149
Under The Mango Tree, 115
United Kingdom, 53
United Nations Association Australia Media Peace Prize, 64
United States, 15
United States First Nations' literature, 140, 156, 162, 166, 182, 184–6
    see also Blaeser, Kimberley M.; Bruchac, Joseph; Erdrich, Louise; Harjo, Joy; King, Thomas; Seale, Doris; Slapin, Beverly
university market, 62, 93, 102
    Aotearoa, 203
    Canada, 165, 171, 173–4
University of Alberta, 182
University of Arkansas, 182
University of Melbourne, 150–1
University of NSW Press, 98
University of Oklahoma, 185
University of Queensland, 11, 66, 93, 145
University of Queensland Press (UQP), 61, 129, 147–9
    Black Australian Writers Series (BAWS), 5, 28, 37, 61, 67, 104, 149
    editing, 72, 73, 75–6, 143
    marketing and distribution, 91–2, 94–5, 98
    see also David Unaipon Award
University of Toronto, 187
University of Victoria, 184
University of Waikato, 203
University of Western Australia, 149
University of Western Australia (UWA) Press, 62–3, 88, 98, 149
Up Rode The Troopers, 151
Up The Road, 151
UQP, see University of Queensland Press
"Urban Dreaming", 131
Us Mob, 5, 37
Utemorrah, Daisy, 40
UWA Press, 62–3, 88, 98, 149

Van Camp, Richard, 156, 160, 177, 178, 187
van den Berg, Rosemary, 7, 12, 23, 32–3, 105
   at literary festivals, 128, 132
van Toorn, Penny, 25, 76
Vance, Sylvia, 172, 179
Victoria University, 154
Victoria University Press, 212
Victorian Fellowship of Australian Writers, 150
Victorian Writers' Centre, 114
Virago, 53
visual arts and design, 95, 115, 119, 141, 143
   Aotearoa, 203: Maori, 197, 217
   awards, 147, 151, 152
   on book jackets, 91
   illustrations, 55, 57
   as story telling, 25
   support and advisory organisations, 110, 111, 112
voice, *see* style

W.K. Kellogg Foundation, 186
WA State Literature Office Inc, 117–18
Waia, Walter, 124
Waiariki and Other Stories, 191
Waitangi, Treaty of, 206
Wakefield Press, 73, 98
Walgar, Monty, 34–5
Walker, Geoff, 192, 193, 197, 200, 215
   on editing, 209, 213
   on style, 198–9
Walker, Kath, *see* Noonuccal, Oodgeroo
Wall, Colleen, 108
Wallan, Angus, 149
Walley, Joe, 132
Walley, Richard, 132, 142, 150
Walsh, Linda, 150
Wandering Girl, 53, 102, 103
Warana Writers' Week, 130
Ward, Glenyse, 27, 53, 102, 103, 128
Warlpiri people, 25
Warrigal's Way, 131, 148
Watego, Cliff, 101
Wathaurong Aboriginal Co-operative, 60
Watson, Maureen, 60, 137, 141
Watson, Sam, 128, 130, 131, 132, 133, 135, 145, 148
   awards, 150
Watts, Walbira, 136, 137

We Are Going, 191
Wedde, Ian, 191
Wednesday to Come, 191–2
Weickhardt, Patricia, 150
Weller, Archie, 8, 60, 95–6
    awards, 150
    literary festivals, 128, 129, 132
Wellington, Louise, 52
Wendt, Albert, 46, 197–8
West, Ida, 115, 146
Western Australian State Literature Office, 117–18
Westralian Aborigine, 49
Whaitiri, Reina, 196–7
Whakapohane, 209–10
Wharton, Herb, 41, 61, 149
    conferences, 145
    editorial experiences, 73–4
    literary festivals, 129, 131, 133, 137
    on marketing and distribution, 104
    Writer-in-Community Project, 116–17
    on writing, 28: post-colonial, 44–5
Wheatley, Nadia, 14, 85
Wheeler, Jordan, 156, 160, 175
When Darkness Falls, 148
When You Grow Up, 103
Whetstone, 182
White, Rawinia, 193, 211
white writers, *see* non-Aboriginal writers
Whitebeach, Terri Anne, 115–16, 121–3, 143
Wight, Rose, 133
Wild, Stephen, 57
Wildcat Falling, 4, 59–60
Wilkes, Richard, 62
Wilkins, Andrew, 5
Willie, Janine A., 165–6, 170, 171, 173–4, 180
Wilmot, Eric, 36, 150
Wilson, Gary, 207, 211, 213, 215
W.K. Kellogg Foundation, 186
Women Of The Sun, 64
Woodford Folk Festival, 91, 136–7
Woodward, Tony, 115
The Wool Pickers, 31
Woorunumurra, Banjo, 84
Wordcraft Circle of First Nations' Writers and Storytellers, 184–5
"Wordpool", 117

workshops and seminars, 86, 115–16, 117–18, 123, 142, 145–6
    Aotearoa, 212, 215, 217, 218, 219
    Australian Society of Authors, 119
    Canada, 160, 174, 176
    Gadigal Information Services, 111
    Master Classes for Aboriginal writers (1998), 111, 120, 146
    see also conferences; literary festivals
Wright, Alexis, 41, 61, 96, 121, 149
    on Aboriginal identity, 42
    on Aboriginal languages, 29
    at literary festivals, 131, 133
    on literary festivals, 126–7, 133
    on reviews, 99
    on writing, 26, 34, 38, 42: by whites about blacks, 12, 13
Wright, Judith, 26, 27, 99–100
"Write Off Centre" project, 117–18
Writer-in-Community Project, 116–17
Writing from the Fringe, 4, 31, 35
Writing the Circle, 172, 179–80
written form, translation into, *see* transcription
Wu, Anthea, 62–3, 88
Wymarra, Goie, 111

Yinto Desert Child, 128
Young-Ing, Greg, 159, 175, 180–1, 187
    on Aboriginal literature, 164
    on publishing, 174, 178
    on writing, 167, 171: by non-Native people, 171–2, 178
youth literature, 40–1, 64, 115, 130, 132
    North American First Nations' works, 186
    print runs, 92
Yunupingu, Galarrwuy, 16